ALWAYS SEPARATE, ALWAYS CONNECTED

Independence and Interdependence in Cultural Contexts of Development

ALWAYS SEPARATE, ALWAYS CONNECTED

Independence and Interdependence in Cultural Contexts of Development

Catherine Raeff

LEA LAWRENCE ERLBAUM ASSOCIATES, PUBLISHERS

2006 Mahwah, New Jersey   London

Lawrence Erlbaum Associates, Inc., Publishers
10 Industrial Avenue
Mahwah, New Jersey 07430
www.erlbaum.com

Cover design by Kathryn Houghtaling Lacey

Library of Congress Cataloging-in-Publication Data

Raeff, Catherine, 1964-
   Always separate, always connected : independence and interdependence in
cultural contexts of development / Catherine Raeff.
       p.   cm.
   Includes bibliographical references and index.
   ISBN 0-8058-4248-9 (alk. paper)
   1. Child development.   2. Culture.   3. Identity (Psychology) in children.
4. Dependency (Psychology).   5. Autonomy (Psychology).   I. Title.

HQ767.9.R33   2005
305.231—dc22
                                                              2005055300
                                                                   CIP

Books published by Lawrence Erlbaum Associates are printed on acid-free paper,
and their bindings are chosen for strength and durability.

Printed in the United States of America
10   9   8   7   6   5   4   3   2   1

For my parents and sister

Contents

Preface   xi

1   Theoretical Foundations, Part 1   1

Some Preliminaries 3
Dichotomous Conceptions of Independence
and Interdependence 8
Uncovering the Complexities of Independence
and Interdependence 14
Moving Beyond Dichotomous Conceptions of Independence
and Interdependence 28
Some General Remarks 35

2   Theoretical Foundations, Part 2   38

Toward a New Conceptual Approach to Independence
and Interdependence 38
Conceptualizing the Dynamics of Independence and
Interdependence in Cultural Contexts of Development 46
Some General Remarks and a Few Words
About Terminology 55

3   A Historical Case Study: Independence and
Interdependence in Euro-American Cultural Traditions   58

Puritan Beginnings 59
The Revolutionary and Early National Periods 69
Nineteenth-Century Families 81

Parents' Magazine *in the Early 20th Century*   *91*
Some General Remarks   *97*

4   Independence and Interdependence
in Parent–Child Relationships   102

Parents' Childrearing Ideas and Goals   *103*
Parent–Child Interactions During Infancy and Childhood   *122*
How Parents Talk About Independence and Interdependence
     During Parent–Child Interactions   *129*
Parent–Child Relationships During Adolescence   *135*
Independence and Interdependence in Japanese
     Childrearing Practices   *138*
Some General Remarks   *146*

5   Independence and Interdependence
in Educational Settings   150

American School Practices   *150*
Preschool and Elementary School in Japan   *162*
Some General Remarks   *176*

6   Independence, Interdependence, and Self-Construction   179

Three Classic Western Theories of Self-Construction   *180*
Self-Constructing Activities   *192*
Self-Construction During Childhood and Adolescence   *196*
Self-Construction in Japan   *204*
Some General Remarks   *209*

7   Independence and Interdependence in Late Adolescent
Self-Constructions   211

Overall Self-Constructions   *212*
Constructing Oneself as Independent   *217*
Why Independence Is Good or Important   *222*
Feeling "Really" Independent   *228*
Constructing Oneself as Interdependent   *231*
Why Interdependence Is Good or Important   *234*
Feeling "Really" Interdependent   *237*
Some General Remarks   *239*

8   Recurring Themes   242

Stepping Back   *242*
Future Directions   *250*

References   256

Author Index   277

Subject Index   285

Preface

As psychologists have struggled in recent years to understand human functioning in relation to cultural processes, issues of both human separateness or independence and human connectedness or interdependence have emerged as useful constructs for understanding cultural differences in behavior and development. The central goal of this book is to offer a conceptual approach to independence and interdependence that moves cultural and developmental analyses beyond investigating whether some cultures value independence or interdependence more or less than do other cultures, to investigating how independence and interdependence issues are construed and particularized during development around the world. In brief, I argue for a conceptualization of independence and interdependence that is based on the premise that people everywhere are physically and mentally separate individuals and simultaneously socially connected beings. Furthermore, the conceptual approach that I am asserting holds that independence and interdependence are multifaceted and inseparable dimensions of human functioning that may be defined and enacted differently in different cultural practices. In turn, children's development toward culturally valued modes of both independence and interdependence is taken to occur as children participate in cultural practices with others.

To contextualize and explicate this conceptual position, in chapter 1, I spend considerable time debunking an approach that has dominated recent discussions of independence and interdependence. This dominant approach holds that independence and interdependence are essentially dichotomous and opposing aspects of human functioning, and that development within a culture follows either an independence trajectory or an interdependence trajectory, but not both. In chapter 1, I also consider some approaches to independence and interdependence that have been offered recently, as social scientists are increasingly recognizing some of the limitations of the dominant perspective.

Then, in chapter 2, I present an alternative conceptualization of how independence and interdependence are particularized in cultural contexts of development. The remaining bulk of the book is taken up with using this conceptualization to consider research from varied academic disciplines, including history, psychology, anthropology, and education. Chapter 3 offers a selective historical analysis of independence and interdependence within Euro-American cultural traditions, including childrearing practices. Moving on to contemporary social science research, chapter 4 explores how issues of independence and interdependence are particularized in parent–child relationships during infancy, childhood, and adolescence. Chapter 5 includes a consideration of independence and interdependence in relation to educational practices. In chapters 6 and 7, I consider how independence and interdependence are particularized in self-construction during childhood and adolescence.

Although chapters 2 through 7 are connected by an overarching conceptual approach, each one also stands on its own to some extent. Thus, readers with different specific interests may delve more deeply into a particular set of independence and interdependence issues. In addition, although my concern in this book is with how independence and interdependence are particularized in children's developmental experiences, I see the conceptual approach that I am offering as having broader applicability to human functioning at any time during the life span.

I am keenly aware that each of the specific topics addressed in these chapters could be the source of separate books in and of themselves, and that my treatment of independence and interdependence issues is limited and incomplete. Nevertheless, the current conceptual framework can hopefully advance our understanding of the complexities of independence and interdependence. It can also provide some productive directions for organizing further empirical and theoretical analyses of the ongoing dynamics of independence and interdependence as they are particularized around the world.

ACKNOWLEDGMENTS

For over 10 years now, my work on issues of independence and interdependence has been supported by varied institutions and people whom I am now pleased to acknowledge and thank. My ideas about culture and development were first formally nurtured when I was a graduate student at Clark University, where I spent 5 years happily engaged in classes and discussions with Ina Č. Užgiris, Bernard Kaplan, James V. Wertsch, Nancy Budwig, Michael Bamberg, and Seymour Wapner. My greatest debt is to the late Ina Č. Užgiris, whose trenchant observations of culture and development continue to provide me with an enduring framework for my work. The good memories of her simultaneously challenging and supportive guidance also continue to sustain me.

After Clark, I went on to a postdoctoral position at UCLA, where discussions with Patricia Greenfield and Blanca Quiroz enabled me to begin formulating my ideas about independence and interdependence. My time at UCLA was also enriched by Deborah Stipek and Carollee Howes, who provided me with opportunities to pursue my interests.

Some of the research presented in this book was supported by Indiana University of Pennsylvania (IUP) Senate Research Committee Awards, an IUP Senate Fellowship Grant, and a grant from the Pennsylvania State System of Higher Education Faculty Professional Development Council. Work on this book was also made possible by a sabbatical from IUP during the fall of 2003. I am indebted to Sara Matteson for her 4 years as a research assistant, and I also thank Danielle Swoboda and Julie Shrager for their assistance with some of the research reported in this book. I thank my sister, Anne Raeff, for facilitating my research with Vietnamese adolescents in Albuquerque, and I am indebted to Trang Huynh and Cuong Phan for coordinating this research. I am also deeply grateful to all the people who participated in the research reported in this book.

I am appreciative of Lawrence Erlbaum Associates for understanding how much time would be needed to complete this book while teaching four courses per semester. I thank Bill Webber for his support of this project since its inception. I also thank Lori Stone and Heather Jefferson for overseeing its completion. I am grateful to two reviewers for their constructive comments.

I am indebted to Nancy Budwig for reading several chapter drafts and for providing supportive and constructive feedback. I am grateful to Michael F. Mascolo for his ongoing support of my work and for providing invaluable comments on several chapter drafts. I also thank Marc Raeff, Lillian Raeff, Anne Raeff, and Lori Ostlund for reading several chapter drafts and for providing helpful suggestions.

I am forever grateful to my parents, Marc and Lillian Raeff, for a home filled with appreciation for and never-ending discussions of culture, history, and ideas. I am deeply grateful to my sister, Anne Raeff, for *her* companionship and for long hikes in the deserts and mountains of the American Southwest during which her vivid, firsthand descriptions of life in varied cultures helped me clarify my ideas about independence and interdependence.

Theoretical Foundations, Part 1

As people go about their lives in all corners of the world, they are separate individuals, and they are also connected to others. Thus, as children develop in all corners of the world, issues of human separateness or independence, and issues of human connectedness or interdependence, abound. For about 10 years now, I have been seeing both independence and interdependence in almost everything, from TV commercials and programs, to popular songs, to political speeches, to children at play. One time, before leaving an airplane bathroom, I copied down a notice that said, "As a courtesy to the next passenger, may we suggest that you use your towel to wipe off the wash basin." To me, this statement exudes both independence and interdependence. It begins with interdependence, in the form of consideration for others, and then it includes independence by pointing out that each washroom towel becomes the property of an individual passenger. Also, by suggesting, rather than demanding, that each person clean up, the notice implies that it is ultimately up to each individual to make a relational decision about cleaning up for the next passenger. Another example is of a friend and her 2-year-old son who picked up toys while singing,

> We always clean up, clean up
> To show we really care.
> We always clean up, clean up
> 'Cause we like to do our share.

In this cleanup song, I see interdependence in the use of the pronoun *we* and in the form of caring for others. I also see links between independence and interdependence in the idea that individuals contribute to common goals by doing their share. One day, as I looked at a college bulletin board, my attention was caught by a sorority recruitment sign stating that the sisters are "individually unique, together complete." In this way, the sorority promised to preserve the important independent individuality of each member, but also emphasized that individuals are complete in relation to others. I have further noticed how Hollywood award ceremonies are replete with actors using their acceptance speeches to talk about and thank a long list of people without whom, they claim, their individual achievements would be nonexistent and meaningless.

As a developmental psychologist, I have been concerned with elaborating on these kinds of informal observations to discern how issues of human separateness, or independence, and issues of human connectedness, or interdependence, are played out in children's developmental experiences. During these last 10 years, investigating developmental and cultural aspects of independence and interdependence have been hot topics in the social sciences, building on flames that have actually been fanned for centuries. As may be expected of any hot topic, confusion abounds as different investigators have dealt with different aspects of very complex phenomena. With this book, I do not present an exhaustive account of the varied and complex strands that constitute ideas about independence and interdependence. My much more limited goal is to offer a conceptual framework for considering issues of independence and interdependence as they are particularized in the cultural practices in which children participate. I also use this conceptual framework to review research from varied sources, thereby integrating disparate developmental studies. Ultimately, I seek to offer a basis for further research into the many unknowns that remain regarding how independence and interdependence are particularized in cultural contexts of development. To provide a sense of where this book is headed, I begin with a short overview of my conceptual approach and its derivation.

Briefly, the conceptual approach that I explicate in this book takes off from the premise that all people are physically and mentally separate or independent individuals, and simultaneously socially connected or interdependent beings. Going beyond recognizing these two essential aspects of the human condition, the conceptual approach holds that independence and interdependence are multifaceted and inseparable dimensions of human functioning that may be defined and enacted differently in different cultures. This systems approach highlights two points. First, concerns with human independence and interdependence are assumed to be particularized in all cultures, albeit in some different ways. Second, this approach goes beyond claiming that concerns with both independence and interdependence are evident in some way in all cultures to claiming that independence and interdependence are inseparable or interrelated dimensions of behavior in all cultures. That is, any cultural manifestations of independence are likely to implicate cultural manifestations of interdependence and vice versa.

Based on this conceptual approach, the focus of the current volume is to delineate how cultural contexts of development are structured in terms of multifaceted and inseparable independence and interdependence issues. Analyzing cultural contexts of development in this way enables us to further our understanding of the complexities and multidimensionality of children's developmental experiences in varied cultures. Moreover, to ultimately study the development of children's independent and interdependent functioning, it is first necessary to discern how the cultural contexts in which children participate provide opportunities for them to act both independently and interdependently.

The current conceptual position stands in contrast to and has been conceived partly in reaction to an approach that has dominated the social sciences during the last 20 years: namely, that independence and interdependence are dichotomous and opposing aspects of human experience. Thus, before explicating my approach in greater detail, most of this first chapter includes a consideration of this dominant view, and I also point to some of the complexities of independence and interdependence that it tends to obscure. Chapter 1 ends with a consideration of a few alternative conceptual approaches that have been offered recently. With this wider theoretical context as a backdrop, chapter 2 includes a full explication of the current conceptual approach to independence and interdependence. Armed with this conceptual framework, subsequent chapters include considerations of how multifaceted and interrelated independence and interdependence issues are particularized in parent–child relationships, educational settings, and self-construction during childhood and adolescence. Before proceeding to the dominant dichotomous approach, I now turn to some preliminary comments about how independence and interdependence issues have been treated within developmental psychology.

SOME PRELIMINARIES

Until approximately the mid- or late 1980s, considerations of independence and interdependence issues were mostly embedded in debates about how development happens. Indeed, the developmental roles of individual and social aspects of human functioning have been a perennial source of debate in developmental psychology, not to mention for our intellectual ancestors in philosophy or our contemporary colleagues in varied social sciences. The end of the 20th century and the beginning of the 21st century have seen a resolution to this debate in the consolidation, even mainstreaming, of the systems view that individual and social factors are not only both essential to human development, but also interact throughout development. For example, research on parent–child relationships has focused not only on how parent–child interactions shape children's development, but also on how children, beginning during infancy, contribute their individual predispositions and competencies to the structuring of those interactions, and also to their own development (e.g., Bell, 1968; Bell & Harper, 1977; Užgiris, 1989). Such research indicates that development happens through interactions between the contributions of separate or independent individuals, and social connections or interdependence.

It has additionally become clear that social connections are structured differently in different cultures, and thus considerations of how culture frames developmental processes have also now found a place in the mainstream of contemporary developmental psychology. For example, much empirical effort has been and continues to be directed toward discerning how varied patterns of parent–child interactions around the world reflect varied cultural values, and how parent–child interactions provide children with opportunities to practice culturally valued modes of behavior.

With the consolidation of an interactive approach to understanding *how* development happens, it has also become increasingly clear that there are cultural differences in *what* happens during development. For example, in one part of the world a 5-year-old child may be going to kindergarten, whereas in another part of the world a 5-year-old may be taking care of a younger sibling. Whereas middle-class Westerners may grow up to make choices about their adult social roles, including what career to pursue and whom to marry, children in some non-Western cultures will grow up to accept a contractual marriage arranged by their parents. In recognition of such cultural diversity in developmental trajectories, developmental analyses are increasingly focused on investigating the development of specific modes of behavior around the world in relation to cultural values and meanings.

As well, since the 1980s investigations of culturally varied social connections and culturally varied developmental trajectories have revolved around considerations of individual separateness and social connectedness, or independence and interdependence. Indeed, developmentalists have been captivated by notions of independence and interdependence, and these constructs have been identified as central for describing and explaining cultural variability in children's developmental experiences.

Despite agreeing on the utility of investigating culture and development in relation to independence and interdependence, different investigators have used different terms to study different specific independence and interdependence issues, often based on different conceptual approaches.

In psychology, considerations of independence and interdependence have often been cast in terms of individualism and collectivism. The term *individualism* is typically equated with issues of human separateness, and other terms—including *independence, individuality, autonomy, separation, freedom*, and *egocentrism*—have also been used to characterize the values and meanings of individualism. The term *collectivism* is typically equated with issues of human connectedness, and other terms—including *interdependence, relatedness, sociocentrism*, and *social connectedness*—have also been invoked to characterize the values and meanings of collectivism. Before delving further into how these constructs are conceptualized and used by some contemporary social scientists, a few words about my own usage of the terms *independence* and *interdependence* are in order. In particular, I wish to explain why I do not use the popular terms *individualism* and *collectivism* as the book proceeds, except at times when considering the work of others who do use these terms.

Although I have used the *individualism/collectivism* terminology in some of my own previous work, my current decision to move away from that terminology is based on what I see as problems with the common contemporary practice of characterizing the United States and its mainstream Euro-American values as individualistic. In many contemporary accounts, characterizing the United States as individualistic is tantamount to saying that the United States is an independence-oriented culture, dominated by Euro-Americans who are focused on pursuing individually defined goals and achieving individual self-fulfillment, with little regard for relationships. For example, prototypical American self-conceptions are said to involve defining oneself "as an independent, self-contained, autonomous entity who (a) comprises a unique configuration of internal attributes (e.g., traits, abilities, motives, and values) and (b) behaves primarily as a consequence of these internal attributes" (Markus & Kitayama, 1991, p. 224). I return to contemporary perspectives in more detail shortly, but for this introductory discussion of terminology, it is useful to quote Waterman (1981), who pointed out, "It should be obvious that self-containment is a practical impossibility" (p. 767). Moreover, such sweeping descriptions of American culture and its European roots have always struck me as problematic because, as I argue throughout this book, they ignore the varied ways in which Americans are also interdependent, or concerned with social connectedness.

I have also decided to move away from the individualism/collectivism terminology because I find it problematic to trace the equation of American individualism with independence back to Alexis de Tocqueville's (1835/1945) *Democracy in America*. de Tocqueville did indeed use the term *individualism* in his treatise on 19th-century American culture, and his analysis is still often invoked in contemporary descriptions of American culture as independence oriented. However, a one-sided conceptualization of individualism as basically synonymous with independence simplifies de Tocqueville's definition and usage of the term *individualism*, as it is embedded in his detailed two-volume analysis of American political and civil life in the 1830s. Granted, de Tocqueville was struck by the modes of independence that he observed in the United States (e.g., being self-reliant, pursuing self-interest), but there is more to his analysis as he also characterized American culture in terms of varied modes of interdependence. I take up a consideration of some historical modes of independence and interdependence in greater detail in chapter 3, but for now let us turn briefly to de Tocqueville's (1835/1945) specific discussion of the term *individualism*, which he presents about one third of the way through the second volume of *Democracy in America*. de Tocqueville defined individualism by contrasting it with selfishness in the following way:

> *Individualism* is a novel expression, to which a novel idea has given birth. Our fathers were only acquainted with *égoïsme* (selfishness). Selfishness is a passionate and exaggerated love of self, which leads a man to connect everything with himself and to prefer himself to everything in the world. Individualism is a mature and calm feeling, which disposes each member of the community to sever himself from the mass of his fellows and to draw apart with his family and his friends, so that after he has thus formed a little circle of his own, he willingly leaves society at large to itself. (Vol. 2, p. 104)

It is noteworthy that this definition of individualism involves a kind of social withdrawal, but not into a vacuum of self-contained isolation. Instead, such individualism turns on the value of a network of direct relationships and involves withdrawing from wider, or indirect, networks of societal functioning. In a similar vein, but much more recently, Gans (1988/1991) pointed out that "the goal of popular individualism is hardly separation from other people. Instead, it is to live mainly, and participate actively, in a small part of society, the array of family, friends, and informal relations and groups which I refer to as *microsociety*. Popular individualism is, therefore, very much a social phenomenon" (pp. 3–4). According to Gans, average American individualists do not eschew social connections, but rather tend to avoid "involuntary conformity" and "obligatory membership in institutions and organizations" (p. 2).

After defining individualism, de Tocqueville then went on to describe how American political institutions actually enable Americans to successfully *avoid* the dangers of individualism that isolate people from wider societal functioning. More specifically, he noted:

> The Americans have combated by free institutions the tendency of equality to keep men asunder, and they have subdued it . . . if the object be to have the local affairs of a district conducted by the men who reside there, the same persons are always in contact, and they are, in a manner, forced to be acquainted and to adapt themselves to one another. . . . Local freedom, then, which leads a great number of citizens to value the affection of their neighbors and of their kindred, perpetually brings men together. (Vol. 2, 1835/1945, pp. 110–111)

These observations indicate how the dangers of individualism (as defined by de Tocqueville) are avoided through political freedom, which promotes social connections among individuals by requiring them to cooperate as they establish and maintain the collective goals of their communities. This link between political freedom and pursuing collective goals is noteworthy because the term *freedom* may be viewed as a form of independence that excludes or stands in opposition to social connectedness. That is, to be free may be defined as being separate from other people; to seek freedom may be defined as seeking separation from others. In contrast, de Tocqueville's analysis indicates how one form of freedom—namely, political freedom—enhances rather than undermines people's social connections. Thus, valuing freedom does not necessarily occur in opposition to valuing social relationships. Indeed, de Tocqueville's analysis suggests that valuing freedom may be inseparable from valuing social connections.

Building on de Tocqueville, I have argued that the term *individualism* may be defined as a broad cultural value system that revolves around the assumptions that all people are ideally free and equal, both politically and personally. I have also argued that these assumptions have implications for the development of both independent and interdependent functioning (Raeff, 1997a, 1997b). Although some of my earlier empirical work was tied to a more "independence only" view of individualism than I advocate today, my main interest has always been to explore the implications of American individualism for both independence and interdependence in American culture and development (Raeff, 2000, 2004). However, because of the popular tendency to equate individualism with independence issues, I have chosen to abandon the terms *individualism* and *collectivism* in favor of *independence* and *interdependence*. The terms *independence* and *interdependence* are also frequently used terms, and thus have been subjected to diverse conceptualizations. Nevertheless, I have come to prefer *independence* and *interdependence* as versatile terms for considering some of the cultural and behavioral complexities of human separateness and human connectedness.

For the time being, independence may be defined generally as those aspects of human functioning and experience that involve being a mentally and physically separate, or distinct, individual. Interdependence may be defined generally as those aspects of human functioning and experience that involve connections among people, including direct relationships and wider societal networks. At this point in our analysis, these general definitions are meant to serve as working definitions, and a more elaborate conceptualization of independence and interdependence is offered later. But first, let us now turn to an overview of some of the most common treatments of the independence and interdependence constructs that have shaped psychological discussions since the 1980s.

DICHOTOMOUS CONCEPTIONS OF INDEPENDENCE AND INTERDEPENDENCE

During the 1980s, the individualism/collectivism terminology and considerations of independence and interdependence began to proliferate in psychology to the extent that the 1980s have been called the "decade of I/C [a frequently used abbreviation for individualism/collectivism]" (Kâğitçibaşi, 1994, p. 52). Although this distinction was "discovered" by psychologists in the 1980s, it actually enjoys a longer heritage in neighboring social sciences. For example, with regard to child development, in a 1959 *American Anthropologist* article Barry, Child, and Bacon hypothesized that cultural differences in childrearing patterns could be linked to differences in modes of subsistence. They speculated that interdependence would be encouraged in agricultural societies, where food is grown over a period of time and then stored before it is consumed. Childrearing in agricultural communities would involve inculcating "faithful adherence to routines," and "Individual initiative in attempts to improve techniques may be feared because no one can tell immediately whether the changes will lead to a greater harvest or to disastrous failure" (p. 52). Alternatively, in hunting and fishing societies, "with low accumulation of food resources adults should tend to be individualistic, assertive, and venturesome" (p. 53). Applying this subsistence analysis to Euro-American culture would highlight its agricultural origins, thus leading to considerations of the importance of interdependence for Euro-Americans. Somehow, however, it has not quite worked out that way because many analyses have focused on the value of independence in Euro-American culture.

In introducing a comparative study of middle-class Japanese and American parents and their infants, Caudill and Weinstein (1969) claimed that there are:

> differing emphases on what is valued in behavior . . . when life in Japan is compared with life in America. These differing emphases seem to be particularly sharp in the areas of family life and general interpersonal relations. . . . Japanese are more "group" oriented and interdependent in their relations with others, while Americans are more 'individual' oriented and independent . . . in normal family life in Japan there is an emphasis on interdependence and reliance on others, while in America the emphasis is on independence and self-assertion. (pp. 14–15)

Focusing on American culture in the 1970s, Sampson (1977) characterized the United States in terms of self-contained individualism, and further claimed that "The self-contained person is one who does not require or desire others for his or her completion or life; self-contained persons either are or hope to be entire unto themselves. Self-containment is the extreme of independence: needing or wanting no one. It is fundamentally antithetical to the concept of interdependence" (p. 770).

Along similar lines, in a widely cited statement, Geertz (1974/1988) held that:

> The Western conception of the person as a bounded, unique, more or less integrated motivational and cognitive universe, a dynamic center of awareness, emotion, judgment, and action organized into a distinctive whole and set contrastively both against other such wholes and against its social and natural background, is, however incorrigible it may seem to us, a rather peculiar idea within the context of the world's cultures. (p. 126)

The 1980s then began with Hofstede's (1980) book, *Culture's Consequences*, to which a key role in instigating the widespread use of the individualism and collectivism constructs in psychology is often attributed. In this work, Hofstede presented analyses of cultural differences based on surveys given to IBM subsidiary employees in 40 nations. In a second edition of *Culture's Consequences*, published in 2001, analyses included over 50 countries. These data suggest that cultures differ along several dimensions, including individualism/collectivism, which is defined in the following way: "*Individualism* on the one side versus its opposite, *collectivism*, is the degree to which individuals are supposed to look after themselves or remain integrated into groups, usually around the family. Positioning itself between these poles is a very basic problem all societies face" (Hofstede, 1980/2001 p. xx). Within this conceptual framework, individualism and collectivism constitute opposite ends of a "single, bipolar, dimension" (Hofstede, 1994, p. xi) or continuum, whereby some cultures may be classified at the bipolar extremes, with others falling somewhere in between the bipolar extremes (Greenfield, 1994).

More specifically, countries in Hofstede's analysis received an individualism score based on participants' 5-point Likert scale responses to the following 14 questions about their work goals:

How important is it to you to have challenging work to do—work from which you can get a personal sense of accomplishment?

How important is it to you to live in an area desirable to you and your family?

How important is it to you to have an opportunity for high earnings?

How important is it to you to work with people who cooperate well with one another?

How important is it to you to have training opportunities (to improve your skills or learn new skills)?

How important is it to you to have good fringe benefits?

How important is it to you to get the recognition you deserve when you do a good job?

How important is it to you to have good physical working conditions (good ventilation and lighting, adequate work space, etc.)?

How important is it to you to have considerable freedom to adapt your own approach to the job?

How important is it to you to have the security that you will be able to work for your company as long as you want to?

How important is it to you to have an opportunity for advancement to higher level jobs?

How important is it to you to have a good working relationship with your manager?

How important is it to you to fully use your skills and abilities on the job?

How important is it to you to have a job which leaves you sufficient time for your personal or family life? (Hofstede, 2001, p. 256)

In the 2001 analysis, the United States was classified with the highest individualistic rating, and Guatemala emerged with the lowest individualism rating. Factor analyses revealed further that the highest positive correlation of .86 was between a country's individualism score and responses to the question, "How important is it to you to have a job which leaves you sufficient time for your personal or family life?" In addition to questioning the utility of using one questionnaire about work goals to investigate issues of independence and interdependence in different cultures, it seems somehow ironic that the question with the highest *positive* correlation to a country's individualism score invokes the importance of family ties. It is also possible that the issue of "personal" life in the same question could be understood by questionnaire respondents to include social activities or time with friends, especially in the context of the term *family life* that immediately follows.

Conceptualizing individualism or independence, and collectivism or interdependence, as a continuum means that they represent opposing aspects of one dimension of human functioning. Accordingly, analyses may focus on the extremes of the continuum, and how a particular culture emphasizes independence or interdependence concerns. At the same time, the nonextreme points along a unidimensional continuum, especially around the midpoint, represent instances of overlap between the bipolar extremes. Therefore, the theoretical possibility also exists for discerning how both independence and interdependence are evident in human behavior across cultures—at the very least, for those cultures that are categorized around the middle of the continuum.

However, as research proceeded through the 1980s and into the 1990s, a tendency emerged to focus on the extremes, and thus on how cultures emphasize either independence or interdependence, rather than on how both independence and interdependence are evident in varied cultures. Thus, dichotomous conceptions and treatments of independence and interdependence took hold and remain prevalent, building on a long tradition of dualistic thinking in Western culture, going back at least to Descartes' mind/body dichotomy. As Schwartz (1990) explained:

> the overall individualism-collectivism dichotomy implicitly postulates that individualist and collectivist values form two coherent syndromes that are in polar opposition. That is, different types of individualist values vary together consistently to form one set, and this set regularly opposes the types of collectivist values that also vary together consistently to form a second set. (pp. 141–142)

More specifically, in cultures that are classified as independence oriented, people are assumed to define themselves separately from others as self-contained units, with stable and context-free internal attributes. Also, people in independence-oriented cultures are alleged to value individual freedom, concern for individual goals, making individual choices, individual self-expression, seeking individual self-fulfillment, and disengagement from others. Within a dichotomous framework, the central cultural endpoint of development in such independence-oriented cultures is taken to be the achievement of autonomy or independence in the form of separation from others.

Such independence is viewed in contrast to cultures that are classified as interdependence oriented, in which people are assumed to define themselves in relation to others and in terms of social roles within specific social relationships. According to a dichotomous perspective, the values emphasized in interdependence-oriented cultures include conformity, enacting social roles, concern for others' needs, pursuing group goals, and maintaining social cohesion. Furthermore, within an interdependence orientation, a person is allegedly viewed "not as separate from the social context but as more connected and less differentiated from others. People are motivated to find a way to fit in with relevant others, to fulfill and create obligation, and in general to become part of various interpersonal relationships" (Markus & Kitayama, 1991, p. 227).

In varied cultures that are assumed to follow such a dichotomously defined interdependence orientation, "A premium is placed on emphasizing collective welfare and on showing a sympathetic concern for others" (Markus & Kitayama, 1991, p. 228). There is also an emphasis on "interrelatedness and kindness" and on the "ability to both respect and share others' feelings" (Markus & Kitayama, 1991, p. 228). Moreover, "To members of sociocentric organic cultures the concept of the autonomous individual, free to choose and mind his own business, must feel alien, a bizarre idea cutting the self off from the interdependent whole, dooming it to a life of isolation and loneliness" (Shweder & Bourne, 1984/1988, p. 194). Within a dichotomous framework, the central cultural goals of development in such interdependence-oriented cultures are to view oneself in relation to others and to maintain strong interpersonal connections.

Sometimes explanations of the independence/interdependence dichotomy are presented in terms of a series of opposites that are taken to represent essential differences between independence-oriented and interdependence-oriented cultures. To highlight the opposition between independence and interdependence, linguistic markers such as "in contrast to," "on the other hand," and "whereas" are often used. For example, a dichotomous approach holds that:

"Independence" refers to a set of tasks or psychological tendencies to separate the self from the social context; it encompasses goals of agency, autonomy, and disengagement from others. "Interdependence," on the other hand, refers to a set of tasks or psychological tendencies to connect the self with others; it encompasses such goals as affiliation, communion, and engagement with others. (Kitayama, Markus, & Matsumoto, 1995, p. 442)

Or:

Childrearing patterns are believed to differ between collectivist and individualist cultures in developmentally meaningful ways. Parents in collectivist cultures (as can be found in Japan) tend to emphasize obedient, reliable, and proper behavior in children, whereas parents in individualist cultures (as can be found in the U.S.) tend to emphasize self-reliant, independent, and creative behavior. In the one, children are encouraged to follow rules and conform to norms; in the other, children are allowed a good deal of autonomy and are encouraged to confront and engage in independent exploration of their environment. (Bornstein, Tal, & Tamis-LeMonda, 1991, pp. 73–74)

Or:

On the one hand, there are conceptions of competence that emphasize individual ability, cultivation of the individual mind, exploration, discovery, and personal achievement. . . . On the other hand, competence is considered as moral self-cultivation, a social contribution, discouraging individual celebration of achievement. (Keller, 2003, pp. 288–289)

Similarly, throughout the individualism/collectivism chapter in *Culture's Consequences* (Hofstede, 1980/2001), there are several tables entitled "Key Differences Between Collectivist and Individualist Societies," and each table is composed of binary statements that show how individualism and collectivism are oppositionally evident in different spheres of human functioning. For example, the following binary statements are included in tables that list differences in individualistic and collectivistic modes of family life, school activities, and consumption patterns: In cultures low on individualism, "mothers expect to live with children in their old age," and in cultures high on individualism, "mothers expect to live apart in their old age" (p. 236). In cultures low on individualism, "children learn to think in terms of 'we,' " and in cultures high on individualism, a "child learns to think in terms of 'I' " (p. 236). In cultures low on individualism, there are "strong family ties, [with] frequent contacts," and in cultures high on individualism, there are "weak family ties [with] rare contacts" (p. 236). In cultures low on individualism, "teachers deal with pupils as a group," and in cultures high on individualism, "teachers deal with individual pupils" (p. 237). In cultures low on individualism, people "live with human companions," and in cultures high on individualism, people "live with cats and/or dogs" (p. 245).

The foregoing definitions and contrasts show how the dominant discourse about independence and interdependence has been, and continues to be, framed dichotomously (Harter, 1999; Murray, 1993). Moreover, it has been pointed out that as investigations of cultural differences were subsumed under dichotomous conceptions of independence and interdependence, "until very recently . . . one dared speak only in the most reverential terms about the so-called 'I/C' distinction" (Chandler, Lalonde, Sokol, & Hallet, 2003, p. 110). This "common tendency to pit individualism against collectivism and use them as general traits across time and space" (Kağitçibaşi, 1994, p. 56) has provided some useful information about culture and development. However, as is the case with most (if not all) dichotomies, these dichotomous conceptions of independence and interdependence are also limited and problematic in several ways. A consideration of some of these limitations and problems can shed light on numerous theoretical issues regarding culture and development that ultimately serve as a basis for offering an alternative conceptual approach to independence and interdependence.

UNCOVERING THE COMPLEXITIES OF INDEPENDENCE AND INTERDEPENDENCE

Some Basic Theoretical Problems and Empirical Discrepancies

A consideration of the binary statements presented earlier quickly points to several theoretical problems with dichotomous conceptions of independence and interdependence, as well as to some empirical discrepancies. First, mothers living on their own in old age does not preclude families from being actively involved with, or connected to, their aging mothers. In addition, a mother may want to live on her own, not only to maintain some individual control over her life, but also because she does not want to be a burden to her children. Not wanting to be a social burden points to the importance of consideration and respect for others, and thus to how a valued mode of interdependence is implicated in separate living. It may be argued that the very notion of one person being a burden to another person is emblematic of an independence orientation. However, by recognizing the possibility of being a burden or disruption, living on her own may provide an aging mother with a way to maintain harmonious relationships with her children. This analysis suggests that living separately does not have to entail social isolation. Instead, living separately may be understood in relation to maintaining culturally valued modes of social connectedness. In addition, a mother's consideration for the children, and maintaining a relationship with them by living on her own, may be indicative of a noninstrumental conception of relationships.

Second, thinking in terms of "we" does not preclude a sense of self as separate, nor does thinking in terms of "I" preclude a conception of self in relation to others. With regard to the American case, the U.S. Constitution begins with a statement about "We the people," and the Declaration of Independence refers to a "people" making their own political decisions.

Third, if the United States is the epitome of individualism, to say that there are weak family ties in the United States ignores the virtual obsession contemporary Americans seem to have with family. From mainstream media discussions of "family values" to a personal Web site I read recently stating that "family is everything," the value of family pervades many areas of American life. The saying "Blood is thicker than water" also points to a primacy of family relationships. In Japan—a culture that is often dichotomously opposed to the United States—sibling ties may actually be weakened in traditional families as siblings marry out of their families of origin to become members of new households (Nakane, 1970/1986). Thus, family ties may be valued universally, with cultural differences lying in how specific family ties are understood, established, and maintained.

Fourth, with regard to school, the binary statement about dealing with individual students in contrast to dealing with students as a group is partly based on Tobin, Wu, and Davidson's 1989 book, *Preschool in Three Cultures*. In my reading, this book and its accompanying videotape showed how children in a typical American preschool often congregate in one group and engage in common activities that are led by the teacher. Moreover, varied analyses (discussed later in this volume in chap. 5) indicate how American education is characterized by whole-class instruction, whereby the teacher lectures to the class as a whole, with little opportunity for children to contribute as individuals to their own learning.

Finally, with regard to contrasting living with human companions to living with cats or dogs, it may indeed be the case that house pets are more common in some cultures than in others, but having house pets does not preclude living with others or valuing human companionship. Indeed, many people live with both animal and human companions.

I admit that I have been selective in my choice of table entries to emphasize from Hofstede's analysis, and I also admit that not all of the entries are so problematic. Hofstede himself claimed that a country's individualism score, based on his work goals questionnaire, does not reveal "all there is to be known about the backgrounds and structures of relationship patterns in that country. It is an abstraction that should not be extended beyond its limited area of usefulness" (1994, p. xi). The main point that I am trying to make is that when independence and interdependence are conceptualized in opposing and mutually exclusive terms, there is then an implication that what is characteristic of one cannot, logically, be characteristic of the other. Accordingly, there seems to be an implication here that if people in so-called interdependence cultures value "concern for others," "kindness," and "the ability to both respect and share others' feelings," then people in so-called independence cultures do not.

Although many dualists do acknowledge that all human beings in all cultures must deal with issues of both independence and interdependence, these acknowledgments often remain rather perfunctory, as many treatments still end up dividing the world into cultures that emphasize independence and cultures that emphasize interdependence. Interestingly, in some recent treatments, there seems to be an increasing tendency for theorists and researchers to explicitly dissociate themselves from dichotomous conceptions of independence and interdependence by stating that both independence and interdependence are universal aspects of human functioning, or that independence and interdependence are not mutually exclusive. For example, Keller (2003) stated that "We associate the two modes of competence with independent and interdependent construals of the self. In order to avoid misunderstandings, we need to stress that the two construals of the self do not represent a dichotomous framework, one that is mutually exclusive nor is it meant to represent another grand divide theory" (p. 290).

However, because some treatments then go on to explore how either independence or interdependence is emphasized in one or another culture, they maintain, for me, a distinctly dichotomous flavor. It seems theoretically problematic to first acknowledge that all cultures and all people are multidimensional and heterogeneous, but then go on to analyze how a culture emphasizes either independence or interdependence. If indeed cultures and people are conceptualized as multidimensional and heterogeneous, why not explore how heterogeneous and multidimensional modes of both independence and interdependence are particularized in human functioning in different cultures?

In some cases, when the value of relationships in allegedly independence-oriented cultures is explicitly acknowledged, it is described rather pejoratively. For example, it has been pointed out that social obligations are carried out by people within individualistic cultures "when their computations of the advantages and disadvantages suggest they would derive a clear benefit" (Triandis, 1995, p. 11), and thus, "Individualists rationally analyze the advantages and disadvantages of maintaining and fostering relationships" (p. 12). Similarly, Markus and Kitayama (1991) noted that:

The independent self must, of course, be responsive to the social environ-ment. This responsiveness, however, is fostered not so much for the sake of the responsiveness itself. Rather, social responsiveness often, if not always, derives from the need to strategically determine the best way to express or assert the internal attributes of the self. Others, or the social situation in gen-eral, are important, but primarily as standards of reflected appraisal, or as sources that can verify and affirm the inner core of the self. (p. 226)

By contrasting relationships within allegedly independence-oriented cultures with relationships "for the sake of the responsiveness itself," there seems to be an implied idealization of relationships within alleg-edly interdependence-oriented cultures. However, relationships in some allegedly interdependence-oriented cultures are structured hierar-chically, with those at the top of the hierarchy accruing all kinds of per-sonal benefits at the expense of people in less powerful positions. Re-search in the patriarchically stratified Arab Druze cultural community indicates that both men's and women's social judgments include the im-portance of independence and personal entitlements for men, but not for women (Turiel & Wainryb, 2000; Wainryb & Turiel, 1994). In addi-tion, many Druze females see the patriarchy of their culture as unfair, but they may refrain from openly protesting these social arrangements not "for the sake of the responsiveness itself" (Markus & Kitayama, 1991, p. 226), but instead for the sake of personal survival.

Individual Inviolability Across Cultures

It has also been suggested that within independence-oriented cultures, "the individual qua individual is seen as inviolate, a supreme value in and of itself," thus supporting the development of an "inviolate self" (Shweder & Bourne, 1984/1988, p. 192). As it turns out, conceptions of individual inviolability have actually been associated with some long-standing Native American cultural traditions. For example, ethnographic analyses of the Navajo point to the "inviolability of the individual," which is taken to be "singularly important to the Navajo" (Downs, 1972/1984, p. 24). Further-more:

Despite close and absolutely essential familial ties, the Navajo remain highly individualistic people. Their primary social premise might be said to be that no person has the right to speak for or to direct the actions of another. . . . In summary, despite the importance of group ties in this area, it should be remembered that the group must and often does make major adjust-ments to fit the behavior of an individual. (Downs, 1972/1984, pp. 24–25)

A similar conception of individual inviolability has also been identified within the White Mountain Apache worldview as "individuals of any age [including children] have the right to make their own decisions with respect to personal action, and . . . it is rude or improper to directly order or force them to do something against their will" (Greenfield, 1996, p. 492). Along similar lines, research in some New Mexico Pueblo communities indicates that rather than working toward a simple majority for handling community concerns:

> What is deemed crucial is the consensus of the group. If the topic that the individual raises is one that generates debate, a council meeting may last throughout the night until each man present has had the opportunity to be heard. No one is to leave the meeting without some sense of satisfaction, even if the basic issue has not been resolved as each individual would have wished. (Suina & Smolkin, 1994, p. 121)

Interestingly, in the wider context of American political organization that is dominated by Euro-American political traditions, a simple majority vote is often all that is needed in decision making. This practice may leave many individuals "without some sense of satisfaction," other than knowing that certain democratic procedures were followed. In presenting these examples, I do not mean to suggest that interdependence is not highly valued in Native American cultural traditions. The point here is that modes of independence have also been found to be critically important in many cultures that are often characterized as essentially interdependence oriented (e.g., Hewlett, 1992/1994; Hollan, 1992; Howard, 1985; Lienhardt, 1985/1991; Spiro, 1993).

Also along these lines, in a cross-cultural study that included Guatemalan Mayan and middle-class American parents, both groups of parents generally supported their 12- to 24-month-old toddlers' autonomy (Rogoff, Mistry, Göncü, & Mosier, 1993). From a dichotomous approach to independence and interdependence, one might assume that as non-Westerners, the Mayan parents would not place much, if any, value on their children's autonomy. Moreover, in an analysis of teaching practices in these two cultural communities, the American parents appeared almost less independence oriented than did the Guatemalan Mayan parents. More specifically, the parents were given several unfamiliar objects and were asked to "get the child to operate them" (p. 26). In teaching the children, it was the Mayan, and not the American, parents who "were more responsive to their children's own efforts to understand and work the objects. They were poised in readiness to assist the toddlers. . . . Being poised ready to help is a responsive way of assisting the children that leaves the pace and direction of children's efforts up to them" (p. 81).

In contrast, the American parents more actively structured and managed the children's engagement with the novel objects, "even to the point of overruling the toddlers' desires" (Rogoff et al., 1993, p. 85). Indeed, the American "caregivers more often tried to supersede the children's will, not accepting children's refusal or insistence on a course of action. They went beyond coaxing (which occurred to similar extents in the two communities), attempting to force the children" (p. 83). Going back to the notion of individual inviolability, Rogoff et al. noted that the findings of nonintervention among the Mayans are consistent with the Mayans' "respect for personal autonomy that cannot be breached even to achieve something that is regarded as necessary for the well-being of another. (For example, family members have been observed not to hold a child against her will for a medical procedure—'She doesn't want to.')" (p. 84).

Recently, these and other Guatemalan Mayan behavioral patterns have been characterized as a cultural pattern of "interdependence with autonomy" (Rogoff, 2003, p. 200), which stands in contrast to traditional, dichotomous classifications of non-Western cultures as essentially interdependence oriented. At the same time, this kind of "interdependence with autonomy" is also viewed in contrast to Euro-American modes of socialization toward "separate individualism" (Rogoff, 2003, p. 200). Characterizing some cultures in terms of "interdependence with autonomy" while characterizing Euro-American culture in terms of "separate individualism" seems to implicitly suggest that the dichotomy still applies to Euro-American culture, but not to varied other cultures. It seems to me that if some cultures have been erroneously characterized as essentially interdependent, it is likely, or at least theoretically possible, that some cultures (including Euro-American) have also been erroneously characterized as independent. In other words, if the dichotomy does not hold up for some cultures, why not go a step further and wonder whether it holds up for any cultures?

Context-Dependent and Context-Independent Selves

Another problematic issue raised by dichotomous conceptions of independence and interdependence involves the claim that people in so-called independence-oriented cultures conceptualize themselves in terms of stable and context-independent personal attributes, whereas people in so-called interdependence-oriented cultures conceptualize themselves in dynamic and context-dependent terms. It is sometimes argued that when people conceptualize themselves in terms of unchanging personal attributes, little attention is paid to how self-conceptualization occurs in relation to others or to how people define themselves contextually (e.g., Markus & Kitayama, 1991; Shweder & Bourne, 1984/1988). For example, a person might describe him or herself as "hardworking" or "friendly," suggesting that he or she is always hardworking or friendly no matter what the situation. In contrast, when self-construction is understood as context dependent, a person might say, "I help my neighbors when their cars break down."

However, viewing some aspects of oneself as context dependent does not preclude viewing other aspects of oneself as context independent (Spiro, 1993). As Spiro pointed out, a cross-cultural study of self-conceptualization (Shweder & Bourne, 1984/1988) indicated that even though Indians are more likely than Americans to describe themselves in context-dependent ways, half of the Indians' self-descriptions were categorized as context independent. Furthermore, defining oneself in relation to a particular social context does not preclude thinking of oneself as a distinct being with a past and a future who makes decisions and constructs subjective experiences in varied social contexts. After all, someone is engaging in the process of self-definition. Also, over time, defining oneself contextually does not preclude constructing a sense of individual continuity that links one's contextual selves together in some way (Chandler, 2000; Chandler et al., 2003).

With regard to the notion of context independence, viewing oneself as a constellation of fairly stable personal attributes does not preclude defining oneself in relation to others. Although we consider self-issues in greater detail in chapters 6 and 7, it is pertinent at this point to consider an example of how describing oneself in terms of stable personal attributes does not preclude a social conceptualization of self. In a study of late adolescent self-constructions that I conducted, one 21-year-old Euro-American female described herself as follows: "I'm outgoing. Uh. Very friendly. Easy to talk to, good listener." This person defined herself in terms of personal attributes that are indeed independent of any specific social situation, and she also did not define herself in terms of a specific collective. But one would be hard-pressed to argue that she conceptualized herself in isolation from others or in isolation from social concerns.

In addition, studies of Euro-American adolescents show that they define themselves differently in relation to different people, such as their parents, friends, and romantic partners (Harter & Monsour, 1992), indicating that there is even a "proliferation of multiple selves across roles" (Harter, 1999, p. 65). Thus, as Euro-Americans define themselves in terms of personal attributes, these attributes are socially situated and may be understood differently in the context of different social relationships.

Along similar lines, interviews with Americans about situations of embarrassment point to how the "self is unabashedly defined in terms of both relationships to, and the opinions of, others" (Holland & Kipnis, 1994, p. 336). Such findings suggest that just because people do not define themselves in terms of a particular, or tightly structured, collective, it does not necessarily mean that their self-definitions are asocial or antisocial. Similarly, just because people pursue goals that do not serve a particular collective or ingroup, it does not necessarily mean that their goals are asocial or antisocial (Schwartz, 1990). For example, promoting world peace or volunteering in a homeless shelter are activities that involve social goals, even if they do not revolve around contributing to a specific, explicitly structured ingroup.

Investigating Cultural Meanings, Not Amounts of Independence and Interdependence

In some cases, the complexities and variability of independence and interdependence within and across cultures have been obscured because cultural comparisons often focus on one or possibly a few aspects of behavior that can support a dichotomous approach. Of course one study can only do so much, and I am not suggesting that single studies try to encompass all the complexities of independence and interdependence. However, there is a need to integrate existing studies to move beyond considering one or a few aspects of behavior at a time, toward discerning the bigger picture of independence and interdependence. The tendency to focus on single or unidimensional aspects of independence and interdependence may stem in part from attempts in traditional, experimental psychology to follow the natural science paradigm, with its particular analytic implications (Danziger, 1990/1998; Taylor, 1985/1991; Valsiner, 1997). This paradigm has led to manipulating human behavior in artificial experimental situations, to analyzing human functioning in terms of isolated, quantifiable acts, to discerning how these acts are caused by the effects of single variables, and to discerning whether individuals, aggregated into groups, differ statistically with regard to the frequency of committing various acts.

In terms of independence and interdependence issues, these traditional empirical practices involve analyses that focus on issues of more or less. That is, the empirical focus becomes one of discerning differences in the overall amount of independence and interdependence across cultures or across individuals. Accordingly, the dominant empirical question has been: Do people in Culture X value independence or interdependence more than do people in Culture Y? However, unlike the objects of natural science, human beings are meaning-making creatures (Bruner, 1990; Taylor, 1985/1991). Thus, focusing on amounts of independence and interdependence may be useful, but ultimately limited, because it distracts us from discerning different cultural meanings of independence and interdependence.

In raising this issue, I am not suggesting that quantitative analyses be wholly abandoned in psychology because it is often quite useful to discern whether certain values or forms of behavior are more or less prevalent across varied groups of people. Instead, I am suggesting that quantitative analyses be integrated with more focused analyses of cultural meanings. For example, rather than simply discerning whether a culture values independence or interdependence more than some other culture, it is important to discern whether there are cultural differences in how independence and interdependence are understood and defined. Then, quantitative analyses could be conducted to discern whether people in one culture value a particular definition of independence or interdependence more or less than do people in some other culture. Similarly, with regard to cultural expectations for development, quantitative and qualitative analyses may involve discerning changing patterns of both independence and interdependence, rather than investigating whether development in one or another culture tends toward either independence or interdependence.

Along these lines, as psychologists have acknowledged some of the limitations of more or less questions for understanding the complexities of human functioning, qualitative and culturally contextualized analytic paradigms are being used with increasing vigor and rigor to complement traditional experimental methods. Accordingly, some theoretical and empirical analyses suggest that there are different conceptions of independence and interdependence, both within and across cultures.

For example, with regard to different cultural conceptions of independence within a culture, Kusserow (1999) identified different patterns of American individualism in the childrearing goals of parents living in three different urban communities. One pattern, known as *hard defensive individualism*, revolves around protecting individuals from a harsh world. Within the context of hard defensive individualism, "self-reliance, minding one's own business, and a dogged self-determination were the traits that would help their children buck up, toughen, harden, and keep going through some challenging situation that would arise" (p. 217). Another urban community favored *hard offensive individualism*, whereby individuals are concerned more with asserting themselves in the world than with protecting themselves from the world. More specifically, according to Kusserow, hard offensive individualism "was seen as that which helped one to gain success and achievement in life, to build momentum in order to arrive and stay 'on top' of a recently reached status or level of success" (p. 220). Finally, within the context of *soft offensive individualism*, "the goal was to puff the delicate layers of the child's self out, so that the child could open out into the world and realize his or her full potential" (p. 223).

With regard to different forms of independence across cultures, a comparative analysis of middle-class Americans and the Gusii of Kenya indicated that:

> Americans expect a boy to learn to clean his room, while the Gusii expect a boy to learn how to build his new house. In that respect, the Gusii youth becomes more self-sufficient. But the traditional Gusii son was expected to consult both parents in the choice of a wife and to bring her home to his mother for help in setting up their household, while the American youth is expected to make his own marital choice and set up an independent household. In this domain, the American is more autonomous. (LeVine, 1990, p. 472)

This example suggests that cultural differences do not necessarily lie in a prevalence of independence per se, but in how independence for young men is defined and enacted.

In addition to shedding light on different cultural conceptions of independence and interdependence, such findings raise questions about using specific a priori definitions of independence and interdependence that do not allow for the possibility that these aspects of human functioning may be understood and structured differently within and across cultures. Since the now-classic attempts to transport Western assessments of cognitive development, such as Piagetian conservation tasks, to varied non-Western cultures (Cole, 1996), the field of developmental psychology is increasingly embracing the idea that the psychological constructs and assessment procedures identified in one culture may be understood differently in other cultures.

Similarly, distinguishing between etic and emic methods in cultural research (Berry, 1969) has also provided a framework for discerning how universal aspects of human functioning may be particularized and understood differently in different cultures. An etic approach involves investigating some aspect of behavior across cultures by using constructs that are defined within one cultural system. An emic approach involves investigating some aspect of behavior in one culture to discern how that aspect of behavior is understood and particularized locally. Ultimately, etic and emic approaches may be integrated into a derived etic approach that involves identifying similarities and differences in behavior across cultures based on emic constructs.

Accordingly, I now wish to extend these ideas to issues of independence and interdependence by suggesting that we not adhere too loyally to a priori and nonculturally specific definitions of these constructs. For example, rather than etically assuming that valuing independence means valuing self-containment and disengagement from others, I suggest that cultural ways of defining human separateness and connectedness be investigated emically to discern specific or local cultural ways of construing and enacting independence and interdependence. Then a derived etic approach can be used to identify similarities and differences in cultural conceptions and enactments of independence and interdependence.

Dynamic Cultural Conceptions of Independence and Interdependence

Specific a priori definitions also imply relatively static cultural conceptions of independence and interdependence, but cultures are not static over the course of historical time. Thus, a more dynamic approach would facilitate our understanding of how independence and interdependence issues are played out historically. I take up some historical concerns in more detail in chapter 3, but for now we may generalize, and consider the tendency for historical analyses to suggest that there is an increasing cultural emphasis on independence over time.

For example, in a study that included urban American, Estonian, and Russian parents (Tudge et al., 1999), conducted after the disintegration of the Soviet Union, it was hypothesized that the American parents would be more likely to value aspects of children's self-direction, including self-control and sound judgment, than would parents in Estonia and Russia. To assess these parental values, Kohn's (1969/1977) Q sort of parental values was used, and this Q sort included statements taken to be characteristic of values regarding self-direction and conformity to authority. Overall, according to Kohn, valuing self-direction "implies that one is attuned to internal dynamics—one's own, and other people's" (1969/1977, p. 35), thus suggesting how self-direction is actually inseparable from issues of connectedness. The results of the study indicated that "mothers and fathers (on average) scored surprisingly similarly in each of the cities" (Tudge et al., 1999, p. 77). It seems to me that this finding is really only "surprising" from a dichotomous approach to independence and interdependence, whereby the United States is viewed as essentially independence oriented, and Russia and Estonia are viewed as essentially interdependence oriented. To explain these findings, the researchers speculated that since the fall of the Soviet Union, Russian and Estonian parents would have experienced cultural changes from collectivism toward individualism such that, "once the ability to compromise and conform may have been the characteristics most conducive to a successful work life, now initiative and independence in thought and action may be perceived to be more important" (p. 87).

Alternatively, the findings may be understood by taking into account that the Soviet system was maintained through coercion and repression. Thus, despite trying to foster cooperation and unity, there was concurrently much in the daily realities of life under Soviet communism that actually served to alienate people from one another. For example, if people cannot express themselves openly, and if they cannot trust their neighbors or colleagues at work for fear that they may be government informants, then self-direction, especially in the forms of self-control and sound judgment, are probably quite adaptive. Being attuned to others' "internal dynamics" would also be adaptive when explicitly speaking one's mind could have dire consequences. In addition, maintaining an active private or personal world of ideas and opinions may have been one important way in which people could defy the system that controlled so much of their lives. This interpretation suggests that, rather than assuming there is an increase in independence over historical time, conceptions and modes of both independence and interdependence may have changed with the fall of the Soviet Union.

In addition to not being static across or within cultures over time, independence and interdependence as aspects of human behavior are not static during development. Thus, there may be different expectations or conceptions of appropriate modes of independent and interdependent functioning for infants, children, and adolescents, or even later in the life span. For example, parents may support a 1-year-old's self-reliance by allowing self-feeding with his or her fingers, but by the time the child is a 3-year-old, expectations for self-reliance might include self-feeding with culturally appropriate utensils. A young child's food-related self-reliance may also be linked to modes of interdependence, as parents enforce expectations for table manners and engaging with others during meals. Ultimately, self-feeding might involve multifaceted and interrelated modes of both independence and interdependence, including budgeting one's own hard-earned money for food, shopping, cooking for oneself and others, eating with others, and cleaning up. This example points to the importance of identifying how changing expectations may shape the developmental trajectories of both independence and interdependence in different cultural settings.

Trying to Understand the Rise of Dichotomous
Conceptions of Independence and Interdependence

Clearly, there are some limitations to dichotomous conceptions of independence and interdependence because they tend to obscure evidence regarding the variability and complexities of behavior and development in different cultural contexts over time (e.g., Chirkov, Ryan, Kim, & Kaplan, 2003; Fijneman et al., 1996; Gjerde, 2004; Gjerde & Onishi, 2000; Harkness, Super, & van Tijen, 2000; Harwood, Handwerker, Schoelmerich, & Leyendecker, 2001; Holland, 1997; Killen & Wainryb, 2000; Mascolo, Misra, & Rapisardi, 2004; Neff, 2003; Shwalb, 2000; Sinha & Tripathi, 1994; Stephan, Stephan, Saito, & Barnett, 1998; Suizzo, 2004; Takahashi, Ohara, Antonucci, & Akiyama, 2002; Turiel & Perkins, 2004). Indeed, as we have already begun to see, there is much evidence pointing to the importance of interdependence in so-called independence-oriented cultures, and there is also evidence for the importance of independence in varied so-called interdependence-oriented cultures. Some of the studies discussed thus far also indicate that independence and interdependence are inseparable or interrelated aspects of human functioning. Such evidence is a basis for this book, and thus is discussed in more detail in subsequent chapters.

However, in general, it is perhaps not surprising that a comprehensive meta-analysis of studies based on the individualism/collectivism dichotomy indicates that cultures are far too heterogeneous and complex to be characterized and contrasted with one another in unidimensional terms (Oyserman, Coon, & Kemmelmeier, 2002). Such findings suggest that even if the first-glance analyses of cross-cultural studies point to a comparative emphasis on either independence or interdependence, further analyses are required to explore the complexities of both independence and interdependence. In particular, further analyses are required to discern how both independence and interdependence are understood and enacted in the cultures being studied.

I find it interesting that dichotomous conceptions of independence and interdependence emerged, and then persisted, even though evidence against this dichotomy was abundant before and during the 1980s and has continued to be generated since the 1980s. Moreover, I have found that at least some of the research that has been used to support the dichotomy can be interpreted nondichotomously. (Again, I consider some of this research later, as this book proceeds.) In addition to such evidence, some scholars have been speaking out against the dichotomy for decades. For example, with regard to independence in the American case, already in 1916 John Dewey commented that philosophers were basically mistaking individualism "as an assertion that each individual's mind was complete in isolation from everything else" (1916/1997, p. 305). We have also seen how in 1981 Waterman pointed out the practical impossibility of self-containment. In 1983, Turiel (1983/1985) cautioned developmentalists against unidimensionally dividing the world up into cultures of independence and interdependence.

I have not analyzed the reasons for the emergence and persistence of the dichotomy in great detail, but there are, no doubt, several reasons for its endurance. One may be that it is simply heuristically useful and offers a straightforward way to understand some cultural differences. Second, dichotomous conceptions of independence and interdependence were embraced and promulgated by social scientists in the 1980s in part to combat the predominance of Western psychology, with its focus on the individual, that did not seem to adequately account for non-Western cultural practices (Hofstede, 1980/2001; Howard, 1985; Murray, 1993). For example, Hofstede (1980/2001) wrote:

> Since the first edition of *Culture's Consequences* appeared in 1980, the individualism/collectivism dimension has gained great popularity . . . The dimension provides psychologists with a paradigm implying that traditional psychology is not a universal science: It is a product of Western thinking, caught in individualist assumptions. When these are replaced by more collectivist assumptions, another psychology emerges that differs in important respects. (p. 215)

This effort to overcome Western dominance in the social sciences serves a generally liberal framework that advocates inclusiveness and cooperation over competition and self-interest. Although identifying the individualism/collectivism dimension has helped to move psychological inquiries beyond focusing on individual aspects of behavior, the preceding quotation from Hofstede (1980/2001) and its exhortation that Western assumptions be "replaced by more collectivist assumptions" once again leaves us with a one-sided approach. Furthermore, although Western notions may pervade psychology, there are some notable exceptions to the general rule that Western psychology has been single-mindedly asocial and focused on the individual. Thus, in addition to addressing how independence and interdependence are both evident in infants', children's, and adolescents' developmental experiences, in chapters 5 and 6, I examine conceptions of independence and interdependence in some classic Western theories of human behavior.

It is also possible that several other interrelated sociocultural trends during the 1980s contributed to the emergence and consolidation of dichotomous conceptions of independence and interdependence. For example, the strengthening momentum of the feminist movement was shedding light on apparently female meanings and modes of interdependence. Indeed, it was also during the 1980s that discussions of gender differences in behavior and development were offering a kind of parallel independence and interdependence dichotomy regarding gender (e.g., Gilligan, 1982). The argument that men are relatively independent, whereas women are relatively interdependent, is certainly familiar by now. However, it is not my intention in this book to analyze independence and interdependence in relation to gender. I now point out only that although this gender dichotomy has elucidated some important differences in male and female socialization and behavior, it has also been criticized based on research revealing patterns of both independence and interdependence for men and women. In addition to these feminist trends, the 1980s saw the conservative independence-oriented policies of the Reagan years. The late 1970s and early 1980s also saw a waning of the liberal social activism of the 1960s that emphasized cooperation and promoting collective goals. Taken together, the time was ripe for a way to overcome patterns of self-interest, competition, and Western domination in psychology by pointing to an alternative cultural model of human functioning.

MOVING BEYOND DICHOTOMOUS CONCEPTIONS OF INDEPENDENCE AND INTERDEPENDENCE

However, in the context of increasingly apparent limitations, calls to look beyond dichotomous conceptions of independence and interdependence have been advanced, and initial attempts to do so involved presenting empirical examples (some of which have already been discussed in this chapter) of independence in so-called interdependence cultures and of interdependence in so-called independence cultures. In addition to offering a list of examples of both independence and interdependence in varied cultures, some attempts have been made to conceptualize the dynamics of how independence and interdependence are coordinated in human functioning. Nevertheless, these varied conceptual approaches still leave us with some unresolved theoretical issues regarding the roles of independence and interdependence in human experience. To date, I have found that there are several specific approaches that can be subsumed under one of two general coordination models, which I refer to as the "sometimes independence, sometimes interdependence" model and the "co-occurrence of independence and interdependence" model.

"Sometimes Independence, Sometimes Interdependence" Models

According to the "sometimes independence, sometimes interdependence" model, people around the world sometimes engage in independence-oriented action and sometimes engage in interdependence-oriented action. Similarly, people sometimes conceptualize themselves as independent and sometimes conceptualize themselves as interdependent. I have further identified four specific "sometimes independence, sometimes interdependence" models.

Independence and Interdependence as Primary and Secondary Orientations. One "sometimes independence, sometimes interdependence" model revolves around the idea that any particular culture may be characterized by an overarching or primary cultural value orientation, toward either independence or interdependence, but that secondary value orientations may also be particularized within a culture (e.g., Greenfield, 2000; Greenfield & Suzuki, 1998). For example, in analyzing American culture, Bellah, Madsen, Sullivan, Swidler, and Tipton (1985/1986) proposed that an independence orientation is dominant in the United States, but that connectedness concerns comprise an American "second language" (p. 154). Within this view, people act according to the primary orientation most of the time, but the secondary orientation may be invoked on occasion. For example, Bellah et al. discussed how a participant in their interview research tended to think of his marriage in terms of a "utilitarian individualist vocabulary," explaining that "he wants a long lasting relationship" because "he has found the best possible partner, the one who will bring him the most happiness" (p. 104). Bellah et al. then noted that, "when pressed to explain why he remains in a long marriage, his several attempts to do so in cost/benefit terms finally break down" and he began "groping for words that could express his marriage as a community of memory and hope" (p. 157). According to Bellah et al., the secondary interdependence orientation is invoked in this case because the primary independent orientation does not seem adequate for explaining the significance of a long-term relationship.

Cultural Emphasis, Individual Variability. Another "sometimes independence, sometimes interdependence" model involves the idea that, although a specific culture emphasizes either an overall independence or interdependence orientation, individuals within a culture express contrasting or conflicting independent and interdependent self-dimensions, and thus may behave in independent or interdependent ways depending on the situation (e.g., Dennis, Cole, Zahn-Waxler, & Mizuta, 2002; Hofstede, 1980/2001; Singelis, 1994; Triandis, 1989, 1995). Even those whom I have associated with explicating dichotomous approaches to independence and interdependence have acknowledged that within-culture variability may occur in this way (e.g., Hofstede, 1980/2001; Markus & Kitayama, 1991). For example, after explaining that Western self-conceptions are generally independence oriented, whereas non-Western self-conceptions are generally interdependence oriented, Markus and Kitayama (1991) noted that, "Within a given culture, however, individuals will vary in the extent to which they are good cultural representatives and construe the self in the mandated way" (p. 226). In addition, Triandis (1995) suggested that, although cultures may generally be characterized either in terms of individualism or collectivism, individuals within cultures may be characterized as relatively allocentric or idiocentric. More specifically, Triandis (1995) explained:

> In every culture there are people who are *allocentric*, who believe, feel, and act very much like collectivists do around the world. There are also people who are *idiocentric*, who believe, feel, and act the way individualists do around the world. For example, we know Americans who would not hesitate to marry someone their parents dislike, but we also know Americans who would never do such a thing. In China those who press for human rights are likely to be idiocentric in a collectivist culture. In the United States, those who join communes are likely to be allocentric in an individualistic culture. (p. 5)

Within this model, a distinction is sometimes made between applying conceptions of independence and interdependence to cultures and applying them to individual behavior. That is, independence and interdependence are conceptualized here as a single dimension, or continuum, to be used for characterizing cultures. However, independence and interdependence are conceptualized differently, as multiple dimensions, for characterizing individual behavior. This distinction draws on Hofstede's (1980/2001) conceptualization of individualism and collectivism in unidimensional terms only for understanding overarching cultural values. With regard to individual behavior, Hofstede (1994) pointed out that his conceptualization of individualism/collectivism in *Culture's Consequences*:

> makes no assumption about the suitability or dimensionality of individualism and collectivism as *psychological* concepts. If one were to ask me, I would suppose that at the individual level a multidimensional model would be more useful than a unidimensional one. . . . A culture does not consist of modal personalities; culture is no king-size personality. . . . Thus it is quite

possible that the same set of variables produces a bipolar dimension at the culture level and two or more unipolar dimensions at the level of individuals. (p. xi)

Similarly, according to Triandis (1994), although "individualism and collectivism are opposite poles of one dimension, individual-level factor analyses suggest that the two can coexist" (p. 42).

Cultural and Individual Heterogeneity. A third "sometimes independence, sometimes interdependence" model rejects the notion of an overarching cultural value orientation toward either independence or interdependence on the grounds that it supports homogeneous and stereotypical characterizations of cultures (Killen & Wainryb, 2000; Turiel, 1996; Turiel, Smetana, & Killen, 1991; Turiel & Wainryb, 2000; Wainryb, 1995; Wainryb & Turiel, 1994). Instead, it is argued that cultures are heterogeneous and made up of social situations that may involve varied independence and interdependence issues that are sometimes in harmony and sometimes in conflict. As individuals negotiate their ways through different social situations, sometimes they will act according to their independence orientations, and sometimes they will act according to their interdependence orientations. In this way, individuals are conceptualized as active agents who emphasize independence or interdependence concerns in varied social contexts. The role of culture is not so much to offer overarching values regarding independence or interdependence as it is to structure social contexts in ways that involve different independence and interdependence issues.

In a fourth "sometimes independence, sometimes interdependence" model that can also be classified in terms of cultural and individual heterogeneity, it is argued that there is a worldwide historical trend toward "emotional interdependence" (Kağitçibaşi, 1994, 1996). Within this model, independence and interdependence are understood as "contrasting tendencies" that coexist culturally and "in the same person or family, though one or the other orientation may take over at different times and regarding different issues" (Kağitçibaşi, 1996, p. 90).

These "sometimes independence, sometimes interdependence" models have moved discussions of independence and interdependence beyond static and unidimensional dichotomies, and they also provide a way to explain some of the empirical data on coexisting modes of independent and interdependent functioning in varied cultures. Nevertheless, several theoretical issues and questions remain unresolved or unaddressed. For example, in the face of the mounting empirical evidence mentioned earlier, it does not seem adequate to conceptualize independence and interdependence only in terms of being relatively primary or secondary in different cultures, as is the case in the first and second models. This conceptualization may easily lead to quantifying independence and interdependence and to characterizing cultures in terms of a quantitative primacy of either independence or interdependence. However, by quantifying independence and interdependence, we risk lapsing back into a dichotomous approach. With regard to the second model, the focus on independence and interdependence as contrasting dimensions of human experience precludes the theoretical possibility that independence and interdependence may be compatible dimensions of human experience.

Also, with regard to the second model, evidence of within-culture heterogeneity calls into question the view that independence and interdependence represent multiple and coexisting dimensions only in relation to individual behavior, but not in relation to cultural processes. Viewing independence and interdependence as culturally unidimensional but individually multidimensional is theoretically problematic when individual and cultural processes are conceptualized as inseparable aspects of human functioning. Based on such a conceptualization (e.g., Bruner, 1990; Miller & Goodnow, 1995; Rogoff, 1990, 2003; Wertsch, 1998), it makes more theoretical sense to conceptualize cultural and individual aspects of independence and interdependence commensurately. I am not suggesting that individuals are mirror images of culture or passive recipients of culture, but if individual behavior is multidimensional, how are unidimensional cultural values embedded in multidimensional modes of behavior? In addition, how are unidimensional cultural values constructed by people who engage in multidimensional modes of behavior?

Although it points to the importance of individual construals of varied social situations, the first of the two cultural and individual heterogeneity models, runs the risk of overemphasizing the role of the individual at the expense of considering how cultural processes frame individual construals and social situations. Thus, I wonder if it is possible for general cultural values regarding *both* independence and interdependence to partly shape the development of individual constructions without invoking the notion of an overarching cultural orientation toward either independence or interdependence.

Finally, although the second cultural and individual heterogeneity model addresses how varied cultures may change historically, conceptualizing independence and interdependence as "contrasting tendencies" forecloses the possibility that they may be compatible aspects of human experience. Also, viewing cultural change in terms of a single historical trend toward emotional interdependence runs the risk of obscuring how cultures may continue to differ, even in the face of some common worldwide historical trends.

The "Co-Occurrence of Independence and Interdependence" Model

To further address issues regarding the coordination of independence and interdependence, there have been some efforts to conceptualize independence and interdependence as co-occurring aspects of human functioning. Overall, the difference between this model and the previous models is that in the "sometimes independence, sometimes interdependence" models there is little theoretical room for modes of independence and interdependence to occur simultaneously. Instead, one or the other is invoked by a person, usually depending on the situation. In contrast, the "co-occurrence of independence and interdependence" model allows for the possibility that modes of independence and interdependence can be enacted simultaneously by a person in a given situation. In other words, a person can be simultaneously separate from and connected to others.

According to the co-occurrence model, it is argued that some aspects of independence and interdependence can be compatible, whereas others may be conflicting. However, whether compatible or conflicting, independence and interdependence are conceptualized as modes of functioning that are interrelated or inseparable in varied ways in human behavior (Damon, 1983). For example, Strauss (2000) suggested that, in the United States, people's causal explanations of behavior involve a mixture of independence and interdependence, or inseparable aspects of independence and interdependence. Specifically, her interviews with working-class and middle-class adults indicate how some of them explained human behavior in terms of both individual dispositions that interact with social circumstances and personal characteristics that are shaped through socialization experiences. In this way, independence and interdependence are inseparable, and further theoretical elaborations to this "co-occurrence" model can be found in developmental analyses of human functioning.

For example, with regard to social development, Shantz and Hobart (1989) noted that independence and interdependence can be variably complementary and conflicting aspects of social development that "overlap at a psychological level in important ways. For example, how one individuates and defines oneself presumably is highly related to experiences in close relationships with others, and the types of connected relations one has with others is influenced by one's degree of individuation and self-definition" (p. 87). Similarly, Buhrmester (1996) pointed out:

Social life seems to involve a dynamic interplay between the pursuit of agentic and communal forms of satisfaction. In some instances, agentic and communal needs may be in direct competition with one another, such as when beating a friend in a game brings individual glory at the expense of hard feelings in the friendship. In other instances, agentic and communal aims are in concert with one another, such as when a team victory simultaneously engenders an agentic sense of achievement for each individual team member, along with a communal sense of close comradeship among teammates. (p. 161)

With respect to the foundations of self-conceptualization during infancy and early childhood, varied theorists and researchers converge on the point that a child's individual sense of self is fundamentally linked to his or her relationships with others (e.g., Bowlby, 1969/1982, 1973; Emde & Buchsbaum, 1990; Pipp, 1990; Sroufe, 1990; Stern, 1985). For example, according to Bowlby (1973), for a young child's sense of self or working model of self, "a key feature is his notion of who his attachment figures are, where they may be found, and how they may be expected to respond. Similarly, in the working model of the self that anyone builds a key feature is his notion of how acceptable or unacceptable he himself is in the eyes of his attachment figures" (p. 203).

Focusing on self-conceptualization issues among Japanese adolescents, Shimizu (2000) argued that conceptions of independence and interdependence "need to be integrated from an ontological perspective which decenters *either* of the two orientations as the primary constituting agent of individual or collective experience, and recasts *both* elements as mutually and dynamically constituting elements of the individual's personal experience" (p. 196). Answering this call (actually before it was even made!), Youniss and Smollar (1985) described how independence and interdependence are integrated during adolescent self-development as adolescents construct conceptions of themselves in the context of relationships with their parents and friends. Youniss and Smollar (1985) explained further:

In neither relationship—between adolescents and parents nor between friends—is development toward the point when an individual asserts self by turning inward with recourse to self-reflective reasoning alone seen. Self-reflection is only part of a larger process, which ultimately requires that reasoning done on one's own must stand the test of social criticism and verification. (pp. 168–169)

Varied other investigations of adolescent identity development, many of which are informed by an Eriksonian approach to identity, also point to how identity involves an ongoing, lifelong interplay between independence and interdependence (Adams & Marshall, 1996; Roeser, Eccles, & Sameroff, 2000) such that "the result is a dialectical system in which achievements in one sphere make possible further developments in the other" (Guisinger & Blatt, 1994, p. 108). As Josselson (1994) noted:

> Adolescents, to be sure, do undergo a separation-individuation process on the road to identity. But at the same time, they are not becoming "lone selves" needing no one, standing to face the forces of life alone. Rather, they are editing and modifying, enriching and extending their connections to others, becoming more fully themselves in relation. Individuation is reinvested in revised relatedness, and in these commitments lies the integration of identity. (p. 83)

Similarly, Grotevant and Cooper (e.g., Cooper, 1999; Grotevant & Cooper, 1986, 1998) conceptualized identity formation, as well as social development, in terms of integrating aspects of individuality and connectedness.

Overall, the "co-occurrence" model addresses some of the complexities of independence and interdependence, but we are still left with some unresolved issues and questions. For me, a major unresolved issue is whether the terms *independence* and *interdependence* represent cultural values that shape development, or dimensions of human activity, or both. To further clarify this issue, it would seem important to delineate how independence and interdependence as cultural values, and independence and interdependence as dimensions of activity, are interrelated in children's developmental experiences. Also with regard to culture, it remains unclear whether independence and interdependence can be conceptualized in ways that allow for both cultural universality and variability in how independence and interdependence are particularized in children's developmental experiences.

SOME GENERAL REMARKS

The main goals of this introductory chapter were to review the dichotomous view of independence and interdependence that has dominated the social sciences for approximately 20 years, and to point out some of the limitations to conceptualizing independence and interdependence as dichotomous constructs. Empirically, an ever-increasing number of studies shows that both independence and interdependence are evident around the world. In this chapter, studies conducted in a range of cultures have been reviewed, and they suggest that cultures do not necessarily differ in relative amounts of independence and interdependence, but rather in how both independence and interdependence are understood and enacted in specific contexts.

More than pointing to cultural conceptions of both independence and interdependence, several theoretical issues regarding independence and interdependence were also raised in this chapter. Building on the idea that conceptions of independence and interdependence may vary across cultures is the theoretical issue of within-culture variability regarding independence and interdependence. For the most part, independence and interdependence have been conceptualized as rather static cultural and individual characteristics, even traits. However, it is possible that independence and interdependence may be particularized in different ways in different specific contexts within a particular culture. Within-culture variability in conceptions of independence and interdependence may also be found over the course of historical time. Moreover, within-culture variability in how independence and interdependence are understood may be evident during the course of development, as children's abilities to engage in valued modes of independence and interdependence are transformed.

Another central theoretical issue that can be raised in the context of this chapter involves the claim that not only do independence and interdependence not preclude each other, but they may even entail each other as they are particularized in specific contexts. In other words, some of the research discussed in this chapter suggests that independence and interdependence are inseparable or interrelated aspects of human functioning that mutually influence and constitute each other. For example, an aging Euro-American mother's desire to live on her own may be inseparable from her conceptions of how to maintain harmonious relationships with her children. Another example of how independence and interdependence may be interrelated is evident in Kohn's conceptualization of self-direction. Although self-direction involves making choices about one's own behavior as a separate physical and mental individual, Kohn's definition ties self-direction to consideration for others. Thus, self-direction involves making choices in relation to others.

Within an empirical and theoretical landscape that is rather inhospitable to traditional, dichotomous conceptions of independence and interdependence, developmentalists are now groping for ways to conceptualize how both independence and interdependence are particularized as children develop around the world. In this chapter, it was suggested that recent conceptual attempts fall into two broad categories, dubbed the "sometimes independence, sometimes interdependence" and the "co-occurrence" models. Although these models have taken us beyond unidimensional dichotomous approaches, varied conceptual issues and questions were raised that require clarification to further our understanding of how independence and interdependence enter into children's developmental experiences. In an effort to resolve some of these issues and questions, I now turn to an alternative approach to independence and interdependence.

CHAPTER TWO

Theoretical Foundations, Part 2

TOWARD A NEW CONCEPTUAL APPROACH
TO INDEPENDENCE AND INTERDEPENDENCE

It has been useful to consider the independence and interdependence constructs in general terms, with independence referring to aspects of human functioning and experience that involve being a mentally and physically separate or distinct individual, and interdependence referring to aspects of human functioning and experience that involve connections among people. The issue before us now is to elaborate on these general definitions with a conceptualization that addresses how, more specifically, independence and interdependence are particularized in cultural contexts of development. In brief, the conceptual approach presented in this chapter is based on the following two assumptions about human functioning: (a) Human functioning universally involves dimensions of both independence and interdependence because people everywhere are physically and mentally separate and also socially connected, and (b) human functioning is cultural. The conceptual position is further based on a synthesis of three theoretical approaches to human behavior and development; namely, systems theory (e.g., Ford & Lerner, 1992; Gottlieb, 1991; Gottlieb, Wahlsten, & Lickliter, 1998; von Bertalanffy, 1968, 1969), organismic developmental theory (Kaplan, 1967; Werner & Kaplan, 1963/1984), and sociocultural theory (e.g., Cole, 1996; Miller & Goodnow, 1995; Rogoff, 2003; Užgiris, 1989, 1996; Valsiner, 1997; Wertsch, 1998).

To derive this conceptual approach to independence and interdependence, it is necessary to consider these basic assumptions in conjunction with these theoretical approaches to human behavior and development. I begin by placing the current conceptual approach within a systems framework because systems theory provides an overarching perspective and basic starting point for the current conceptual approach.

A Systems Framework

Within a systems framework, human functioning is taken to consist of multifaceted constituent processes that are systemically organized within specific contexts. Systemic organization means that the constituents of human functioning are interrelated and inseparable as they mutually influence and regulate each other. As just noted, I assume that human beings everywhere are always separate physical and mental individuals, as well as connected to others. By considering this assumption within a systems perspective, I start from the position that human functioning partakes of interrelated or inseparable independence and interdependence constituent processes. This basic systems premise immediately leads to discerning how independence and interdependence are particularized in relation to each other within specific contexts during development.

In keeping with a systems conceptualization, the current approach is also guided by the orthogenetic principle of organismic developmental theory that, when applied to individuals, holds that development involves progressive differentiation and integration in the systemic organization of a person's functioning. As Kaplan (1967) put it, "Insofar as development occurs in a process under consideration, there is a progression from a state of relative undifferentiatedness to a state of increasing differentiation and hierarchic integration" (pp. 82–83). In turn, such progression in systemic functioning is defined in relation to cultural expectations, values, and conceptions about optimal human functioning. The current approach to independence and interdependence is further guided by the premise of sociocultural theory that the development of individual children occurs as they participate actively with others in cultural practices. Synthesizing these developmental theories leads to claiming that children's abilities to engage in culturally valued modes of behavior are differentiated and integrated as they participate with others in varied cultural practices.

By synthesizing these basic theoretical premises, we may now ask: How do the cultural practices in which children participate with others involve independence and interdependence? To use different words, how do independence and interdependence enter children's lives as they participate in cultural practices with others? Answering this question first requires us to explain the term *cultural practices*, which has not been easy for social scientists to pin down (e.g., Cole, 1995). Very generally, I take cultural practices to be made up of activities that are systemically organized or structured in terms of goals that are co-constructed by the participating individuals. The goals and systemic organization of activities within cultural practices may be fairly stable over time while simultaneously open to ongoing negotiation and change. Moreover, cultural practices include activities "that are repeated, shared with others in a social group, and invested with normative expectations and with meanings or significances that go beyond the immediate goals of the action" (Miller & Goodnow, 1995, p. 7). In part because cultural practices are flexible, it may be difficult to clearly demarcate their boundaries. To further clarify what counts as activities within cultural practices, I find it helpful to think about segmenting what I do during the day into meaningful chunks. Rather than including activities in isolation, I think about how varied activities are systemically organized in terms of some wider goals and meanings, such as getting up, teaching a class, or eating dinner.

Conceptualizing Independence and Interdependence as Dimensions of Activity

In keeping with systems theory and the basic assumption that people everywhere are both separate and connected, cultural practices are further considered to partake of multifaceted and interrelated independence, interdependence, and cultural activity dimensions. In this way, the current approach goes beyond simply acknowledging that cultural practices around the world involve both independence and interdependence, to claiming that independence and interdependence activity dimensions are mutually constitutive of one another. The interrelatedness or inseparability of these activity dimensions makes it quite impossible to explain any single dimension in isolation from the other dimensions. Indeed, defining any one dimension requires at least mentioning issues pertaining to the other dimensions. Although such interrelatedness or inseparability may be confusing at times to disentangle, understanding can be facilitated "when one opens one's eyes to the multifaceted and untidy interrelationships that characterize everyday life" (Briggs, 1992, p. 48).

As children participate in a cultural practice with others, the multifaceted interdependence dimensions of their activities involve how the individuals are connected to each other, including the relationship they share, the wider social roles being enacted, the patterning of their interactions, and how they are linked to wider societal functioning. For example, the individuals may be connected as parent and child, as siblings, or as teacher and student, and different interaction patterns may characterize a child's participation in cultural practices with these different social partners. That is, a child may sometimes participate in dyadic interactions and sometimes in group interactions. Interactions among peers may be relatively egalitarian, whereas interactions between some teachers and students may be structured hierarchically. A child's interactions with varied social partners may also be sustained over differing periods of time, and the ensuing relationships may differ in the extent to which they are characterized by strong affectional ties. The cultural practices in which children participate may also be linked to wider societal functioning in varied ways. For example, when adolescents take on part-time summer jobs, they are engaging in work activities that link them to socioeconomic institutions. When American schoolchildren and adolescents participate in their school governments, they are engaging in activities that link them to wider sociopolitical functioning.

Insofar as such interdependence involves connections among individuals, already in this brief definition of the interdependence dimensions of activity we cannot help but include a consideration of the independence dimensions of activity. Multifaceted independence dimensions of activity involve each individual's functioning as a separate physical and mental being, including subjectivity, self-awareness/reflection, self-direction, and individuality. That is, each individual who participates in a cultural practice constructs his or her own subjective experience of the situation. For example, a grandmother may experience personal fulfillment while playing basketball with a grandchild, and the child may experience enjoyment, as well as some personal frustration, at not always being able to get the basketball through the hoop. In addition to such subjectivity, each individual is also aware of his or her behavior and experience and, as symbolic abilities permit, may reflect on his or her behavior and experience. Insofar as each individual regulates aspects of his or her own behavior, another independence dimension of activity involves individual agency or self-direction. For example, when playing basketball, each individual regulates the movement of his or her own arms and legs and makes decisions about throwing the ball and running in different directions. In addition, the independence dimension of activity includes individuality insofar as each participant is a distinct physical and mental individual with his or her own physical features, behavioral predispositions, and personal preferences.

Thus far, independence and interdependence are being conceptualized as constructs that refer to fundamental dimensions of human activity, and neither independence nor interdependence is viewed as more or less important than the other. If we start with neonatal functioning, there is much empirical support for this basic premise insofar as both independence and interdependence are constituents of human functioning from the outset (Pipp, 1990; Stern, 1985). For example, not only do human infants require interpersonal connections for survival, but varied studies of infant abilities suggest that human infants come to the world predisposed to actively engage in and contribute to social interactions (Užgiris, 1989). Human infants are also predisposed to individual self-direction by being able to sustain some physiological self-regulation. In addition, they are able to engage in organized perceptual and sensorimotor activities that enable them to begin acting on the world, and to subjectively construe their experiences as separate mental beings (Piaget, 1953).

Although often studied separately, a systems conceptualization of cultural practices focuses our attention on how these multifaceted foundational independence and interdependence activity dimensions are interrelated or inseparable from the outset. For example, infants contribute their individual preferences to the structuring of social interactions (e.g., Bell, 1968; Stern, 1977; Užgiris, 1989), and infant physiological self-regulation is shaped through social interactions with others.

Moving beyond the infancy years, dimensions of independence and interdependence continue to be inseparable. For example, experiencing subjective fulfillment may be a dimension of independence, but for many individuals fulfillment may only be achieved through maintaining satisfying relationships with others. Going back to the example of a grandmother and grandchild playing basketball, each individual's subjective experience of fulfillment or enjoyment in that situation requires the other person. Also, during the course of interpersonal interaction, an individual's self-direction is not purely self-generated, but instead occurs in relation to others. When playing basketball together, the grandmother and grandchild are regulating their activities in relation to each other, as, for example, each individual's decision to throw the ball depends in part on where the other player is standing or how the other player is blocking the thrower's attempts. In such different ways, dimensions of independence and interdependence are inseparable and are particularized in human activities in relation to each other. Thus, understanding the independence dimensions of some cultural practice requires understanding its interdependence dimensions and vice versa.

These examples of interrelated independence and interdependence activity dimensions suggest that independence and interdependence represent compatible dimensions of activity. At the same time, however, it is also theoretically possible that dimensions of independence and interdependence may come into conflict as people engage in varied cultural practices. For example, an individual may find that, in some situations, connections to other people enable him or her to pursue varied individual goals, or the individual may find that some interpersonal connections could hinder his or her individual goal pursuits. Nevertheless, whether independence and interdependence activity dimensions are in harmony or conflict, they may still be conceptualized as inseparable or interrelated. Only empirical analyses can reveal the varied ways—both harmonious and conflicted—in which independence and interdependence dimensions are interrelated within specific cultural practices.

Conceptualizing Independence and Interdependence in Relation to Culture

The independence and interdependence dimensions of activity may be structured differently in different cultures, and thus are inseparable from the cultural dimension of activity. For example, there may be cultural differences regarding when and how individuality is expressed or suppressed. With respect to self-direction, there may be cultural differences regarding when and how to take initiative or when and how to control one's emotional reactions. With regard to interdependence, there may be cultural differences in the patterning of interactions between parents and children, between peers, or between teachers and students. There may also be cultural differences in how varied social roles are construed, such as what it means to be a mother, father, sibling, or teacher. The structuring of wider societal functioning in the form of political, economic, and educational institutions also varies across cultures.

The word *culture* is one of those many terms that has been debated and defined in innumerable ways by generations of social scientists. A useful approach holds that culture may be defined as a dynamic system of meaningful patterns of activity that is constructed and enacted by individuals through social interactions (e.g., Bruner, 1990; Cole, 1996; Geertz, 1973; Miller & Goodnow, 1995; Rogoff, 2003). As such, human functioning within cultural practices consists of patterns of activity that are meaningful beyond the immediate face value of their physical or quantifiably observable behavioral components. In other words, and as mentioned earlier, cultural practices consist of activities "that are repeated, shared with others in a social group, and invested with normative expectations and with meanings or significances that go beyond the immediate goals of the action" (Miller & Goodnow, 1995, p. 7). Within this approach, to claim that human activity is cultural is to claim that human activity reflects or enacts shared meanings about human behavior and being.

For example, it is commonplace to see American parents encouraging young, often preverbal, children to shake their hands in the air. One way of analyzing such hand shaking would be to count the number of times a child shakes his or her hand, or one could quantitatively measure the vigor with which children shake their hands back and forth. One could also investigate whether American children shake their hands in the air more or less often or vigorously than do children in other cultures. Many might also jump to investigate the brain processes that are associated with this kind of hand shaking. Although informative, none of these approaches tells us much about the meaning or significance of this kind of hand shaking, and how it fits into the complex and ongoing dynamics of human activity within cultural practices.

Another way to analyze this hand shaking would be to discern its cultural meaning; that is, understanding that the hand movements are part of a culturally meaningful practice in which a child is being encouraged to wave goodbye to someone who is leaving. "Waving bye bye" also often includes thanking the departing person for visiting, saying how nice the visit was, telling the departing person to get home safely, or asking the person to come again soon. Children are additionally often encouraged to "wave bye bye" when they are departing, and in this social context waving may be accompanied by thanking one's hosts for their hospitality and perhaps making plans for some future meeting. In these ways, the meaning of a departing hand wave is multifaceted and suffused with cultural values and expectations about how to behave in relation to others. In the next few pages, when I use the term *cultural meanings*, I am using it rather generally to refer to a culture's values about, expectations for, and conceptions of human behavior.

As children actively participate in taking leave, their leave-taking competencies also develop, and children are increasingly able to take leave on their own without protracted episodes involving parental queries about their hand-waving abilities. Also, by participating in varied cultural practices, the meaning of "waving bye bye" would further come to be differentiated from other culturally meaningful hand-moving activities, such as eagerly raising and waving one's hand to answer a teacher's question, holding up one's arm to take a time out while playing catch, or stiffly holding one's raised arm and hand in the air to hail a New York City taxi. Moreover, because human activity is culturally meaningful, what might look like the same physical or observable form of activity may take on different meanings within different cultural contexts. For example, in Germany during the 1930s and 1940s, the meaning of stiffly holding one's raised right arm and hand in the air certainly had nothing to do with hailing taxis.

To be sure, hand waving is part of leave taking in varied cultures. Furthermore, in some cultures, leave taking may involve other specific activities, such as shaking hands, hugging, kissing, bowing, back slapping, cheek pinching, or rubbing noses. The point of this hand-waving example is to illustrate that human activity is culturally meaningful or significant. Thus, human activity not only involves independence and interdependence, but it is also necessarily cultural. According to the current view of culture, this example of Euro-American children taking leave can be seen as a cultural practice in which varied American cultural meanings (i.e., expectations for, values about, and conceptions of human behavior) are enacted.

In addition to being varied or multifaceted, the meanings that are enacted in cultural practices are conceptualized as interrelated or inseparable parts of a system. As such, specific cultural meanings cannot be understood except in relation to other cultural meanings. For example, as we see in subsequent chapters, within Euro-American cultural traditions, some expectations for being independent involve being able to pursue one's own self-chosen goals and finding individual self-fulfillment. However, such expectations do not exist in isolation from varied interdependence expectations. That is, pursuing one's own goals is ideally carried out with consideration and respect for others, and the value of achieving individual self-fulfillment is often viewed in relation to the value of establishing and maintaining varied kinds of interpersonal connections.

It is also important to point out that cultural meanings are historically derived and, therefore, any cultural meanings that are enacted in specific cultural practices are moments in the ongoing construction of cultural meanings. As an example, contemporary school practices in varied cultures have been borne out of previous generations' values, conceptions of pedagogy, and conceptions of the school's role as a wider societal institution in shaping child and adolescent development. To understand the historical roots of cultural independence and interdependence meanings and activity dimensions, we obviously cannot go back in time to observe the cultural practices in which children participated. Nevertheless, cultural meanings as well as information about cultural practices from earlier times remain available to us in varied historical sources.

Insofar as cultural meanings are multifaceted and also subject to change, cultures are not necessarily comprised of homogeneous or logically consistent meanings (Archer, 1988/1994). In addition, not all people within a particular culture will necessarily always agree about their value orientations or the specific meanings embedded in varied cultural practices (e.g., Gjerde, 2004; Turiel, 1996; Turiel & Perkins, 2004; Turiel & Wainryb, 2000; Wainryb & Turiel, 1994). For example, at this time in the United States, many Americans may define themselves as "patriotic." However, for some of these Americans, being patriotic means supporting the invasion and occupation of Iraq, and for others, being patriotic means protesting the invasion and occupation of Iraq. Nevertheless, cultures may endure as people continue to engage with one another to negotiate shared meanings and practices.

Based on this view of culture and cultural meanings, independence and interdependence may be conceptualized as constructs that refer to multifaceted and interrelated cultural meanings about human separateness and human connectedness that are enacted by people in varied cultural practices. In conjunction with our earlier discussion of independence and interdependence as constructs that refer to inseparable dimensions of activity, the terms *independence* and *interdependence* may be used to represent cultural meanings, as well as dimensions of activity. Before proceeding further, it is crucial to explain that an analytic distinction is being made here between using the terms *independence* and *interdependence* to represent cultural meanings and using them to represent dimensions of activity. In making this analytic distinction, I am not suggesting that independence and interdependence meanings and activity dimensions are separate aspects of human functioning and experience; quite the contrary. Because I follow the position that cultural independence and interdependence meanings are enacted in how the independence and interdependence activity dimensions of cultural practices are structured, I assume that they represent inseparable aspects of human functioning and experience.

CONCEPTUALIZING THE DYNAMICS
OF INDEPENDENCE AND INTERDEPENDENCE
IN CULTURAL CONTEXTS OF DEVELOPMENT

Putting these theoretical points together, I am now in a position to officially state my conceptual approach to independence and interdependence with two basic claims. First, the current conceptual approach holds that independence and interdependence are constructs that refer to multifaceted and inseparable dimensions of the activities that comprise the cultural practices in which children participate. As noted earlier, independence activity dimensions refer to an individual's functioning as physically and mentally separate, including an individual's self-direction, self-awareness/reflection, subjectivity, and individuality. Interdependence activity dimensions refer to the social arrangements of a cultural practice, including the relationship shared by the interacting individuals, the social roles being enacted, the patterning of their interactions, and the links to wider societal functioning. It is important to point out that this first component of the current approach does not specify a particular culture, and therefore is meant to be applicable to any culture. That is, in any culture, independence and interdependence may be conceptualized as multifaceted and inseparable dimensions of activity that are particularized in cultural practices during development. What remains to be considered is how such independence and interdependence activity dimensions are structured in relation to the cultural dimension of activity, thus bringing us to the second basic claim of the current conceptual approach.

Second, the current conceptual approach holds that independence and interdependence are constructs that refer to multifaceted and interrelated cultural meanings regarding human separateness and human connectedness that are enacted in the cultural practices in which children participate. We may recall that, in the previous section, I explained that I was using the term *meanings* to generally encompass cultural values about, expectations for, and conceptions of human behavior. In the context of this second conceptual claim, the term *meanings* may now be tied more specifically to independence and interdependence. Throughout this book, the terms *independence meanings* and *interdependence meanings* are used to refer inclusively to cultural values about, expectations for, and conceptions of human separateness and human connectedness, respectively. Rather generally, the term *independence and interdependence conceptions* refers to varied cultural ways of defining or understanding what it means to be a separate individual and connected to others. The term *independence and interdependence values* adds a judgment of preference to particular conceptions of human separateness and connectedness. The term *independence and interdependence expectations* incorporates a developmental component into the notion of conceptions and values, and refers to how particular independence and interdependence conceptions or values may be encouraged or fostered as children participate in cultural practices. Specific cultural values, expectations, and conceptions are identified as the book proceeds.

As part of this second claim, multifaceted independence and interdependence meanings are taken to be interrelated or inseparable parts of historically situated cultural systems that are not necessarily defined, valued, or encouraged in the same way in all cultures. As with the first claim, this second claim of the current approach does not specify a particular culture, and therefore is meant to be applicable to any culture. That is, in any culture, independence and interdependence may be conceptualized as multifaceted and interrelated meanings about human separateness and human connectedness that are enacted in cultural practices. In this way, the current conceptualization is general enough to be universally applicable while simultaneously leaving room to account for cultural variability and specificity in independence and interdependence meanings. Further understanding of how independence and interdependence are defined, valued, and encouraged within a particular culture during development requires a consideration of that culture's cultural practices. Understanding may also be enhanced by historical analyses of cultural traditions.

Putting these two conceptual claims together, the current conceptual approach holds that multifaceted and inseparable cultural independence and interdependence meanings are enacted in the structuring of multifaceted and inseparable independence and interdependence activity dimensions as children participate with others in varied cultural practices. Within this approach, the notion of inseparability applies to independence and interdependence in the following three ways:

1. Independence and interdependence meanings are taken to be inseparable.
2. Independence and interdependence activity dimensions are taken to be inseparable.
3. Because independence and interdependence meanings are enacted in the structuring of independence and interdependence activity dimensions, independence and interdependence meanings and independence and interdependence activity dimensions are taken to be inseparable from each other.

These notions of inseparability take us beyond merely accepting that cultural practices in all cultures involve some of both independence and interdependence because people everywhere are inherently separate and connected. Instead, these notions of inseparability lead us to considering how independence and interdependence are interrelated as they are particularized in varied cultural practices. In other words, we are led to considering how a cultural independence meaning *entails* a cultural interdependence meaning and how a cultural interdependence meaning *entails* a cultural independence meaning. With regard to activity dimensions, we are led to considering how the cultural structuring of independence activity dimensions *entails* the cultural structuring of interdependence activity dimensions and how the cultural structuring of interdependence activity dimensions *entails* independence activity dimensions.[1]

The theoretical premises that undergird this conceptual position lead to asking varied questions about how independence and interdependence are particularized in children's developmental experiences. For example, this conceptual position leads to the question: What are the multifaceted ways in which both independence and interdependence are defined and valued in different cultures? The key point of this question is to highlight that independence and interdependence are not only aspects of cultural practices in all cultures, but that in all cultures there may be varied ways of defining and valuing independence and interde-

---

[1]Although these forms of inseparability represent interfunctional interrelations between independence and interdependence, it is readily recognized that, theoretically, inseparability may also be apparent intrafunctionally. That is, the varied independence activity dimensions (individuality, subjectivity, self-direction, and self-awareness/reflection) are inseparable from each other, as are the interdependence activity dimensions (the patterning of social interactions, social roles, and links to wider societal functioning). Similarly, varied cultural independence meanings may be interrelated, and varied cultural interdependence meanings may be interrelated. Although important, these interrelations are not discussed in this book to maintain a focus on the inseparability between independence and interdependence.

pendence. Answering this question can further our understanding of the complexities of cultural independence and interdependence meanings.

The theoretical premise that cultural independence and interdependence meanings are enacted in cultural practices leads to the question: How are multifaceted independence and interdependence meanings enacted in the structuring of multifaceted independence and interdependence activity dimensions, as children participate in varied cultural practices? The main point of this question is to focus attention on how cultural meanings are particularized in the cultural practices in which children participate. Answering this question would further our understanding of how cultural practices provide children with opportunities to engage in culturally valued modes of independence and interdependence.

The theoretical premise that independence and interdependence meanings are inseparable, as they are particularized in children's developmental experiences, leads to the question: How are multifaceted independence and interdependence meanings inseparable within different cultural practices? The main point of this question is to go beyond compiling lists that consist of both independence and interdependence meanings for different cultures, to discerning how independence and interdependence meanings are interrelated in different cultural practices. Answering this question can further our understanding of how independence and interdependence meanings are interrelated in similar and different ways, both within and across cultures.

The theoretical premise that the independence and interdependence activity dimensions of cultural practices are inseparable leads to the question: How are multifaceted independence and interdependence activity dimensions interrelated or inseparable as children participate in varied cultural practices? The main point of this question is to go beyond simply compiling lists of both independent and interdependent activities in varied cultures, to discerning how cultural practices entail inseparable independence and interdependence activity dimensions. Answering this question would further our understanding of some of the similar and different ways in which independence and interdependence activity dimensions implicate and mutually constitute each other within and across cultures.

The theoretical premise that independence and interdependence meanings and activity dimensions may sometimes be compatible and sometimes conflicting leads to the question: How may independence and interdependence meanings and the structuring of independence and interdependence activity dimensions be conflicting and compatible in different cultural practices? The main point of this question is to counter the premise that independence and interdependence are essentially conflicting aspects of the human condition. Answering this question can further our understanding of how and when independence and interdependence may be compatible or conflicting as they are particularized in different cultural practices.

Finally, the theoretical premise that independence and interdependence meanings and activity dimensions are historically situated leads to the question: What do historical sources reveal about independence and interdependence meanings and activity dimensions in different cultures? The main point of this question is to emphasize that independence and interdependence meanings and activity dimensions are not static characteristics of cultures or individuals. Answering this question would further our understanding of how contemporary cultural patterns of independence and interdependence are derived from the ongoing historical construction of independence and interdependence meanings and activity dimensions in different cultures.

Overall, this conceptualization not only involves a synthesis of several theoretical approaches to human behavior and development, but it also generates new questions about the roles of independence and interdependence during development. These questions move us beyond asking if a culture values independence more or less than it values interdependence, or if a culture values independence or interdependence more or less than does some other culture. These new questions also move us beyond asking whether certain cultural practices involve more or less independence or interdependence than do other cultural practices. Indeed, to ask whether a cultural practice involves more or less independence or interdependence than does some other cultural practice makes no sense within the current conceptual framework, just as it makes no sense to ask whether some cultural practice involves more or less culture than does another cultural practice.

As dimensions of activity within cultural practices, independence and interdependence, like culture, are taken to be essential constitutive dimensions of cultural practices. Accordingly, we may assume that when children participate in any cultural practice with other people, independence and interdependence activity dimensions are involved. Thus, as the questions presented previously imply, once independence and interdependence are conceptualized as essential constitutive dimensions of cultural practices, the analytic focus involves investigating cultural meanings of both independence and interdependence, and how they are enacted in the structuring of independence and interdependence activity dimensions.

The implications and advantages of this conceptual approach are manifold. In general terms, this approach fills a conceptual void that has emerged as mounting evidence against dichotomous approaches points to the importance of both independence and interdependence in varied cultures. Moreover, the current conceptual approach goes beyond simply claiming that children's developmental experiences in all cultures involve both independence and interdependence in some way, to claiming that independence and interdependence are defined and interrelated in culturally distinct ways.

For some time now, systems conceptualizations that focus on the interrelations that comprise phenomena have done much to advance our understanding of human behavior and development. For example, analyzing the interrelations between inseparable biological and environmental processes has advanced our understanding of how development happens. Similarly, sociocultural approaches to development have pointed to the utility of examining development in terms of interrelations among inseparable individual, social, and cultural processes. Given this successful track record, and given the basic premise that human beings are both separate and connected, further understanding of human behavior and development would seem to require discerning how independence and interdependence are interrelated in children's developmental experiences. Ultimately, by analyzing independence and interdependence in relation to each other, the current conceptual approach may be a voice in efforts to achieve an integrated understanding of the complexities and dynamics of human behavior and development.

These kinds of advances in understanding behavior and development are possible within the framework of the current approach because it provides specific conceptual tools for systematically discerning how independence and interdependence are construed and inseparable in cultural contexts of development. That is, within the current approach, independence and interdependence are specifically defined as constructs that refer to inseparable cultural values about, expectations for, and conceptions of human separateness and connectedness. In addition, independence and interdependence are specifically defined as constructs that refer to inseparable activity dimensions of cultural practices. Independence activity dimensions have further been defined in terms of individuality, subjectivity, self-awareness/reflection, and self-direction. Interdependence activity dimensions have further been defined in terms of the patterning of social interactions, the social roles being enacted, the links to wider societal functioning, and the relationship shared by the participants in a particular cultural practice. Finally, independence and interdependence as meanings and as activity dimensions are specifically defined as interrelated or inseparable from each other.

These specific ways of defining independence and interdependence make it possible to systematically investigate the complexities of how independence and interdependence are particularized in any of the cultural practices in which children participate with others in any cultural community. For example, it is common for developmentalists to conduct observational studies of parent–child play practices. Although analyses may start with a particular independence or interdependence activity dimension, employing the tools of the current conceptual approach leads to analyzing how multifaceted independence and interdependence activity dimensions are structured in relation to each other during the course of parent–child play. That is, the current approach leads to analyzing how each participant's individuality, subjectivity, self-awareness/reflection, and self-direction are structured in relation to the patterning of the participants' interactions, their social roles, their relationships, and their links to wider societal functioning. Starting with interdependence, we may say that the current conceptual approach leads to analyzing how the patterning of the participants' interactions, their social roles, their relationships, and their links to wider societal functioning are structured in relation to the structuring of each participant's individuality, subjectivity, self-awareness/reflection, and self-direction.

My point in writing out the analytic possibilities of the current conceptual approach in these two ways is to emphasize that no matter where the analytic road starts (i.e., with some dimension of independence or interdependence), it goes on to include varied and inseparable independence and interdependence activity dimensions. Similarly, when it comes to analyzing historically situated cultural values about, expectations for, and conceptions of human separateness and connectedness, the current conceptual approach leads to considering how independence and interdependence meanings are multifaceted and inseparable as they are enacted in cultural practices.

It is certainly possible that a particular independence or interdependence activity dimension or meaning may jump out as dominant in a particular cultural practice. For example, during parent–child play in some cultures, children may have latitude in choosing what and how to play, suggesting that play practices revolve around the independence activity dimension of self-direction. Analyses may further suggest that the structuring of self-direction during parent–child play reflects cultural expectations for children to grow up to be self-reliant. However, according to the current conceptual approach, identifying the structuring of this one activity dimension is but a first analytic step that must be supplemented by identifying the structuring of the cultural practice's remaining independence activity dimensions, as well as its multifaceted interdependence activity dimensions that presumably reflect cultural interdependence meanings. In other words, the current conceptualization calls on us to ask what else is going on in this cultural practice, and the current conceptualization provides us with ways to specifically discern what else is going on. In doing so, the current conceptualization moves analyses away from trying to discern whether a cultural practice involves more or less independence or interdependence to analyzing how varied independence and interdependence meanings and activity dimensions are structured in relation to each other.

The current conceptualization of independence and interdependence is also of value because it provides a universal starting point for defining independence and interdependence that simultaneously leaves room for cultural specificity and variability in how independence and interdependence are construed, interrelated, and enacted in cultural practices. This aspect of the conceptual approach can facilitate systematic cross-cultural comparisons of independence and interdependence within varied cultural practices. Such research can further our understanding of the complex interplay between universal aspects of human independence and interdependence, and culturally distinct ways of dealing with human separateness and connectedness. Ultimately, such analyses may also enhance worldwide intercultural communication and understanding by enabling people to see how some of their differences represent variations on substantial commonalities.

Although research based on the current conceptual approach has yet to be conducted, it can be used to consider some of the extant developmental and cultural research. Doing so requires us to cast a wide empirical net that encompasses a range of studies to consider what is known about both independence and interdependence within and across varied cultures. The current conceptual approach provides a framework for integrating varied studies that may deal with different, often isolated, independence and interdependence issues by prodding us to ask what else we know about a culture and its cultural practices. Then, as explicated earlier, the current conceptual approach provides us with some tools for discerning how complex aspects of both independence and interdependence may be particularized in varied cultures. Integrating a range of studies within the current conceptual framework also suggests that there is room for productive collaboration among scholars who focus on particular aspects of independence or interdependence.

In subsequent chapters, a range of studies is discussed through the lenses of the current conceptual approach to explore how independence and interdependence are enacted in varied cultural contexts of development. The research to be discussed from the vantage point of the current conceptual approach does not simply show that both independence and interdependence are valued in some way in diverse cultures around the world. Rather, it demonstrates how independence and interdependence may be conceptualized and enacted in multifaceted ways, both within and across cultures. The research also shows that independence and interdependence meanings and activity dimensions are inseparable in varied ways in cultural practices, both within and across cultures. Thus, as more and more studies are discussed, different independence and interdependence meanings are introduced, as are different interrelations between independence and interdependence activity dimensions.

As cultural practices within different cultural communities are discussed, it also becomes possible to discern some cultural similarities and differences in independence and interdependence meanings, as well as in the structuring of independence and interdependence activity dimensions. Furthermore, different studies enable us to consider a variety of conceptual issues pertaining to how independence and interdependence are particularized during development. Some of these conceptual issues include changes in independence and interdependence expectations over the course of development, the deception of first-glance analyses that seem to point to a relative cultural preference for either independence or interdependence, how independence and interdependence may vary both within and across cultures, and how independence and interdependence may sometimes come into conflict within some cultural practices. Taken together, these analyses can advance our understanding of some of the complexities of children's experiences within cultural contexts of development. By considering research on different cultural practices, it is also possible to see that the inseparability of independence and interdependence pervades children's developmental experiences.

Throughout the book, my analyses of independence and interdependence issues are guided by three organizing goals. One goal is to show that independence meanings are prevalent in cultures that have traditionally been characterized as interdependent, as well as to show that interdependence meanings are prevalent in cultures that have traditionally been characterized as independent. However, as already noted, I seek to go beyond simply suggesting that all cultures have some ways of dealing with both independence and interdependence. Thus, the second and third organizing goals are based on the position that cultures differ in terms of how independence and interdependence are construed and interrelated, rather than only in the extent to which either independence or interdependence is valued. Accordingly, a second goal is to explore how independence and interdependence may be understood and valued in multifaceted ways as they are enacted across cultures in the varied cultural practices in which children participate. Third, and I think most important for furthering our understanding of the complexities of independence and interdependence, I examine some of the ways in which independence and interdependence meanings are interrelated or inseparable as they are particularized in cultural practices, and some of the ways in which independence and interdependence activity dimensions are interrelated or inseparable in the cultural practices in which children participate.

In the chapters that follow, varied independence and interdependence meanings are considered in relation to the structuring of varied independence and interdependence activity dimensions in varied cultural practices. Despite this variability, some independence and interdependence issues appear fairly often. Many of these recurring independence and interdependence issues have been prominent in dichotomously based discussions of independence and interdependence during the last 20 years. That is, the independence issues have often been conceptualized in opposition to the interdependence issues, and cultures have often been characterized in terms of either the independence or interdependence issues. The current conceptual approach offers an alternative framework for understanding some of the complexities of how these independence and interdependence issues are particularized and interrelated in children's developmental experiences in different cultural contexts.

More specifically, the recurring independence issues that generally represent aspects of human separateness include varied forms of self-direction, such as acting on one's own, pursuing individual goals, valuing freedom, valuing self-reliance, and making one's own choices, decisions, and judgments. Other recurring independence issues include forms of individuality, such as conceptualizing oneself and others as physically and mentally separate individuals and in terms of individual characteristics, conceptualizing oneself and others as self-contained individuals, valuing the unique individuality of all people, and valuing the expression of one's individual preferences and opinions. Some discussions of independence also include conceptions of self-awareness. The recurring interdependence issues that generally represent aspects of human connectedness include conformity, maintaining social cohesion, following social standards, obedience, respecting others, and being considerate of others. Other recurring interdependence issues include valuing relationships, conceptualizing oneself and others as inherently connected, and conceptions of dependence.

SOME GENERAL REMARKS AND A FEW WORDS ABOUT TERMINOLOGY

It may seem almost banal and unnecessary to point out that human beings everywhere are both separate and connected. Indeed, many dualists acknowledge that all cultures have some ways of dealing with issues of both independence and interdependence. However, these essential facets of the human condition have so often been glossed over in the rush to quantify independence and interdependence and to differentiate cultures in terms of relative amounts of independence and interdependence. In my view, it is precisely because being separate and being connected are both so basic to the human condition that it is necessary to seriously consider how issues of both independence and interdependence are construed and particularized in varied cultures. Within this context, I assume that most readers will readily agree on the basic independence and interdependence of all people. The point of this book, then, is to go further and begin a discussion of how both independence and interdependence enter into children's developmental experiences. Although the current perspective does not provide a definitive account of independence and interdependence, it does offer a way to fill the conceptual gap that has been left in the wake of mounting evidence against dichotomous approaches.

The current conceptual approach provides an alternative to traditional conceptions of independence and interdependence by asking new questions that focus analytic attention on how both independence and interdependence are understood in different cultures, and on how specific independence and interdependence meanings and activity dimensions are interrelated in the cultural practices in which children participate. The current conceptualization is a kind of "co-occurrence" model of independence and interdependence in that independence and interdependence are taken to represent inseparable aspects of human functioning. The current approach goes beyond the "co-occurrence" model mentioned at the end of chapter 1, as well as beyond the "sometimes independence, sometimes interdependence" models in several ways. That is, the current approach explicitly focuses on how independence and interdependence are particularized in the context of specific cultural practices. In addition, the current approach provides conceptual tools to disentangle some of the complexities of independence and interdependence by making an analytic distinction between using the terms *independence* and *interdependence* to refer to cultural meanings about human separateness and connectedness, and also to refer to dimensions of activity.

Before proceeding, I wish to explain how I use certain terms and phrases in subsequent chapters. First, the term *independence and interdependence issues*, as well as the unaccompanied terms *independence* and *interdependence*, are used as widely encompassing terms when I am referring generally to cultural independence and interdependence meanings, as well as the cultural structuring of independence and interdependence activity dimensions. Second, I use the term *independence meanings* to refer broadly to cultural values about, expectations for, and conceptions of human separateness. Third, I use the term *interdependence meanings* to refer broadly to cultural values about, expectations for, and conceptions of human connectedness. Fourth, I use the term *independence activity dimension* to refer to how a cultural practice involves self-direction, individuality, subjectivity, and self-awareness/reflection. I also include the traditional independence issues, listed earlier, under the rubric of independence meanings and activity dimensions. Fifth, I use the term *interdependence activity dimension* to refer to the social arrangements of a cultural practice, including the social roles being enacted, the patterning of interpersonal interactions, and the links to wider societal functioning. I also include the traditional interdependence issues, listed earlier, under the rubric of interdependence meanings and activity dimensions. Finally, I use the terms *interrelated* and *inseparable* interchangeably when referring to how independence and interdependence are particularized in relation to each other.

A Historical Case Study: Independence and Interdependence in Euro-American Cultural Traditions

There are certainly many ways to analyze and present the historical roots of contemporary independence and interdependence meanings and activity dimensions around the world. However, I am not a historian, and I do not take it as my task in this chapter to provide a comprehensive historical chronicle of these issues. Instead, I consider some highly selective aspects of this history by limiting my analyses to a few Euro-American historical sources that provide insight into some independence and interdependence issues. I realize that such a focus is somewhat risky because analyses of Euro-Americans have fallen into disfavor as they have dominated the social sciences, and as Euro-Americans have been held up as the standard against which other cultures are analyzed and, all too often, misjudged.

In focusing on Euro-American cultural traditions, I in no way mean to perpetuate these kinds of cultural biases. However, I am focusing on the Euro-American case for two reasons. First, because I am lacking in historical expertise and limited in space, I feel that it is prudent to focus my attention on one culture, and so I have chosen the one culture whose history is most familiar to me. Second, considering the practices and traditions of a culture that is typically characterized in terms of independence offers the greatest challenge to the current conceptual position that independence and interdependence meanings, as well as independence and interdependence activity dimensions, are multifaceted and inseparable in all cultures. Thus, if there is historical evidence for this position in relation to the Euro-American case, it bodes well for moving on to considerations of how independence and interdependence are particularized during infancy, childhood, and adolescence around the world in more recent times. In addition, if this conceptual approach is compelling in the Euro-American case, it can serve as a guide for analyzing the historical roots of independence and interdependence in other cultures.

I begin this historical analysis with the Puritans of Colonial North America, who were essentially the original Euro-Americans. The analysis then addresses some independence and interdependence issues that were evident during the Revolutionary War and early national periods. Next, the chapter moves on to the 19th century and ends with a consideration of some mainstream American childrearing ideas from the pre-World War II years of the 20th century. In this historical overview, I summarize some secondary historical analyses, and I also offer my own analysis of at least one relevant written document from each of these eras. Although this chapter addresses varied independence and interdependence issues, much of it anticipates chapter 4 by addressing how independence and interdependence are particularized in ideas about childrearing and parent–child relationships. As these eras are discussed, we are introduced to multifaceted independence and interdependence meanings, as well as to some of the varied ways in which independence and interdependence meanings may be interrelated. The discussion also points to some of the different ways in which independence and interdependence activity dimensions may be interrelated within varied cultural practices.

PURITAN BEGINNINGS

Protestant Premises: Some Fundamental Conceptions of Independence and Interdependence

In keeping with centuries of Christian theology, the Puritans, who began settling in the New World in 1620, believed that all individuals have separate souls, thus reflecting a Christian conception of independence (Morris, 1972). At the same time, such separate souls were taken to engage in personal relationships with God, indicating that this conception of separate souls is inseparable from conceptions of interdependence. Of course, one can question whether such a "relationship" is social in the way that relationships among people are social. Nevertheless, within the Protestant framework, separate souls are defined in relation to something beyond the individual, thus pointing to a basic inseparability between individuality and interdependence.

As heirs to Luther's and Calvin's Protestant Reformation, it is instructive to further consider Puritan beliefs in the context of some central Protestant writings. Beginning with the posting of his *Ninety-Five Theses* on the Wittenberg castle church door in 1517, Luther's protest against the Catholic Church's system of salvation through good works turned Christianity toward practices whereby individuals found proof of their own salvation through faith alone, rather than through institutional mediation (e.g., Rice, 1970). Three years later, in *A Treatise on Christian Liberty*, Luther "set down . . . two propositions concerning the liberty and bondage of the spirit" (1520/1943, p. 251).

The first of these propositions stated that "A Christian man is a perfectly free lord of all, subject to none" (p. 251). At first glance, Luther's protest against Church practices, and his first proposition regarding freedom, point to the primacy of the individual in attaining salvation. Indeed, it has been argued that with this first proposition, "Individual autonomy took center stage, simultaneously freeing persons from the former institutional ties that had so tightly bound them while establishing increasingly strong boundaries around the individual as an autonomous entity apart from others" (Sampson, 2000, p. 1427). Based on this premise, Sampson argued further that Protestant Christianity set the foundation for conceptions of interdependence whereby "others serve primarily instrumental functions for the person" (2000, p. 1428). Although Luther's position may have elaborated on the individual's unmediated relationship with God, it seems important to note that Luther's first proposition was immediately followed by the second proposition: "A Christian man is a perfectly dutiful servant of all, subject to all" (1520/1943, p. 251). Thus, a contextualized understanding of the meaning and implications of the first proposition may be gained by considering both propositions together and also by considering Luther's explication of the two propositions.

With regard to the first proposition, Luther began by pointing out that he was referring to a form of spiritual freedom whereby an individual's salvation is achieved through that individual's faith alone, thus freeing people from what he took to be the Catholic Church's corrupt and insincere system of good works. Reiterating this claim many times throughout the treatise, Luther wrote, "The Word of God cannot be received and cherished by any works whatever, but only by faith" (p. 254), and "It is clear then that a Christian man has in his faith all that he needs, and needs no works to justify him" (p. 258).

In addition to freeing people from performing good works, having faith within Luther's framework also promised people freedom from evil, sin, and death. For example, Luther noted that "true faith in Christ is a treasure beyond comparison, which brings with it all salvation and saves from every evil" (p. 255), and "The believing soul by the pledge of its faith is free in Christ, its Bridegroom, from all sins, secure against death and against hell, and is endowed with the eternal righteousness, life and salvation of Christ" (p. 261). Such freedom from sin and eternal death further implies that the faithful are able to triumph over all evil, weakness, and danger, thus clarifying the first proposition that a faithful Christian is "a perfectly free lord of all, subject to none" (p. 251). Luther also explicitly pointed out that with such spiritual freedom it is "Not as if every Christian were set over all things, to possess and control them by physical power" (p. 264). Thus, Luther's explication of the first proposition indicates that being lord of all does not entail using others for self-serving purposes. Moreover, defining freedom as freedom from sin and evil indicates that conceptions of freedom do not necessarily involve doing solely as one pleases to further one's self-contained interests.

With regard to the second proposition, that a Christian "is a perfectly dutiful servant of all, subject to all," it becomes clear that Luther did not consider people to be wholly separate from one another. Instead, he explained that because people "live in the flesh . . . in this mortal life on earth," they must "have dealings with men" (p. 268). Accordingly, a person "does not live for himself alone in this mortal body, so as to work for it alone, but he lives also for all men on earth, nay, rather, he lives only for others and not for himself" (p. 275). Moreover, in all that a person does:

> he should be guided by this thought and look to this one thing alone, that he may serve and benefit others in all that he does, having regard to nothing except the need and the advantage of his neighbor . . . in this way the strong member may serve the weaker, and we may be sons of God, each caring for and working for the other, bearing one another's burdens, and so fulfilling the law of Christ. (pp. 275–276)

Luther then maintained that because having faith is the ultimate of all goods, a faithful Christian needs nothing more, and thus is free to serve others for their own sake, and not with an eye toward some kind of self-serving reward. Accordingly, he advised people to "Give your gifts freely and for nothing" (p. 282). Ultimately, Luther did not seem to conceptualize relationships in terms of self-serving functions, but rather in terms of acting for the sake of others and in terms of their needs. Finally, Luther concluded that a Christian "lives not in himself, but in Christ and in his neighbor" (p. 283), suggesting a cultural conception of people as fundamentally connected to others, or interdependent. More specifically, human connectedness is understood in terms of service to others.

In addition to these basic premises regarding independence and interdependence, the doctrine of predestination was a dominant theological force in the religious practices and daily lives of the Puritans who transported Lutheranism and Calvinism to the New World. The doctrine of predestination offers a view of human functioning in which the individual's

role in ensuring salvation is severely limited, thus actually placing individual self-direction well to the side of center stage. According to the doctrine
of predestination, an individual's salvation is predestined by God, and
thus salvation is beyond the individual's control, leaving the individual
quite powerless to affect, much less determine, his or her own destiny. Indeed, the Puritans were rather wracked with anxiety over predestination
because a person could never know for sure if he or she was saved or
doomed to eternal damnation. The most an individual could hope for was
to find proof of his or her salvation by having faith, working hard, and
achieving worldly success (e.g., Silverman, 1984/2002).

Individual self-direction and the extent to which a person could define
him or herself as separate from others were further limited within the Puritan cultural framework because the Puritans were intensely committed
to communal modes of living, thus introducing us to another conception
of human connectedness. Accordingly, when they set off for the New
World to escape religious persecution in Europe, they traveled in groups,
not as individuals. Once in the New World, their religion came to be called
Congregationalism as they organized themselves into religious communities or congregations (Demos, 1970; Shain, 1994; Silverman, 1984/2002).
Granted, the numerous congregations that eventually spread across the
New England countryside were considered to be autonomous from one
another before they (and their Southern neighbors) eventually organized
themselves into a nation. Nevertheless, within the congregations, community concerns took center stage. Within this context, the Puritan conception of religious freedom did not entail a wholly individual pursuit of freedom, but instead involved the freedom of a group of like-minded
individuals to communally practice their religion. An individual may have
been viewed as free to choose a religion, but in making such a choice, he
or she was choosing a communal way of life. Thus, to the extent that individual freedom was valued, it was inseparable from the interdependence
value of living a communal life.

These and yet other interrelated Puritan conceptions of independence
and interdependence are reflected in a sermon delivered by John Winthrop (1588–1649), the first governor of the Massachusetts Bay Colony,
on arriving in Salem, Massachusetts, in 1630. Winthrop began his sermon,
entitled "A Model of Christian Charity," by introducing the fact of human
individuality and the uniqueness of all people, claiming that God, "in his
most holy and wise providence hath soe disposed of the Condicion of
mankinde, as in all times some must be rich, some poore, some highe and
eminent in power and dignitie; others meane and in subjeccion" (1630/
1988, p. 22). He then went on to explain that these individual differences
serve communal purposes because they require "That every man might

have need of other, and from hence they might be all knitt more nearly together in the Bond of brotherly affeccion" (p. 23), and thus there is an "ordering [of] all these differences for the preservacion and good of the whole" (p. 22). In these words, we can discern a conception of people as physically and mentally separate individuals. However, this conception of independence is related to interdependence values because these human differences are considered important insofar as they serve cooperative ends. In addition, Winthrop further described individuals not as independent self-contained entities, but instead as "a Company professing our selves fellow members of Christ" (p. 24).

Much of the remaining bulk of Winthrop's sermon focused on how the Company should pursue its communal life, and he identified justice and mercy as the "two rules whereby wee are to walke one towards another" (p. 23). Within the current conceptual approach, such justice and mercy represent conceptions of how interpersonal interactions among people (an interdependence activity dimension) should be structured. The rule of justice requires people to treat each other equally despite their varied individual differences. The rule of mercy requires "that every man afford his help to another in every want or distress" (p. 23). Ultimately, Winthrop was concerned that "the care of the publique must oversway all private respects" (p. 25), and, as community members, "wee must love brotherly without dissimulation, wee must love one another with a pure hearte fervently, wee must beare one anothers burthens, wee must not looke onely on our owne things but allsoe on the things of our bretheren" (p. 25). Also, to establish a religious community in Massachusetts, Winthrop exhorted his congregation to serve each other and their community by pointing out:

> wee must be knitt together in this worke as one man, wee must entertaine each other in brotherly Affecion, wee must be willing to abridge our selves of our superfluities, for the supply of others necessities, wee must uphold a familiar Commerce together in all meekness, gentleness, patience and liberallity, we must delight in each other, make others Condicions our owne, rejoyce together, mourne together, labour and suffer together, allwayes haveing before our eyes our Commission and Community in the worke, our Community as members of the same body, soe shall we keepe the unitie of the spirit in the bond of peace. (p. 26)

Enacting Conceptions of Independence and Interdependence in Puritan Cultural Practices

These multifaceted and interrelated independence and interdependence meanings were enacted in the New World as the Puritans organized their communities mostly around farming households that typically consisted of a nuclear family as well as servants and apprentices from other families (e.g., Demos, 1970). Insofar as the family household was the basic unit of economic production, all household members, including children, contributed to its maintenance, and all were dependent on one another for survival (Coontz, 1988/1991, 1992; Demos, 1970; Mintz & Kellogg, 1988; Ryan, 1981/1998). Although individual households may have experienced some autonomy in production, they were bound together as a community, and as family historian Coontz pointed out, "[S]elf-sufficiency was never attained or even aspired to. A constant circulation of goods and services filled gaps in production or shortages of labor" (1988/1991, p. 78). These households also provided varied "social services," such as taking in the elderly, the infirm, and orphans even if they were not blood relatives (Demos, 1970; Hareven, 1992; Mintz & Kellog, 1988). Indeed, there were no "single" people and unmarried individuals, including men, were required to live within some household (Coontz, 1988/1991; Getis & Vinovskis, 1992). Accordingly, "Connecticut imposed a fine of one pound for each week a bachelor lived on his own" (Coontz, 1988/1991, p. 83).

Also, in the context of valuing communal life and the maintenance of social connections within and across households, individual privacy was limited in several ways. First, people in these fairly densely populated households lived together in relatively small houses (Demos, 1970), suggesting that there was little in the way of a room of one's own for most household members. Second, minding one's own business does not seem to have been a highly valued practice, and instead was precluded by neighborly surveillance as "neighbors constantly intervened to report departures from the norm" (Coontz, 1988/1991, p. 75). Third, virtually all aspects of life were subject to church and civil regulation, "from sexual conduct to prices of goods to whether a person could build a fence or take up a trade [to] where people should live, [and] what they should wear" (Coontz, 1988/1991, p. 75).

To maintain this kind of highly regulated and closely knit society, interdependence was also understood and structured in terms of conformity and obedience to community standards. Indeed, as Hester Prynne's fate in *The Scarlet Letter* poignantly indicated (Hawthorne, 1850/1994), individual deviations from community standards were not tolerated. The Puritans expected individuals to subordinate their desires to the wider common good, and individuality in the form of dissenting opinions was disparaged. Within this context, people conceptualized themselves in relation to their communities, and a person was considered to be "radically incomplete outside a defining, nurturing, and morally intrusive communal environment" (Shain, 1994, p. 57). Thus, self-definition was achieved interdependently through pursuing common goals and adhering to community norms. In other words, conceptions of independence (e.g., self-awareness and individuality) and interdependence (e.g., pursuing common goals, obedience, and conformity) were interrelated as individuals contributed to their communities and as communities made individual lives possible.

Applying Puritan Conceptions of Independence and Interdependence to Childrearing

Within the context of these multifaceted and interrelated independence and interdependence meanings, Puritan parent–child relationships and childrearing practices revolved around ensuring children's salvation, as well as their obedience to parental, church, and community standards. In keeping with the view that individuals have separate souls, some analyses suggest that the Puritans viewed children as individuals with "unique personalities" (Harari & Vinovskis, 1989, p. 387), and they were accordingly concerned with each child's individual soul and salvation. At the same time, "Egalitarianism formed no part of seventeenth-century assumptions about the proper relationships of parents and children" (Demos, 1970, p. 100). Parents, especially fathers, continued to maintain even their adult children in dependent positions, as they exerted absolute control over the transfer of property, and often only transferred property upon death (Beales, 1985; Demos, 1970; Mintz & Kellogg, 1988).

During the Colonial era, Puritan ministers were a main source of childrearing advice, and their writings provide us with some insight into the childrearing practices and goals of the time. Cotton Mather (1663–1728), ordained in 1685, was a most influential and active minister in Massachusetts, and during the course of his long career, he participated in many of the major events and debates of his times, from regulating relations between England and Colonial Massachusetts, to the Salem witch trials, to Christianizing the local Indian population, to advocating the introduction of inoculations during a smallpox epidemic (Silverman, 1984/2002). According to one biographer, "Mather enacted his domestic role with great thoughtfulness and affection. He viewed parental love and responsibility as, next to devotion to God, the supreme human fact" (Silverman, 1984/2002, p. 265). Included among Mather's written works are a piece entitled *A Family Well-Ordered*, first published in 1699, in which he offered childrearing advice, and a 1706 excerpt from his diaries (1706/1973), in which he reported how he treated his own children. These writings point to how some of the Puritan conceptions of independence and interdependence already mentioned were specifically particularized in relation to childrearing and child development.

Reflecting the patriarchal organization of Puritan life, Mather's advice in *A Family Well-Ordered* was mostly geared toward fathers, even though he did claim that mothers "have more than a little to do for the souls of your children" (p. 21). Reflecting the value of wider community interdependence, Mather also noted that fathers and mothers are not the only parents responsible for children. As he put it, "There are parents in the commonwealth as well as in the family; there are parents in the church, and parents in the school" (p. 40). Moreover, "The civil authority, and the whole vicinity, cannot be true to their own interest" (p. 50) if they do not participate in nurturing children. In other words, and in accord with Puritan conceptions of community connectedness, Mather realized that it took a congregation to raise children.

The subtitle of Mather's work (1699/2001) *A Family Well-Ordered* addressed two basic questions about parent–child relationships and childrearing, namely: "What are the duties to be done by pious parents to promote piety in their children?" and "What are the duties that must be paid by children to their parents that they may obtain the blessings of the dutiful?" Mather began with the parental question and immediately raised issues of interdependence by pointing out that, insofar as God "has made man a sociable creature," childrearing requires "well-ordered families" (p. 1) to ultimately maintain an orderly society. Also reflecting interdependence values, he noted that "Every serious Christian is concerned to be serviceable in the world," and by maintaining a well-ordered family, people may be serviceable to others (p. 1). Overall, well-ordered or well-regulated families are ones "that through the blessing of God . . . would generally keep his way and his law" (p. 2), indicating that adherence to the community's religious practices was at the heart of childrearing.

Accordingly, Mather went on to enumerate how "pious parents" can "promote the piety and salvation of their children" (p. 3). Pointing to a Puritan conception of individuality, Mather claimed that parents must be aware that "children have precious and immortal souls within them" (p. 4). However, insofar as "children are born with deadly wounds upon their souls" and "There is a corrupt nature in your children, which is a fountain of all wickedness and confusion" (p. 5), parents must attend to their children's souls even more than to their physical well-being. In this discussion, Mather explained that, "Till your children are brought home to God, they are the slaves of devils" (p. 6), thus echoing one aspect of Luther's position that freedom means being free from evil and sin. More specifically, in attending to their children's souls, parents can, first of all, pray for and with their children. Mather asserted:

> Prayer must be the crown of all. . . . Family prayer must be maintained by all those parents who would not have their children miss salvation. . . . Carry the child with you into your secret chambers; make the child kneel down by you while you present it unto the Lord, and implore His blessing upon it. Let

the child hear the groans and see the tears, and be a witness of the agonies wherewith you are travailing for the salvation of it. (pp. 19–21)

Mather (1706/1973) reported that in his own household, "When the children are capable of it, I take them alone, one by one; and . . . I pray with them in my study and make them witnesses of the agonies, with which I address the throne of grace on their behalf" (p. 45). These descriptions of his prayer sessions with each child, one after the other, not only illustrate the Puritan anxiety over salvation, but also a recognition of each child as an individual with whom Mather prayed separately. Although individualized, such prayer links individuality to interdependence as parent and child engage in prayer together.

Along with prayer, parents can provide children with religious instruction and see to it that their children are baptized with a genuine understanding of the meaning of baptism. In addition to religious instruction, Mather advocated "instruction in civil matters" so that "our children should be well-informed with, and well-informed in, the rules of civility, and not be left as clownish, sottish, and ill-bred sorts of creatures" (1699/2001, p. 9). Similarly, the importance of teaching children to attend to others was evident in Mather's report that:

> Betimes I try to form in the children a temper of benignity. I put them upon doing of services and kindnesses for one another, and for other children. I applaud them, when I see them delight in it. I upbraid all aversion to it. I caution them exquisitely against all revenges of injuries. I instruct them, to return good offices for evil ones. (1706/1973, p. 43)

Finally, with regard to instruction, Mather (1699/2001) suggested that parents arrange for their children's education, so that they can "read, write, cypher, and be put into some agreeable callings. And not only our sons, but our daughters also should be taught such things as will later make them useful in their places" (pp. 9–10). These suggestions reveal the importance of educating children for the interdependent purpose of serving others, thus demonstrating how a conception of children as separate mental individuals is related to interdependence, conceptualized as service to others. Also, with regard to conceptions of interdependence, referring to children as "our" children again suggests that Mather considered children to be members of the wider community, and not only the responsibility of their mothers and fathers.

To further ensure their children's pious development, Mather suggested that parents "charge them to work about their own salvation" (1699/2001, p. 14) by commanding them to believe in Christ, "to retire for secret prayer every day" (p. 16), and "to avoid the snares of evil company" (p. 16). Mather also brought up another conception of independence—namely, individual self-reflection—by advising parents to command children "to set apart a few minutes now and then for consideration, and in those minutes, charge them to consider what they have been doing, what they should have been doing ever since they came into the world, and if they should immediately go out of the world, what will become of them throughout eternal ages" (p. 15). Such self-reflection clearly involves a concern with oneself and a focus on one's own personal characteristics. However, in conjunction with the importance of adhering to community standards of conduct, reflecting on one's own behavior by considering "what they should have been doing" implies that self-reflection involves placing oneself in relation to community standards. Rather than isolating oneself from others, such self-reflection could strengthen one's connections to others and one's commitment to the wider community. In this way, expectations for independent self-reflection are inseparable from the interdependence expectation of adhering to community standards.

With regard to the children, Mather enumerated varied "Duties of children to their parents" (1699/2001, p. 23), of which obedience to and respect for parents are most important. He informed children that "The heavy curse of God will fall upon those children who make light of their parents" (p. 24), and that "there is no sin more usually revenged by the sensible and notable curses of God than that sin of the contempt of parents" (p. 26). In addition to obedience, Mather claimed that children must engage in multifaceted modes of interdependence by offering ongoing "reverence" (p. 36) and "recompense" (p. 39) to their parents. Mather explained that "There is first an inward reverence that children owe unto their parents," and also that "this reverence must have some outward expression given of it" (p. 36). The overt expression of reverence may include speaking to and of one's parents with reverence, as well as obeying them. Similarly, recompense involves fulfilling filial obligations to parents through obedience and respect, and by repaying "their parents for all the vast benefits which their parents have heaped upon them" (p. 40). Because parents include people outside of the immediate household, such as church leaders and schoolteachers, obedience to and respect for wider community norms were also required of children.

From their religious beliefs, to their communal daily lives, to their childrearing practices, the Puritans stressed interdependence, conceptualized in terms of obeying community standards, service to others, and treating parents with respect. Even as they valued some independence, such as recognizing the individuality of all people, including children, they harnessed individual abilities to serve communal goals. This brief analysis indicates that the Puritans not only valued both independence and interdependence, but that the lives of the original Euro-Americans were enactments of multifaceted and inseparable independence and interdependence meanings.

THE REVOLUTIONARY AND EARLY
NATIONAL PERIODS

As the Colonial era entered the 18th century, life for the transplanted Europeans in North America was still largely characterized by basic Puritan customs and values, insofar as people generally "believed it was the legitimate and necessary role of local religious, familial, social, and governmental forces to limit, reform, and shape the sinful individual" (Shain, 1994, p. 13). Individuals continued to be viewed as incomplete without a community, and a person was considered to be a contributing community member. Although people could serve their communities with their individual talents, they continued to subordinate themselves to cooperative goals and maintained communities that did not tolerate dissension or differences of opinion.

However, as these communities moved toward the Revolutionary War era during the second half of the 18th century, some Puritan customs, including patterns of family life, slowly began "showing strains" (Coontz, 1988/1991, p. 108). With the birth of subsequent generations of Puritans, a growing population encountered an increasing scarcity of land within congregations. This population growth made it difficult for fathers to pass land on to their sons, thus often forcing sons to leave their native congregations in search of farm land (Coontz, 1988/1991; Mintz & Kellogg, 1988). Some young adults even began to abandon farming to pursue livelihoods in the expanding commercial opportunities of the times. This trend further introduced an element of individual choice into occupational pursuits (Coontz, 1988/1991), thus pointing to an emerging conception of independence during this era. Also, toward the end of the 18th century, children were less likely to be characterized in terms of innate sinfulness and willfulness, and they were increasingly viewed as individuals with unique needs and abilities that required parental nurturing (e.g., Mintz & Kellogg, 1988; Ryan, 1981/1998). Obedience to parental, church, and town authorities may still have been required, but these modes of obedience were increasingly tempered by affectional ties between parents and children.

Multifaceted and Interrelated Conceptions
of Independence and Interdependence
in Thomas Jefferson's Family Letters

Examples of such attitudes toward children and childrearing may be found in Thomas Jefferson's letters to his "official" daughters and grandsons (Betts & Bear, 1966/1986).[2] Jefferson's daughter Martha was born in 1772, was married to Thomas Mann Randolph, gave birth to 12 children, and died in 1836. Martha's oldest son, Thomas Jefferson Randolph, known in the family as Jefferson, was born in 1792. Thomas Jefferson's daughter Mary was born in 1778, was married to John Wayles Eppes, bore three children, and died in 1804. Of Mary's three children, only Francis Wayles Eppes, born in 1801, survived into adulthood.

As a member of the Virginia elite and as a widower taking on the primary care of two daughters, Jefferson's parental experience is clearly not representative of 18th-century American parents. Nevertheless, these letters furnish us with useful information about how independence and interdependence were construed at the time, and they also indicate how a man who is so often associated with independence recognized and valued the importance of interdependence in human life. In general, Jefferson's letters to his daughters were replete with reports about the activities of varied people, including relatives, friends, and acquaintances, thus linking both himself and his daughters to others. In addition, as Martha and Mary got older, the letters were full of instructions and comments on varied practical matters, from purchasing wigs for Martha, to sending mattresses to Monticello (Jefferson's Virginia plantation), to when it was best to plant endives for the winter.

General Independence and Interdependence Expectations. Amid these varied topics, Jefferson's letters to his daughters during their younger years included comments regarding his hopes for their long-term development. Pointing generally to conceptions of people as both mentally separate and socially connected, he hoped that Martha would "lose no moment in improving your head, nor any opportunity of exercising your heart in benevolence" (1786, Betts & Bear, 1966/1986, p. 30). He also wrote to Martha that:

> The object most interesting to me for the residue of my life, will be to see you both developing daily those principles of virtue and goodness which will make you valuable to others and happy in yourselves, and acquiring those talents and that degree of science which will guard you at all times against ennui, the most dangerous poison of life. (1787, Betts & Bear, 1966/1986, p. 41)

---

[2]I use the term *official* here in recognition of the fact that Thomas Jefferson is known to have fathered children with at least one of his slaves. Only recently, and still surrounded by controversy, have these children and their descendants been recognized as members of the Jeffersonian lineage.

To Mary, he wrote of his hopes "in seeing you improved in knowledge, learned in all the domestic arts, useful to your friends and good to all. To see you in short place your felicity in acquiring the love of those among whom you live, and without which no body can ever be happy" (1791, Betts & Bear, 1966/1986, pp. 83–84). In these last two quotes, we can discern a Puritan interdependence concern with being useful to others. Also, reflecting conceptions of independence and interdependence as interrelated dimensions of human experience, happiness in life (or individual self-fulfillment) appears to entail relationships with and love of others.

In the following lines to Martha, Jefferson indicated his general hopes for the long-term development of his grandson, Jefferson:

> Of Jefferson's disposition I formed a good opinion, and have not suffered myself to form any other good or bad of his genius. . . . I set much less store by talents than good dispositions: and shall be perfectly happy to see Jefferson a good man, industrious farmer, and kind and beloved among all his neighbors. By cultivating those dispositions in him, and they may be immensely strengthened by culture, we may ensure his and our happiness: and genius itself can propose no other object. (1801, Betts & Bear, 1966/1986, p. 195)

In addition to reflecting the value of structuring interdependence in terms of being kind to others, this passage reflects the view that people have individual predispositions that require social nurture. Thus, conceptualizing people as separate individuals with distinct predispositions is inseparable from the value of engaging in interactions with others. This letter also suggests that Jefferson envisioned a life for his grandson that would take place in relation to a network of neighbors.

Maintaining Family Ties. In addition to these overall expectations, Jefferson's letters point to how human connectedness was more specifically understood in terms of maintaining family ties. With regard to their familial connections, the letters are filled with Jefferson's explicit expressions of affection for his daughters. For example, in telling Martha that he had taken care of a request from her, he wrote, "The commission to me has given me the greatest pleasure, as it always would that you would say to me freely at all times what want you have which I could gratify. My wishes are always to do what would be pleasing to you" (1805, Betts & Bear, 1966/1986, p. 272). To Mary, he wrote, "My only object in life is to see yourself and your sister, and those deservedly dear to you, not only happy, but in no danger of becoming unhappy" (1798, Betts & Bear, 1966/1986, p. 153).

Jefferson's letters also clearly indicated that he did not like being separated from his daughters, and he often sang the praises of family life, especially as an antidote to the frustrations and conflicts of political life. In the first preserved letter to Martha, written while he was making plans to go to Paris as Minister to France, Jefferson wrote, "I expect to be at Paris about the middle of next month. By that time we may begin to expect our dear Polly [nickname for daughter Mary]. It will be a circumstance of inexpressible comfort to me to have you both with me once more" (1787, Betts & Bear, 1966/1986, p. 41). From Philadelphia in 1791, he wrote to Mary, "Would to god I could be with you to partake of your felicities, and to tell you in person how much I love you all, and how necessary it is to my happiness to be with you" (Betts & Bear, 1966/1986, p. 86). Similarly, he declared to Martha that "The bloom of Monticello is chilled by my solitude. It makes me wish the more that yourself and sister were here to enjoy it. I value the enjoiments of this life only in proportion as you participate them with me" (1797, Betts & Bear, 1966/1986, p. 142). Three months later, he wrote to Mary from Philadelphia, "I feel the desire of never separating from you grow daily stronger, for nothing can compensate with me the want of your society" (1797, Betts & Bear, 1966/1986, p. 145).

Reflecting his not only positive but also rather sentimental view of family life, Jefferson wrote in 1797, "When I look to the ineffable pleasures of my family society, I become more and more disgusted with the jealousies, the hatred, and the rancorous and malignant passions of this scene, and lament my having ever again been drawn into public view" (Betts & Bear, 1966/1986, p. 146). Also in 1797, Jefferson wrote the following to Mary in anticipation of her impending marriage: "It promises us long years of domestic concord and love, the best ingredient in human happiness, and I deem the composition of my family the most precious of all the kindnesses of fortune" (Betts & Bear, 1966/1986, p. 148).

To ensure that they would be together as much as possible, Jefferson hoped that both daughters, along with their husbands and children, would settle at Monticello. In 1790, he wrote to Martha, "I think both Mr. Randolph and yourself will suffer with ennui at Richmond. . . . I hope Mr. Randolph's idea of settling near Monticello will gain strength; and that no other settlement will in the mean time be fixed on" (Betts & Bear, 1966/1986, p. 54). In 1801, he wrote to Mary, "If Mr. Eppes undertakes what I have proposed to him . . . I should think it indispensable that he should make Monticello his headquarters. . . . It would be a great satisfaction to me to find you fixed there in April" (Betts & Bear, 1966/1986, p. 210). In the end, only Martha, Mr. Randolph, and their children settled at Monticello.

Within this general context of apparent paternal affection and the value of family ties, Jefferson continuously exhorted his daughters to write to him, expressing distress when he did not hear from them often enough, and using rather manipulative tactics to get them to write. For example, in early letters to Martha, he claimed, "Your long silence had induced me almost to suspect you had forgotten me and the more so as I had desired you to write to me every week" (1784, Betts & Bear, 1966/1986, p. 23). Or, "I have not received a scrip of a pen from home since I left it which is now eleven weeks. I think it so easy for you to write me one letter every week" (1790, Betts & Bear, 1966/1986, p. 67). To Mary, he wrote:

> I did not write to you, my dear Poll, the last week, because I was really angry at receiving no letter. I have now been near nine weeks from home, and have never had a scrip of a pen, when by the regularity of the post, I might receive your letters as frequently and as exactly as if I were at Charlottesville. I ascribed it at first to indolence, but the affection must be weak which is so long overruled by that. (1791, Betts & Bear, 1966/1986, p. 67)

Along with such manipulations, Jefferson also demanded that Martha and Mary be obedient to him, suggesting that Jefferson's affection for his daughters did not displace the traditional value of filial obedience. For example, in his first preserved letter to Martha, Jefferson wrote, "If you love me then, strive to be good under every situation and to all living creatures, and to acquire those accomplishments which I have put in your power, and which will go far towards ensuring you the warmest love of your affectionate father" (1783, Betts & Bear, 1966/1986, p. 20). He also admonished Martha that "I shall be very much mortified and disappointed if you become inattentive to my wishes" (1783, Betts & Bear, 1966/1986, p. 22).

Connections Beyond the Immediate Family. Jefferson's letters also included some explicit instructions about how he expected his daughters and grandsons to conduct themselves in relation to others beyond the immediate family. For example, in the first preserved letter to Martha, Jefferson instructed her to "Consider the good lady who has taken you under her roof" (1783, Betts & Bear, 1966/1986, p. 19). He further instructed Martha to maintain relationships with one of his acquaintances and to write weekly to different aunts. He also wrote to Mary that "I hope you are a very good girl, that you love your uncle and aunt very much, and are very thankful to them for all their goodness to you" (1785, Betts & Bear, 1966/1986, p. 29). While in New York, as Secretary of State, Jefferson wrote to Mary, "I send you some prints of a new kind for your amusement. I send several to enable you to be generous to your friends" (1790, Betts & Bear, 1966/1986, p. 55).

In addition to their behavior in these direct relationships, Jefferson expressed his expectations for their treatment of and interactions with people in general. For example, he wrote that he hoped Mary would "never suffer yourself to be angry with any body, that you give your playthings to those who want them, that you do whatever any body desires of you that is right, that you never tell stories" (1785, Betts & Bear, 1966/1986, pp. 29–30). Pointing to varied ways of interacting with others, Jefferson wrote to Martha, in anticipation of Mary's arrival in France:

> When she arrives, she will become a precious charge on your hands. The difference of your age, and your common loss of a mother, will put that office on you. Teach her above all things to be good: because without that we can neither be valued by others, nor set any value on ourselves. Teach her to be always true. No vice is so mean as the want of truth, and at the same time so useless. Teach her never to be angry. Anger only serves to torment ourselves, to divert others, and alienate their esteem. And teach her industry and application to useful pursuits. I will venture to assure you that if you inculcate this in her mind you will make her a happy being in herself, a most inestimable friend to you, and precious to all the world. In teaching her these dispositions of mind, you will be more fixed in them yourself, and render yourself dear to all your acquaintance. (1787, Betts & Bear, 1966/1986, p. 36)

In addition, this passage highlights the importance of family obligations and enumerates varied aspects of social engagement that serve as criteria for self judgment, thus placing individual self-reflection into a social framework.

Jefferson's letters to his grandsons also include comments regarding appropriate comportment as individuals in relation to others. For example, he wrote in 1814, "My first wish, my dear Francis, is ever to hear that you are in good health, because that is the first of blessings. The second is to become an honest and useful man to those among whom we live" (Betts & Bear, 1966/1986, p. 407). Reflecting the value of wider civic or political participation, in 1820, Jefferson wrote that Francis should "Be assured that no one living is more anxious than myself to see you become a virtuous and useful citizen, worthy of the trusts of your country and wise enough to conduct them advantageously" (Betts & Bear, 1966/1986, pp. 434–435). This hope demonstrates how individual mental abilities, in particular being "wise," have implications for contributing to wider common goals. In other words, valuing independence in the form of valuing people for their individual abilities is inseparable from conceptualizing interdependence in terms of contributing to common societal goals.

The Inseparability of Independence and Interdependence in Conceptions of Self-Reliance. In the second preserved letter to Martha, Jefferson introduced the value of self-reliance by writing, "I am glad you are proceeding regularly under your tutors. You must not let the sickness of your French master interrupt your reading French, because you are able to do that with the help of your dictionary" (1783, Betts & Bear, 1966/1986, p. 21). Several years later, in 1787, Jefferson offered Martha a somewhat lengthier consideration of self-reliant learning:

> I do not like your saying that you are unable to read the antient print of your Livy, but with the aid of your master. We are always equal to what we undertake with resolution. A little degree of this will enable you to decypher your Livy. If you always lean on your master, you will never be able to proceed without him. It is a part of the American character to consider nothing as desperate; to surmount every difficulty by resolution and contrivance. In Europe there are shops for every want. It's inhabitants therefore have no idea that their wants can be furnished otherwise. Remote from all other aid, we are obliged to invent and to execute; to find means within ourselves, and not to lean on others. Consider therefore the conquering your Livy as an exercise in the habit of surmounting difficulties, a habit which will be necessary to you in the country where you are to live, and without which you will be thought a very helpless animal, and less esteemed. (Betts & Bear, 1966/1986, p. 35)

Many years later, he wrote to Francis:

> I am sorry you are disappointed in your teacher, but it depends on yourself whether this is of any consequence. A master is necessary only to those who require compulsion to get their lessons. As to instruction a translation supplies the place of a teacher. Get the lesson first by dictionary; and then, instead of saying it to a master go over it with the translation, and that will tell you whether you have got it truly. Dacier's Horace is admirable for this. As to parsing you can do that by yourself both as to parts of speech and syntax. You can perfect yourself too in your Greek grammar as well alone as with a teacher. Your Spanish too should be kept up. All depends on your own resolution to stick as closely to your book as if a master was looking over you. (1819, Betts & Bear, 1966/1986, p. 428)

It is interesting that these comments on self-reliance specifically address language studies, and thus do not necessarily imply self-reliance in all matters. Indeed, at the same time that he was giving advice about academic self-reliance, other letters indicate that Jefferson did not eschew learning from others. For example, Jefferson expressed his pleasure with Martha's living situation, claiming that "[N]othing could give me more pleasure than your being much with that worthy family wherein you will see the best examples of rational life and learn to esteem and copy them" (1784, Betts & Bear, 1966/1986, p. 23). To Mary, Jefferson wrote, "You must make the most of your time while you are with so good an aunt who can learn you every thing (1790, Betts & Bear, 1966/1986, p. 58).

Jefferson also admonished both grandsons to follow school rules, thus placing individual academic self-reliance within a social institutional framework. For example, to grandson Jefferson he wrote:

> I received by the last post your letter of 9th expressing your desire to study half the day in your own room rather than in the school . . . and I have consulted your father on the subject. We both find ourselves too much uninformed of the regulations of the school to form a proper judgment on the proposition. If it would break through any rule which Mr. Gerardin thinks necessary for the government of his school, and would set a precedent which he could not extend to others under equal circumstances, we should be entirely unwilling to infringe the regular course by which he wishes to conduct the institution. (1810, Betts & Bear, 1966/1986, pp. 395–396)

Moreover, when interpreted in relation to his comments on how his daughters and grandsons should find personal happiness through social connections, Jefferson did not seem to value self-reliance to the point of self-containment or social isolation. As he wrote to Mary in 1802:

> I am convinced our own happiness requires that we should continue to mix with the world, and to keep pace with it as it goes; and that every person who retires from free communication with it is severely punished afterwards by the state of mind into which they get, and which can only be prevented by feeding our sociable principles. (Betts & Bear, 1966/1986, p. 219)

Some Conceptions of Freedom

Of course, Thomas Jefferson is not known primarily for his role as a devoted father, but instead as an American founding father. As the author of the Declaration of Independence and as the third president of the United States, he is typically associated with the issues of independence that permeated the political upheaval of the American Revolutionary War era and the subsequent early national period. During this time, issues of freedom or liberty were hotly debated, and it is tempting, even easy, to characterize this era in terms of independence. Indeed, as noted in chapter 1, the term *freedom* may be understood as an aspect of human separateness that precludes or opposes social connectedness. However, conceptions of freedom or liberty have varied historically, and as one renowned philosopher of liberty pointed out, "the meaning of this term is so porous that there is little interpretation that it seems able to resist" (Berlin, 1958/1969, p. 121). Following Berlin's example, I do not attempt in any way to consider "the history or the more than two hundred senses of this protean word recorded by historians of ideas" (Berlin, 1958/1969, p. 121). Instead, I confine myself to briefly arguing that early American conceptions of freedom were multifaceted, as well as intertwined with conceptions of interdependence.

The Inseparability of Individuality and Wider Societal Functioning in Conceptions of Political Freedom. First and foremost, it seems important to point out that conceptions of freedom, as particularized in documents such as the Declaration of Independence, reflect the founders' pursuit of a particular kind of freedom—namely, political freedom. As such, they were concerned with promoting the public welfare and establishing the freedom of a collective, not only with promoting forms of individual freedom (e.g., Shain, 1994). Accordingly, the Declaration of Independence explains why it is "necessary for one *people* to dissolve the political bands which have connected them with another" people (italics added). Similarly, the Preamble to the American Constitution makes clear that the American *people* were uniting to establish a democratic system of government that would enable them to maintain and enhance social cohesion, as well as pursue common goals. That is:

> We the People of the United States, in Order to form a more perfect Union, establish Justice, insure domestic Tranquility, provide for the common defence, promote the general Welfare, and secure the Blessings of Liberty to ourselves and our Posterity, do ordain and establish this Constitution for the United States of America.

In addition, the American founders were concerned with establishing a government whose legitimacy was determined by its inhabitants and not coerced by others; in their case, the British monarchy. Thus, political freedom was defined in terms of a group's independent self-direction, which in turn was based on the consent of individuals who were considered to be politically equal. Admittedly, the American founders by no means granted equal political participation to all who inhabited the United States at the time, as they notably excluded women, slaves, and men without property from political freedom. However, within the context of 18th-century norms, those who were deemed worthy of political freedom enjoyed it equally. Accordingly, political freedom involved freeing individuals and groups from arbitrary rule, and to the extent that individuals enjoyed political freedom it meant that each could participate equally in the government of the collective to which he belonged. In this way, the soon-to-be Americans were being transformed from subjects into citizens. With regard to the pursuit of political freedom, Berlin (1958/1969) pointed out:

> It is not a demand for *Lebensraum* for each individual that has stimulated the rebellions and wars of liberation for which men were ready to die in the past, or, indeed, in the present. Men who have fought for freedom have commonly fought for the right to be governed by themselves or their representatives—sternly governed, if need be, like the Spartans, with little individual liberty, but in a manner which allowed them to participate, or at any rate to believe that they were participating, in the legislation and administration of their collective lives. (pp. 161–162)

In other words, conceptualizing freedom in terms of political participation by equal individuals entailed neither doing solely as one pleases, nor self-containment, but instead was inseparable from conceptualizing interdependence in terms of pursuing collective organization and common goals.

Within the context of 18th-century political discourse, conceptions of political freedom also involved concerns with limiting the regulatory role of government so that democratic citizens could be further freed from governmental coercion. Accordingly, de Tocqueville (1835/1945) observed that early 19th-century Americans adhered to the view that "[E]veryone is the best and sole judge of his own private interest, and that society has no right to control a man's actions unless they are prejudicial to the common weal or unless the common weal demands his help" (Vol. I, p. 67). Thus, individuals were conceptualized as free to make their own life choices, and, in tandem with the principle of equality, no one person could decide another individual's personal fate or force another individual to think in any particular way. Nevertheless, as the quotation from de Tocqueville indicates, such freedom regarding individual interests is ultimately subordinated to, and thus inseparable from, the common weal.

To achieve and maintain these aspects of political freedom, and also to protect the common weal, de Tocqueville observed further that individuals in America had to unite because "in a state where the citizens are all practically equal, it becomes difficult for them to preserve their independence against the aggressions of power. No one among them being strong enough to engage in the struggle alone with advantage, nothing but a general combination can protect their liberty" (Vol. I, p. 56).

This analysis points to how political freedom is both derived from and protected through social engagement, rather than by individual isolation or self-containment. Moreover, insofar as the organization and practices of a democracy revolve around pursuing common goals through the participation of its individual and equal members, political freedom may serve to enhance their social contacts. Indeed, as de Tocqueville pointed out, "[G]reat political freedom improves and diffuses the art of association" (Vol. II, p. 148). de Tocqueville also noted that in their personal equality, Americans were personally or individually powerless and even "insignificant" (Vol. II, p. 56). Therefore, great value was placed on interpersonal cooperation and social ties because the only way to preserve political freedom is to unite in the pursuit of common endeavors. de Tocqueville claimed to "have often seen Americans make great and real sacrifices to the public welfare; and I have noticed a hundred instances in which they hardly ever failed to lend faithful support to one another" (Vol. II, p. 112). Moreover, de Tocqueville observed that:

> It is difficult to say what place is taken up in the life of an inhabitant of the United States by his concern for politics. To take a hand in the regulation of society and to discuss it is his biggest concern, and so to speak, the only pleasure an American knows. . . . In some countries the inhabitants seem unwilling to avail themselves of the political privileges which the law gives them; it would seem that they set too high a value upon their time to spend it on the interests of the community; and they shut themselves up in a narrow selfishness, marked out by four sunk fences and a quickset hedge. But if an American were condemned to confine his activity to his own affairs, he would be robbed of one half of his existence; he would feel an immense void in the life which he is accustomed to lead, and his wretchedness would be unbearable. (Vol. I, pp. 259–260)

In this way, through political participation, specific political units or communities may not be viewed as prior to the individuals who establish them but, once established, they are viewed as essential to human functioning. Indeed, as we have already seen, for these new Americans who were heirs to Puritan modes of community interdependence, once individuals came together to establish a community, the importance of the community in shaping people's lives and cultural practices cannot be underestimated.

Further pointing to how conceptions of freedom did not preclude the importance of interdependence, de Tocqueville explained that "It was never assumed in the United States that the citizen of a free country has a right to do whatever he pleases; on the contrary, more social obligations were there imposed upon him than anywhere else" (Vol. I, p. 73). During his visit to the United States, de Tocqueville was also struck by an apparent "zeal for regulation" (Vol. I, p. 40), as he described how Americans were strictly guided by their numerous social obligations and concerns for social regulation. According to de Tocqueville, social regulation in the

United States of the 1830s was evident in a tendency for Americans to conform not only to religious percepts, but also to public opinion and the will of the majority (Meyer, 1986). For example, he wrote, "I know of no country in which there is so little independence of mind and real freedom of discussion as in America. . . .In America the majority raises formidable barriers around the liberty of opinion; within these barriers an author may write what he pleases, but woe to him if he goes beyond them" (Vol. I, pp. 273–274). He explained further that:

> If the influence of individuals is weak and hardly perceptible among such a people, the power exercised by the mass upon the mind of each individual is extremely great . . . public favor seems as necessary as the air we breathe, and to live at variance with the multitude is, as it were, not to live. The multitude require no laws to coerce those who do not think like themselves: public disapprobation is enough; a sense of their loneliness and impotence overtakes them and drives them to despair. (Vol. II, p. 275)

These observations indicate that, in keeping with their Puritan heritage, conformity to social standards was still valued by early American citizens, as was being in harmony with others. In addition to such conformity in daily life, the democratic system that these citizens established was, and continues to be, sustained in part by conformity to majority decisions.

Household Freedom and Conceptualizing Independence in Opposition to Dependence. Within local communities during the Revolutionary War and early national periods, conceptions of freedom also included household freedom (e.g., Shain, 1994). According to Shain (1994), this conception of freedom involved "the household's freedom to be uncontrolled economically, politically, or socially by outside individuals," and thus "freed men and their households from dependence on other individuals" (p. 179). At the same time, however, as people continued to live their Puritan lives of communal interdependence and regulation, this household freedom "did not free them from communal controls or the need to serve the public good" (Shain, 1994, p. 179).

This kind of household freedom points to how independence was increasingly conceptualized in opposition to dependence, but not in opposition to interdependence or connectedness per se. Overall, people, both as groups and individuals, should ideally not be dependent on others and thus subject to their arbitrary control. Moreover, the economic freedom of households enabled each household to contribute to the wider community, and thus relationships among households could be organized around mutuality and reciprocal obligations rather than a one-sided kind of dependence. In this way, household freedom was inseparable from conceptions of interdependent ties among households within the community.

NINETEENTH-CENTURY FAMILIES

The changing conceptions of parent–child relationships and childrearing that had begun to emerge during the Revolutionary War and early national periods were further consolidated during the course of the 19th century, as household economic production was usurped by industrialization and rapidly expanding capitalism. In addition, the 19th century saw the settlement of the Western frontier, where independence and interdependence meanings were also enacted in varied cultural practices.

Middle-Class Lives

For the middle class that was emerging in the context of urban capitalist industrialization, conformity to social norms was still valued, but this basic childrearing goal was now being supplemented by new childrearing goals and by increasingly egalitarian conceptions of parent–child relationships. In the new political and economic order, absolute parental authority continued its decline as democratic principles of equality became entrenched in daily civil life, as economic production moved out of the household, as land distribution among children became even more circumscribed, and as there were fewer fixed adult roles and prescribed occupational directions awaiting 19-century youth (Coontz, 1988/1991; Gadlin, 1978; Harari & Vinovskis, 1989; Hareven, 1992; Mintz & Kellogg, 1988). In addition, the Puritan view of children as innately sinful was being replaced by Rousseau and Lockean views of children as naturally innocent and full of individual potentials that required a nurturing environment rather than a rigidly controlling one (Gadlin, 1978; Mintz & Kellogg, 1988; Ryan, 1981/ 1998; Sunley, 1955; Wishy, 1968). For example, Lydia Child, a 19th-century abolitionist and activist who also wrote a childrearing advice book, entitled *The Mother's Book* (1831/1972), pointed out that the child's mind "is a vessel empty and pure" (p. 9). Insofar as this empty vessel of a mind could potentially be affected by any kind of experience, the role of social connections in shaping children's development was not to be underestimated.

Within this context, the structuring of interdependence within parent–child relationships became increasingly egalitarian and revolved increasingly around fostering emotional and affectional ties among individual family members. In the face of increasingly flexible adult roles and occupational opportunities, parents were less able to train their children for the future in specific ways or in terms of traditional modes of production. Thus, the parent–child relationship became a key focus of family life. Lydia Child (1831/1972) advised mothers to encourage sibling connections, and pointing to the interdependence value of family connections,

Child noted that, "To have the various members of a family feel a common interest, as if they were all portions of the same body, is extremely desirable" (Child, 1831/1972, p. 155). Accordingly, Child maintained that family members should be encouraged to always do for each other, and she also suggested that "It has a very salutary effect for whole families to unite in singing" (p. 156). These overall trends in family relationships were observed by de Tocqueville, who, focusing on father–son relationships, wrote, "I think that in proportion as manners and laws become more democratic, the relation of father and son becomes more intimate and more affectionate; rules and authority are less talked of, confidence and tenderness are often increased" (Vol. II, p. 205). Ultimately, de Tocqueville observed that democracy "brings kindred more closely together" (Vol. II, p. 208).

The transformation of family relationships toward strong emotional ties, and the movement of economic production out of the household, were also related to an increasing division between public and private life. Thus, during the 19th century, earlier practices of community surveillance and intervention gave way to the increasing privatization of the nuclear family (Coontz, 1988/1991, 1992; Gadlin, 1978; Hareven, 1992; Mintz & Kellogg, 1988; Ryan, 1981/1998). This trend also involved defining the family as a private haven or sanctuary from the realm of industrial capitalism, which, within the changing but still strong Protestant framework, was increasingly perceived by some to revolve around greed, cut-throat competition, and materialism. To counterbalance these tendencies, the family was idealized as the site of "devotion to people and principles beyond the self" (Demos, 1986, p. 31). The division between public and private life also led to a sharper division between male and female social roles, leaving women at home to raise children. Accordingly, mothers became the main target of childrearing advice. For example, in addition to addressing her childrearing advice book's title to mothers, Lydia Child (1831/1972) rather dramatically dedicated her book "To American mothers, on whose intelligence and discretion the safety and prosperity of our republic so much depend."

Fostering Individuality and Self-Direction in Relation to Multi-faceted Conceptions of Interdependence. Within the context of rapidly expanding 19th-century capitalist occupational opportunities, adult roles were increasingly based on individual choices (Coontz 1988/1991; Wishy, 1968). Preparing children to be self-directed by making their own life choices was, in turn, related to emphasizing individuality, insofar as choosing an individually suitable occupation requires at least some understanding of an individual's abilities and preferences. Furthermore, in *The*

Mother's Book, Child (1831/1972) noted that the "business of parents is to develope each individual character so as to produce the greatest amount of usefulness and happiness" (p. 155). This point indicates that individuality was conceptualized as a source of individual fulfillment. At the same time, in the context of Protestant conceptions of usefulness, individuality was also conceptualized in relation to interdependence because it enables people to be of service to others.

Emphasizing the development of individuality and self-direction has also been associated with the idea that people experienced the 19th century as a time of incredibly rapid change and increasing uncertainty (e.g., Coontz, 1988/1991; Ryan, 1981/1998; Wishy, 1968). Thus, preparing children for survival in ever-changing and uncertain social situations meant preparing them to rely on what seemed to be the only factor subject to some stability and control—namely, their own personal or individual resources. Accordingly, as childrearing goals revolved around issues of individuality and self-direction, those two independence issues were conceptualized in relation to changing modes of social engagement.

Moreover, rather than implying license to do as one pleases, self-direction was conceptualized in terms of being "governed by internal principle" (Child, 1831/1972, p. 39), in contrast to the dependence of relying on others for direction. Toward that end, obedience to parents was encouraged in children so they would grow up to be adults capable of directing their own activities without control by others. Child explained that, "The necessity of obedience early instilled is the foundation of all good management" (p. 27), and "Wilful disobedience should never go unpunished" (p. 27). In this way, self-direction was also conceptualized in relation to the interdependence value of obedience to parents. This analysis further points to how self-direction was increasingly being conceptualized in opposition to dependence, rather than in opposition to interdependence.

According to Child, self-direction also requires self-reflection to ensure that, as adults, people would make wise choices and direct their actions in socially acceptable ways, suggesting again that self-reflection was understood in relation to social life. To foster self-reflection, Child noted that, "Children should always be taught to judge whether their actions are right, by the *motives* which induced the actions" (pp. 66–67). More specifically, "actions are right" if they are motivated by a desire to be useful, not by a desire to gain rewards or a concern with others' opinions. Thus, reflecting on one's individual motives is inseparable from the interdependence value of being useful to others. At the same time that Child cautioned readers against too much concern for others' opinions, she also took care to point out that she did "not mean to inculcate a defiance of public opinion; such contempt springs from no good feeling" (p. 38). Similarly, she did not seem particularly keen on encouraging children's imagination and creativity. For example, when discussing what books children should be given to read, Child warned that, "To read every new thing fosters a love of novelty and a craving for excitement; and it fritters away time and intellect to little purpose" (p. 95). In general, encouraging imaginative activities and fostering creativity do not seem to have been overwhelmingly endorsed by childrearing advisers of the 19th century (Wishy, 1968).

Conceptualizing Interdependence in a Diverse Society. Being generally sociable and able to get along with a wide variety of people in diverse situations was also becoming increasingly important in the rapidly changing and socially expanding world of the 19th century (e.g., Gadlin, 1978). Thus, childrearing involved fostering children's connections within diverse direct relationships. For example, Child (1831/1972) advised parents to encourage "social intercourse between the children of different families" (p. 60), and to "early accustom your children to an intercourse with strangers" (p. 114). Child's (1831/1972) advice was also replete with comments on the importance of teaching children to do for and be kind to others. For example, she implied that children are naturally sociable and pointed out:

> The disposition to help others should be cherished as much as possible. Even very little children are happy when they think they are useful. "I can do *some* good, can't I, mother?" is one of the first questions asked. To encourage this spirit, indulge children in assisting you, even when their exertions are full as much trouble as profit. . . . In the house, various things may be found to employ children. They may dust the chairs, and wipe the spoons, and teach a younger brother his lessons. (pp. 62–63)

According to Child, children should also be taught "to abhor what is selfish, and always prefer another's comfort and pleasure to their own" (p. 109). More specifically, "A child should always be taught to give away the *largest* slice of his apple, or his cake, and to take his whistle immediately from his mouth, if a sick little brother or sister is anxious for it" (p. 112). In addition, children should be encouraged "in laying up money to buy an orange for a sick neighbor, a pair of shoes for a poor boy, or a present to surprise his sister on her birth-day—anything,—no matter what,—that is not for himself alone" (p. 41). This kind of interdependence can also be encouraged through "Kindness toward animals" (p. 6), and if possible children should feed animals because "it excites kindness, and love of usefulness" (p. 58).

Frontier Lives

As middle-class families were negotiating independence and interdependence in the new context of industrial capitalism, many other families were settling the Western frontier, and the popular image of the lone Western cowboy has come to represent the independent spirit of the American frontier. However, that unidimensional image, like so many other images fabricated partly by Hollywood, may be as much myth and fantasy as reality (Murdoch, 2001). More realistically, we may recognize that from herding, to branding, to rounding up cattle, even a cowboy was adept at modes of interdependence. Rather than revolving only around independence values, the Western expansion was multidimensional, as people enacted their customary conceptions of independence and interdependence (West, 1989) and transformed some of them along the way. To begin dispelling the myth of a kind of pure frontier independence, we may first consider some of the varied ways in which interdependence was practiced on the frontier.

The Interdependence of Frontier Life. As the pioneers went West, they traveled mostly in groups that often included networks of extended families. A man may have gone West before sending for his family, and some single men also went West, but rather than traveling alone, they typically joined other groups of travelers (e.g., Boatright, 1968; Schlissel, 1982, 1992). Historical records show that:

> Within this massive movement of people, the westward migration remained a migration of families. Branches of families were gathered in from different states. . . . And the families of old friends and neighbors were gathered in. The extra men who were working their passage across the continent were drawn into the family. (Schlissel, 1982, p. 77)

As the pioneers traveled West in family caravans, they did not leave their Eastern homes lightly, and they were not typically seeking to radically separate themselves from their families, friends, and customary patterns of activity. Accordingly, they often consciously sought to maintain some connections to the people and lives they had left behind in varied ways. For example, according to West (1989), as the pioneers packed up and moved:

> Almost always there were some small items linking settlers with a specific past—framed photographs of parents and relatives and painted scenes from the home country. Nearby was a mirror, another piece of family heritage laden with personal memories. Usually it was hung among pictures of distant loved ones, so those who saw themselves reflected would be reminded

of their parent stock. . . . Other articles connected the family as a group to a common past. At mealtime parents and children ate food from dishes given by grandparents and packed carefully in flour barrels for the trip west. Covering the table might be a meticulously embroidered cloth, a daily reminder of the care of the one who had made and given it. (p. 61)

A concern for physical objects may be interpreted as a sign of materialism that is easily associated with valuing independent achievement over social connections. However, the quoted description suggests that the pioneers endowed their physical objects with deep social significance. Insofar as they lived in an age before telephones, Federal Express, and the Internet were available to facilitate the establishment and maintenance of social ties, they relied on other symbolic ways of maintaining connections to people whom they could not see regularly.

In addition to working together as members of a traveling group, the pioneers were often met with hospitality from local inhabitants along the way West. For example, Miriam Davis Colt's (1862/1966) diary entries indicate that they were taken in by local inhabitants on several occasions. She wrote on May 5, 1856, "This family are very kind to give up their beds and floor to the weary travelers and take themselves to the loft above" (p. 38). On May 8, 1856, she recorded, "Our good host of last night, of whom we bought a cow and calf, paying him $25 in gold, said he would see us all safely over the river, and would pilot us through the water that had flowed over the river's bank for some distance in consequence of the late rain" (p. 39).

When Mrs. Colt's 3-year-old son died, she described how her "stranger friends" (p. 184) gathered to comfort her. Similarly, when her husband died, "The hand of charity was extended" (p. 200). Also pointing to the interdependence value of providing aid to others, according to Boatright (1968), "a bona fide traveler could . . . enter a house in the absence of the owner, and so long as he took only food required for his needs, no frontier court would convict him. He might use the kitchen, but he was expected to leave the dishes clean" (p. 49). A pioneer description of one of the many gravestones that marked the way West indicates how "The gravestone carried a plea to all emigrants who might pass to repair the grave" (Schlissel, 1982, p. 135). According to one passerby, "It *was repaired* and a pen of logs built around it" (Schlissel, 1982, p. 135). Thus, even strangers helped each other and were connected not only across time and space, but also in death.

When groups of pioneer families reached their destinations, they typically settled together in small communities that centered around a mutually protective fort. Eventually, one community often branched out into several communities and ultimately into larger and more permanent towns (Boatright, 1968; Coontz, 1992; Doyle, 1978; Lingeman, 1992; Mintz & Kellogg, 1988; Ryan, 1981/1998). Often beginning as farming and ranching communities, expectations for cooperation and mutual aid continued to permeate the pioneers' lives (West, 1989). That is, the settlers:

> erected their homes, their schools, and their churches by cooperative labor. The log-rolling and the house-raising became characteristic frontier institutions. They helped each other plow and harvest. . . . If a widow had no men in her family, her cattle would be gathered and her calves branded with her own brand. If a neighbor were sick, his corn would be plowed for him. If his house burnt down, neighbors contributed food and labor and clothing. If a school or church was to be built, each contributed his share of materials and labor. (Boatright, 1968, p. 47)

In keeping with this analysis, Miriam Davis Colt (1862/1966) described how initially there was "only one plough in the company" (p. 56) for all the men to share. In addition, she recorded that she "had Mrs. Herriman's baby here for a few days, she is so very sick" (p. 65).

The Inseparability of Independence and Interdependence in Frontier Life.   Although the value of individual self direction and dreams of individual achievement played a role in decisions to go West, social connections were also critical to the pioneers' survival. Moreover, the ways in which the pioneers structured social connections among individuals point to inseparable independence and interdependence meanings.

For example, in addition to some rather loosely organized traveling groups, many groups drew up "constitutions" before they set forth as a way to organize their efforts and ensure that everyone contributed to a group's common goals. As Miriam Davis Colt wrote in her diary on January 5, 1856, "We are going to Kansas. The Vegetarian Company that has been forming for many months, has finally organized, formed its constitution, elected its directors, and is making all necessary preparations for the spring settlement" (1862/1966, p. 13). Another pioneer woman, Catherine Haun, wrote:

> Among those who formed the personnel of our train were the following families—a wonderful collection of many people with as many different dispositions and characteristics, all recognizing their mutual dependence upon each other and bound together by the single aim of "getting to California." . . . After a sufficient number of wagons and people were collected at this rendezvous we proceeded to draw up and agree upon a code of general regulations for train government and mutual protection—a necessary precaution when so many were to travel together. Each family was to be independent yet a part of the grand unit and every man was expected to do his

individual share of general work and picket duty. (Schlissel, 1982, pp. 171–172)

This excerpt indicates how people were understood and valued as separate beings with their own individual characteristics, which in turn could be used to promote the common weal. In this way, as their Puritan predecessors had chosen congregations, pioneers were making individual choices about a social way of life.

The inseparability of independence and interdependence also permeates *Interwoven: A Pioneer Chronicle*, by Sally Reynolds Matthews (1936/1992). Born in 1861, Matthews participated in the settlement of Texas and wrote her chronicle as an adult for the benefit of her children and grandchildren. Her delusion that slaves were treated well notwithstanding, the chronicle serves as an informative source for understanding aspects of frontier life during the second half of the 19th century. Matthews' chronicle of ranching life basically tells a story of cattle and people. Although she described periods of social isolation because people sometimes lived far apart, her narrative often focused on the people and social events in the many communities she inhabited, beginning with her birth in the company of "kindly neighbor women who took care of each other at such times" (p. 8).

In her descriptions of cooperation and social connections on the Texas frontier, I find it interesting that Matthews sometimes referred to the people of the varied communities, with an implied inclusion of herself, as "citizens." For example, she wrote, "The establishing of the fort brought many worth-while things to the citizens, not the least being the social contacts" (p. 51). She could have used several other terms, such as *people*, *individuals*, *families*, or *men and women*. Using the word *citizens* directs the reader's attention to the democratic framework being established on the frontier, in which citizens were viewed as individuals who contributed to a wider collective. In other words, people were viewed not as self-contained individuals, but as individuals in relation to others.

Also, as self-directing individuals, people on the frontier made other individual choices about their social ties, including joining work-related associations. For example, Matthews described how her husband, John, decided to join a ranching partnership "[a]fter due consideration" (p. 153). At the end of the initial 5-year term of the partnership, Matthews explained that "Although there had been no business troubles, they having been agreeable with each other, John decided to withdraw, feeling that he might become too dependent upon the older men of the firm. He wanted to try his own right arm, so land and cattle were divided" (p. 163). In this case, John's decision points to the value of independent self-direction for the sake of not being dependent on others. However, eschewing dependence is not necessarily seen in opposition to being socially connected.

Raising Individuals in Relation to Others on the Frontier. As families traveled and then settled throughout the Western territories, parent–child relationships and childrearing goals were similar in some ways to those that characterized the emerging urban middle class (West, 1989), as discussed in the previous section. However, there was at least one key difference between urban middle-class children's experiences and those of frontier children. That is, although middle-class homes were no longer sites of economic production, frontier homes were. Thus, frontier children participated in household activities in ways that their urban middle-class counterparts did not. In his analysis of frontier childhood, West (1989) pointed out that, by approximately the age of 5, "Tens of thousands of children . . . spent countless hours doing much of the essential work of western settlement" (p. 73). They cooked, planted, plowed, gathered wild plants, cared for siblings, did laundry, hunted, and fetched water. They herded and fed animals. They ironed, chopped wood, scrubbed floors, churned, and canned. Some of this cooperative work took children beyond the household, thus requiring them to direct themselves as they sometimes ventured off alone. Insofar as they were carrying out household tasks, such self-direction was inseparable from interdependence expectations. More generally, as children participated with their parents in settling the West, their self-direction and individuality were particularized in relation to frontier patterns of interdependence.

The Inseparability of Independence and Interdependence in the Emergence of Voluntary Associations

Whether for work or other purposes, from literary societies to fire companies to fraternal lodges to mothers' groups to temperance societies, voluntary associations proliferated in communities, towns, and cities throughout the United States and the Western territories during the 19th century. These voluntary associations generally provided opportunities for diverse individuals to come together in the pursuit of common interests and goals (Coontz, 1992; Doyle, 1978; Ryan, 1981/1998). Already in the 1830s, de Tocqueville was struck by how the spirit of social cohesion, in tandem with the relative equality of individuals, was enacted in the American propensity to form voluntary associations. He described a kind of association mania whereby:

> The political associations that exist in the United States are only a single fea-
> ture in the midst of the immense assemblage of associations in that country.
> Americans of all ages, all conditions, and all dispositions constantly form as-
> sociations. They have not only commercial and manufacturing companies,
> in which all take part, but associations of a thousand other kinds, religious,
> moral, serious, futile, general or restricted, enormous or diminutive. . . . I
> met with several kinds of associations in America of which I confess I had no
> previous notion; and I have often admired the extreme skill with which the
> inhabitants of the United States succeed in proposing a common object for
> the exertions of a great many men and inducing them voluntarily to pursue
> it . . . the Americans form associations for the smallest undertakings . . .
> [and] seem to regard it as the only means they have of acting. (1835/1945,
> Vol. II, pp. 114–115)

As the power of religion in regulating people's lives waned, due in part
to denominational disagreements and the influx of immigrants who practiced different religions, voluntary associations represented a new institutional form of social cohesion and social regulation among individuals. In
describing the settlement of Jacksonville, Illinois, from 1825 to 1870,
Doyle (1978) noted that many of the voluntary associations enforced strict
rules of conduct, thus indicating how the structuring of social connections
was taking place within new cultural practices.

As the nation's population became increasingly diverse, voluntary associations also created connections among people that might not have ex-
isted otherwise. In addition, despite differences of opinion among diverse
association members, orderly meetings were conducted by using demo-
cratically agreed-on procedures, as members made motions, debated, and
voted. In Jacksonville and no doubt in other communities across the
country:

> associations, and the social discipline they instilled, helped an extraordi-
> narily mobile and discordant people to live together with a certain stability
> and order—not because they were basically alike or because they always
> agreed on fundamental ideals, but because, despite their differences, they
> accepted certain rules of order in dozens of small societies and, conse-
> quently, in the society at large. (Doyle, 1978, p. 192)

As some fraternal associations became organized nationally, men could
transfer their memberships if they moved, thus serving as social "sources
of stability and continuity amid all the movement of the nineteenth century" (Doyle, 1978, p. 186). In keeping with many of the independence
and interdependence meanings already discussed, individuals could make
independent choices to join and leave these voluntary social groups, and
as members they contributed their individual abilities and votes to promote common goals and interests.

PARENTS' MAGAZINE IN THE EARLY 20TH CENTURY

In the years before World War II, the first half of the 20th century saw an increasing popular interest in the scientific study of child development, and in October 1926, *Parents' Magazine* (initially called *Children, a Magazine for Parents*) was launched as a monthly publication. The first issue's editorial, entitled "Parents, We are Here!", promised to help parents with "the all-important, often bewildering, yet always loving task of caring for your children." The editorial went on to explain that the goal of the magazine was "to bring to you who are out on the firing-line, the scientific findings of the specialists concerning the child's needs of mind, body and spirit from birth to the twenty-first year." Setting the stage for the kind of childrearing advice to be offered in subsequent issues, the editorial also claimed that "It is a new world of loving understanding, wise tolerance and humility into which today's pioneers in child study lead us."

Because World War II has been used to mark a changing point between early and late 20th-century childrearing goals (e.g., Bronfenbrenner, 1958; Coontz, 1992; Mintz & Kellogg, 1988; Vincent, 1951; Wolfenstein, 1953), and because my own considerations of contemporary analyses of childrearing (discussed in chap. 4) are based on postwar studies, I confined my reading of *Parents' Magazine* articles to the pre-World War II period. The pre-World War II period was defined as the period prior to American military involvement in World War II following the Japanese invasion of Pearl Harbor on December 7, 1941. After the opening issue, I further confined myself to choosing one article from the magazine every 4 months—including January, May, and September of each year—from 1927 to 1941.

During this period, the magazine encouraged women to establish or join groups (forms of voluntary association) in their local communities to discuss varied childrearing issues. Each month, a particular magazine article was designated as the basis for discussion in these groups, and I used this criterion as the basis for my own reading. By September 1931, two articles in each issue were being designated for the groups—one focusing on general childrearing issues and the other on preschoolers. From that point, I focused on the article dealing with general childrearing issues. When I got to the September 1935 issue, I found that one group article was focusing on preschoolers and the other article was focusing on school-age children. From that point, I alternated between the two age groups, beginning with the preschool article. This pattern of alternating was briefly interrupted by the September 1939 issue, in which I found only one group article.

These early *Parents' Magazine* articles are rich and fascinating sources of information about the early 20th-century period in general, and they also provide much information about how independence and interdependence meanings were particularized in childrearing practices. A detailed analysis of these articles could be the subject of an entirely separate book, and so I limit my current consideration to a few key points that are relevant to issues of independence and interdependence.

Flexible Childrearing Methods: The Inseparability of Individuality, Self-Direction, and Following the Rules

In general, the advice offered to parents about childrearing methods built on 19th-century tendencies to downplay the use of control and dominance in favor of understanding and tolerating children's individual abilities and preferences (e.g., Benedict, 1939). In addition to recognizing differences among individuals in general, it was also increasingly recognized that there are "the greatest varieties of tradition in our social make-up" (Gruenberg & Gruenberg, 1932, p. 58). Within this framework, children were often described as active individuals who need their parents' (mostly mothers') loving and cheerful guidance. For example, mothers were advised that "Most of the problems which a small child meets are new to him. It is the mother's task to watch these problems, as they arise, to see how the child attempts to meet them, and, out of her greater experience, carefully to guide the child into efficient habits of behavior" (Preston, 1929, p. 62).

Insofar as children were viewed as active individuals, parents were further advised to provide them with enriching opportunities to enable them to learn for themselves. For children moving into adolescence, parents were advised "increasingly to give growing boys and girls a chance to explain their positions objectively" (Gruenberg, 1930, p. 63). This kind of flexibility was also advocated as the best way to handle raising children during times of rapid and intense societal change. For example, one article pointed out that, "In one generation our means of locomotion, our dwellings, the rate of living, and the closely related ways of thinking, have been so completely revolutionized that it is very difficult to keep up with the change" (Gruenberg, 1930, p. 17). In the context of these changes, traditional standards were seen to now "conflict with new scales of values, new ways of interpreting the facts of our common life. . . . One thing at least we may learn: it is impossible to generalize either from the old formulas or from any particular situation" (Gruenberg & Gruenberg, 1932, p. 25).

In the midst of this flexible and tolerant guidance, however, permissiveness was not the order of the day. As one article author made sure to point out, "I am certainly not advocating too great laxity in discipline" (Benedict, 1939, p. 25). Instead, the articles generally renounced "docile obedience" (Meek, 1928, p. 43) and promoted the idea that children should ultimately comply with rules willingly, based on a genuine understanding of the reasons for having rules. Accordingly, a mother "must plan deliberately to give her child enough understanding of the situation and enough experiences so that he will gradually begin to *choose* to do what she requires" (Meek, 1928, pp. 9, 43).

Thus, following rules was not necessarily considered to be inherently incompatible with individuality or with making self-directed choices. Instead, an American disdain for coercion and dependence was evident in the view that requiring "docile obedience" was not considered to be an effective childrearing method. In an interesting twist on the link between obedience and self-direction that echoed Child's 19th-century advice, the first *Parents' Magazine* article asserted that "The wise parent regards obedience as a mere stepping stone to independent, self directed activity, and knows how to secure the child's intelligent compliance with reasonable rules and regulations" (Woolley, 1926, p. 10). In this way, the independence expectation of being self-directed is possible through a kind of *appropriation* (to use a term from contemporary developmental psychology) of earlier obedience to others, thus irrevocably linking ideas about self-direction to interdependence values.

Moreover, once a child goes to school, this approach allowed him or her to "adapt himself to reasonable school rules, while making his own contribution to school procedure" (Woolley, 1926, p. 10). This point about school rules first of all suggests that a child's individual behavior continues to be shaped by wider social rules in school. Second, this point indicates how, ideally, individuals contribute to the formation of those social rules, rather than following them docilely. In both cases, independence and interdependence expectations are inseparable.

Fostering Self-Reliance, Self-Direction, and Security: Multifaceted Conceptions of Independence in Relation to Multifaceted Conceptions of Interdependence

A January 1931 article, entitled "What the Preschool Child Needs," enumerated several childrearing goals, pointing to some basic meanings of independence and interdependence that were discussed throughout the pre-World War II period (Pearson, 1931). More specifically, during the preschool years:

> the child must learn the mechanics of living—to see, hear, handle, walk, comprehend, talk, feed himself, dress himself, etc. He must learn the thousand and one social customs which we term manners. Most important of all, he must learn that he is an individual living among other individuals in a real world, and that he has to adjust himself both to the realities of the world and

to the other individuals in it. To do this he has to learn to give up his feeling that he is the center of his world and that the other inhabitants are placed there solely to minister to his pleasures. . . . He has to learn by experience that there is greater pleasure in caring for his own needs and taking his own responsibilities than in being dependent on others. . . . He has to learn the give and take attitude necessary for him to be a welcome member of his group of companions. He has to learn to give up willingly habits and behavior that may be pleasing to him, but which interfere with the happiness and comfort of other people. He has to learn that he cannot always have pleasurable experiences, but that he must accept the realities of life even though some of his experiences with it may be unpleasant. (Pearson, 1931, p. 12)

This list of childrearing goals begins with practical self-reliance, including feeding and dressing oneself. Encouraging children to prefer "caring for [their] own needs" rather than "being dependent on others" further points to a recurring theme throughout the period: Instrumental self-reliance was viewed in opposition to being dependent, but not in opposition to the conceptions of interdependence discussed in the remainder of the excerpt. These multifaceted conceptions of interdependence involved learning manners and learning to adjust oneself to others. Other self-reliance issues were addressed in articles throughout the period, further pointing to how this independence goal was understood in relation to interdependence. For example, a May 1941 article, entitled "Cultivating Self-Reliance," began with the following question about self-reliance: "What kind of adult do you want your child to be? One who will adapt the home's standards to his adult life instead of overthrowing them?" (Hattwick, 1941, p. 24). This question indicates that self-reliance, as an independence expectation, is inseparable from the interdependence expectation of living according to social standards learned at home.

Elaborating on this idea is the childrearing goal of getting a child "to accept the standards and behavior which we believe are best, and still let him have the responsibility of making choices for himself" (Hattwick, 1941, pp. 25, 44). To achieve this goal, it was explained to parents that, "Gradually a child should be allowed to make more and more choices, choices that affect his own well-being and the comfort of the family" (Meek, 1928, p. 43). This advice also indicates that a child's individual decisions and choices are understood as affecting not only him or herself, but the family as a whole, thus tying self-direction to social concerns. Some other articles throughout the period further addressed issues of self-direction, conceptualized as being able to make one's own decisions about how to behave in varied situations. For example, in May 1932, parents were told that "more and more we must expect the individual to find his guide within rather than without; and that in full recognition of his obligations to others" (Gruenberg & Gruenberg, p. 60). Again, we can see how interdependence meanings are implicated in self-direction insofar as the expectation is for a person to direct him or herself in relation to social obligations.

In relation to wider societal functioning, self-direction further involves being able to "face new ideas" (Fowler, 1934, p. 22) in a rapidly changing and diverse society. Within this context, parents were advised to help children evaluate and analyze new ideas for themselves, which in turn would lead to "constructive action" (p. 23). In addition, such self-directed analysis is linked to the interdependence value of "group discussion which attempts to bring out all sides of a question and consider proposed plans of action [and] is absolutely essential" for analyzing new ideas and situations (Fowler, 1934, p. 23). Further linking self-direction with conceptions of interdependence, thinking and judging for oneself ultimately are "the only sure means of achieving enlightened group action. A competent society must be composed of competent individuals" (Fowler, 1934, p. 67).

Taken together, these points about independent analysis (a form of self-direction) through group discussion, and composing competent societies with competent individuals, suggest that there are ongoing interrelations between independent judgment and group practices. That is, independent judgment is viewed as necessary for the enlightened group action of a competent society, and, in turn, group discussion is part of what makes independent judgment possible. This analysis further suggests that trying to determine which comes first, valuing independence in the form of independent judgment or valuing interdependence in the form of group action, is a version of the chicken and egg problem. Insofar as independence and interdependence are viewed as inseparable dimensions of activity, neither comes first, and neither is necessarily valued more or less than the other.

To further understand the perspectives on childrearing that are reflected in these *Parents' Magazine* articles, it is important to point out that most of the articles in the time period under consideration were written during the Great Depression. On several occasions, the articles made explicit reference to the upheavals and uncertainties experienced by families during this time. For example, pointing to a conception of independence that we have not yet encountered, one article entitled "Your Child's Need of Security" (Zachry, 1933) stated:

> Many parents have been shocked since 1929 to realize that after hard work and saving they have little or nothing to pass on to their children. Parents who set great value on economic security find the fact that there is no economic security very difficult—sometimes impossible—to face. Other parents who were not so concerned with material values felt comforted in the past because they thought they were able to pass on to their children a feeling of security in the social order or definite institutions such as the church, the

school, community social groups, and even certain modes and customs which they believe have stood the test and which in the past have provided them with a source of security. (p. 15)

However, in the midst of the Depression, neither of these sources of security could be counted on, thereby pushing security in oneself to the foreground. In this article, security in oneself was defined as being sure of oneself and believing in one's own abilities. It was then pointed out that such individual security develops out of "the sense of being wanted, of belonging to a family group" (Zachry, 1933, p. 62), thus associating individual security with social connections. Moreover, the ultimate goal is to achieve a "deep inner security that frees a person to look outward and see other people, instead of always looking inward" (Keliher, 1941, p. 23). In this way, a subjective sense of security is inseparable from interdependence expectations.

Understanding Societal Cohesion in Relation to Individuality

The last of the prewar articles that I read was written in September 1941, under the looming imminence of American involvement in World War II. The article was called "Understanding Themselves and Others." Pointing to the importance of interdependence values, the article's subtitle promised to offer "Important steps toward that friendly and cooperative approach to living which is essential to our democracy" (Keliher, 1941, p. 23). The article began by explaining the importance of understanding people as separate individuals with their particular life experiences. Pointing to the inseparability of individuality and social connectedness, the article also explained that, "Each human being has a life history. This is a network of experiences with parents, grandparents, relatives and friends, preachers, teachers, places and things. These experiences have colored the history of the person, have left attitudes, prejudices, convictions, beliefs" (Keliher, 1941, p. 72).

According to this article, understanding one another as separate individuals with varied social experiences is important because it facilitates interpersonal relationships in a diverse society and makes a democratic collective way of life possible. More specifically, "Understanding is an avenue of communication that each of us longs to deepen and broaden as life goes on. It makes possible all our mutual efforts. It clears the way for us to walk side by side and forward toward a better life" (Keliher, 1941, p. 23). In this way, rather than isolating people from one another, understanding others as separate individuals is what strengthens relationships among people. Interestingly, this perspective seemed to presage a contemporary view in developmental psychology that intersubjectivity is achieved when people recognize and treat each other as separate individuals. In doing so, "the joining of subjective psychic experience" (Stern, 1985, p. 127) becomes possible, thus enhancing interpersonal connections and facilitating the co-construction of a shared world. Extending this logic, one could also argue that the ability to fully understand and empathize with others requires an understanding of others as separate individuals. Indeed, this point is a basic premise of contemporary theory of mind research, suggesting that understanding others as separate individuals, with their own goals and beliefs, is related to being able to establish and maintain social connections (e.g., Dunn, 1996; Dunn, Cutting, & Fisher, 2002).

Ultimately, back in 1941, "The new world must be built on the understanding of the needs of all people" (Keliher, 1941, p. 70). To achieve that end, parents were advised to provide children with opportunities to engage with varied people, thus promoting understanding and cooperation among diverse individuals. Such experiences were taken to provide the foundation for "the sharing of the joint quest for better community life" (Keliher, 1941, p. 73). The article ended on a simultaneously urgent and optimistic note, stating:

> We have a great task in the defense of democracy before us. We will need ships and guns and men to man them but we will need as much, if not more, the quality of understanding on which democracy itself rests. We have not created a perfect democracy. Our children will come upon rude experiences with intolerance and prejudice and the miserable lack of understanding in our adult world. . . . We must give them the sense that while our frontiers have been largely those of space and speed, soil and forest, theirs is the challenge to build human understanding that will carry them far beyond what we have been able to accomplish. (Keliher, 1941, p. 73)

This vision for human understanding not only requires understanding people as separate individuals, but also implies an ever-widening sphere of individuals contributing to relationships and cooperative goals in a democratic world.

SOME GENERAL REMARKS

This historical overview points to some of the varied and complex ways in which independence and interdependence can enter into human experience, including children's developmental experiences. Rather than trying to figure out whether independence or interdependence was valued more or less during one historical era or another, the current approach focuses our attention on discerning how both independence and interdependence, as dynamic cultural meanings and activity dimensions, have been understood and structured within Euro-American cultural traditions. Accordingly, a variety of interrelated independence and interdependence meanings were introduced in this chapter, and some of the varied ways in which independence and interdependence activity dimensions may be structured in relation to each other were also discussed.

With regard to multifaceted independence meanings, Euro-American cultural traditions include viewing people as separate individuals with individual personality predispositions, unique abilities, and active learning processes. Although self-direction was initially limited for the Puritans, opportunities for making self-directed life choices were expanded for later generations of Euro-Americans. Independence within Euro-American traditions has also included the importance of self-reliance, self-reflection, and subjective feelings of security in oneself. With regard to human connectedness, multifaceted conceptions of interdependence within Euro-American cultural traditions have included the importance of family ties, service to others, living within communities of reciprocal obligations, and being able to establish and maintain relationships with a diverse range of people. In addition, varied forms of obedience and conformity have been valued by generations of Euro-Americans, including obeying parents, conforming to wider social standards, and conforming to public opinion.

Going beyond simply listing multifaceted independence and interdependence meanings, this chapter also pointed to how independence and interdependence have been interrelated in varied ways for generations of Euro-Americans. For example, we have seen how the independence of self-direction was at first inseparable from the interdependence of living a communal life, and later came to be inseparable from the interdependence of social roles, as individuals made self-directed choices about their occupations. In addition, self-direction was structured in relation to the interdependence of fulfilling one's obligations to others and obeying social standards. The analyses of freedom during the Puritan and Revolutionary War eras also indicated that self-direction was understood and structured in relation to interdependence, and that freedom was not synonymous with doing as one pleases. Instead, religious, political, and household freedom were all defined in relation to interdependence. Throughout this historical overview, we have also seen how individuality was inseparable from the value of pursuing common societal goals as individuals made unique contributions to the common weal in their Puritan communities and on the frontier. In addition, understanding people as separate and unique individuals was viewed as central to strengthening both direct relationships and wider societal cohesion. Since the Revolutionary War era, individuality was also taken to require social nurture, suggesting that individual development was understood partly in relational terms.

The research discussed in this chapter additionally pointed to how multifaceted and interrelated independence and interdependence meanings and activity dimensions have changed over the course of approximately 300 years. However, complex historical trends are not easily explicated with the broad brush strokes of a selective review, and I am keenly aware that I have not only glossed over, but also left out, huge portions of American history.

Moreover, while I have suggested that conceptions of interdependence have been key to Euro-American culture since its inception, I am keenly aware that American history has not been a picture of idyllic harmony between independence and interdependence. For example, as the American founders expounded their ideas of freedom and equality, slavery and racism thrived. During the 19th century, as middle-class family life was increasingly structured around egalitarianism and affective ties, women occupied subordinate social positions, and the competition, self-interest, and worker exploitation of industrial capitalism were running rampant. As the frontier was settled by mutually cooperative pioneers, the Indians suffered, slavery endured in the South, and racism continued to thrive. Even as voluntary associations promoted social cohesion, men also joined voluntary associations for the sake of individual self-interest because association membership could bolster their business or political aspirations. Instead of a rise in worldwide understanding, as anticipated by the last *Parents' Magazine* article (Keliher, 1941), the post-World War II era saw the escalating arms race of the cold war and continued capitalist economic oppression throughout the world.

Today, Americans are known for their self-interested litigiousness (Glendon, 1991) and declining community participation (Bellah et al., 1985; Putnam, 2000). They also seek psychotherapy in record numbers to find individual self-fulfillment and liberation (Cushman, 1995). As I write these words (December 2003–December 2004), the monied interests of a few prevail in Washington, DC. These patterns of independence have been the subject of innumerable analyses of American culture, as well as Western cultural patterns more generally, indicating that independence values have basically run amuck.

Nevertheless, the point of this overview remains. While some extreme independence meanings have been prevalent in American culture, other independence meanings have also thrived, along with and in relation to interdependence meanings, as people have gone about their daily lives. The current historical overview indicates that, although Euro-American cultural patterns may be characterized in terms of increasingly differentiated conceptions of an independent individual, relationships among individuals were not abandoned. Instead, they were transformed. With this differentiation of individuals came a new kind of organizational integration of individuals in relation to each other, not a disintegration of relationships.

With regard to parent–child relationships and childrearing practices, we have seen that children's individuality as separate mental beings with personal or individual characteristics and motives was increasingly emphasized over the years. However, this trend toward valuing separate individuality was tied to interdependence in varied ways. That is, attending to separate or personal characteristics was seen as a way to promote understanding and connections among diverse individuals whose social roles were not clearly prescribed. Moreover, each individual's voice counted in the democratic process of maintaining the wider common weal, and, as equals, people's individual talents also provided them with a way to contribute to achieving common social goals.

The trend toward emphasizing the independence value of self-direction was tied to conceptions of interdependence in varied ways as well. For example, making one's own choices and directing one's own behavior occurred in social situations and was ideally related to following social norms and standards. Indeed, our historical overview suggested that Euro-Americans have long preferred conformity to social norms and standards over pursuing isolated individual desires. Such conformity further enabled people to direct themselves in the pursuit of common goals and community cohesion. The shift toward raising children to make their own choices was related to a shift in the focus of family life from economic production to fostering affective and egalitarian ties among individual family members. Accordingly, the interdependence of enhancing family relationships, along with supporting each member's self-directedness and individuality, became the center of family life.

By briefly analyzing Euro-American cultural traditions with the analytic tools of the current conceptual framework, some of the complexities of independence and interdependence have been elucidated. In particular, this historical overview indicated that both independence and interdependence have pervaded Euro-American lives, and that understanding the independence of Euro-American culture involves understanding its interdependence traditions. Versions of these historical meanings of independence and interdependence continue to be particularized in Euro-American developmental experiences during infancy, childhood, and adolescence. As we now turn to contemporary developmental analyses, we return to some of these issues, and we also explore how independence and interdependence within Euro-American cultural practices may stand in contrast to some independence and interdependence meanings, and the structuring of independence and interdependence activity dimensions in other cultures. Limited space and a lack of expertise preclude me from situating other cultural perspectives on independence and interdependence in proper historical perspective, and thus the upcoming analyses may seem deficiently nonhistorical. Nevertheless, some understanding of cultural independence and interdependence meanings and activity dimensions can be gained by considering contemporary studies. Ultimately, comprehensive analyses of cultural variability in independence and interdependence require historical analyses in cultures throughout the world.

CHAPTER FOUR

Independence and Interdependence in Parent–Child Relationships

To state the obvious, parent–child relationships play central roles in infant, child, and adolescent development, and thus it is perhaps not surprising that there is a voluminous corpus of research on these issues. This research ranges from detailed descriptions of parent–infant interactions, to analyses of parents' childrearing goals and ideas, to investigations of how parents discipline their children in varied situations. Rather than attempting to present an exhaustive overview of this research, a central goal for this chapter is to show that parents in different parts of the world think about childrearing in terms of both independence and interdependence. Another goal is to consider multifaceted or varied cultural ways of thinking about independence and interdependence. This chapter also points to some of the varied ways in which independence and interdependence meanings may be interrelated, as well as to some of the varied ways in which independence and interdependence activity dimensions may be structured in relation to each other. As different studies are considered, several conceptual issues regarding independence and interdependence are addressed, including the importance of going beyond first-glance analyses that seem to point to a cultural preference for either independence or interdependence, how independence and interdependence may vary both within and across cultures, how parents' independence and interdependence expectations change as children develop, and how independence and interdependence may come into conflict.

Toward these ends, this chapter begins with a section on parents' childrearing ideas and goals. The chapter then includes a section on how independence and interdependence are embedded in the structuring of parent–child interactions during infancy and childhood. The discussion of parent–child interactions also includes a presentation of a study that I conducted on how independence and interdependence issues are particularized in parents' utterances during parent–child interactions. Eventually, the chapter presents a section on parent–child relationships during adolescence and ends with a consideration of how independence and interdependence meanings and activity dimensions are particularized in Japanese parent–child relationships.

PARENTS' CHILDREARING IDEAS AND GOALS

Although the study of parents' childrearing ideas and goals has been popular in developmental psychology for decades now, there is much debate about how to assess parents' ideas. There is also debate about how parents' goals may be related to parent–child interactions and to children's development. What does not seem to be subject to debate is that parents' ideas and goals represent key aspects of a developing child's sociocultural context insofar as they are enacted while parents and children engage in cultural practices together. As such, parents' ideas and goals can be understood as reflections of cultural meanings (Raeff, 2003), including independence and interdependence meanings.

Within this general area of inquiry, studies have covered specific topics as varied as parents' ideas about children's eating habits, sleeping arrangements, dependence, conformity, relationships with family and peers, and household work. Discussing these varied topics links us to a wide range of studies that enables us to consider some of the complexities of independence and interdependence as they are enacted in children's developmental experiences. To enter into these issues, we begin with some general parental ideas that point to multifaceted and interrelated independence and interdependence meanings, and then we move on to a consideration of parents' ideas in the context of specific cultural practices.

Some General Independence and Interdependence Expectations

Explicitly highlighting the importance of social connections, middle-class American parents' claims reveal multifaceted conceptions of interdependence, as they typically report wanting their children to "be generous, honest, and respectful of the rights of others" (Richman, Miller, & Solomon, 1988, p. 68), and also "well mannered, well socialized, and cooperative"

(Tobin et al., 1989, p. 142). In addition, Euro-American mothers of 1-year-olds are known to make interdependence requests and rules that involve consideration and respect for others, such as "not being too rough with other children" (Gralinski & Kopp, 1993, p. 576). American parents of preschoolers also report wanting their children to go to preschool to be able to play with other children (Tobin et al., 1989). Taken together, these varied interdependence expectations point to the importance of general sociability, which emerges in other studies of Euro-American parents' childrearing goals as well (Raeff, 2000). Indeed, research suggests that "Children are bombarded constantly with social communications from their parents about how best to get along with other people" (Pettit & Mize, 1993, p. 118), and parents' expectations for general sociability typically increase as children move through the preschool years (Gralinski & Kopp, 1993). Harking back to chapter 3, being able to get along with people in general is required in a heterogeneous and democratic society, characterized in part by relationships that are established through negotiation and mutual consent.

With regard to independence, American parents of preschoolers report wanting their children to be "independent" (Tobin et al., 1989, p. 142), which is defined in opposition to "overdependence" (p. 138). This definition again takes us back to chapter 3, where viewing independence in opposition to dependence, but not to interdependence, was first encountered. Others have also found that middle-class Euro-American parents want their children to eventually "make their own decisions and establish separate existences" (Richman et al., 1988, p. 68). With regard to wanting children to make their own decisions, it is unclear from the research reports—but it is possible and even likely—that being self-directed by making individual decisions could include varied decisions and choices about social engagement, such as whom to be friends with, whom to date, or what kind of career to pursue. In fact, other studies indicate that Euro-American parents typically view playmate and friendship choices as issues that belong largely to a child's personal domain of functioning, and therefore such choices are less subject to parental interference than are other domains of functioning (Nucci & Smetana, 1996). Overall, childrearing ideas that appear to emphasize self-direction not only do not preclude the importance of relationships, but are also inseparable from interdependence as self-direction occurs in social situations.

The Inseparability of Independence
and Interdependence in Eating and Sleeping Practices

In addition to these general conceptions of independence and interdependence, parents' conceptions of independence and interdependence are also evident in studies of parents' ideas about specific cultural practices. An early systematic analysis of childrearing patterns conducted in the 1950s by Sears, Maccoby, and Levin (1957) provides a useful springboard from which to discuss how independence and interdependence meanings are particularized in parents' ideas about different cultural practices. Amid varied topics, the Sears et al. interviews with working- and middle-class New England suburban mothers of 5-year-old children included discussions of how they handled their children's feeding during infancy. The mothers' reports revealed conceptions of children as separate physical beings, given that most mothers (48%) who tried to establish a feeding schedule "modified the schedule according to the needs of the child" (p. 78). Although some mothers (22%) claimed to have adhered to "fairly rigid" or "rigid" feeding schedules, others (29%) did not try to set up a schedule at all, allowing their children to eat on demand.

The findings that some mothers followed some kind of schedule, whereas many mothers followed the child's lead, reflect the concurrent changes that were taking place in the ideas of so-called experts about feeding routines. That is, some of the mothers in this study "reported that while doctors had advised them to use a schedule with their older children, the same doctors had begun to advocate self-demand by the time the younger children were born" (p. 79). Sears et al. went on to point out that, "This shift is in accord with the general tendency for child-rearing advice to move in the direction of less rigidity and less severity" (p. 79). Indeed, before World War II, strict feeding schedules were imposed on middle-class infants (Bronfenbrenner, 1958; Vincent, 1951; Wolfenstein, 1953), and many mothers "forced exactly six ounces of formula down a baby's throat exactly every four hours" (Escalona, 1949, p. 159).

In the 40-odd years since the Sears et al. study, the trend toward feeding on demand appears to have been consolidated, and more recent research with middle-class Euro-American parents shows that they encourage early self-feeding (New & Richman, 1996; Schulze, Harwood, Schoelmerich, & Leyendecker, 2002) and are known to let their children "regulate their own eating habits" (New & Richman, 1996, p. 396) by allowing them to eat on demand. Along similar lines, working-class African Americans have been found to stress the importance of early weaning and self-feeding (Bartz & Levine, 1978). All in all, these findings about feeding practices point to conceptions of independence in the form of treating children as separate physical and mental individuals who will eventually feed themselves and make self-directed eating choices.

Once past infancy, eating practices change somewhat for Euro-American children, as their parents are increasingly likely to make food-related requests and rules (Gralinski & Kopp, 1993). Thus, while children and adolescents may be allowed to choose what to eat (Nucci & Smetana, 1996), parents' food-related rules and requests point to how eating does not just involve independence expectations for self-direction and conceptions of children as physically and mentally separate individuals. Eating as a separate and self-directed individual takes place in relation to social standards for behavior, including "eating etiquette, such as 'not eating like a complete pig,' using a fork, and not spilling or throwing food" (Gralinski & Kopp, 1993, p. 576). These findings also suggest that independence and interdependence expectations, within the general cultural practice of eating, may change in relation to each other during development. That is, we have seen that, during infancy, feeding practices are largely structured by parents in terms of their conceptions of infants as separate physical and mental individuals. With development, these conceptions are integrated with parents' interdependence expectations for children to follow social norms. In this way, parents' conceptions of children's self-directed eating are inseparable from their expectations for children's engagement with others.

Including and also going beyond feeding, Gaskins (1999) reported that in a small, traditional Mexican Mayan village, 5-year-old children:

> are usually expected to take responsibility for doing almost all of their own maintenance activities, even though they may be prompted or checked on by adults. They decide what they wish to eat and how much of it . . . what to wear; and when to bathe (as long as they choose to bathe a minimum of once a day in the afternoon, which is the cultural norm). (p. 40)

In a similar vein, 3- to 5-year-olds on the Marquesas Islands "know how to wash, dress, and feed themselves" (Martini & Kirkpatrick, 1992/1994, p. 211). Analyses of Marquesas childrearing practices also point to a view that "Households run more smoothly when children care for themselves" (p. 210). This view reveals an ongoing interrelation between independence and interdependence expectations insofar as pursuing common household goals requires some self-reliance on the part of its individual members. In this case, it may be that group goals provide an orienting framework for some socialization experiences. However, identifying that organizing framework is only part of the picture because independence expectations for physical self-reliance are fully implicated in the realization of interdependence goals.

In addition to eating, sleeping constitutes a basic physical necessity that is socially regulated for infants in ways that reflect complex cultural independence and interdependence meanings. In recent years, much attention has been paid to the typical Euro-American practice of having children, beginning in infancy, sleep in their own beds and in their own rooms, in contrast to the cosleeping arrangements that are more common among some African Americans, some working-class Euro-Americans and Europeans, as well as in varied non-Western cultures (e.g., Abbott, 1992; Caudill & Plath, 1966; Greenfield & Suzuki, 1998; Lutz, 1985; Martini & Kirkpatrick, 1981; Morelli, Rogoff, Oppenheim, & Goldsmith, 1992; Rogoff, 2003; Shweder, Jensen, & Goldstein, 1995; Whiting & Edwards, 1988; Wolf, Lozoff, Latz, & Paludetto, 1996). As some researchers have pointed out, sleeping alone reflects independence meanings because the child is treated as a physically separate person who is being trained to care for him or herself and be generally self-directed. It has also been argued that cosleeping reflects interdependence values, such as establishing close family ties.

However, even if it is the case that sleeping alone and cosleeping are used by parents to foster self-direction and family ties, respectively, it does not necessarily follow that parents who send their children off to sleep alone do not value and promote interdependence in other cultural practices (Wolf et al., 1996). Similarly, parents who cosleep with their children may also value and promote independence in other ways. For example, although cosleeping is a common practice on the Marquesas Islands, we just saw how 3- to 5-year-old children there are physically self-reliant. In addition, observations and interviews indicate how Marquesas Islanders believe that an infant "from birth, has a complex personality of his own. Complex motivations are ascribed to the infant in the first months . . . and caregivers interpret infant behaviors as indices of or attempts to deal with internal states" (Martini & Kirkpatrick, 1981, p. 195). Within this context, "Marquesan adults hold babies as if they were separate beings. They either attend to the baby or put the baby down. They tend not to carry infants in a 'blending' fashion or strapped to their bodies" (Martini & Kirkpatrick, 1992/1994, p. 209). In addition, infants "were rarely cuddled, even if they tried to cling when distressed" (Martini & Kirkpatrick, 1981, p. 208). By the time children are between 1½ and 2 years old, they learn that "parents will not comfort them until they begin to comfort themselves" (Martini & Kirkpatrick, 1992/1994, p. 210).

Furthermore, it is not clear that sleeping alone reflects purely independent expectations or that cosleeping is structured only in terms of interdependence expectations. That is, in some studies, Euro-American parents have provided reasons for why they want their children to sleep alone that are either tangential to fostering self-direction or that point to how separate sleeping arrangements involve interdependence meanings. For example, many parents, especially first-time parents, are concerned with lying on or rolling over their infants while sleeping (Ball, Hooker, & Kelly, 1999). In addition, parents often claim to want children to sleep in their own rooms so that the parents may sleep better, and also so that the parents can have time for themselves, including for their own dyadic relationship (e.g., Richman et al., 1988; Shweder et al., 1995). In this way, the independence value of self-direction that is fostered through sleeping separately takes place in a social context where children are expected to be respectful and considerate of other family members' needs and desires. Moreover, the perceived needs and desires of the other family members in this case are partly social, thereby further highlighting the cultural importance of interdependence. Thus, expectations for children's self-direction within the cultural practice of sleeping are inseparable from interdependence expectations about how to engage with other people.

Not only do Euro-American parents expect children to sleep on their own for different reasons, they also actively try to shape children's sleeping schedules in accord with their own scheduling preferences (New & Richman, 1996; Richman et al., 1988). In fact, as Sears et al. (1957) noted, it was common for parents "to establish a certain time at which their children were to go to bed, and to put them to bed at this time whether the children were sleepy or not" (p. 292). Almost 40 years later, in a study of middle-class Euro-American families, New and Richman (1996) found:

> Strategies for putting infants to sleep were carefully orchestrated. . . . At the designated hour, infants were removed from the social stimulation of the dinner table or family room to their own quiet bedrooms. Mothers attached considerable importance to infants getting enough sleep . . . even when the infants showed great resistance to naps and bedtime, including prolonged crying. (p. 395)

Setting up bedtime in this way actually requires infants to conform to others and indicates how their individual physical needs are inseparable from social connections. It may be that children are being removed from a specific social situation, but they are not being removed from social connectedness, conceptualized in terms of conforming to others' preferences. In this way, Euro-American parents' expectations for children's self-direction are inseparable from their conformity expectations.

Interestingly, these scheduling practices for sleeping stand somewhat in contrast to the self-direction that characterizes contemporary Euro-American infant feeding routines. Taken together, it is possible to discern how somewhat different independence and interdependence meanings are enacted in these different cultural practices (i.e., eating and sleeping) during infancy and early childhood. That is, Euro-American parents seem to see feeding during infancy as a forum for fostering children's self-direction, and then, as children develop, parents' conceptions of self-direction during feeding are integrated with expectations for following social standards. In contrast, beginning already when their children are in infancy, Euro-American parents seem to see sleeping as a forum for fostering children's self-direction in relation to fostering conformity to others and consideration of others.

Just as separate sleeping arrangements implicate interdependence expectations for Euro-Americans, cosleeping arrangements may be inseparable from independence expectations in other cultures. For example, in the Mexican Mayan community introduced previously in this chapter, cosleeping arrangements are typical, but children are allowed to sleep on demand (Gaskins, 1999), and once children are about 5 years old, they are allowed to choose "when, how long, and with whom to sleep" (Gaskins, 1999, p. 40). These practices point to how the child is treated as a separate self-directing individual, with his or her own preferences that are enacted in a social situation, and that are also particularized in relation to the interdependence value of fostering family ties.

Life at Home and the Structuring of Independence and Interdependence

Changes in Independence and Interdependence Expectations Over Time and Potential Conflict Between Independence and Interdependence. Within the context of family relationships and home life, Euro-American parents of 1- to 4-year-olds report making requests and having rules for varied aspects of children's functioning as family members, including "Waiting when Mom is on the telephone" or "not interrupting others' conversations" (Gralinski & Kopp, 1993, p. 576). Encouraging children to wait or not to interrupt others provides them with opportunities to understand that there are social dimensions to their individual needs and preferences. Such expectations for "socially required or approved behavior, even if this means effort or sacrifice of some immediate personal objectives" (Maccoby & Martin, 1983, p. 35), become increasingly prevalent during the second year of life. These kinds of rules are also compatible with a finding from the Sears et al. (1957) study that many mothers expected their children to be reasonably quiet so as not to disturb other family members. As Sears et al. pointed out, "children must be taught to be co-operative in the living arrangements of the family. . . . They must be quiet when others are resting. . . . They have to curb their enthusiasm and free movements to some degree, and develop the necessary skills and attitudes that will make them agreeable family members" (p. 272).

In these examples, there is an implication that children are seen initially as separate individuals, with individual predispositions, who must be taught how to relate to others. There is also an implication in these examples that dimensions of independence and interdependence may come into conflict as a child finds the pursuit of his or her individual goals constrained by social parameters. Let us explore each of these implications in turn.

The implication that children are separate individuals first, and connected to others only later, may be interpreted as indicating that human separateness is of greater value than is human connectedness. However, in conjunction with other studies discussed thus far (and ones that soon follow), Euro-American parents are concerned with fostering their children's connectedness to others, as well as their children's individuality and self-direction. Thus, instead of concluding that Euro-Americans value independence more than interdependence, it may be concluded that some forms of independence are understood as temporally prior to an ultimate goal of engaging in harmonious relationships with others.

Furthermore, we may recall that Euro-American parents expect their children to eventually "establish separate existences" (Richman et al., 1988, p. 68), suggesting that some aspects of children's independence are considered to develop after a period of interdependence. Taken together, these findings indicate that Euro-American parents see their children as both separate and connected, and that parents' conceptions of children's independence and interdependence may be understood and interrelated differently during the course of a child's development.

With regard to the implication of conflict between independence and interdependence in children's developmental experiences, the findings at issue suggest that interdependence expectations may take precedence in some situations because children are expected to "sacrifice" some individual goals. With this interpretation, I am not trying to turn Euro-Americans into "collectivists." Instead, I am suggesting that, in some situations, some interdependence meanings may be emphasized over some independence meanings. In this case, consideration for others may take precedence over pursuing individual goals. However, consideration for others is ideally being coordinated with self-direction insofar as the expectation is for children to be considerate of others on their own. In this way, parents conceptualize self-direction and consideration for others in relation to each other. It is also important to point out that the Sears et al. (1957) descriptions of mothers wanting their children to "curb their enthusiasm and free movements to some degree" (p. 272, emphasis added) does not require children to fully suppress their individual goals and preferences. Instead, families may negotiate ways of living as individuals in relation to each other.

Such negotiation is in keeping with Euro-American "authoritative" discipline practices that are characterized by parental demandingness and responsiveness (Baumrind, 1967, 1989, 1996). More specifically, authoritative parents:

encourage verbal give and take and share with their children the reasoning behind their policies. They value both expressive and instrumental attributes, both autonomous self-will and disciplined conformity. Therefore, they exert firm control at points of parent–child divergence but do not hem their children in with restrictions. Authoritative parents are demanding in that they guide their children's activities firmly and consistently and require them to contribute to family functioning by helping with household tasks. They willingly confront their children in order to obtain conformity, state their values clearly, and expect their children to respect their norms. (Baumrind, 1989, pp. 353–354)

This description indicates how authoritative parents treat their children as separate individuals with distinct perspectives. At the same time, children are treated as social beings who are expected to contribute to the family and conform to social standards. Independence and interdependence meanings are thus interrelated within authoritative childrearing practices as a child's individuality is socially nurtured, and as parents conceptualize children's individuality and self-direction in relation to family ties and conformity to social standards.

The Inseparability of Independence and Interdependence in the Context of Household Work. Life at home may also include rules and requests for children to participate in varied practices that "contribute to a neat, orderly household, such as putting away toys, clearing the table, and throwing away trash" (Gralinksi & Kopp, 1993, p. 576). The ways in which middle-class Western parents construe and structure children's participation in household work or chores are permeated by varied and interrelated independence and interdependence meanings. Although it is not economically necessary, because the household is no longer the primary site of economic production, by the time middle-class children are about 9 or 10 years old, many parents have some expectations that their children will participate in varied household chores (Whiting & Edwards, 1988). Although children, especially younger children, do not always carry out these chores in particularly efficient or effective ways, parents are still likely to assign chores because the tasks are viewed as a way to foster children's self-reliance and build family unity and cohesion (e.g., Goodnow & Delaney, 1989; White & Brinkerhoff, 1981).

Contributing to household maintenance is also seen as a way to foster varied interdependence expectations, including helpfulness, a sense of responsibility to others, a sense of reciprocal obligations among family members, and sensitivity to others' needs (Goodnow, 1996; Goodnow & Warton, 1991). As Goodnow (1996) asserted, "For many Anglo [in this case, Australian-born English-speaking] mothers the ideal appears to be one of help given willingly, without being requested, and with signs of alertness to the other's needs" (p. 327), thus pointing to the importance of consideration and empathy for others. We also see another way in which independence expectations are inseparable from interdependence expectations, insofar as children are being encouraged to make decisions on their own as self-directed individuals in relation to consideration for others.

Similarly, picking up one's toys is conceptualized by parents as a household chore, and therefore provides another way in which the individual child, with his or her own personal property, is considered to be connected to, or inseparable from, a wider social unit. In addition, many mothers expect children to pick up their own toys because leaving them for someone else to pick up is burdensome to the other person and also implies that the other is viewed as something of a servant (Goodnow & Warton, 1991). In this way, picking up one's toys is inseparable from treating others with respect and involves being responsive to others "for the sake of the responsiveness itself" (Markus & Kitayama, 1991, p. 226; see chap. 1, this volume, for a discussion of this quotation in relation to dichotomous conceptions of independence and interdependence).

A few studies with Euro-American and Western samples also show that some of the first household chores parents assign to children are making their own beds and keeping their own rooms neat (e.g., Gralinski & Kopp, 1993; Sears et al., 1957; White & Brinkerhoff, 1981; Whiting & Edwards, 1988), thus taking us back to the issue of children's sleeping arrangements. The idea that making one's own bed and keeping one's own room neat are household chores (Hill & Holmbeck, 1987), and not only ways to foster eventual self-reliance, points to another interrelation between independence and interdependence expectations in children's lives. In this case, a child's separate room becomes a forum for learning how to live as a separate individual in relation to others within a family unit. As a household chore, a child's individual room or space is part of a wider social space and is also subject to some social regulation, thereby providing children with experiences as individuals who participate in a wider social system.

Gaskins' (1996, 1999) descriptions of children's early work experiences in a traditional Mexican Mayan village, with approximately 800 inhabitants, also enable us to discern how independence and interdependence meanings may be interrelated in a culture where children's experiences are far removed from the experiences of middle-class Western children. According to Gaskins, the daily life of this village is centered around the adults' work activities, which are required for the community's survival. The men's work revolves around farming corn, beans, and squash, and the women's work revolves around grinding the corn and making it into edible tortillas. Women also wash, garden, tend to infants, and supervise older children who care for younger siblings.

In this and other cultural communities where economic subsistence is based within or across several households, children often engage in work that contributes to community subsistence and enables them to participate directly in the work that will constitute their adult roles (e.g., Martini & Kirkpatrick, 1992/1994; Rogoff, 2003; Whiting & Edwards, 1988). Within these contexts, children as young as 2 years old may be asked to carry out relatively short and easy tasks, and they are expected to be available to fulfill these requests at any time. Gaskins observed that, "By the time children are 5 years old, it is not unusual to see them do some chores spontaneously and take responsibility for tasks beyond those assigned to them" (1999, p. 53). This kind of individual self-direction continues, and as children get older and are able to do chores that take more time, they may end up at a distance from their homes "to go shopping, run errands, or to deliver messages throughout the village" (Gaskins, 1999, p. 50). At the same time, this self-direction is socially supervised as "Parents retain authority for making sure that children's work is done and done well, that they demonstrate proper respect for those above them and proper responsibility for those below them, and that they not cause trouble in the larger community" (Gaskins, 1996, p. 356). The ultimate goal is for children to regulate work activities on their own, and most children then make the transition into adulthood in their mid-teens, when they become partners in the community's work.

Although there may not be much room in subsistence-based communities for individual choice regarding one's adult social roles, fairly prescribed social roles are structured in relation to self-direction. In these cultural contexts, self-direction is inseparable from community subsistence and, in turn, the community relies on its individual members to make their contributions through self-directed work. As we saw earlier in this chapter, modes of self-direction in some subsistence communities are also evident in parents' expectations for young children's physical self-reliance (e.g., feeding, washing, and dressing themselves). Even as such self-direction may serve group goals, realizing group goals implicates and requires dimensions of independence, making for ongoing interrelations between independence and interdependence expectations. In this way, it is evident how a first-glance analysis that focuses attention on the importance of community cooperation obscures the inseparability of community cooperation from other dimensions of cultural practices, such as individual self-direction.

Fostering Independence and Interdependence Through Neighborhood Connections and Peer Relationships

Self-Direction in Social Situations. Going back to the Sears et al. (1957) study, many of the mothers indicated that, although they made sure to know of their children's whereabouts, they did not keep a constant eye on their children, allowing the children to play by themselves and sometimes to venture beyond their own homes to play with other children in the neighborhood. This kind of time alone reflects an independence expectation for being self-directed. However, by including play with other children as well as going out into the neighborhood, we can also see how this independence expectation is inseparable from interdependence expectations. In this case, a child's ability to make his or her way through the neighborhood, and to make decisions about playing with other children, points to how independent self-direction is inseparable from parental expectations for engaging with others in direct relationships and also in a wider social environment.

Just as these New England children were allowed some independence within their neighborhoods, Whiting and Edwards' (1988) now-classic ethnographic analyses of another middle-class American community in 1950s New England, fictionally known as Orchard Town, indicated that children there were also granted some independence or autonomy to venture beyond their homes. However, the American children were granted less independence to venture beyond their homes in comparison to children in varied non-Western cultural communities, nationally situated in Liberia, Kenya, India, Mexico, the Philippines, and Okinawa. Noting the inseparability of individual self-direction from interdependence, Whiting and Edwards (1988) explained that, "The degree to which families know and trust one another and the safety of the environment are predictors of the amount of autonomy granted to young children to leave the home setting" (p. 82). In this way, interdependence, structured in terms of wider community ties, makes individual self-direction possible.

Along similar lines, Rogoff (2003) suggested that when children are included in ongoing community and adult activities, people beyond the immediate family are involved in caring for each other's children. No doubt, this kind of communal child care reflects the value of community interdependence and stands in contrast to the private nuclear family life of contemporary middle-class Westerners. However, at the same time, such community interdependence is related to independence by making forms of individual self-direction possible. For example, Rogoff (2003) described how a 3-year-old Guatemalan Mayan girl "usually went to evening church meetings by herself. She would put on her shawl at about 7:30 P. M. (well after dusk) and walk the four blocks to church, returning about two hours later" (p. 132). According to Rogoff, "If responsibility for caregiving is widely shared by a community . . . children have the freedom to watch ongoing community activities and to engage in them according to their interest and emerging skills" (p. 132). Although many Americans may currently lament the erosion of neighborhood connections in the United States, this erosion may also result in more limited opportunities for children to practice some forms of self-direction. Also, I suspect that even some Euro-Americans would be surprised by the 3-year-old Mayan girl's self-direction.

Cultural Differences in the Inseparability of Independence and Interdependence in the Context of Peer Relationships. In this Mayan village, and in some other cultural contexts, children's community-embedded independence may occur in peer groups, involving 3- to 5-year-olds who wander about their communities together and take care of themselves (e.g., Martini, 1994; Martini & Kirkpatrick, 1981, 1992/1994; Rogoff, 2003). These fairly autonomous peer groups often include siblings, with the older sibling primarily responsible for taking care of the younger sibling. Indeed, sibling caregiving has been, and continues to be, a prevalent mode of peer interaction in some nontechnological cultural contexts (Weisner & Gallimore, 1977; Zukow-Goldring, 1995). The optimal sibling caregiver may be a girl between 5 or 6 and 10 years old (Whiting & Edwards, 1988), but as formal education becomes more and more widespread, even younger children may also be charged with sibling care. For example, on the Marquesas Islands, children's first peer experiences typically begin when they start walking and "mothers release them into the care of preschool siblings who play with them near the house" (Martini & Kirkpatrick, 1992/1994, p. 208). Then:

> two-year-olds go to quite dangerous places (the boat ramp, elevated bridges, and the stream bed) with preschool siblings. . . . However, they [the preschool siblings] teach toddlers that they can stay with the group only if they keep themselves safe, stay out of the way of the group activity, and make few demands on the older sibling. (Martini & Kirkpatrick, 1992/1994, p. 211)

This description suggests that mixed-age peer groups and sibling caregiving may provide toddlers with opportunities not only for social engagement, but also for self-direction. Eventually, such peer group experiences provide opportunities for Marquesas Island children to learn how to direct themselves in activities with peers, or "how to exercise autonomy in a world of consociates" (Martini & Kirkpatrick, 1992/1994, p. 208). Conceptions and dimensions of independence and interdependence are thus interrelated because self-direction is inseparable from mixed-age peer interaction.

As mentioned earlier, studies with Euro-American parents also point to the importance of childhood peer relationships. However, in contrast to the structuring of mixed-age peer groups in some cultural communities, the structuring of American peer relationships indicates different interrelations between independence and interdependence in the context of peer relationships. For example, some research suggests that Euro-American parents generally view peer relationships as a major source of children's well-being and happiness, and they want their children to establish and maintain friendships (Raeff, 2000; Rubin & Sloman, 1984). In this way, parents see happiness as a relational phenomenon rather than as the property of an isolated child. Within this context, when Euro-American parents claim to want their children to "be happy regardless of the material conditions of their lives" (Richman et al., 1988, p. 68), they may be including social connections in their conceptions of happiness. Thus, the pursuit of happiness does not necessarily revolve exclusively around independence and is inseparable from interdependence. Parents also view early peer relationships as a forum for facilitating children's participation in group activities, especially in school (Tobin et al., 1989), thus demonstrating another Euro-American interdependence expectation.

Not only do Euro-American parents want their children to have positive peer relationships and friendships, but they also make efforts to actively influence and facilitate their children's peer connections (Bhavnagri & Parke, 1991; Ladd, Profilet, & Hart, 1992). More specifically, when making decisions about where to live, parents often consider whether there are other children in a neighborhood (Ladd, LeSieur, & Profilet, 1993; Rubin & Sloman, 1984). In addition, Euro-American parents, particularly of preschool-age children, actively arrange for children to have contact with peers by inviting other children to their homes or by taking their own children to others' homes. Although the almost businesslike arrangements of "play dates" may stand in contrast to the mixed-age peer groups just discussed, they reveal the value that Euro-American parents place on fostering their children's peer connections.

In terms of parental age expectations for varied modes of peer interaction, in one classic cross-cultural study that included Euro-American and Japanese parents of 5-year-olds, the Euro-American parents expressed significantly earlier expectations for the following issues: being "sympathetic to feelings of other children," "resolves disagreements without fighting," and "takes initiative in playing with others" (Hess, Kashiwagi, Azuma, Price, & Dickson, 1980, p. 264). Taking initiative while playing with others occurs in relation to others, thus pointing to how self-direction is inseparable from interdependence. There were no significant differences between Euro-American and Japanese parents' expectations for "waits for his turn in games" and "shares his toys with other children" (p. 264).

What Conceptions of Dependence, Obedience, and Conformity Reveal About Within-Culture Differences in Independence and Interdependence

Issues of dependence, obedience, and conformity have been major players in traditional considerations of independence and interdependence. Within the dichotomous tradition, dependence, obedience, and conformity are typically associated with an overall interdependence orientation, especially among non-Westerners and working-class Westerners. In addition, these issues are typically conceptualized in contrast to middle-class Western independence values that emphasize self-direction and the unique individuality of all people. However, when varied studies, with varied socioeconomic and ethnic samples, are considered in tandem, it starts to become clear that modes of dependence, obedience, and conformity are not related to independence and interdependence in straightforward ways. I try to untangle some of the complexities of these issues by starting out with a general consideration of dependence, and then I move on to more specific conceptions of conformity and obedience.

General Conceptions of Dependence. In conjunction with their expectations for socially situated self-direction (discussed in the previous section), the New England mothers in the Sears et al. (1957) study also generally hoped that their children would become less dependent on them. More specifically, 11% of the mothers indicated that they were not at all permissive of dependence, 26% indicated that they were low on dependence permissiveness, and 30% indicated that they were moderately permissive of dependence. Although decreasing dependence was clearly favored by these mothers, Sears et al. (1957) noted that a decrease in dependence does not entail separation between mother and child. In their words, "The ultimate aim of the socialization process, as it relates to dependency, is for the child to be fond of the mother rather than passionately attached to her, to be pleased by her attention and interest but not incessantly to demand it" (p. 140). This analysis points to both the importance of the parent–child relationship and (recalling chap. 3) a Euro-American theme that independence is being contrasted with dependence, not with relationships in and of themselves. Similarly, as noted earlier in this chapter, contemporary Euro-American parents typically report wanting their children to be self-directed and not overly dependent on others.

Social Class and Conceptions of Independence and Dependence.
Although varied samples of Euro-American parents since the 1950s claim
to generally prefer decreasing child dependence along with increasing
self-direction, some social class differences regarding dependence have
emerged. That is, in the Sears et al. (1957) study, 56% of the working-class
mothers, in contrast to 44% of the middle-class mothers, claimed to be "irritated by dependency behavior and to reject it with a punishing attitude"
(p. 428). Concomitantly, more of the middle-class mothers (42%) claimed
to be permissive of dependency in comparison to the working-class mothers (29%).

These findings are compatible with several more recent studies that
note multifaceted independence meanings among working-class families,
some of which have not been discussed thus far in our considerations of
mostly middle-class American samples. For example, Heath's (1983/1992)
ethnographic analyses in a rural working-class African-American community indicate values of independence in the form of individual effort and
achievement. In a neighboring working-class Euro-American community,
parents reported wanting their children to provide for themselves by
working hard and being able "to garden, sew, can, do woodworking, and
maintain their homes" (Heath, 1983/1992, p. 37). Interviews and ethnographic observations of Euro-American working-class parents in a tough,
violent, drug-infested New York City neighborhood demonstrate the importance of fostering children's independence, defined as " 'not relying
on anyone else,' 'not trusting anyone but yourself,' self-determination,
and keeping to oneself" (Kusserow, 1999, p. 216). In a nearby working-
class Euro-American community, but one that is safe, clean, and populated by long-term residents who know and trust one another, parents expect their children to work hard, persevere, be self-confident, and speak
their minds, all to achieve and move beyond their current circumstances.

Also, a study of working-class Euro-American families showed that 2-
and 3-year-olds have opportunities to construct "autonomous selves"
(Wiley, Rose, Burger, & Miller, 1998, p. 833) as parents engage their toddlers in conarratives of the children's experiences. In particular, children
in this study were expected:

> to give a factual accounting. If this did not occur, a conflict ensued and con-
> tinued until the child produced or agreed to the expected answer or the
> mother got the final word. Mothers were unlikely to soften their oppositions
> or to give in quickly. In this manner, the children gained experience in the
> presentation and defense of their claims in the face of quite resolute opposi-
> tion. (p. 843)

This analysis shows how conceptualizing independence in terms of defending one's own position was prevalent in this working-class commu-

nity. Similarly, other research with urban working-class Euro-American families points to how mothers often structure interactions with their toddlers in ways that enable children to practice defending themselves and standing up for their rights (Miller, 1986; Miller & Sperry, 1987). Toward these ends, the mothers tease their children verbally and also pretend to engage in fistfights with them. According to Miller, verbal teasing practices are used to provoke the children's anger, which can then be channeled toward self-defense. These studies also show how independence, conceptualized in terms of self-defense, is inseparable from interdependence as children learn to defend their individual positions in relation to others.

Social Class and Conceptions of Obedience and Conformity. At first glance, these working-class parents' conceptions of independence, and the Sears et al. (1957) finding that working-class mothers claim to be irritated by dependence, may seem at odds with other research on socioeconomic differences in parental ideas. That is, at least since Kohn's (1963, 1969/1977) studies of middle- and working-class families, researchers have consistently found that working-class parents are more likely than are middle-class parents to value conformity to authority and to want their children to be obedient (Hoff-Ginsburg & Tardif, 1995). These findings have been interpreted as suggesting that working-class families are more interdependence oriented than are middle-class families.

In contrast, according to Kohn (1969/1977), middle-class Euro-American parents are more likely to value initiative and to want their children to be self-directed. To make sense of this array of studies, we may turn back to Kohn (1969/1977), who maintained that working-class parents' values and conceptions of obedience and conformity to authority can be understood in relation to the parents' expectations that their children would eventually have working-class jobs that typically revolve around obeying authority and conforming to others' standards and demands. Also, the value of obedience may be related to concerns regarding children's safety in dangerous environments (e.g., Hoff-Ginsberg & Tardif, 1995; Kelley, Power, & Wimbush, 1992). In contrast to these working-class experiences, advancement in middle-class professional occupations depends in part on taking initiative and being generally self-directed.

Taken together, these varied findings indicate that, although obedience and conformity to authority may be valued in relation to future job expectations and/or safety concerns, working-class parents may still want their children to show independence by being self-reliant and by not being dependent. Thus, obedience and conformity to authority, as ways of enacting conceptions of interdependence, do not preclude conceptualizing independence in terms of self-reliance. In fact, keeping a job in the context of difficult economic circumstances may be essential to self-reliance and also to being less dependent on parents who themselves may experience financial difficulties.

In addition, being able to defend oneself and stand up for one's rights as a working-class person in a society dominated by monied interests would also be adaptive. Accordingly, occupational obedience and conformity to authority, in tandem with self-defense in some social situations, may serve as means toward achieving a valued independence goal. Indeed, it has been suggested that some children of working-class families become financially self-reliant earlier than do children of middle-class families "[b]y dropping out of school to seek employment," thus enabling them to "escape the pattern of dependency which is the common lot of their middle-class counterparts" (Fasick, 1984, p. 152). An interview study of barely surviving inner-city African-American adolescents and adults showed that achieving economic self-sufficiency as early as possible is considered to be a key to becoming an adult, along with maintaining close family and community ties (Burton, Allison, & Obeidallah, 1995). Thus, when independence goals are conceptualized partly in terms of financial self-reliance, middle-class adolescents may actually appear to be less independent than are their working-class counterparts.

However, rather than trying to discern who is more or less independent or interdependent, the current analysis points to how independence and interdependence may be understood and interrelated in different ways for working- and middle-class families. In particular, these studies with working-class samples show that not only do conformity to authority and obedience not preclude self-reliance, they are inseparable insofar as conformity to authority and obedience provide some foundations for eventual self-reliance. For the middle-class samples, there is also an inseparability, albeit a different one, between independence expectations, in the form of self-direction, and interdependence expectations. We may recall from a brief consideration of Kohn's analyses in chapter 1 that the self-directed initiative required for advancement in middle-class professional occupations does not involve "isolation, or insensitivity to others; on the contrary, it implies that one is attuned to internal dynamics—one's own, and other people's" (Kohn, 1969/1977, p. 35). Thus, the middle-class expectation is for people to be self-directed in social situations by understanding and engaging with others as separate people with their own perspectives, goals, and opinions.

Obedience, Conformity, and Dependence Within Cultural Practices. As with so many aspects of human behavior, defining and investigating conformity, obedience, and dependence are not straightforward endeavors. In chapter 3, we saw how dependence, as well as conformity and obedience to arbitrary authority or coercion, have been disavowed by Euro-Americans for centuries, beginning with the Puritans who settled in America so as not to conform to European religious practices. Studies conducted in varied cultural contexts suggest that conformity or obedience to what is perceived as arbitrary authority or coercion is disavowed by many. For example, on the Marquesas Islands, people "value group participation but reject the idea of persons submitting to authority" (Martini & Kirkpatrick, 1992/1994, p. 218). Similarly, among the Inuit of the Central Arctic, "children are not expected to develop blind obedience" (Briggs, 1991, p. 269). Among the Kaluli of Papua New Guinea, there is "a profound respect for personal autonomy" (Schieffelin, 1990/1993, p. 243) and a belief that "One can never compel another to act" (Schieffelin, 1990/1993, p. 245).

Even when obedience is expected of children, as has consistently been found in research with poor rural African-American families, these expectations are "tempered with an enjoyment and valuing of the child's spirited challenges to authority and testing of adult rules and limits" (Brody & Stoneman, 1992, p. 416). Within the wider context of African-American historical experiences in the United States, this research also shows that African Americans value "the ability to influence situations and persons to achieve desired goals, rather than unquestioning compliance with conventional rules and standards of conduct" (p. 416).

However, conformity and obedience to agreed-on social standards and forms of institutional regulation are not necessarily considered to be problematic. With regard to the American case, the Puritans are well known for their community conformity, and the United States of the 1950s is known for its suburbanite modes of conformity. Moreover, a democracy is sustained in part by a willingness to conform to (or at least temporarily accept) majority decisions. In terms of ideas about independence and interdependence, it would seem important to specify what kinds of conformity and obedience are valued and not valued in different cultures and in relation to different cultural practices. To say generally that a culture values conformity or obedience could be applicable to virtually any culture, and thus by itself does not tell us much about the meanings of independence and interdependence in that culture. Knowing that working-class American parents are less likely than are middle-class American parents to tolerate dependence, and more likely to encourage children's conformity and obedience to authority in relation to job expectations, enables us to construct a contextualized understanding of how conceptions of independence and interdependence may be interrelated for different socioeconomic groups.

Interim Summary

This discussion of parents' ideas and goals has taken us in varied directions, pointing to some of the complexities of independence and interdependence in children's developmental experiences. In the context of this discussion, some general statements about independence and interdependence may be made. First, independence values and expectations are enacted in various non-Western cultures that are typically characterized as interdependence oriented. For example, observations of Marquesas Islanders demonstrate how infants are viewed as separate motivational individuals, and studies with Mexican and Guatemalan Mayans show the value of self-direction in different situations. Second, we have seen how multifaceted interdependence values and expectations are enacted in Euro-American children's developmental experiences as children are expected to engage with peers, be considerate of others, follow rules, contribute to household organization, and even conform to others' preferences.

Third, the research just discussed indicates how independence and interdependence may be interrelated in varied ways, within as well as across cultures. For example, we have seen the inseparability of self-direction and peer interaction, self-reliance and conformity to authority, self-direction and the pursuit of common goals, self-direction and consideration for others, as well as individual self-expression and consideration for others. Although self-direction has emerged as an important developmental expectation in varied studies, we have seen how it is related to community child care in some cultures, but for Euro-Americans it is nurtured in the private nuclear family. In addition, although self-direction may be related to the pursuit of common goals in varied cultures, the structuring of common goals may be quite different across cultures. For example, although Euro-American children direct themselves in the pursuit of household chores within their nuclear families, Mexican Mayan children direct themselves in the pursuit of village subsistence goals.

These examples of interrelated or inseparable independence and interdependence meanings and activity dimensions also point to the inadequacy of first-glance analyses, which might suggest that a culture appears to emphasize some form of either independence or interdependence. If a culture appears to emphasize independence, further analyses are required to understand how that form of independence is inseparable from interdependence. Similarly, if a culture appears to emphasize interdependence, further analyses are required to understand how that form of interdependence is inseparable from independence.

PARENT–CHILD INTERACTIONS
DURING INFANCY AND CHILDHOOD

Independence and interdependence meanings are also enacted in the specific structuring of independence and interdependence activity dimensions during parent–child interactions in varied cultural practices. The current discussion of parent–child interactions during infancy and child-hood is based on some classic studies of parent–child interactions among Euro-Americans, African Americans, the Kaluli, and Marquesas Islanders. These studies show that children in varied cultures are viewed as separate individuals whose individuality is inseparable from their social connections. However, although there may be some similarities in conceptualizing children as individuals in relation to others, the studies discussed in this section demonstrate cultural differences in how these interrelated conceptions of independence and interdependence are particularized. This section of the chapter ends with a more general consideration of independence and interdependence in relation to dyadic and group interaction patterns.

Individuals in Relation to Others:
Euro-American Patterns

Not only does the prolonged period of physical dependence that characterizes human infancy necessarily and universally place infants in relation to others, but human infants also come to the world with varied specific abilities that facilitate engaging in social interactions (Užgiris, 1989). For example, during the first months of life, infants prefer to look at and listen to people (e.g., Brazelton, 1982; Spelke & Cortelyou, 1981; Stern, 1977). They also mold their bodies toward another person's body when being held, and they can be soothed and comforted by other people (e.g., Brazelton, 1982). Elaborating on these kinds of abilities, Euro-American parents engage their infants socially from the outset by establishing periods of mutual gazing (Schaffer, 1984), which may be extended into prolonged periods of face-to-face interaction to "have fun, to interest and delight and be with one another" (Stern, 1977, p. 71). Parents also adjust their behavior in relation to an infant's activities, arousal states, and individual tolerance for stimulation (e.g., Kaye, 1982; Ochs & Schieffelin, 1984/1988; Schaffer, 1979, 1984; Stern, 1977; Trevarthen, 1979). Similarly, parents are likely to modify their expressiveness by exaggerating their facial expressions and using high-pitched and elongated vocalizations (e.g., Schaffer, 1984; Stern, 1977). When not revolving around basic caregiving, Euro-American parent–infant interactions during the first half of the first year of life are relatively nonverbal, as parents mostly hold and look at infants (Richman, Miller, & LeVine, 1992). Then during the second half of the first year, talking becomes the dominant medium of interaction used by Euro-American parents (Richman et al., 1992).

Euro-American parents also typically interact with infants by trying to discern and then talk about what seems to be of most individual interest to an infant. As middle- and working-class Euro-American parents spend time talking to their infants, they often comment on and ask infants about their ideas, feelings, interests, and actions (e.g., Heath, 1983/1992; Kruper & Užgiris, 1987; Schaffer, 1984; Trevarthen, 1979). Indeed, as Kaye (1982) noted, an infant "is plunged into ongoing discourse on topics very largely selected by his own interests" (p. 103). When asking infants questions, parents are likely to pause, as if to leave time for the infant to answer, and just about anything the infant does (from burping to wiggling) is then usually accepted as a reasonable response (Kruper & Užgiris, 1987; Ochs & Schieffelin, 1984/1988; Rogoff et al., 1993; Schaffer, 1979, 1984). These interaction patterns show how parents impute meaning to their infants' actions, thereby treating the infants as both separate mental individuals and active social partners from the outset (e.g., Bruner, 1983; Kruper & Užgiris, 1987; Ochs & Schieffelin, 1984/1988; Trevarthen, 1979, 1980). Commenting on and asking questions about the infant reflect the values of treating people as relatively equal separate physical and mental individuals who have their own interests, goals, and preferences that can eventually be expressed to interested others, thus making the child's individuality inseparable from social connections.

Imitation is another characteristic of early dyadic parent–child interactions. Although imitation is often viewed as a mode of learning for children, or as an indicator of individual cognitive competence, it is the adults who actually do most of the imitating during a child's first year of life (e.g., Užgiris, Benson, Kruper, & Vasek, 1989). Studies of Euro-American parent–infant dyads indicate that gradually, during the course of the first year, imitation becomes more reciprocal as infants imitate parents more frequently, sometimes leading to several rounds of mutual imitation. Insofar as this early imitation takes place during the course of interpersonal interaction, imitation has been conceptualized as a medium used by parents to engage their infants socially as communicative partners, and to express understanding of and similarity to their babies (e.g., Užgiris, 1984, 1990). Observations of mother–infant interactions demonstrate that by adjusting their actions to the infant's actions through imitation, there "can be a realization of mutuality for both the infant and mother: to do the same thing as the other is to confirm a similarity in capability, interest, or feeling with the other" (Užgiris, 1981, p. 6). Through imitation, a child's individuality is inseparable from interdependence values as parents build on the child's individual actions to establish and maintain social engagement. Along similar lines, Stern's (1985) discussion of affect attunement described how parents imitate an infant's individual emotional states as a way of sharing the infant's subjective experience, thus linking the infant's subjectivity and individuality to others.

Individuals in Relation to Others:
African-American Patterns

An early study of working-class African-American families in the rural South also showed how infants were engaged verbally in face-to-face interactions (Young, 1970). Although adults often interrupted infants' activities, requiring the children to conform to others' preferences, they also often asked infants questions about their own individual preferences and desires (e.g., Young, 1970). Physical and verbal modes of interaction were often coordinated as adults frequently engaged infants and young children in physical teasing play routines. According to Young's descriptions, these teasing practices build on the infants' sensorimotor tendencies to explore the world, including other people, with their mouths. When such mouthing occurred, the adults would teasingly accuse the baby of biting or fighting and would further characterize the baby as "an individual capable of bold initiative" (p. 279). Moreover, the infant's assertiveness would be admired and encouraged, and an infant would generally be treated as a "willful assertive individual" (p. 280). Then, once capable of walking, a child "has free rein in his behavior, but he is expected to cause his mother no trouble" (p. 280).

These interaction patterns are in keeping with the research discussed in the previous section that African-American parents value obedience, as well as "spirited challenges to authority" in their children. Similarly, Ogbu (1985) concluded that, for African-American families, the "few extended observational studies we have show that during infancy children receive a great deal of nurturance, warmth and affection. Investigators generally agree that the infant's individuality is stressed" (p. 59).

Another way of structuring individuality through social interaction is evident in Heath's (1983/1992) descriptions of how rural working-class African Americans engage children in the practice of storytelling. Children are encouraged to tell stories about themselves and their achievements as a way "to assert individual strengths and powers" (p. 184). Heath also pointed out that to get an audience's attention, "story-tellers, from a young age, must be aggressive in inserting their stories into an on-going stream of discourse. Story-telling is highly competitive. Everyone in a conversation may want to tell a story, so only the most aggressive wins out" (p. 185). A good story includes individual creativity through exaggeration and fictionalization, and "The 'best stories' often call forth highly diverse additional stories, all designed not to unify the group, but to set out the individual merits of each member of the group" (p. 185). Moreover, stories "do not teach lessons about proper behavior; they tell of individuals who excel by outwitting the rules of conventional behavior" (p. 187).

These aspects of African-American storytelling practices, and the expression of individuality through "verbal facility" (Levine, 1977, p. 128), are part of a long-standing oral tradition, reaching back before the period of slavery to African cultural traditions.

Individuals in Relation to Others: Kaluli Patterns

In contrast to both Euro-American and African-American interaction patterns, Ochs and Schieffelin (1984/1988) described how the Kaluli of Papua New Guinea believe that "infants 'have no understanding' " (p. 289), and therefore mothers:

> never treat their infants as partners (speaker/addressee) in dyadic communicative interactions. Although they greet their infants by name and use expressive vocalizations, they rarely address other utterances to them. Furthermore, a mother and infant do not gaze into each other's eyes, an interactional pattern that is consistent with adult patterns of not gazing when vocalizing in interaction with one another. Rather than facing their babies and speaking to them, Kaluli mothers tend to face their babies outward so that they can see, and be seen by, other members of the social group. (p. 289)

In addition, once children start speaking, rather than building on a child's initiatives, mothers explicitly teach children what to say in different situations. More specifically:

> The mother pushes the child into ongoing interactions that the child may or may not be interested in and will at times spend a good deal of energy in trying to get the child verbally involved. This is part of the Kaluli pattern of fitting (or pushing) the child into the situation rather than changing the situation to meet the interests or abilities of the child. Thus mothers take a directive role with their young children, teaching them what to say so that they may become participants in the social group. (p. 293)

Ochs and Schieffelin (1984/1988) explained that although children are treated as group members, the Kaluli do not believe in talking about other people's internal states and motives—not because such phenomena are not considered to exist, but because the Kaluli do not think one can really know another's perspective. Thus, "the responsibility for clear expression is with the speaker, and child speakers are not exempt from this. Rather than offering possible interpretations or guessing at the meaning of what a child is saying, caregivers make extensive use of clarification requests" (p. 294). This practice indicates how the Kaluli understand people as separate mental beings. It also suggests that social interaction is facilitated in part by clear statements of one's individual perspective, thus making group social interaction inseparable from expressing one's individuality. Ultimately, "Learning how to talk and become independent is a major goal of socialization" (p. 288), and these parent–child interaction patterns provide Kaluli children with opportunities for constructing individual positions within group networks.

The Inseparability of Independence and Interdependence in Dyadic and Group Interaction Patterns

In addition to elucidating some different cultural ways in which individuality and social interactions are interrelated, the findings from these three cultural groups show how children in different parts of the world participate variably in dyadic and group interaction patterns. Moreover, the findings from these three cultural groups suggest that interpreting group and dyadic interactions in relation to independence and interdependence issues is not straightforward. At first glance, dyadic interactions may be interpreted as reflecting independence meanings because they involve recognizing each partner's separate individuality. Commensurately, group interactions may be interpreted as reflecting interdependence meanings because they appear to emphasize wider group cohesion over individual preferences or goals.

Although it may be the case that group interactions are more common in some cultures than in others, it is not clear that group interactions are necessarily "more" social or interdependent than are dyadic interactions. By definition, any kind of interpersonal interaction is a social or interdependent phenomenon. Similarly, insofar as group interactions are made up of distinct individuals who are self-aware, can direct themselves, and can experience subjectivity, independence activity dimensions are implicated in the structuring of group interactions. Accordingly, rather than conceptualizing interactions as more or less interdependent or independent, the current conceptual approach leads to discerning how independence and interdependence activity dimensions may be structured differently in different cultures, and how they may be related to each other in different ways. With regard to dyadic patterns, research with Euro-American families shows how parents build on infants' and children's actions and individual preferences to engage with them as relatively equal social partners. With regard to group patterns, studies of the Kaluli suggest that group interactions are inseparable from individual self-expression, and group storytelling among African Americans provides a forum for asserting and expressing one's individuality.

The research with African Americans also indicates that children from a particular culture may participate in both dyadic and group interactions.

Investigations on the Marquesas Islands similarly suggest that infants and children engage in both dyadic and group interactions with varied social partners. As mentioned earlier in this chapter, Marquesas Islanders see infants as separate mental and motivational beings. Within this context, "an infant is cared for almost exclusively by the mother for the first 2 or 3 months" (Martini & Kirkpatrick, 1981, p. 192). Once a baby can sit up, he or she begins to be cared for by "other children in the household and is passed around to other women at church or public events" (Martini & Kirkpatrick, 1981, p. 193). In addition to participating in interactions with multiple people, "All routine caregiving activities are performed while the baby faces outward" (Martini & Kirkpatrick, 1981, p. 193), pointing to a group orientation. When a baby is about 5 or 6 months old, "young children carry the baby around the valley where they care for him while watching their friends play. In this situation, the infant is engaged in intensive face-to-face play with many of the valley children" (Martini & Kirkpatrick, 1981, p. 193). Then, when they are about 6 or 8 months old, infants participate in games involving "three or more people" (Martini & Kirkpatrick, 1981, p. 193). As noted earlier in this chapter, preschoolers then spend much of their time in autonomous peer groups. By the time children go to school, they:

> are considered to be competent conversational partners and adults draw on children's superior knowledge of valley events. At home, children sit near adults and participate in all but the most serious conversations. They initiate topics, take long speaking turns, and adults listen to their input. Mothers report that they enjoy their children's company and discuss events with older children in much the way they talk with adult friends. (Martini & Kirkpatrick, 1992/1994, p. 213)

Taken together, these analyses show how Marquesas children's individuality as well as self-direction are inseparable from dyadic face-to-face and group interactions.

To further muddy these waters, some analyses suggest that conceptualizing the structuring of children's interactions with others as either dyadic or group may represent another false dichotomy that is not applicable in all situations. For example, a comparative study of middle-class Euro-American and Colombian families (with toddlers between 18 and 20 months old, and at least one older sibling) pointed to dyadic, group, and semigroup interaction patterns (Ramirez, 2003). In this study, *semigroup interaction* was defined as "The parent or sibling was watching the child play with another family member, but did not actively engage in the activity" (p. 91). During a 20-minute interaction period, the American and Colombian families spent some time (a mean of at least 17% of the time) in all three interaction states. In addition, there were no statistically significant differences in the amount of time the Euro-American and Colombian families each spent in group interactions. However, the Euro-Americans spent a statistically significant greater amount of time in dyadic interaction in comparison with the Colombian families, who spent more time in semigroup interaction. Taken together, these varied studies show how children's interactions with others, as they occur in dyads, groups, or semigroups, involve different ways of engaging as individuals in relation to others.

HOW PARENTS TALK ABOUT INDEPENDENCE AND INTERDEPENDENCE DURING PARENT–CHILD INTERACTIONS

Although studies of Euro-American parent–child interactions during early childhood are abundant, little explicit attention has been paid to how independence and interdependence are structured by parents during parent–child interactions. Thus, rather than focusing only on discerning whether Euro-American parents are more or less concerned with independence or interdependence, the current conceptual approach leads us to discern how these parents incorporate certain independence and interdependence issues into their interactions with their children. For example, when talking about interdependence issues, do Euro-American parents tend to talk about other people, do they talk about social standards, or do they talk about a particular joint activity that they may be engaging in with their children? The current approach also leads to discerning how parents talk about independence and interdependence in relation to each other.

In addition, it is important to discern how parents' discussions of independence and interdependence issues are related to parents' and children's ongoing activities. As noted in the previous section, much research demonstrates how Euro-American parents engage their children dyadically and comment on the children's individual preferences and actions. However, it is unclear how parents' comments about children's preferences and actions are embedded in specific activities beyond infancy.

For example, it is not clear whether parents' comments about children's preferences occur when a parent is watching a child who is engaging in some activity alone or when a parent and child are jointly pursuing a common goal. Although the parent may be commenting on the child's independent action in both cases, different independence and interdependence issues are emphasized in each case. That is, commenting on a child's actions while the child is doing something alone emphasizes the child's separateness, but also may serve to make the child's separate activity socially meaningful. Commenting on a child's actions within a joint activity emphasizes how the child's individual action is related to the ongoing social interaction. It would thus seem important to analyze how parents' utterances during parent–child interactions are linked to the child's actions within different ongoing activities. Such analyses can help to disentangle some multifaceted and interrelated independence and interdependence issues as they are particularized in parent–child relationships, and they can further our understanding of the structuring of children's behavior as individuals in relation to others.

Toward these ends, I conducted an observational study of Euro-American families with 1- to 3-year-olds. For current purposes, I present analyses of the form and content of parents' utterances in the context of the parents' and children's ongoing activities. Fifty-six Euro-American middle- and working-class parents with children (26 boys, 30 girls) between 12 and 42 months of age, living in and around a small, rural university town, participated in the study. In most cases, the participating parents were mothers, but fathers who wanted to participate were also included. Thus, 91% of the participants included mothers only, 7% included both mothers and fathers, and one parent–child pair (2%) included only the father. Because mostly one parent participated in the study, a child and his or her parent or parents taken together are referred to as a parent–child pair or dyad. All of the children could walk, and the parent–child pairs were divided into three groups based on the children's ages. Twenty of the parent–child pairs consisted of 1-year-old children (10 boys, 10 girls) who were between 12 and 18 months old ($M = 15$ months), 18 of the parent–child pairs consisted of 2-year-old children (8 boys, 10 girls) who were between 24 and 30 months old ($M = 26$ months), and 18 of the parent–child pairs included 3-year-old children (8 boys, 10 girls) who were between 36 and 42 months old ($M = 39$ months).

Videotaped observations of parent–child interactions were conducted at the participants' homes, and the parent–child pairs were told to spend 15 minutes doing what they would normally do when at home together. All of the parents' utterances were transcribed and then coded from the transcripts while simultaneously watching the videotapes to interpret the utterances as they were embedded in the children's and parents' ongoing activities. Coding the parents' utterances first involved categorizing utterances as statements, questions, or commands. Interrater reliability between two judges for counting utterances as statements, questions, or commands, calculated in terms of kappa coefficients on 20% of the observations, was .95. These utterances were then coded according to the following system of theoretically and empirically derived independence and interdependence issues. Each coding category is presented with an example from the observations. Interrater reliability between two judges for these utterance coding categories, calculated in terms of kappa coefficients on 20% of the observations, was .82.

I. Statements
   A. About the overall joint activity: "We'll have to put this here."
   B. About the child's separate action or individual perspective while engaged in a separate activity: "You love to dig in there." (The shorthand term for this category is *child's separate action/ perspective*.)
   C. About the child's action or role in a joint activity: "This one's done."
   D. About the parent's separate action or individual perspective while engaged in a separate activity: "I need to toss this." (The shorthand term for this category is *parent's separate action/ perspective*.)
   E. About the parent's action or role in a joint activity: "I broke it."
   F. About another person: "He might be a doctor some day."
   G. About a social rule or standard: "We don't hit."
   H. Other: This coding category included statements that could not be classified according to any of the preceding statement coding categories.

II. Questions
   A. About a joint activity: "What do we do next?"
   B. About the child's separate action or individual perspective while engaged in a separate activity: "What did you do?" (The shorthand term for this category is *child's separate action/perspective*.)
   C. About the child's action or role in a joint activity: "Are you gonna be able to catch it?"
   D. About the parent's separate action or individual perspective while engaged in a separate activity: "Do I have black on my pants?" (The shorthand term for this category is *parent's separate action/perspective*.)
   E. About the parent's role or action in a joint activity: "Where should I make it?"
   F. About another person: "Which grandma's a nurse?"
   G. About a social rule or standard: "We only color on?"
   H. Other: This coding category included questions that could not be classified according to any of the preceding question coding categories.

III. Commands
   A. For joint attention: "Look."
   B. For the child to act separately: "Ride your bike."

    C. For the child to act in a joint activity: "Roll it."
    D. For the child to follow a social rule or standard: "Only take one."

One way to discern how parents structure independence and interdependence during parent–child interactions involves analyzing their utterance forms. In particular, the use of questions provides a way for parents to structure children's individuality in relation to interdependence, or to treat their children as individuals in relation to others. We have already mentioned the Euro-American practice of posing questions in the previous section. Asking questions may be interpreted in terms of Euro-American values regarding independence insofar as asking questions indicates that parents view their children as separate individuals who have their own individual opinions, preferences, choices, and needs. However, based on the current perspective that independence and interdependence are inseparable dimensions of activity, asking questions and expecting answers may be seen as ways to highlight the importance of communicating one's individual opinions and preferences to others within a social world. Thus, asking children questions enables them to articulate their own perspectives as independent individuals, not for the sake of individual self-aggrandizement, but rather as individuals who live in relation to others who want to know about those perspectives. In this way, individuality is irrevocably linked to interdependence.

As can be seen in Table 4.1, across all age groups, parental utterances consisted primarily of statements, followed closely by questions for the 2- and 3-year-olds. In addition, parents of 2- and 3-year-olds posed more questions than did parents of 1-year-olds. This finding points to how parents may be responding to children's changing capacities for behaving as individuals in relation to others. In this case, as children develop and are able to answer questions linguistically, their parents are providing them with even more opportunities to express their individual perspectives socially by asking them questions.

In addition to utterance form, independence and interdependence issues may also be particularized in the content of parents' statements,

TABLE 4.1

Mean Proportions of Parental Utterance Forms for Each Age Group

Age Group	Statements	Questions	Commands
1 year	.47 (.10)	.31 (.08)	.22 (.11)
2 years	.45 (.08)	.43 (.08)	.13 (.07)
3 years	.46 (.11)	.41 (.13)	.12 (.08)

Note. Values in parentheses represent standard deviations.

questions, and commands. With regard to interdependence issues, the parents' statements revolved around the joint activity, as did their questions. The parents' statements did not emphasize other people, nor did their questions, thus revealing a child-centered orientation that is known to be typical of Euro-American parents. This finding may also be peculiar to the research situation, and the parents may have focused on the children based on the assumption that the study addressed child development issues. The parents' statements and questions also did not emphasize social rules and standards. Interdependence was additionally particularized in the parents' commands for joint attention, and to a lesser extent in their commands for children to act according to a social rule or standard. Utterances about social rules or standards may have been relatively rare because the children did not frequently break any social rules or standards during the observation session.

With regard to independence issues, the parents' utterances included statements and questions about the children's separate action/perspective. The parents also sometimes commanded the children to act separately. Independence issues were particularized less frequently in terms of parents' statements or questions about their own separate action/perspective.

The parents' utterances about the child's action within an activity that a parent and child are pursuing jointly point to how independence and interdependence are interrelated insofar as such utterances link the child's action as a separate person to a joint activity. For this sample, a mean of 28% of the parents' statements included statements about the child's action within a joint activity, a mean of 32% of their questions included questions about the child's action within a joint activity, and a mean of 43% of their commands included commands for the child to act within a joint activity.

Differing patterns of parental statement and command topics across the three age groups further demonstrate how independence and interdependence issues are particularized in relation to each other, and also in relation to children's changing abilities over time. The distribution of the most common statement topics for parents of each age group is given in Table 4.2. Across age groups, parents of 2- and 3-year-olds made fewer statements about the child's separate action/perspective than did parents of 1-year-olds. By itself, this finding indicates how the parents were less focused on the child's action as a self-contained individual over time.

The pattern of findings presented in Table 4.2 also shows that parents of 1- and 2-year-olds talked somewhat more about joint activities than did parents of 3-year-olds. On its own, this finding might suggest a decrease in parents' concern with interdependence as their children get older. However, when considered in tandem with the small increase in statements

TABLE 4.2
Mean Proportions of Parental Statement Topics for Each Age Group

Age Group	Joint Activity	Child's Action in Joint Activity	Child's Separate Action
1 year	.32 (.11)	.27 (.13)	.21 (.09)
2 years	.32 (.15)	.24 (.09)	.13 (.10)
3 years	.26 (.10)	.32 (.13)	.10 (.07)

Note. Values in parentheses represent standard deviations.

about the children's action within joint activities (from 1 to 3 years) and the decrease in statements about the children's separate action/perspective, the findings as a whole suggest that parents are concerned with the implications of their children's individual actions for the ongoing social interaction. Developmentally, these differences suggest that as children can direct themselves in more complex ways and can contribute to increasingly complex joint activities, parents' utterances are more likely to focus on the child's role in the joint activities. Thus, these differences indicate that parents are not necessarily more or less concerned with either independence or interdependence per se over time, but rather with how children's individual actions are socially significant. Paralleling the children's development, the parents' utterances seem to reflect an increasing concern with how children's individual actions are integrated with interpersonal engagement.

The changing distributions of parental command topics across the three age groups parallel the changes just discussed regarding parental statements. That is, parental commands for joint attention were lower for dyads with 3-year-olds than for dyads with 1-year-olds. In addition, parental commands for the child to act within a joint activity were higher for dyads with 3-year-olds than for dyads with 1-year-olds. These differences suggest that the older children were increasingly able to enter into joint activities on their own, with less explicit parental prodding. With joint attention easier to establish, parents' commands for the 3-year-olds focused more on the child's action within a joint activity, providing opportunities for children to refine their skills as individuals who contribute to joint activities with others.

Taken together, these analyses reveal that independence and interdependence issues are particularized in parents' use of questions, as well as in their utterances about joint activities, the child's role in joint activities, and the child's separate action/perspective. The changing patterns of statement topics and command topics, coupled with the increase in posing questions, further indicate that parents do not necessarily emphasize either independence or interdependence over the other. Instead, the changes over time in parental utterances demonstrate a transformation in parents' constructions of their children's independence in relation to interdependence. In addition, these findings point to the utility of analyzing parents' utterances to children in relation to their ongoing activities. If parents' utterances are interpreted in isolation from the ongoing activity, a statement such as "You did it" seems to focus on the child as a separate individual. However, knowing that a statement such as "You did it" refers to a child's action as it occurs in a joint activity helps us to understand how interdependence expectations for contributing to a joint activity are implicated in conceptions of the child's independent action. Again, such analyses show how these Euro-American parents are treating children as individuals in relation to others.

PARENT–CHILD RELATIONSHIPS DURING ADOLESCENCE

Individualized Family Members

In reading about parent–adolescent relationships, one may be struck by how common it is for researchers to point out that the popular description of Western parent–adolescent interactions as riddled by virtually constant and dramatic conflict is not supported empirically. This common description has been promulgated by the popular media and has roots in psychoanalytic theory (Steinberg, 1990), but a review of research indicates that "less than 10 percent of families endure serious relationship difficulties during adolescence (i.e., parent–adolescent relationships characterized by chronic and escalating levels of conflict and repeated arguments over serious issues)" (Holmbeck, Paikoff, & Brooks-Gunn, 1995, p. 108). Instead, investigations of adolescents and their parents typically show that, although some conflict may inevitably occur, parent–adolescent interactions are generally characterized by continuity with earlier patterns of interaction, as well as by open, supportive, and mutual communication patterns (Collins & Laursen, 1992; Collins & Luebker, 1994; Holmbeck et al., 1995; Laursen, Coy, & Collins, 1998; Youniss & Smollar, 1985).

Overall, a sweeping questionnaire study of 13- to 19-year-old adolescents from varied socioeconomic backgrounds in Australia, Bangladesh, Hungary, Israel, Italy, Japan, Taiwan, Turkey, the United States, and what was then West Germany indicated that "[i]tems measuring family relationships showed the most agreement across countries. The overwhelming majority of teenagers in all ten countries disclaimed negative attitudes toward their families" (Offer, Ostrov, Howard, & Atkinson, 1988, p. 63). Even as adolescents spend more unsupervised time with peers, they typically assert that relationships with parents remain salient and important to them (Collins & Laursen, 1992; Csikszentmihalyi & Larson, 1984; Furman & Buhrmester, 1992; Holmbeck et al., 1995; Laursen, Coy, & Collins, 1998; Youniss & Smollar, 1985).

Within this context, a revealing picture of parent–adolescent relationships is evident in adolescents' reports that one of their preferred activities is to simply talk to their parents (Youniss & Smollar, 1985). These conversations are characterized by mutuality as "ideas and feelings are exchanged" (p. 91) between parents and children, pointing to how ongoing interactions between communicative partners are structured in relation to individual self-expression. Also building on earlier interaction patterns, parents have been found to make efforts to engage with their adolescent children in terms of the children's interests, to respect their adolescents' individuality, and to grant them more latitude in decision making. Accordingly, in many families, parents allow adolescents to contribute more input into family decisions, thus pointing to how parents view adolescents as separate individuals with their own perspectives (Bumpus, Crouter, & McHale, 2001; Holmbeck et al., 1995) that are inseparable from the interdependence of the wider family unit.

This process of transformation in the mutuality of parent–child relationships during adolescence has been called *individuation*. Although it may be tempting to interpret the construct of individuation in terms of cultural expectations for independence during adolescence, many researchers of adolescent development define individuation in relational terms (Grotevant & Cooper, 1985, 1986, 1998; Youniss & Smollar, 1985). According to Grotevant and Cooper, it is the parent–child relationship that undergoes individuation during the child's adolescence, not the adolescent alone. In keeping with the current conceptual approach, "Individuation is defined as a quality of dyadic relationships generated by both its members, and is seen in the interplay between the individuality and connectedness of the partners" (Grotevant & Cooper, 1986, p. 87). More specifically, according to Grotevant and Cooper's definition of an individuated relationship, the partners see themselves and each other as distinct individuals with their "own feelings and thoughts," and each partner expresses "willingness to accept responsibility for [his/her] own feelings and thoughts, as well as the ability to communicate [his/her] ideas clearly and directly" (1986, p. 89). According to Grotevant and Cooper, connectedness in an individuated relationship involves "the demonstration of sensitivity to and respect for the beliefs, feelings, and ideas of others," as well as partners who support each other "to develop a point of view" (1986, p. 89).

Such relational individuation also seems to be characteristic of middle-class African-American parent–child interactions, as family members report feeling comfortable in expressing their ideas and opinions (Smetana, Abernethy, & Harris, 2000). In addition, interaction observations of parents and their adolescent children reveal mutual support and receptivity to each other's ideas, as well as tolerance for differences of opinion. These findings build on and corroborate a study of working- and lower-middle-class African-American adolescent girls and their mothers, which indicated that the mothers support and respect their daughters' individual preferences and self-reliance while also supporting "the development of attachment and loyalty to parents and community" (Cauce et al., 1996, p. 113).

Conflict Between Independence and Interdependence in Parent–Adolescent Relationships

As noted, in the context of generally positive and individuated relationships, some conflict does indeed occur in "all families some of the time and some families most of the time" (Montemayor, 1983, p. 83). Some conflict is perhaps not surprising as parents continue to set rules for their adolescent children to follow, including rules about religious practices, family activities, keeping one's room clean, helping out at home, watching TV, doing homework, physical appearance, spending money, and eating habits (Hill & Holmbeck, 1987). Also, even (or perhaps especially) in individuated relationships, which are characterized in part by parents and children who express their individual opinions and points of view, some conflict is inevitable.

To further understand some of the sources of parent–adolescent conflict, Smetana and her colleagues conducted several studies with working- and middle-class Euro-American and African-American families that have generally shown how conflict is played out in relation to different behavioral domains (e.g., Smetana, 1988, 1989, 1994, 2000; Smetana & Asquith, 1994; Smetana & Gaines, 1999). These studies have consisted of analyzing parents' and adolescents' reactions to hypothetical scenarios about commonly occurring family conflicts, as well as parents' and adolescents' conceptions of their actual family conflicts.

Across several decades of studies, parents and adolescent children have been found to disagree "over the everyday, mundane details of family life" (Smetana, 1989, p. 1063), including household chores, homework, physical appearance, the adolescent's room, and time with friends (Montemayor, 1983). It is interesting to note that the adolescent's room is part of this list, taking us back to our previous discussion of how a child's individual room is inseparable from relational issues and represents a socially negotiated individual space. Parent–adolescent disagreements about these varied daily life issues more substantively involve differing conceptions and expectations of parental authority and children's self-direction (Collins & Luebker, 1994). That is, although parents and adolescents generally agree that varied domains of an adolescent's functioning legitimately fall under parental authority, parents are more likely than are adolescents to endorse this claim. In addition, adolescents tend to view more issues as personal, whereas parents tend to view more issues as conventional, involving "the arbitrary and consensually agreed-upon behavioral uniformities that structure social interactions within social systems" (Smetana, 1988, p. 322).

Overall, these findings "suggest that conflict emerges when adolescents' attempts to assert autonomy . . . compete with parents' conventional goals of regulating the household, maintaining authority, and upholding conventional standards" (Smetana, 1989, p. 1064). In other words, conflict appears to occur between children's conceptions of their own self-direction and parents' interdependence expectations. As the children develop, parents' claims of authority over adolescents' lives wane, and they are also more likely to expand what is included in their adolescent children's personal domains of functioning. In this way, an adolescent's self-direction is socially negotiated and co-constructed during development. These studies point to how adolescents' conceptions of independence may come into conflict with parental interdependence expectations, including maintaining family cohesion and adhering to social standards. The practice of negotiating to resolve parent–adolescent conflict suggests that, rather than either independence or interdependence expectations prevailing, their interrelations are reconstituted in ways that are sensitive to family relationships, social standards, adolescent individuality, and adolescent self-direction.

INDEPENDENCE AND INTERDEPENDENCE
IN JAPANESE CHILDREARING PRACTICES

Japanese childrearing practices, as well as differences between American and Japanese childrearing practices, have often been viewed from the vantage point of a dichotomous understanding of independence and interdependence. From this vantage point, Japanese culture and childrearing are characterized as essentially interdependence oriented, in contrast to the independence orientation of Euro-American culture and child socialization patterns. However, as we have already seen in this chapter as well as in chapter 3, Euro-American cultural practices do not revolve exclusively around independence issues. Based on the current theoretical position that independence and interdependence are universally inseparable dimensions of cultural practices, it is likely that characterizing Japanese childrearing practices in terms of interdependence obscures Japanese independence meanings. Indeed, some students of Japan have criticized descriptions of Japanese culture that revolve around interdependence as being inadequate (e.g., Holloway, 1999; Shimizu, 2000; Toma & Wertsch, 2003; Yamada, 2004), thus further pointing to the importance of exploring how independence and interdependence are particularized in Japanese ideas about children and in the structuring of Japanese parent–child interactions.

Enacting Multifaceted and Interrelated Conceptions of Independence and Interdependence in the Context of Inner and Outer Cultural Practices

Multifaceted and interrelated independence and interdependence meanings are reflected in Japanese modes of behavior in complex ways, especially in relation to the important distinction made in Japanese culture between relatively private, inner, or informal cultural practices and relatively public, outer, or formal cultural practices. Part of socialization toward competence in Japan involves learning the distinction between inner and outer cultural practices, and the modes of behavior considered differentially appropriate to them (e.g., Bachnik, 1992a/1995, 1992b; Doi, 1985/1988; Hendry, 1986; Tobin, 1992/1995).

Public or outer cultural practices, which may take place at school and work, involve formal modes of communication as well as interactions that are structured around sensitivity to others' feelings and wants. In outer or public situations, people are expected to engage in *enryo*, or restraint (Doi, 1973/2001), which involves attending to others, refraining from expressing contrary opinions, adhering to social norms, and generally avoiding overt conflict (Chen, 1996; Clancy, 1986; Hendry, 1986; Lebra, 1994). In keeping with these ends, Japanese social interactions have been described in terms of empathy, and as "intuitive and indirect" (Clancy, 1986, p. 213). If one empathizes with another person, one can nonverbally intuit and then fulfill the other's needs and wishes without direct communication. Moreover, overt conflict is less likely if people communicate indirectly, thus enabling them to maintain social harmony. Within this context, Japanese parent–infant interactions are characterized by verbal communication, as well as nonverbal and physical modes of responsivity (e.g., Caudill & Weinstein, 1969; Clancy, 1986; Fernald & Morikawa, 1993; Fogel, Stevenson, & Messinger, 1992; Fogel, Toda, & Kawai, 1988). The nonverbal dimensions of parent–infant interactions provide infants with opportunities for engaging in intuitive and indirect communication and for learning the "eloquence of silence" (Kondo, 1990, p. 300).

Empathy, indirect communication, and avoiding overt conflict are ways of structuring interpersonal interactions, and they reflect multifaceted interdependence expectations, such as adhering to social norms and maintaining social cohesion. At the same time, they also implicate independence expectations insofar as people are considered to be separate individuals with their own feelings and needs that require understanding by other separate individuals. Furthermore, insofar as "All members of a group expect their unstated feelings to be understood and their unarticulated desires to be anticipated" (Smith, 1983/1993, p. 58), maintaining social harmony seems to depend in part on understanding at least someone's individual feelings and desires.

In addition to being attuned to others as separate individuals, empathy and fulfilling others' expectations require that a person be self-directed and exert voluntary control over the extent to which he or she expresses his or her individual opinions (Lanaham & Garrick, 1996; Lebra, 1994). According to Lebra (1994), the Japanese believe that harmonious and empathic interactions are based on individuals voluntarily engaging in self-restraint and conforming to social expectations. Lebra explained:

> It is implied that social rules cannot be enforced unless the child is subjectively ready to understand and accept them or to comply with them voluntarily. Thus, empathy socialization results in fostering self-reflectiveness, inner motivations, strength, perseverance, and determination to overcome externally encountered adversities. (p. 263)

In this way, structuring interdependence in terms of empathy and maintaining social harmony is derived not only through awareness of others as separate individuals, but also partly through structuring self-direction in terms of self-control and through self-awareness as a separate mental being. Within this context, Japanese parents, in comparison with Euro-Americans, have been found to express significantly earlier expectations for some modes of self-control in children, including "does not cry easily" and "can get over anger by himself" (Hess et al., 1980, p. 264).

Empathy, intuition, and indirect communication are also part of private or inner cultural practices, which may take place at home. In addition, inner cultural practices involve relatively informal modes of communication and may serve as a forum for directly expressing one's individual feelings and opinions, even if they are contrary to others' feelings and opinions (Doi, 1985/1988; Kondo, 1990; Lebra, 1992/1995; Rothbaum, Pott, Azuma, Miyake, & Weisz, 2000). Thus, while Japanese parents are concerned that children learn to "think of others, be kind and sympathetic to them, and to avoid causing people trouble or annoyance" (Hendry, 1986, p. 82), they also think that "the child's individual personality is not to be neglected" (Hendry, 1986, p. 83). At first glance, this analysis of individuality and self-expression seems to be at odds with some findings from the Hess et al. (1980) study that the Japanese parents expressed significantly later expectations than did the American parents for varied modes of "verbal assertiveness," including "states own preference when asked," "asks for explanation when in doubt," "can explain why he thinks so," and "stands up for own rights with others" (p. 264). Given the importance of distinguishing between public and private cultural practices, it may be that Japanese parents would express expectations for knowing when and when not to be verbally assertive, rather than placing less value on verbal assertiveness per se.

The issue of distinguishing inner from outer practices can certainly be found in numerous analyses of ingroups and outgroups in non-Western cultures. However, my impression is that the ingroup–outgroup distinction is not quite the same as the Japanese distinction between inner and outer practices that I am trying to make sense of here. For example, Triandis (1995) defined *ingroups* and *outgroups* as follows:

> Ingroups are groups of individuals about whose welfare a person is concerned, with whom that person is willing to cooperate without demanding equitable returns, and separation from whom leads to anxiety. . . . Ingroups are usually characterized by similarities among the members, and individuals have a sense of "common fate" with members of the ingroup. . . . Clear outgroups are groups with which one has something to divide, perhaps unequally, or are harmful in some way, groups that disagree on valued attributes, or groups with which one is in conflict. (p. 9)

The Japanese conception of inner or private practices seems to be in line with this definition of ingroups, but outer or public practices do not seem equivalent to Triandis' definition of outgroups. Instead, outer relationships in Japan are populated by " 'meaningful' outsiders, with whom one must *enryo* [show restraint]" (Kondo, 1990, p. 150). In other words, outer cultural practices do not necessarily involve interactions with members of an outgroup, as it is commonly described in the research literature. With regard to Japan, the common definition of outgroups seems more in keeping with a third Japanese social category known as *tannin*, or strangers, that includes "someone who has no connection with oneself" (Doi, 1973/2001, p. 36). With strangers, "there is no need, even, to bring *enryo* into play," and people may act "with complete indifference towards outsiders who have no connection with [them]" (Doi, 1973/2001, p. 40). As Nakane (1970/1986) explained, a person who is considered to be a stranger even "ceases to be considered human. Ridiculous situations occur, such as that of the man who will shove a stranger out of the way to take an empty seat, but will then, no matter how tired he is, give up the seat to someone he knows, particularly if that someone is a superior in his company" (p. 186).

Kondo (1990) corroborated these analyses by pointing out that, in Japan, "the stranger is a socially meaningless person, and usual social norms do not apply" (p. 151). Pointing to even subtler distinctions, Mann, Mitsui, Beswick, and Harmoni (1994) suggested that, in Japan, there is a "primary group, a secondary group of friends and associates, a third category of functional, service contacts (including teachers) and a fourth category of strangers who are often seen as 'outsiders' and 'nonpersons' " (p. 142).

Much of the research on Japanese childrearing goals and parent–child interactions seems to have yielded information about the socialization of appropriate behavior in relatively public or outer cultural practices because the focus has been on issues of outer interdependence, including empathy, indirect communication, and social harmony. However, it does not necessarily follow from these findings that independence meanings, and other interdependence meanings, are not enacted in Japanese cultural practices. Instead, it is possible that expectations for interdependence in outer practices have been highlighted in analyses of Japanese parent–child interactions partly because participating in a scientific study is construed as an outer or public practice even if observations are conducted at home. Reflecting on her experiences of conducting research on Japanese parent–child interactions, Clancy (1986) pointed out that the mothers "seemed to seize upon these visits as occasions for socializing their children into appropriate patterns of polite interaction with people outside the family circle" (p. 219). This comment suggests that it might be quite difficult to conduct research on expectations for independence and interdependence in inner practices because the very presence of a researcher supports the cultural construction of a public, outer practice. Along similar lines, Hendry (1986) noted that one Japanese mother whom she interviewed about childrearing practices "explained that while many Japanese say in public that they want only for their child to be average, in private they would admit higher ideals" (p. 92).

The Inseparability of Independence and Interdependence in the Context of *Amae* Relationships

As part of inner cultural practices, a central aspect of parent–child interactions is found in the Japanese practice of *amae*. Although varied analyses point to the importance of *amae* in Japanese culture, there is apparently little consensus among scholars regarding how to conceptualize *amae* and its function in Japanese relationships (Behrens, 2004). To organize the discussion of *amae* in this section, I confine myself to Doi's analysis because it focuses on how *amae* emerges in parent–child relationships. According to Doi (1962/1974/1986), *amae* "is the noun form of *amaeru*, an intransitive verb that means 'to depend and presume upon another's benevolence' " (p. 121). In the context of *amae*, " 'Freedom' in Japan, in other words, has traditionally meant freedom to *amaeru*, that is to behave as one pleases, without considering others" (Doi, 1973/2001, p. 84). Similarly, as Peak (1991) explained, "The home, Japanese believe, should be a place where one can freely demonstrate feelings of *amae*, or the desire to be indulged. This legitimate desire for indulgence encompasses the free display of feelings that in other settings would be termed selfishness, regressive dependence, irritability, and even petty tyranny" (pp. 5–6).

Amae is first evident in the parent–infant relationship, especially between mother and infant, when the infant is dependent on a caregiver who anticipates and satisfies his or her needs and desires (Hendry, 1986). According to Doi, the ability to *amaeru* is not given at birth, but emerges during the second half of the first year of life. A central goal of Japanese mother–infant interactions is to establish a close *amae* relationship by promoting the infant's sense of security and trust in their relationship (Hendry, 1986).

This goal is achieved in part by not restricting young children's behavior and allowing them to openly express their needs and preferences. By not restricting young children's behavior, the private, personal world of Japanese parent–child interactions reflects the independence value of treating people as separate mental beings with their own preferences and characteristic modes of behavior. Accordingly, individual infants are valued in part for their individuality, and thus are taken to require special attention rather than restrictions (Lebra, 1994; Osterweil & Nagano, 1991; Shwalb, Shwalb, & Shoji, 1996). These interrelated conceptions of independence and interdependence are reflected in studies showing that Japanese parents are not particularly controlling of infants and young children and generally allow them to express and satisfy their wants (Fogel et al., 1992). According to Lebra (1994), Japanese assume that children will naturally outgrow their willfulness, or "obstreperous conduct" (p. 262), once they become capable of understanding how to behave in different settings, during what is considered to be the natural course of development. Comparative studies indicate that American parents of 3- to 6-year-olds are actually more controlling of young children's behavior than are Japanese parents. American parents also report having more rules and making more demands of young children than do Japanese parents (Power, Kobayashi-Winata, & Kelly, 1992).

At the same time, Japanese parents are indeed concerned with fostering children's compliance and conformity to social standards. Thus, although parent–child *amae* relationships constitute a forum for the child to express individuality, they may also serve as a forum for fostering children's compliance to parents and conformity to social standards. The importance of compliance is reflected in findings from the Hess et al. (1980)

study that Japanese parents expressed significantly earlier expectations than did the Euro-American parents for varied compliance goals, such as "comes or answers when called" and "does not do things forbidden by parents" (p. 264). Although the differences were not significant, the Japanese parents also expressed earlier expectations for "stops misbehaving when told" and "does task immediately when told" (p. 264).

The Inseparability of Independence and Interdependence in the Context of Indirect Discipline Practices

In keeping with the value of empathizing with others through intuition and indirect modes of communication, Japanese parents are likely to use indirect persuasion as a strategy to promote child compliance and conformity to social norms (Conroy, Hess, Azuma, & Kashiwagi, 1980). Japanese middle-class mothers of preschoolers are also likely to endorse the use of persuasion over direct commands and negotiation (Yamada, 2004). According to Conroy et al. (1980), persuasion "does not explicitly require compliance but attempts to persuade the child to obey. The mother may or may not require the child to conform; her expectations are implicit and are defined by individual contexts and cultural norms" (p. 162).

As an example of indirect persuasion, Conroy et al. (1980) offered the "response of a Japanese mother persuading her child to cease drawing on the wall: 'You drew very well. You can draw even better if you use paper instead of the wall' " (p. 169). As Conroy et al. explained, the Japanese mother in this example was not specifically requesting compliance, but was still making it known to the child that she wanted him or her to draw on paper. In addition, there was room for the child to construct some understanding, from his or her own independent perspective, of why drawing on paper would be beneficial for him or her. Indeed, it is interesting to note that the mother's statement in this case appealed to the child's individual achievement, thus further pointing to how interdependence, in the form of compliance to social norms, is inseparable from conceptions of independence.

In contrast to Japanese indirect persuasion practices, Conroy et al. (1980) presented the following example of an American mother's reaction to the wall-drawing situation:

> Mark, you know better than that. You've been taught you don't use crayons any place but on paper. If you can't use crayons properly, we will put them away. When you think you can use them in their right place, let me know

and I'll take them out. But right now they are going back on the shelf and then we're going to clean off the wall. (p. 169)

This statement is clearly more longwinded and direct than was the Japanese statement just quoted, and, in its own way, it too reflects interrelated independence and interdependence meanings. The mother here began by highlighting what the child, as a separate mental being, already knew, and then immediately pointed out that this knowledge had been taught to the child by others. The mother also placed the child in relation to social standards for behavior by reminding him that there was a way to use crayons "properly" and in a "right" location. Finally, by twice using the pronoun *we*, the mother indicated that the child's individual use (rather misuse) of crayons had consequences for the ongoing social interaction.

Construing Self-Reliance and Self-Direction in Relation to Interdependence

Thus far, we have considered how varied independence activity dimensions, including, self-direction, individuality, and self-awareness, are particularized in Japan in relation to the structuring of interdependence activity dimensions, including *amae* relationships, maintaining social harmony, and conforming to social norms. In addition, some Japanese childrearing practices are geared toward encouraging instrumental self-reliance, thus pointing to an independence goal of development (e.g., Chen, 1996; Hendry, 1986; Osterweil & Nagano, 1991). In particular, children are expected to do for themselves and may be teased if they "insist on having things done for them by their parents (e.g., to be carried when the child is old enough to walk by him or herself)" (Chen, 1996, p. 37).

With regard to self-reliance issues in the Hess et al. (1980) study, the Japanese parents expressed significantly earlier expectations than did the Euro-American parents for the following conceptions of self-reliance: "stays home alone for an hour or so," "takes care of own clothes," and "sits at table and eats without help" (p. 264). There were, however, no significant differences between the two groups of parents on the remaining self-reliance issues, which consisted of "makes phone calls without help," "does regular household tasks," "spends own money carefully," "can entertain himself alone," and "plays outside without adult supervision" (p. 264).

Some of these examples also point to how self-reliance may be inseparable from interdependence issues. For instance, being able to make phone calls without help links self-reliance to interdependence insofar as making a phone call necessarily involves some kind of connection to another person. Also, as noted earlier in this chapter, doing household chores involves contributing to a wider social unit, and being able to play outside on one's own may involve playing with other children in the neighborhood. Similarly, another Japanese–American comparative study, with middle-class mothers of first and fifth graders (Stevenson et al., 1990), indicated that the Japanese mothers tended to grant children more choice regarding playmates.

In considering issues of self-reliance and self-direction in tandem with issues of dependence in *amae* relationships and conforming to social group norms, we may recall our discussion earlier in this chapter of dependence, self-direction, and conformity to authority in relation to American social class. Now, in Japan, a different picture regarding conformity, dependence, and self-direction emerges, pointing to how these issues may be played out differently in different cultures. For example, although some middle-class American parents may be tolerant of children's dependence, they do not necessarily encourage it. In contrast, some *amae* dependence in certain relationships, such as the parent–child relationship, may be encouraged by Japanese parents. However, insofar as the value of such dependence is reserved for certain relationships, it is not necessarily an absolute value across all Japanese relationships. *Amae* is also not necessarily the only characteristic of a relationship in which *amae* is practiced (Behrens, 2004). Moreover, the value of dependence in the form of *amae* does not preclude multifaceted independence values and expectations, such as self-reliance, individual understanding, and self-direction.

Another difference between our discussion of Japanese conformity and American conformity involves the point that Kohn's (1969/1977) analysis of conformity specifically addresses conformity to authority, but discussions of Japanese conformity tend to address conformity to social norms. Conformity to social norms may, in some instances, include conformity to authority, but it seems important to distinguish these different types of conformity for analyzing specific cultural conceptions of independence and interdependence. More generally, these analyses point to how multifaceted dimensions of independence and interdependence, from conformity to self-direction to expressing and not expressing oneself directly, are understood and interrelated in culturally distinct ways as parents and children engage in cultural practices together.

SOME GENERAL REMARKS

In this chapter, the current conceptual approach has provided a systematic framework for integrating a wide range of studies on parent–child relationships. Moreover, the current conceptual approach provides a coherent framework for making sense of the complex ways in which independence and interdependence enter into children's lives as they participate in varied cultural practices. When the conceptual focus shifts from viewing independence and interdependence as static characteristics that people or cultures can have in greater or lesser quantities to conceptualizing independence and interdependence as cultural meanings and activity dimensions, it is possible to discern how both independence and interdependence pervade the cultural practices in which children participate. To begin summarizing in most general terms, the research discussed in this chapter points to some of the multifaceted ways in which independence and interdependence are understood, enacted, and interrelated in varied cultures during infancy, childhood, and adolescence.

For example, research with Euro-American parents indicates multifaceted independence meanings, including expectations for making self-directed choices, expectations for financial self-reliance, encouraging children to take initiative, viewing children as separate physical and mental individuals, and valuing self-fulfillment. Research with Japanese samples also points to the importance of viewing children as separate physical and mental individuals, and to expectations for children to become instrumentally self-reliant. At the same time that there may be some similarities among Euro-American and Japanese conceptions of independence, the studies discussed in this chapter also suggest that there are important cultural differences as well. For example, some studies of Japanese socialization practices demonstrate the importance of individual self-reflection, but this conception of independence is not typically emphasized in studies of Euro-American socialization practices.

With regard to interdependence, research with Euro-American parents points to multifaceted interdependence meanings and ways of structuring social interactions, including conforming to others' preferences, following social standards, maintaining family ties, pursuing common goals, and being able to establish and maintain relationships with others by being considerate, generous, respectful, and honest. Across cultures, this chapter noted multifaceted interdependence meanings and ways of structuring social interactions in Japan, including valuing dependence in the context of certain relationships, conforming to wider social standards, and maintaining social cohesion through empathy and indirect communication.

Considering the multifaceted nature of independence and interdependence in different cultures is useful, in that it reveals some of the complexities of how human separateness and connectedness are understood and structured in different cultures. It also shows how problematic it is to characterize cultures and development within cultures in terms of either independence or interdependence. However, such analyses are ultimately an incomplete first analytic step, and the research discussed in this chapter demonstrates the utility of going a step further to considering how independence and interdependence are interrelated in parents' ideas and parent–child interactions. Studies in this chapter show that independence and interdependence do not enter children's lives as isolated phenomena. Instead, the research discussed in this chapter shows that understanding independence requires analyzing interdependence and vice versa. For example, in the Euro-American case, we have seen how parents expect children to be self-directed in varied social situations (e.g., with peers and at home). Self-direction is also inseparable from interdependence as parents expect children's self-direction to be structured in relation to following social standards. The inseparability of independence and interdependence in children's developmental experiences also occurs as Euro-American parents talk about how children's separate actions are related to joint activities.

The relative abundance of research with Euro-American and Japanese samples has made it possible to consider varied issues regarding some of the cultural complexities of how independence and interdependence are inseparable within parent–child relationships. Nevertheless, studies that have been conducted in other cultures around the world also show how independence and interdependence are interrelated in culturally distinct ways. For example, for children in cultural communities with subsistence economies, self-direction is implicated in the pursuit of common goals, and community child care not only supports strong community ties but also the development of children's self-direction. In addition, the chapter section on parent–child interactions during infancy and childhood illustrated conceptions of individuality as children in varied cultures (Euro-American, African American, Kaluli, and Marquesas Island) are viewed as separate mental individuals. Insofar as individuality is valued in all of these cultures, cultural differences do not necessarily lie in whether children are viewed as having greater or lesser amounts of individuality. Rather, cultural differences lie in how conceptions of individuality are enacted in cultural practices, and in how individuality is related to the structuring of interdependence in each culture's cultural practices.

Pointing to within-culture differences, some studies suggest that independence and interdependence may be interrelated in different ways for American children of different socioeconomic groups. In particular, research on conformity and obedience shows that they are inseparable from financial self-reliance for working-class families, whereas taking initiative is inseparable from being attuned to other people's perspectives for middle-class families. In Japan, within-culture differences in the structuring of independence and interdependence are apparent in relation to Japanese inner and outer cultural practices.

Within-culture differences also emerge as parents understand and structure independence and interdependence differently for children over the course of development. For example, studies with Euro-American parents indicate that they treat children as separate individuals from the outset and structure interactions in ways that are sensitive even to infants' individual preferences. As infants become young children, parents continue to encourage children's individuality, but they also report expectations for children to express that individuality with consideration for others. During adolescence, as parents and children co-construct individuated relationships, parents support adolescents' individuality by engaging them in conversations characterized by mutuality and by allowing them to contribute to family decisions. In these ways, from infancy through adolescence, parents appear to value children's individuality, but the expression of that individuality is related to interactions that are structured in different ways as the children develop.

To further understand how independence and interdependence enter into children's developmental experiences, it is necessary to consider how independence and interdependence are particularized as children participate in cultural practices with people other than their parents. Accordingly, we now turn to a consideration of how independence and interdependence are particularized in some educational practices in the United States and in Japan.

CHAPTER FIVE

Independence and Interdependence in Educational Settings

To again begin a chapter by stating the obvious, many children around the world participate in cultural practices in formal educational settings. As cultural institutions charged with preparing the young for adult life, schools provide children with opportunities to engage in cultural practices that reflect varied culturally valued modes of behavior. The current conceptual approach leads to considering how cultural independence and interdependence meanings are reflected in educational practices, and how educational practices are structured in terms of inseparable independence and interdependence activity dimensions. Toward these ends, this chapter includes considerations of how independence and interdependence are particularized in American and Japanese educational practices. The section on American school practices begins with a discussion of John Dewey's early 20th-century vision for American schooling and then moves on to a consideration of some contemporary American school practices. The second half of the chapter includes a discussion of Japanese preschool and elementary school practices. Although in this chapter we encounter some of the same independence and interdependence issues that were discussed in chapter 4, some new issues are raised as well, pointing to how independence and interdependence may be particularized in the context of different cultural practices.

AMERICAN SCHOOL PRACTICES

Although different specific goals for American education have been emphasized during different time periods, historical analyses suggest that, since the emergence of public schools in the mid-1800s, American education has generally been geared toward fostering both the academic achievement of individual children and the formation of a competent democratic citizenry (Baker, Terry, Bridger, & Winsor, 1997; Egan, 1992; Labaree, 1997; Nasaw, 1979/1981; Wentzel, 1991). Public schools were additionally supposed to foster cohesion among diverse groups of children by emphasizing certain allegedly common cultural values, and ideally (although not actually) schools offered equal opportunities for all children to learn. Also, since the establishment of public schools, there have been ongoing political and academic discussions about how varied educational methods can be used to achieve these educational goals. It is my intention here neither to review these discussions nor to endorse one or another educational philosophy or teaching method. Instead, I focus briefly on one voice within this discussion, namely John Dewey (1859–1952), who shaped public and academic discussions about education during his own lifetime, and whose ideas continue to be invoked in contemporary discussions of American education. In addition, Dewey's general philosophical approach, as well as his specific ideas about education, point to multifaceted and interrelated conceptions of independence and interdependence in the philosophy of a major Euro-American thinker.

John Dewey and the Education of Individuals in Relation to Others

Certain key themes run through many of Dewey's writings on education as he argued against common early 20th-century educational practices. In general, Dewey was opposed to educational practices that are based on the premise that learning involves transmitting a fixed body of knowledge or information to students (Dewey, 1902/1990), who are expected to have attitudes of "docility, receptivity, and obedience" (Dewey, 1938/1997, p. 18). Put another way, Dewey criticized educational practices that are structured in terms of an "imposition from above and outside" (Dewey, 1938/1997, p. 18). Within this context, he offered suggestions for alternative ways of structuring classroom practices that are inseparable from his ideas about the long-term goals of education. These ideas, in turn, are inseparable from Dewey's ideas about democracy and freedom, all of which, in their turn, are inseparable from his overall philosophy of human functioning.

Dewey's philosophy is part of the pragmatist tradition in American philosophy that emerged in the late 1800s, and is generally based on the view that humans are wholly active and social beings whose functioning both serves and reflects social experiences (e.g., Odin, 1996; Schubert, 1998). In keeping with a pragmatist worldview, Dewey claimed that "all human experience is ultimately social" (1938/1997, p. 38), and he also advanced a systems view of human functioning in which:

the individual and society are neither opposed to each other nor separated from each other. Society is a society of individuals and the individual is always a social individual. He has no existence by himself. He lives in, for, and by society, just as society has no existence excepting in and through the individuals who constitute it. (Dewey, 1897/1974a, p. 109)

This characterization of individuals in relation to others is compatible with the current systems view that independence and interdependence are interrelated or inseparable dimensions of human functioning, and demonstrates how neither individuals nor social connections are differentially dominant in Dewey's philosophy. Elaborating on this general view of individuals in relation to others, Dewey held that the purpose of educating individual children is to enable them to fully participate in and contribute their individual voices and talents to the cooperative pursuit of common social goals. In this way, individual academic achievement serves social purposes because "The educational end and the ultimate test of the value of what is learned is its use and application in carrying on and improving the common life of all" (Dewey, 1934/1974, p. 11).

Even more specifically, Dewey's vision for educational reform revolved around guiding children toward becoming effective participants in and contributors to a democratic society. We may recall that issues of independence and interdependence in relation to democratic processes were raised in chapter 3. For example, political freedom in a democracy was conceptualized in relation to inclusive collective functioning, and the cohesion of democratic societies was viewed in relation to individuality. Building on these traditions, Dewey pondered democratic processes in many of his writings and pointed out that:

A democracy is more than a form of government; it is primarily a mode of associated living, of conjoint communicated experience. The extension in space of the number of individuals who participate in an interest so that each has to refer his own action to that of others, and to consider the action of others to give point and direction to his own, is equivalent to the breaking down of those barriers of class, race, and national territory which kept men from perceiving the full import of their activity. These more numerous and more varied points of contact denote a greater diversity of stimuli to which an individual has to respond; they consequently put a premium on variation in his action. They secure a liberation of powers which remain suppressed as long as the incitations to action are partial, as they must be in a group which in its exclusiveness shuts out many interests. (1916/1997, p. 87)

This characterization of democratic social arrangements sheds some light on how both independence and interdependence may be particularized in a democracy, and also on how Dewey viewed the inseparability of independence and interdependence dimensions in human functioning. Insofar as a democratic society provides opportunities for a wide range of people to contribute to its common interests, those common interests are expanded to account for more individuals with diverse perspectives. Echoing de Tocqueville, Dewey wrote that in democracies there is a "widening of the area of shared concerns, and the liberation of a greater diversity of personal capacities" (1916/1997, p. 87). Thus, social connections are enhanced because more individuals come into contact with each other and join together to pursue common goals. With such widened interdependence, more individuals are included in or have a participatory voice in shaping the common goals of a democracy. Also, as people come into contact while working together toward common goals, independence, in the form of individuality, is expressed as distinct individuals serve wider societal interests. Moreover, widened social connections not only shape but also liberate individual abilities, as individuals act in relation to more and more people with diverse perspectives and concerns. In other words, ongoing interrelations between independence and interdependence meanings are enacted as individuals contribute to common goals and as group life draws on individual contributions.

Also according to Dewey, for individuals to fully contribute to common social goals, they must be free, and thus Dewey's conceptions of freedom are also implicated in his vision for education. In keeping with some of our earlier considerations of ideas about freedom, Dewey viewed it as a "mental attitude rather than external unconstraint of movements" (1916/1997, p. 305). More specifically, Dewey explained:

> Genuine freedom, in short, is intellectual; it rests in the trained *power of thought*, in ability to "turn things over," to look at matters deliberately, to judge whether the amount and kind of evidence requisite for decision is at hand, and if not, to tell where and how to seek such evidence. If a man's actions are not guided by thoughtful conclusions, then they are guided by inconsiderate impulse, unbalanced appetite, caprice, or the circumstances of the moment. (1933/1974, pp. 258–259)

This kind of intellectual freedom involves being able to engage in what I have been referring to as self-direction. According to Dewey, free self-direction occurs when individuals act by making informed or educated choices, decisions, and judgments during the course of participating in varied social situations (Dewey, 1916/1997). Indeed, as Dewey pointed out, the American Bill of Rights guarantees varied forms of intellectual freedom (e.g., freedom of speech, press, and assembly) that enable individuals "to look at matters deliberately" and to direct themselves accordingly. Moreover, these freedoms "are guaranteed because without them individuals are not free to develop and society is deprived of what they might contribute"

(Dewey, 1937/1939, p. 404). Insofar as such self-direction involves making choices in social situations, as well as contributing to social goals, this conception of independence is inseparable from Dewey's view that interdependence involves contributing to wider societal functioning.

Putting these varied strands of Dewey's philosophy together, education involves nurturing children's intellectual abilities so they are able to freely and thus most effectively direct themselves and contribute their individual voices and talents to a democratic society. Toward that end, Dewey suggested that educational practices build on children's individual inclinations by shaping them through and toward social engagement. With regard to building on children's individual inclinations, Dewey conceived of children as actively engaged in constructing knowledge of the world (Dewey, 1900/1990, 1902/1990, 1916/1997). As part of what Dewey called "My Pedagogic Creed," he claimed:

> The child's own instincts and powers furnish the material and give the starting-point for all education. Save as the efforts of the educator connect with some activity which the child is carrying on of his own initiative independent of the educator, education becomes reduced to a pressure from without. It may, indeed, give certain external results, but cannot truly be called educative. Without insight into the psychological structure and activities of the individual, the educative process will, therefore, be haphazard and arbitrary. (1897/1974b, p. 428)

For Dewey, starting with the child also means making classroom practices relevant to the child's experiences, which he viewed as essentially social. As he put it, "The child lives in a somewhat narrow world of personal contacts. Things hardly come within his experience unless they touch, intimately and obviously, his own well-being, or that of his family and friends. His world is a world of persons with their personal interests, rather than a realm of facts and laws" (1902/1990, p. 183).

To further shape children's socially nurtured individual inclinations toward democratic citizenship, Dewey proposed that classrooms function as cooperative communities in which children can clearly discern the social foundations, meanings, and implications of their individual actions, and also of any particular subject that they may be studying (Dewey, 1900/1990, 1916/1997). Accordingly, Dewey suggested that children participate in "joint activity, where one person's use of material and tools is consciously referred to the use other persons are making of their capacities and appliances" (1916/1997, p. 39). This kind of joint activity may occur in varied specific settings, such as "Playgrounds, shops, workrooms, laboratories [which] not only direct the natural active tendencies of youth, but they involve intercourse, communication, and coöperation—all extending the perception of connections" (1916/1997, p. 358).

For example, Dewey explained how sewing and weaving can serve as "the point of departure from which the child can trace and follow the progress of mankind in history, getting an insight also into the materials used and the mechanical principles involved" (1900/1990, p. 20). Dewey then launched into a long description of a lesson he observed that began with children actively "freeing cotton fibers from the boll and seeds," after which they "reinvented the first frame for carding the wool," and continuously moved to "the invention next in historic order, working it out experimentally, thus seeing its necessity, and tracing its effects, not only upon that particular industry, but upon modes of social life" (1900/1990, pp. 20–21). These lessons involved "the study of the fibers, of geographical features, the conditions under which raw materials are grown, the great centers of manufacture and distribution, the physics involved in the machinery of production . . . the influence which these inventions have had upon humanity" (pp. 21–22). Dewey concluded, "You can concentrate the history of all mankind into the evolution of the flax, cotton, and wool fibers into clothing" (p. 22).

Ultimately, through education, Dewey envisioned social progress toward:

> a society in which every person shall be occupied in something which makes the lives of others better worth living, and which accordingly makes the ties which bind persons together more perceptible—which breaks down the barriers of distance between them. It denotes a state of affairs in which the interest of each in his work is uncoerced and intelligent: based upon its congeniality to his own aptitudes. (1916/1997, p. 316)

It almost does not matter where one begins to analyze this societal vision; one ends up considering how multifaceted independence and interdependence meanings are interrelated. For example, if we start with "every person," we have an individual who engages in work that is congenial not only to his or her own individual aptitude, but also an individual who contributes to the improvement of others' lives. In addition, with such improvements come even stronger social ties among individuals. If we start with the idea of an improved society, we quickly see that a society is made up of individuals whose work is uncoerced and individually congenial. In these ways, we can discern ongoing interrelations between independence and interdependence within Dewey's worldview.

Contemporary American Classrooms

Competitive Classrooms: Fostering Independence or Undermining Independence? Although much has changed since Dewey's day, much also remains the same in American education. Despite generations of criticism and attempts at school reform, the American educational system may generally be characterized as a competitive system in which "the possibility or opportunity for one student to attain a goal or receive rewards is reduced when others are successful" (Ames, 1984, p. 179). In addition, competitively structured practices usually emphasize individual performance goals, whereby an individual student's success or achievement is assessed in terms of the quantity of right answers, and not in terms of how a student is thinking about and reflecting on complex issues. With regard to issues of independence and interdependence, such competition discourages the establishment of social connections and cooperation among students. Thus, the American educational system can be seen as a context in which certain independence expectations are enacted at the expense of interdependence expectations. Indeed, to succeed in a competitive school environment, certain forms of independence would be highlighted, such as working alone and looking out for oneself, sometimes even to the extent of undermining others' achievement efforts.

This generally competitive system also typically involves what are known as traditional, whole-class practices. In a traditional, whole-class setting, the teacher can usually be found lecturing to a group of silent students who are discouraged from engaging with one another. When not listening to a lecturing teacher, students are often found engaging in individual seatwork. In this kind of setting, the "teacher is the center of the activity. He/she controls all communication networks and presents the information to the pupils. Students are expected to be largely passive, to listen, and to respond to the teacher only when called upon to do so" (Hertz-Lazarowitz & Shachar, 1990, p. 78). In addition to exams, student learning in a whole-class setting may be assessed through student public recitation, which tends to promote "invidious social comparisons and competition for the teacher's praise and attention" (Sharan & Shaulov, 1990, p. 174). Organizing this kind of public recitation relies heavily on the IRE or IRF format (Cazden, 2001; Mehan, 1979), which is composed of the following three elements: teacher initiation (I), student response (R), and teacher evaluation (E) or feedback (F). For example, I observed many IRE/F sequences in a kindergarten classroom, including:

Teacher: Do you know what day of the week it is? (I)
Student: Wednesday. (R)
Teacher: Wednesday. Good. (E)

Or, while reading a story to the whole class:

Teacher: What happens to elephants on the moon? (I)

Student: They get gravity pull. (R)

Teacher: Right. They start floating because gravity is different. (E, F)

The whole-class structure and its accompanying IRE/F format have been criticized by some not only because they undermine cooperation as part of a generally competitive system, but also because they undermine some forms of independence, including individual creativity, individual self-expression, and active learning on the part of individual children (e.g., Mehan, 1979; Tharp & Gallimore, 1988; Wertsch, 1998). Self-direction and individuality, structured in terms of individual initiative, individual creativity, and individual self-expression, are also undermined in traditional whole-class settings because success is typically assessed in relation to a predetermined set of right answers and not by children's creative intellectual pursuits. Thus, as was the case in Dewey's day, children are still expected to take attitudes of "docility, receptivity, and obedience," and over time these traditional educational practices promote student passivity, conformity, and compliance.

In addition, American teachers have been known to explicitly value passive and compliant students. For example, one early study of teacher goals indicates that, despite being trained in the context of changing social and educational attitudes during the 1960s, student teachers typically favored pupils who engaged in "control, caution, and conformity" (Feshbach, 1969, p. 129). These student teachers further ranked varied student characteristics in the following order, from most favorable to least favorable: "rigid; conforming; orderly; dependent; passive; acquiescent; flexible; nonconforming; untidy; independent; active; assertive" (p. 129). I am inclined to treat these findings with caution given that the prospect of a classroom full of unconforming and assertive pupils is no doubt quite daunting for a student teacher. Nevertheless, some studies suggest that these values continue to be prevalent in more recent times (Minuchin & Shapiro, 1983; Wentzel, 1993) because teachers' preferences involve learning another set of three Rs—namely, being "receptive, reactive and responsive" (Kedar-Voivodas, 1983, p. 418).

This discussion of contemporary American school practices brings out some complex issues regarding independence and interdependence. For example, although whole-class and competitive practices may promote what are considered to be insidious forms of independence (e.g., achieving individually by undermining others' achievement), they may also be criticized for inhibiting other forms of independence, including individual creativity and active individual learning. Thus, independence is not necessarily an absolute value, and claiming that Americans (or any cultural groups) value independence does not mean that all possible conceptions of independence are valued willy-nilly. The same may also be said for interdependence. Another point of complexity inherent to this discussion is that, within cultures, some meanings of independence and interdependence may be valued in some cultural practices but not in others. For example, we are now seeing that, although self-direction in making life choices has been valued in mainstream American culture for generations, it has not dominated American educational practices.

At the same time, however, although traditional, whole-class practices remain common in American education, teachers now seem to agree that students should have regular opportunities to engage in individual self-expression. For example, the Tobin et al. (1989) classic preschool study suggested that individual self-expression is central to educational curricula already in preschool. Their analyses of a typical American preschool showed that much emphasis is placed on children's self-expression and language development as the children "are continually encouraged to use words to describe, evaluate, and name objects in their world and to give verbal accounts of their work and play" (p. 148). Verbal self-expression is viewed as an important component of individual cognitive development, but it is also related to social development insofar as the "preschool parents and staff believe that to be a friend, a group participant, a member of society, a citizen in a democracy, children need to be taught to express their wants, needs, and feelings" (pp. 151–152).

In keeping with historical traditions, this finding indicates how self-expression is valued as a way to facilitate direct relationships and wider societal participation. Self-expression makes social cohesion possible and provides a way to maintain social harmony in a diverse society. The children at this American preschool were also encouraged and expected to use language to resolve their interpersonal conflicts, rather than resort to physical fighting. When teachers intervened to help children resolve interpersonal conflicts, they typically encouraged each child to state his or her case, express his or her feelings about the situation, and verbally work out a solution. In these ways, conceptions of independence and interdependence were interrelated as individual self-expression was inseparable from establishing and maintaining social cohesion.

In addition to individual self-expression, teachers also seem to agree that students should have regular opportunities to make individual choices about some of their academic activities, such as choosing their own project or paper topics (Flowerday & Schraw, 2000; Reeve, Bolt, & Cai, 1999). Teachers may also provide children with opportunities to make choices in social situations, such as "decisions about working in pairs or small groups, seating arrangements, and choosing group members when collaborative projects were assigned" (Flowerday & Schraw, 2000, p. 637). Pointing to interrelated independence and interdependence values, opportunities for making choices are considered to promote not only individual student motivation, creativity, and effort, but also co-operation and respect for others.

Further reflecting multifaceted conceptions of interdependence, teachers have been found to value and encourage honesty, cooperation, manners, sharing, and respecting others (Wentzel, 1991). Elementary school teachers are also typically concerned with fostering children's connections to others through cooperation and positive social interactions, as well as with bolstering each child's individual self-esteem and encouraging each to work hard and try his or her individual best (Prawat, 1985). Pointing to some changes since Feshbach's 1969 study, for some elementary school teachers, their ideal student is open, friendly, cooperative, helpful, caring, considerate, eager to learn, hard working, and not "overly conforming" (Prawat, 1985, p. 592). In keeping with our earlier discussions of conformity, preferring students who are not "overly" conforming suggests that some forms of conformity are valued when tempered by an individual who can think for him or herself, thus making his or her own self-directed decisions in varied situations, including when to conform and when not to conform.

The Inseparability of Independence and Interdependence in the Context of Cooperative Learning Practices

In an effort to solve some of the pedagogical and social problems that have been associated with competitive and whole-class educational practices, cooperative learning practices emerged and proliferated as a kind of panacea for American education in the late 1970s and early 1980s (Eisenberg & Mussen, 1989). Echoing Dewey's vision for American education, cooperative learning practices generally emphasize the importance of student–student interaction and cooperation, as well as active individual participation by all students (Schmuck, 1985). Although different cooperative learning practices have been designed, they are generally based on the view that humans are by nature cooperative beings, and that it is "unnatural to prevent students from sharing what they know" (Kagan, 1985, p. 369). Based on this position, some form of cooperative learning is now considered to be standard educational practice by many teachers and administrators throughout the United States (Antil, Jenkins, Wayne, & Vadasy, 1998; Cohen, 1994; O'Donnell & O'Kelly, 1994). However, cooperative learning techniques have not fully displaced traditional whole-class practices, and, eschewing another potential dichotomy, many elementary and secondary school teachers use some kind of combination of whole-class and cooperative learning practices.

As many cooperative learning theorists and researchers take pains to point out, cooperative learning is not simply a matter of group work, or having students work individually while being allowed to sit together and talk to their classmates (Antil et al., 1997; O'Donnell & O'Kelly, 1994). Instead, it is a complex process, and some of the specific cooperative learning practices that have been designed and studied during the last 20 to 30 years can be seen as requiring students to engage in activities that reflect multifaceted and inseparable independence and interdependence meanings. Despite the heterogeneity of cooperative learning practices that have been designed for different academic subjects and different school grades, there are organizational commonalities among some of them. For example, several methods involve small learning groups that consist of four to six students, and ideally "each group is a microcosm of the class in academic achievement level, sex, and ethnicity" (Slavin, 1985, p. 6). Each student in these heterogeneous groups is then expected to contribute to a common goal, and ways to ensure that one student does not do most of the group's work are built into the design of many cooperative learning methods. In contrast to the traditional, whole-class setup, as students work in their small, heterogeneous groups, they are more likely to:

> exchange information, generate ideas, actively gather information, and participate in multilateral communication. Students take on various social roles in the learning process: leaders, planners, and investigators. . . . In this type of classroom the teachers act as facilitators of learning and as resource persons rather than dispensers of information. (Hertz-Lazarowitz & Shachar, 1990, p. 79)

Within this general framework, one cooperative learning practice, known as Jigsaw, was originally designed in the early 1970s to mitigate racial clashes that were occurring in some Austin, Texas, schools during the initial years of desegregation (Aronson & Patnoe, 1997). In the Jigsaw method, students are assigned to small, heterogeneous groups or teams, and an academic topic is divided into sections. After each team member reads his or her particular section:

> Members of different teams who have studied the same sections meet in "expert groups" to discuss their sections. Then the students return to their teams and take turns teaching their teammates about their sections. Since the only way students can learn the sections other than their own is to listen carefully to their teammates, they are motivated to support and show interest in each other's work. . . . Following the team reports, students may take individual quizzes covering all of the topics, and they receive individual grades on their quizzes. (Slavin, 1983, p. 28)

In ensuring that "success could occur only after there was cooperative behavior among the students in a group" (Aronson & Patnoe, 1997, p. 9), Jigsaw minimizes competition among students and also ensures that each student actively and individually contributes essential information about the issue being studied by the group. In addition, children engage with each other as they discuss material in their expert groups and also when they are presenting that material to their teams. Effective presentation to team members further involves consideration for each individual team member's abilities, thus requiring students to interact to achieve group goals while accounting for the individuals who constitute the group.

Several cooperative learning methods have also been designed by Robert Slavin and his colleagues at The Johns Hopkins University. One of these methods, known as Student Teams-Achievement Divisions (STAD), involves grouping students into heterogeneous teams of four or five. Then, according to Slavin (1991):

> Each week, the teacher introduces new material in a lecture or a discussion. Team members then study worksheets on the material. They may work problems one at a time in pairs, take turns quizzing each other, discuss problems as a group, or use whatever means they wish to master the material. The students also receive worksheet answer sheets making clear to them that their task is to learn the concepts, not simply to fill out the worksheets. Team members are told they have not finished studying until all are sure they understand the material.
>
> Following team practice, students take quizzes on the material they have been studying. Teammates may *not* help one another on the quizzes; they are on their own. The quizzes are scored in class or soon after; then the individual scores are formed into team scores by the teacher.
>
> The amount each student contributes to his or her team is determined by the amount the student's quiz score exceeds his or her past quiz average. This improvement score system gives every student a good chance to contribute maximum points to the team if (and only if) the student does his or her best, showing substantial improvement or completing a perfect paper. . . .
>
> A weekly one-page class newsletter recognizes the teams with the highest scores. The newsletter also recognizes the students who exceeded their own past records by the largest amounts or who completed perfect papers. (p. 9)

Cooperation in learning is encouraged in this STAD method insofar as the group benefits when individual members know the material. Equality is also built into STAD because the use of improvement scores gives each student an equal chance to contribute to the group score no matter what his or her overall individual achievement record may be. At the same time, however, this version of STAD does perpetuate some competition because the weekly newsletter recognizes the highest-achieving teams.

Along similar lines, Slavin and his colleagues have also added the notion of improvement scores to Aronson's Jigsaw method, thus creating Jigsaw II. As in the original Jigsaw, students are grouped into teams of four or five, but before each student goes off to work on an expert topic in expert groups made up of students from other teams, all the team members read some common material. After working in the expert groups, the students go back to their teams, where each team member presents his or her topic. A major change from the original Jigsaw then occurs when "students take individual quizzes, which are formed into team scores using the improvement score system of STAD, and a class newsletter recognizes the highest-scoring teams and individuals" (Slavin, 1991, p. 11).

As these examples indicate, the central components of cooperative learning revolve around "group rewards based on group members' individual learning" (Slavin, 1983, p. 53) or "positive interdependence" and "individual accountability" (e.g., Antil et al., 1998; Aronson & Patnoe, 1997; Cohen, 1994; Johnson & Johnson, 1987). Group rewards or positive interdependence involve:

> the perception that you are linked with others in such a way that you cannot succeed unless they do (and vice versa), and that their work benefits you and your work benefits them. It promotes a situation in which individuals work together in small groups to maximize the learning of all members, sharing their resources, providing mutual support, and celebrating their joint success. (Johnson & Johnson, 1987, pp. 125–126)

Individual accountability ensures that each group member contributes so that the group as a whole, as well as each individual member, would not be able to succeed without the contribution of each other member (Webb, 1982). Moreover, each group member has "a unique and essential contribution to make" (Aronson & Patnoe, 1997, p. 11), and the "different interests, backgrounds, values, and abilities of the members are, in fact, the group's greatest asset" (Sharan & Sharan, 1976, p. 8). Thus, not only do individuals interact to achieve common learning goals, but, in good democratic fashion, cooperation toward common goals is enhanced by the talents and perspectives of individual group members. In other words, cooperative learning involves ongoing interrelations between independence and interdependence activity dimensions that reflect interrelated independence and interdependence values.

PRESCHOOL AND ELEMENTARY SCHOOL IN JAPAN

In this section, I consider some studies that point to how multifaceted and interrelated independence and interdependence issues are particularized in Japanese preschool and elementary school practices. Insofar as many accounts of Japanese children's developmental experiences have emphasized interdependence, I focus on offering some ideas about how interdependence in Japanese school practices may be inseparable from independence in varied ways. In doing so, I do not mean to suggest that the group is not central to Japanese education and culture. Instead, as in chapter 4, I seek to consider how independence meanings may be implicated in the organization of group concerns and practices.

As was the case in our chapter 4 discussion of parent–child relationships in Japan, the important Japanese distinction between outer and inner cultural practices provides a key to understanding how independence and interdependence are particularized in Japanese educational practices. Primary school in Japan, beginning with preschool, is seen as a setting for learning how to behave in public or outer cultural practices. Thus, expectations and standards for behaving as one child among many others stand in contrast to the tolerance and *amae* of relationships at home (Hendry, 1986; Hill, 1996; Peak, 1991; Tobin, 1992/1995; Tobin, Wu, & Davidson, 1987, 1989). As Peak (1991) explained:

> Whereas homes are indulgent, preschools require that children learn they are no longer the center of attention and cooperate smoothly as part of a group. The same child who at home enjoys the patient indulgence of an attentive mother, who eats, sleeps, and plays when he wishes and is largely unused to dressing and toileting alone or picking up after himself, at preschool must suddenly perform these activities on a regular schedule, without assistance, in unison with thirty or more other children. Far from exercising discipline similar to that of the schools, Japanese believe that the home and the school are so dissimilar that it is difficult for the family to teach the behavior the child will need in the classroom. (p. 6)

Structuring Cooperation and Group Life in Relation to Independence

To engage in outer social settings, learning to cooperate and get along with others, as well as learning to be an enthusiastic and active member of a group, are central to the structuring of Japanese preschool and elementary school practices. Despite variability in teaching philosophies, the goals of fostering cooperation and group life appear to be common throughout Japanese schools (Boocock, 1992). In the Tobin et al. (1989) preschool analysis, 31% of the parents, teachers, and administrators in their Japanese sample considered "sympathy/empathy/concern for others" to be the most important thing for children to learn in preschool, and 30% considered "cooperation and how to be a member of a group" to be most important. In keeping with these goals, Japanese preschool and elementary school classrooms have been described as small communities in which children help, support, and encourage each other as they cooperate toward varied common goals (Hendry, 1986; Lewis, 1995/1999; Peak, 1991). In school, children experience "the safety provided by strong, shared class norms of kindness, helpfulness, and 'putting our strength together' " (Lewis, 1995/1999, p. 177).

Cooperation and group identification are fostered through varied specific practices that include the entire class and sometimes the entire school. For example, Lewis (1995/1999) observed how teachers facilitated the production of "puppet shows, dramatic performances . . . that began in the spontaneous play of a few children and grew to involve the whole class or even the whole school in shared dramatic pursuits" (p. 22). Or, there may be a list of each child's birthday in a classroom, but rather than celebrating individual birthdays, there may be monthly celebrations that involve all children, sometimes in the whole school, who have birthdays during that month (Hendry, 1986; Lewis, 1995/1999). Rather than employing janitors, children also cooperate to keep their schools clean, and school property is considered to belong to everyone in the school collectively. In addition, Lewis (1995/1999) described how students in many of the Japanese preschool and elementary classrooms that she observed "studied beneath banners and posters proclaiming their school, class, or group goals" (p. 44). Many of these goals emphasize "friendship, cooperation, and other aspects of social and emotional development: 'Let's become friends'; 'Let's be children who get along well with each other and help each other'; 'Let's be kind children who easily say, I'm sorry and Thank you' " (p. 45). During times set aside for reflection or group discussion, "Under signs that said, 'Let's be friends and help each other,' children spoke earnestly of what they had done during the previous school week to help others—or of ways they had fallen short of this goal" (p. 44).

Group participation and group identification in preschool are also fostered through large class sizes of about 30, thus essentially forcing a child to cope with being one among many and to cooperate with others. Although preschool class sizes are partly driven by economic concerns, many Japanese teachers and school administrators generally claim that a teacher–student ratio of at least 15 children per teacher is optimal for enabling children to learn how to cooperate with others and be part of a group (Tobin et al., 1987, 1989).

Such large-group settings are considered to be beneficial because they allow children the opportunity to have contact with "a broader range of personalities" (Peak, 1991, p. 57). This reasoning brings us to Japanese conceptions of independence because the notion of a broad range of personalities suggests that learning how to get along with others involves dealing with others as separate individuals, and that groups consist partly of separate individuals with their own goals and preferences. Ultimately, part of being a member of a preschool or elementary school group in Japan involves negotiating harmonious relationships among diverse individuals who know and understand each other well (Hendry, 1986; Holloway, 1999). Based on observations of varied first-grade classrooms, Lewis generally found that elementary school students "listened and responded to one another's ideas—clapping for one another, correcting, congratulating, devising explanations for students who were having difficulty" (Lewis, 1995/1999, p. 177). In addition, there is an "infrastructure" in which "all students know and care about one another as people, [and] know how to talk and listen to one another respectfully" (p. 177).

To foster the recognition of each individual group member, Lewis (1995/1999) described how, in many preschool and elementary school classrooms, each child says hello and goodbye to all the other children individually. This practice emphasizes the importance of each individual to the group, and "teachers explained to [Lewis] that greetings are the most basic way to recognize other members of the school community" (p. 47). Greeting practices also provide a way "to make classmates and teachers feel important and cared about" (p. 48), thus suggesting that social engagement is conceptualized in relation to subjective self-fulfillment. Recognizing individual students also occurs as classroom walls are often adorned with each child's individual contribution to a common theme (Hendry, 1986). Along similar lines, a preschool principal interviewed by Tobin et al. (1989) said that, "Everyone doing the same thing at the same time isn't the same as real group life, is it?" (p. 39). This comment suggests that "real group life" involves attending to individuals as well as to common goals.

In addition to being part of a whole class, elementary school children spend much of their time in small groups of about four to eight students (Hoffman, 2000; Lewis, 1995/1999), not only to work on academic activities, but also to eat, play, and contribute to keeping the school clean. As class activities move back and forth between whole-class and small-group practices, each individual child is expected to energetically and enthusiastically contribute to the common activity (Lewis, 1995/1999; White, 1987). When children are working in their small groups, teachers are often found monitoring the groups' activities, in part, to make sure that each child is contributing to the common activity. In this context, a noisy and boisterous classroom seems to be a hallmark of Japanese preschool and elementary school life that is taken as a sign that all children are energetically contributing to the class activities.

One way of ensuring everyone's participation in class activities may occur at the end of the day, when students are often asked to "reflect privately on questions such as, 'Did today's class discussions involve all classmates or just a few classmates?' and 'Did I volunteer my ideas sometime today?' " (Lewis, 1995/1999, p. 113). These practices point to the value that is placed on each individual's perspective, and how without them there would be no group. In addition to reflecting specifically on their individual contributions to the group, Japanese elementary school students are often called on to engage in private self-reflection and self-evaluation about varied aspects of their own behavior and feelings (Hoffman, 2000; Lewis, 1995/1999; White, 1987). For example, White (1987) mentioned how a teacher, when introducing the topic of cubing to a fifth-grade class, asked the students to explain in their diaries how they felt about the new topic. Insofar as appropriate behavior in public settings involves avoiding overt social conflict, in part by not criticizing others, much is left to the individual to privately reflect on him or herself (White, 1987; White & LeVine, 1986). Such practices suggest that social cohesion is inseparable from independent self-awareness, and that independent self-awareness, as well as awareness of others, is implicated in the structuring of social interactions (Hendry, 1986).

The Inseparability of Independence
and Interdependence in Classroom Regulation

To organize and regulate large preschool and elementary school classes, and to encourage social cohesion among the children, teacher control is kept to a minimum, thus leaving children to figure out how to get along among themselves (Lewis, 1995/1999; Peak, 1991; Tobin et al., 1989). In this way, Japanese students are able to exercise much self-direction that is unsupervised and unlimited by authority figures. In her observations of a first-grade class, Lewis (1995/1999) noted how students are expected to be attentive and diligent in their work during class lessons for approximately 45 minutes, but during the 10- or 20-minute breaks between lessons she saw "bedlam" (p. 39) because the children are free to do almost anything. According to Lewis, teachers reason that when there are no rules, children inevitably "bumped up against one another" (p. 109), thus enabling them to realize and understand, for themselves, the necessity of rules to regulate interactions among individuals. In addition, allowing children to create some of their own classroom rules and norms is viewed as a way of enhancing each child's individual commitment to and identification with the classroom community, again pointing to the importance of establishing communities in ways that recognize the individuality of its members. One teacher also explained to Lewis that, "Bumping up against others is important. Children must learn both to form their own ideas and to understand the ideas of others" (p. 85). This comment again demonstrates the importance of understanding oneself and others as separate mental beings.

One way of enabling individual children to be actively involved in classroom regulation is through the widespread use of daily monitors, whereby classrooms are organized and structured by different students each day (Lewis, 1995/1999; Stevenson, 1991). According to Lewis (1995/1999):

> By first grade, monitors—usually one boy and one girl—assembled and quieted the class before the teacher arrived for each lesson. In addition, they often led meetings, evaluated other students' behavior, and led the class in solving disputes or problems that arose. In fact, first-grade monitors—not teachers—managed much of the mechanics of classroom life, freeing teachers to teach. (p. 106)

Students take turns being daily monitors so that all children—not just the ones who are doing particularly well academically, are particularly outgoing and charming, or are considered to have "leadership skills"— have the same opportunity to lead the class, and thus be actively involved in classroom regulation. In addition to leaving much of classroom regulation up to the students, this all-inclusive practice reflects the egalitarian basis of Japanese education (Tobin et al., 1989). In this case, each individual child is considered to be equally capable of leading the class, and everyone enjoys the same chances of being a daily monitor.

In her discussions with teachers, Lewis (1995/1999) found further that, "When Japanese teachers talked about classroom rules and routines, their central concern seemed to be children's autonomy: how to introduce rules and norms without imposing them on children" (p. 108). Accordingly, when teachers involve themselves in classroom discipline, instead of invoking methods of control they often try to get children to understand how to cooperate, get along, and empathize with one another through hints and roundabout questioning. These practices seem to parallel some of the indirect childrearing practices discussed in chapter 4.

It is also interesting to note that, in preschool and elementary school, one way of getting children to understand others' feelings and perspectives involves asking a child to explain how he or she might feel in a similar situation (e.g., Lewis, 1984, 1995/1999). For example, Lewis (1995/1999) explained how elementary school teachers worked to get children to understand the importance of being friendly and greeting people with a smile by asking, " 'What makes you smile?', 'How do you feel when you're smiling?', and 'How do you feel when other people smile at you?' " (p. 47). In this way, empathizing with others is partly derived from understanding one's own individual feelings and perspective. According to Hendry (1986), in Japan, "it is said to be through coming to understand oneself that one comes to understand others, and thus work out appropriate behaviour" (p. 165). Overall, these observations suggest that empathy and getting along with others involve the understanding by a separate mental being of other separate mental beings, all with their own individual feelings and perspectives. In these ways, empathy, group cohesion, and classroom regulation implicate conceptions of independence.

In these kinds of unstructured and socially saturated classroom settings, disputes and conflicts among children are perhaps inevitable. However, unlike their American counterparts, Japanese preschool and elementary school staff do not necessarily consider peer conflict, even physical fighting, to be particularly problematic. Although Japanese teachers may tell children not to hit, they are less likely than American teachers to directly intervene or to adjudicate children's disputes by trying to figure out who started the fight (Killen & Sueyoshi, 1995; Lewis, 1984; Peak, 1991; Tobin et al., 1989). Instead, peer conflicts in Japanese schools are often viewed as arenas for learning how to express one's needs and goals and to understand and accept others' needs and goals. Within this framework, hitting and not being able to get along with others in general are viewed as manifestations of an immature child's inability to understand how to behave in relation to others in outer cultural practices (Peak, 1991). Rather than being concerned that a child might have behavioral problems or aggressive tendencies, it is assumed that with time, encouragement, indirect persuasion, and continued peer interaction, the appropriate understanding will be constructed.

In addition, classroom regulation is related to the independence of self-reliance. That is, self-reliance for a child involves being able to function outside of the mother–child *amae* relationship and being able to contribute to the group without being dependent on others. As Peak (1991) explained:

> in the preschool, basic daily habits include changing clothes quickly and efficiently, looking after one's own belongings, using proper greetings and polite speech, and being cheerful and diligent. These abilities and attitudes all form the child's own portion of the social contract within the small society of the preschool, and fulfilling these responsibilities constitutes upholding one's own end of the social bargain. For this reason, the acquisition of proper daily habits is a prerequisite to full participation in society. (pp. 71–72)

The end of this quotation seems to imply that being able to regulate aspects of one's own behavior is required before one can fully participate in a group, suggesting that some forms of independence are taken to be temporally prior to some forms of interdependence before they are ultimately integrated. Also, characterizing preschool society in terms of a "social contract" or "social bargain" indicates how at least certain groups in Japan may be established and maintained through consent and negotiation among separate individuals.

Within this context, becoming instrumentally self-reliant, especially being able to take care of one's physical needs, is a central goal of Japanese preschool education (Ben-Ari, 1996; Peak, 1991; Tobin et al., 1989). In the Tobin et al. (1989) interviews about what is most important for children to learn in preschool, 49% of the Japanese parents, teachers, and administrators in their sample rated "good health, hygiene, and grooming habits" (p. 190) among their top three choices, and when asked "Why should a society have preschools?" (p. 192), 80% rated "to make young children more independent and self-reliant" (p. 192) among their top three choices.

Toward these ends, in addition to scheduling bathroom breaks for an entire class, preschool children are allowed and "expected to use the toilet whenever they felt the need and simply disappeared from classroom activities" (Peak, 1991, p. 27). Peak also described how preschool children have to change from indoor to outdoor uniforms several times a day, and teachers offer little assistance beyond patient and cheerful encouragement as well as "praise as children gradually become more self-reliant" (1991, p. 166). Moreover, most of the mothers of the preschoolers she observed "believed that the teacher should not help the child, even if the child cried" (p. 36).

At the same time that a great deal of the responsibility for classroom regulation and group cooperation is in the hands of the children, there is also much in Japanese classrooms that is strictly regulated by teachers and institutional sources. For example, although children have their own materials, such as pens, scissors, and crayons (Hendry, 1986), these materials may be subject to all kinds of rules that the children do not devise. Based on her observations of a range of Japanese first-grade classrooms, Lewis (1995/1999) cited varied rules or:

> procedures suggesting that there is one correct way to do things: to arrange desk contents (pencils on the right!), to stow shoes (toes first!), to take notes from the blackboard (reproducing the elaborate system of underlining and boxes used by the teacher). The list goes on: The number of pencils, erasers, and handkerchiefs one brings to school is sometimes a matter of policy, not personal choice, and checks for "forgotten items" are conducted regularly in many classrooms. Schools provide rules governing students' use of time over vacations and weekends, asking, for example, that students rise early, exercise daily, and stay away from video parlors. Schools also regulate how students come to school (in neighborhood walking groups that arrive well before school actually begins), suggest an appropriate bedtime and wake-up time for students, and even suggest the appropriate timing of bowel movements (before school!). (p. 142)

Lewis went on to suggest that these kinds of rules may serve several purposes, including promoting the kind of conformity and obedience that is required in junior high school and adult life, and instilling efficiency in the classroom that can then be generalized to any group. These practices may also inspire loyalty to the group insofar as "Commitment to the group is shown by willingness to stow one's backpack and point one's shoes in the right direction" (Lewis, 1995/1999, p. 143).

Individualized Learning

As Japanese teachers work on fostering children's individual understanding of the importance of cooperation, rules, and regulations, studies suggest that they are extremely tolerant of what they consider to be each child's individual learning pace (Peak, 1991). Although it is assumed that children have basically the same or equal abilities to eventually understand, it is also assumed that these abilities are actualized at different rates by different children. According to Kojima (1986), the view that children are "autonomous learning organisms" (p. 322) is rooted in centuries of Japanese educational traditions. In keeping with those traditions, "teachers are unruffled by demonstrations of selfish or regressive behavior, preferring that a child who has not yet developed an understanding of proper behavior straightforwardly express his feelings rather than attempt an artificial form of behavior beyond his level of genuine understanding" (Peak, 1991, p. 85). Again, we see how independence is conceptualized in terms of treating children as separate mental individuals. At the same time, we also see that Japanese educators take a generally egalitarian approach to children's overall abilities (Hamilton, Blumenfeld, Akoh, & Miura, 1989; Hess & Azuma, 1991; Hoffman, 2000; Lewis, 1995/1999; Peak, 1991; Stevenson et al., 1990; Tobin et al., 1989). That is, all children are considered to be equally capable of eventually understanding how to get along with others and of succeeding academically, although ultimate success may come at different rates.

In keeping with the view that individual understanding is central to varied aspects of educational success, some Japanese elementary school teachers visit each student's home at least once a year so they can learn about and make a personal connection to each child's individual experience (Hendry, 1986; Lewis, 1995/1999). Teachers then may use this knowledge to make class lessons personally relevant to individual children and incorporate all children into the class discussion. Speaking against a unidimensional understanding of Japanese society, Lewis (1995/1999) wrote, "Teachers' interest in personalizing lessons and their attention to the 'thread' with each individual child seem paradoxical in a society known for groupism and conformity. Yet, as teachers explained to me

[i.e., Lewis], 'To nurture the group, you must nurture each individual' "
(p. 57). Thus, to some extent, class lessons are structured around each
child's individual experience and personal engagement with the issues at
hand. The idea that personalized lessons seem "paradoxical" in a society
known for interdependence is rooted in a dichotomous approach to independence and interdependence. However, when independence and interdependence are taken to be not only compatible but also inseparable,
the way is opened for discerning how "groupism and conformity" are related to conceptions of independence—in this case, individual understanding and attention to each child's individual perspective and personal
experience.

Aspects of individualized learning may also be found in the importance
that Japanese society places on individual persistence (Hamilton et al.,
1989; Hendry, 1986; Lewis, 1995/1999; Smith, 1983/1993; Stevenson,
1991; Tobin et al., 1989; White, 1987; White & LeVine, 1986). Indeed, preschool is considered to be a place where children learn how to enthusiastically persist in completing varied kinds of difficult tasks—from buttoning
a shirt to making complex origami figures. Persistence continues to be
stressed as an educational goal throughout Japanese children's school careers and may also be seen in relation to the view held by Japanese educators and parents that academic success is based on individual effort and
persistence (Hamilton, Blumenfeld, Akoh, & Miura, 1989; Hess & Azuma,
1991; Hoffman, 2000; Stevenson, 1991; Stevenson et al., 1990). This approach to academic success seems compatible with the view that children
are endowed with the same basic capabilities, and thus any differences in
achievement would be due in part to individual factors such as effort and
persistence.

It is also important to point out that children are not only encouraged
to persist at school tasks that are defined and structured by the teacher,
but also at tasks or goals that they define for themselves. For example,
Lewis (1995/1999) described how discussing the diligent pursuit of self-
chosen goals was a common topic throughout the school year in several of
the elementary schools that she visited. Moreover, pointing to the value of
independent self-awareness, she explained that, "Later in the year, they
would revisit these goals and reflect on their personal progress" (p. 49).

This approach appears to place a lot of emphasis on the child as a separate mental individual who is responsible for his or her own success as a
self-directing and self-aware individual, further pointing to another conception of children as independent. However, as Kondo (1990) cautioned, the role of individual effort is not necessarily recognized by all Japanese and may represent a particularly middle-class understanding of
independence. Based on interviews and ethnographic observations, Kondo found that, for less-affluent families with working mothers, opportuni-

ties for advancement are restricted, and "Academic excellence was . . . a matter of *umaretsuki*, innate abilities" (p. 283).

Enacting Conceptions of Independence and Interdependence in a Typical Japanese Preschool

These and other independence and interdependence issues are evident in the Japanese segment of the Tobin et al. (1989) now classic *Preschool in Three Cultures* book and accompanying videotape. Their analyses focused on a typical day in Japanese, Chinese, and American preschools. In addition to interviews with parents, teachers, and preschool administrators in each country about why children should attend preschool, the book and videotape provide fairly detailed descriptions of some specific preschool practices in each country, which I interpret through the lenses of the current approach to independence and interdependence. In addition, it is instructive to consider some of this Japanese preschool's practices in conjunction with some of the cultural practices at St. Timothy's, an American preschool located in Honolulu, Hawaii.

It is estimated that over 90% of Japanese children attend at least 2 years of one of two types of preschools (e.g., Lewis, 1995/1999; Tobin et al., 1989). One type of preschool, called a *yochien*, is attended mostly by 3- to 6-year-old children of nonworking mothers and is based on a curriculum mandated by the Ministry of Education. There is also the *hoikuen*, for 6-month-olds to 6-year-olds of working mothers, with a curriculum mandated by the Ministry of Health and Welfare. In a nation that places great emphasis and value on the mother–child relationship, some research suggests that attitudes toward preschool education tend to be positive. Rather than viewing preschool as a necessary evil resulting from economic factors or women's liberation, preschool education is instead seen as an important developmental experience in Japan (Boocock, 1992). Accordingly, preschool is not necessarily considered to be a form of maternal deprivation, and interviews with Ministry of Education and Ministry of Health and Welfare officials suggest that, "Japanese scholars and educators have neither conducted systematic research on the effects of group care on children's cognitive and social development, nor paid much attention to the huge body of American research on this subject" (Boocock, 1992, p. 176).

The Japanese preschool, a *hoikuen*, called Komatsudani is located in Kyoto, and the videotaped class consisted of 28 four-year-olds and their one teacher. In general, the investigators noted that Komatsudani is similar to other Japanese preschools, "which self-consciously and deliberately reflect and cultivate traditional Japanese values" (Tobin et al., 1989, p. 49). At the same time, however, some Japanese teachers and school administrators claimed that Komatsudani is neither a representative nor model Japanese preschool. Thus, any insights into Japanese conceptions of independence and interdependence meanings and the structuring of independence and interdependence activity dimensions that we may extract from this one preschool are not necessarily generalizable to all Japanese preschool experiences.

The Japanese video segment began with shots of children being dropped off at the preschool by their parents who, unlike many American parents, did not go into the school or stay for protracted leave-taking episodes, thus marking a distinction between inner and outer social contexts. As they entered the school, children changed into their indoor shoes and placed their outdoor shoes in their individual cubby holes, thus pointing to how the children had individual spaces for their personal belongings (e.g., Hendry, 1986). A period of free play ensued, and the videotape then focused in on two 4-year-old girls who were carrying infants. At this point, the video commentator explained that toddlers at Komatsudani are encouraged to play with and care for infants in the preschool to foster "empathy" in the older children and provide "stimulation" for the younger children.

After cleaning up, teachers and children gathered together in a circle to perform morning calisthenics. The videotape commentator noted that these calisthenics were performed for the sake of physical exercise and also to create a feeling of "oneness," thus indicating a way in which group identification among the students is fostered. However, no child was overtly forced to participate in these group exercises, reflecting the view that group interaction is derived from, and thus inseparable from, the individuality of each person, as well as individual self-direction. In their book, Tobin et al. (1989) noted:

> each child in the school is given an opportunity to participate in his or her own fashion. Those who cannot or will not join in the activity are periodically encouraged to join in by teachers and other children, but usually they are allowed to refrain from active participation or, more accurately, to participate in their own way even if that way involves seeming not to participate actively. (pp. 41–42)

Rather than explicitly forcing children to participate and punishing them if they did not, preschool and elementary school teachers and other children are likely to try to get children to want to participate in group activities, and to understand and enjoy, for themselves as individuals, the benefits of group life (Hendry, 1986; Peak, 1991; Tsuneyoshi, 1994; White, 1987).

The children then split up into their classrooms, bowed to each other and their teacher, and sang a good-morning song together. A daily monitor could then be seen counting the number of children present that day by patting each child individually on the head. Another song was sung, this time about the date, day, weather, and number of children who were in attendance. After these beginning-of-the-day activities, the videotape showed the children participating in a workbook counting exercise, which constituted the day's single formal academic practice. The teacher lectured to the whole class, and although the children worked individually, they talked to each other throughout the counting exercise. Individual children were not overlooked during this exercise, as the teacher helped one child who was having trouble with the task at hand.

The videotape then focused on a boy named Hiroki, who had been acting out, rather rambunctiously, throughout the workbook session. He was shown interrupting the teacher and other children, singing songs, and making obscene remarks and gestures. Later on in the videotape, Hiroki threw flashcards over a balcony wall and hit and kicked other children. In keeping with the practice of minimal teacher supervision, the teacher, for the most part, did not take any special measures to discipline Hiroki. At one point, when another student told the teacher about Hiroki's behavior, the teacher responded, "Is that so? Why are you telling me? You do something about it." This approach reflects the idea that classroom regulation stems partly from the children's individual initiatives, and later in the video, we see that this approach seemed to be somewhat effective. That is, Hiroki stepped on another boy's (Satoshi) wrist, and as Satoshi cried, a little girl, Midori, appeared at his side to take him out of Hiroki's kicking range. Midori and Satoshi then discussed the situation with two other children, and they told Satoshi that if he did not want to get hurt, he just should not play with Hiroki. From an American perspective, this admonition may seem more punitive to Satoshi than to Hiroki, but in the long run if children stopped playing with Hiroki, the Japanese hope was that he would change his ways to be part of the group.

In trying to understand Hiroki's behavior, the videotape commentator explained how the visiting researchers thought that Hiroki might be gifted, taking his misbehavior as a sign of boredom with class activities that were too easy for him. However, the Japanese preschool staff claimed not to be familiar with the concept of giftedness, and when it was explained to them, they responded that they did not think that Hiroki was gifted, for two reasons. First, the preschool staff explained that Hiroki was an average child, reflecting Japanese values about equality and the preschool staff's "reluctance to explain or excuse behavior in terms of differences in abilities" (Tobin et al., 1989, p. 25). Rather than being persuaded by the concept of giftedness, the Komatsudani staff maintained that Hiroki's behavior represented his attempts to get attention, which had remained unsatisfied for him at home, where he lived only with his father and lacked an effective *amae* relationship. Second, the preschool staff wondered why, if Hiroki was so intelligent, he did not understand how to behave appropriately. This comment indicates that intelligence is culturally understood to involve social dimensions and is not defined exclusively in terms of individual intellectual or academic abilities (Greenfield, 1994). The preschool staff's comment also reflects the view that individual understanding is a key to behaving in culturally appropriate ways.

The remainder of the Japanese videotape segment showed more freeplay time, during which children were allowed to wander freely throughout the preschool building and grounds, pointing to the value placed on self-direction. This kind of free play also stands somewhat in contrast to how issues of freedom were particularized in the American preschool. As Tobin et al. (1989) explained, the American children's day was structured around several learning center periods, during which children could choose to move from one activity to another, reflecting this preschool's emphasis on independence in the form of individual choice or self-direction. Tobin et al. (1989) noted that the children were also given many other opportunities to make their own choices throughout the day. For example:

> At lunchtime children choose whom to sit with. At naptime they sleep wherever they choose to sleep. During outdoor play twice a day they are free to choose from a variety of large-motor activities. Once a week, each child gets a chance to bring something from home to show to the class or to tell about something the child has done or seen. (p. 141)

However, as Tobin et al. (1989) maintained, these children did not experience unlimited freedom of self-direction, as their choices of activities were highly structured by the preschool staff and administration, thus making individual choice inseparable from conceptions of interdependence. Indeed, the authors explained that the children's choices, as well as many of the preschool activities, were organized around all kinds of rules:

> Although the children of St. Timothy's are free to make many choices, these choices are by no means unconstrained. Children are not free to choose to eat junk food or refuse to take a nap or to play war games on the playground. They can freely choose what toys to play with, but they are not free to choose not to clean up. The teachers at St. Timothy's believe that whenever possible children should be given the opportunity to make choices. But they see their job as carefully structuring the range of available choices and setting clear limits on acceptable behavior. (p. 141)

In keeping with earlier discussions, these rules indicate how expectations for being independent were not defined in terms of being a self-contained entity with license to do as one pleases. Instead, independence expectations, including the freedom to make self-directed choices, were carried out in relation to others and wider social standards. Indeed, in the United States more generally, there is much rancorous public debate regarding what aspects of life are to be included within the purview of freedom of choice.

Going back to Japan, the children's free-play sessions were interspersed with cleanup periods, lunch, and a half-hour origami lesson. During lunch, the children and teacher ate together as a group, but during the origami session, each child worked individually to create his or her own paper ball. It was explained that, in addition to fostering "manual dexterity," the origami exercise was used to teach children the value of persistence and completing a difficult task. Many of the students in my undergraduate developmental psychology classes are rather amazed to see 4-year-olds who had just been hitting, throwing things, and generally running around, without any immediately apparent adult supervision, diligently sit and fold paper for about 30 minutes.

SOME GENERAL REMARKS

The research discussed in this chapter demonstrates how varied independence and interdependence issues are construed and particularized in relation to each other within American and Japanese school practices. In addition, some of the research discussed in this chapter has implications for wider conceptual issues regarding independence and interdependence. For example, educational research has long pointed to the competitive nature of American school practices, as well as a strong tradition of criticizing not only those competitive school practices but also traditional whole-class practices. In general, competitive and whole-class practices have been criticized because they undermine students' social connections, self-direction, and individuality. These negative assessments show that conceptions of independence are multifaceted, and that valuing independence does not mean that all independence meanings or ways of structuring independence activity dimensions are necessarily valued. At least theoretically, this point may be applied to interdependence, suggesting that not all interdependence meanings or ways of structuring interdependence activity dimensions are endorsed within a particular culture.

Along these lines, the analysis of some of Dewey's writings indicates that he was not an advocate of any form of either independence or interdependence. More specifically, his writings demonstrate that he was not particularly keen on fostering children's individual achievement simply for its own sake. Instead, Dewey was concerned with shaping children's individual abilities toward productive social participation and with how individual abilities could enhance cooperative ways of living. Similarly, independence in the form of self-direction for Dewey did not involve pursuing self-contained personal interests. Instead, for Dewey, self-direction involved making individual decisions and taking action by considering others' perspectives. In addition, Dewey conceptualized freedom in terms of acting on the basis of informed consideration and choice.

Some of the research discussed in this chapter points to how deceptive first-glance, unidimensional analyses of cultural practices can be. For example, the increasing emphasis on individual self-expression in American school practices could be taken as a sign of an ever-increasing value of independence in American culture. However, as the Tobin et al. (1989) interviews with American parents, teachers, and administrators indicated, self-expression is considered to be important, in part, because it enables children to make friends and participate in groups. Echoing Dewey's ideas about the inseparability of independence and interdependence, these interview participants additionally claimed that self-expression is required to contribute to a democratic society.

The research discussed regarding Japanese educational practices also points to the deception of first-glance, unidimensional analyses. For so long now, Japanese cultural practices have generally been characterized in terms of interdependence, and there is certainly no denying that cooperation and group identification are essential to Japanese educational practices. However, varied studies note how such interdependence is inseparable from independence insofar as children are expected to cooperate with others by expressing their individual perspectives, and by taking initiative to establish and maintain social connections with other students. In addition, in this chapter, we have seen that independence, in the forms of individual self-reflection and individual persistence, are central to Japanese educational practices.

Along similar lines, comparative analyses of American and Japanese educational practices have also typically been based on the position that American practices are more independence oriented than are Japanese practices, which in turn are more interdependence oriented. By discussing American and Japanese education practices from the vantage point of the current conceptual approach, comparative considerations of American and Japanese educational practices are also possible. In this chapter, the discussion of Japanese preschool and school practices does indeed stand in contrast to the discussion of American preschool and school practices. However, in keeping with the current conceptual approach, the contrast does not center around the notion that Japanese school practices involve more interdependence than do American school practices, or that American school practices involve more independence than do Japanese practices. Instead, cultural differences in Japanese and American school practices may be understood in terms of how independence and interdependence meanings are defined and interrelated differently, and how inseparable independence and interdependence activity dimensions are structured differently. Thus, although a first-glance analysis might point to the importance of identifying with the group in Japan (in this case, one's classroom) but not in the United States, other enactments of interdependence are evident in American educational practices, as children are often expected to follow rules set by teachers. Some studies also indicate that American children are expected to be cooperative, helpful, and generally sociable.

In addition, although certain conceptions of independence have been identified in the structuring of American classrooms, other conceptions of independence seem prevalent in Japanese classrooms. For example, individual self-reflection seems to play an important role in Japanese educational practices, but does not figure centrally in any of the analyses of American educational practices with which I am familiar. Interestingly, at least one contemporary effort at educational reform in the United States involves not only fostering cooperation among children, but also bolstering children's abilities to reflect on their own thinking and learning (Brown, 1997).

In conjunction with chapter 4, we have explored some of the ways in which independence and interdependence are particularized as children participate in cultural practices with their parents and in school. We now turn to a consideration of how some of the independence and interdependence issues discussed thus far may be particularized in children's and adolescents' self-constructions.

Independence, Interdependence, and Self-Construction

In chapters 4 and 5, we considered multifaceted and interrelated independence and interdependence meanings and activity dimensions within parent–child relationships and educational settings. However, we did not address children's changing behavior beyond claiming that children may encounter different independence and interdependence expectations during development. Thus, we now turn to a consideration of how children's and adolescents' self-constructions reflect cultural independence and interdependence meanings.

Many analyses of independence and interdependence during the last 20 years have involved studies of self-construction. Although research on self-construction has been used to support dichotomous approaches to independence and interdependence, it is also in relation to self-construction that much evidence for the current conceptual approach can be found. In addition, much of my own thinking about independence and interdependence issues is based on several classic theories of self, and from trying to understand the roles of independence and interdependence in Euro-American self-constructions. Although there is little systematic research specifically designed to investigate how children and adolescents in varied cultures construct themselves in ways that reflect increasingly differentiated and integrated cultural independence and interdependence meanings, considerations of self-construction have pervaded psychology at least since the turn of the 20th century and are also quite the rage in psychology today. Although identifying specific developmental trajectories for independent and interdependent modes of self-construction lies in the future, much theoretical and empirical work exists to provide some insight into how independence and interdependence are implicated in self-construction during childhood and adolescence.

In this chapter, I begin by presenting some early theoretical considerations of the roles of independence and interdependence in self-construction as part of my goal to consider how Western theoretical traditions are not exclusively independence oriented. In particular, because the theories of William James, George Herbert Mead, Charles Horton Cooley, and Erik Erikson have been central to the articulation of my own framework, I start this chapter with a consideration of Mead's, Cooley's, and Erikson's theories. (I include William James later in the chapter.) After considering these classic theories of self, I define self-construction as a form of cultural activity, and this definition then serves as a backdrop for considering how self-construction during childhood and adolescence reflects multifaceted and inseparable independence and interdependence meanings. The chapter ends with a consideration of Japanese self-construction. As has been the case in previous chapters, the goal now is to consider how self-construction involves not only multifaceted but also inseparable independence and interdependence meanings and activity dimensions.

THREE CLASSIC WESTERN THEORIES
OF SELF-CONSTRUCTION

Although Mead, Cooley, and Erikson did not specifically use the terms *independence* and *interdependence* as I am using them now, their ideas about individual and social dimensions of self-construction are quite relevant to our concerns. As we discuss in this section, the current view that human functioning involves multifaceted and inseparable independence and interdependence dimensions is evident, albeit in different ways, in their self-theories.

Independence and Interdependence
in Mead's Theory of Self-Construction

As a figure in the tradition of American pragmatism, Mead (1863–1931), like Dewey, was primarily concerned with formulating a social scientific approach that would be of practical significance for dealing with issues of everyday social life (Stuhr, 2000). Within the philosophical context of pragmatism, Mead claimed that "human nature is something social through and through" (1934/1962, p. 229) and, according to Mead, a self comes into existence and develops only through social interaction. More specifically, it is in terms of communication through the medium of significant symbols that people become objects to themselves, or self-conscious, during the course of social engagement. Within Mead's framework, significant symbols enable people to partake of a common meaning system because they "arouse in an individual making them the same responses which they explicitly arouse, or are supposed to arouse in other individuals, the individuals to whom they are addressed . . . and this particular act or response for which it stands is its meaning as a significant symbol" (Mead, 1934/1962, p. 47). Once an individual learns the significant symbols of his or her wider social group or community, it is possible for a self to arise during social interaction because an individual can then reflexively apply common significant symbols to his or her own conduct, and thus interpret his or her own behavior in terms of others' perspectives and attitudes. According to Mead, "It is as he takes the attitude of the other that the individual is able to realize himself as a self" (Mead, 1934/1962, p. 194).

By being able to view one's own behavior and being from the perspectives of others, Mead conceptualized the self as an active process, and thus rather than having a single self, people engage in self-constructing activity during the course of social interaction. Using different verbs and descriptions of social interaction, Mead asserted that, "When we reach a self we reach a certain sort of conduct, a certain type of social process which involves the interaction of different individuals" (1934/1962, p. 165). Therefore, according to Mead, "The self is not something that exists first and then enters into relationship with others, but it is, so to speak, an eddy in the social current and so still a part of the current" (1934/1962, p. 182). Such self-constructing activity enables a social partner to adjust his or her own action during the ongoing dynamics of social interaction within cultural practices. As Mead explained, the value of this ongoing mutual adjustment that results from self-constructing activity "lies in the superior co-ordination gained for society as a whole, and in the increased efficiency of the individual as a member of the group" (Mead, 1934/1962, p. 179). In this way, inseparable independence and interdependence dimensions constitute self-construction because individual self-consciousness is socially derived and also, in turn, serves the interdependent purpose of maintaining and enhancing social harmony or cohesion.

Taking the attitudes of others toward one's own behavior and being during social interactions with others suggests that it is possible for people to construct multiple selves in relation to varied social partners. As Mead pointed out, "We divide ourselves up in all sorts of different selves with reference to our acquaintances. We discuss politics with one and religion with another. There are all sorts of different selves answering to all sorts of different social reactions" (1934/1962, p. 142). At the same time, however, there is a structure and coherence to self-construction within

Mead's theory insofar as a person ultimately moves beyond taking the attitudes of different specific others to being able to generalize specific social encounters into an understanding of the whole system of attitudes enacted by his or her wider sociocultural group or community. In Mead's view:

> The organized community or social group which gives to the individual his unity of self may be called the "generalized other." The attitude of the generalized other is the attitude of the whole community. . . . This getting of the broad activities of any given social whole or organized society as such within the experiential field of any one of the individuals involved or included in that whole is, in other words, the essential basis and prerequisite of the fullest development of that individual's self. (1934/1962, pp. 154–155)

Mead's conceptualization of the generalized other parallels what is known as the *appropriation of sociocultural norms and values*, in the parlance of contemporary developmental psychology. Insofar as the symbolically mediated attitudes of the generalized other are organized and stable, even if simultaneously dynamic and open to change (Miller, 1973), these generalized attitudes enable an individual's selfing activity to maintain continuity and coherence across a diversity of particular social encounters. In this way, independence, conceptualized as a person's awareness of individual continuity, is inseparable from the social structure that provides its organization.

Although Mead did not specify in great detail how appropriating the generalized other takes place, he did outline a two-step sequence of self-development. Within this framework, the first step occurs during childhood with different kinds of play. One kind of play that some children engage in involves creating imaginary friends that enable children to "organize . . . the responses which they call out in other persons and call out also in themselves" (Mead, 1934/1962, p. 150). Another kind of play involves social role playing, such as when "A child plays at being a mother, at being a teacher, at being a policeman" (Mead, 1934/1962, p. 150), and this kind of play enables a child to take the perspectives or attitudes of varied particular other social actors. The second step in self-development involves playing organized games with rules, whereby a child "must be ready to take the attitude of everyone else involved in that game," and these attitudes or roles of the other players "must have a definite relationship to each other" (Mead, 1934/1962, p. 151). Thus, it is the rule-bound organization of roles that differentiates games from the simpler play of the previous developmental step. Using the game of baseball as an example, Mead pointed out that a player's activity "is determined by his assumption of the action of the others who are playing the game. What he does is controlled by his being everyone else on that team, at least in so far as those attitudes affect his own particular response. We get then an 'other' which is an organization of the attitudes of those involved in the same process" (Mead, 1934/1962, p. 154).

Once fully developed to involve appropriating the generalized other, the process of self-construction more specifically involves two complementary activities: namely, "Me" and "I" activities. According to Mead, "Me" activity is the part of self-construction, just outlined in this discussion, that involves taking the attitudes of the generalized other toward one's own behavior and being. At the same time, however, Mead maintained, "Of course we are not only what is common to all: each one of the selves is different from everyone else" (1934/1962, p. 163). It is the "I" aspect of self-construction that allows for self-consciousness as a separate and unique individual to occur. According to Mead, the "I" activity of self-construction occurs when an individual reacts to the generalized other by:

> expressing himself, not necessarily asserting himself in the offensive sense but expressing himself, being himself in such a co-operative process as belongs to any community. The attitudes involved are gathered from the group, but the individual in whom they are organized has the opportunity of giving them an expression which perhaps has never taken place before. (Mead, 1934/1962, pp. 197–198)

Based on this conceptualization, the "I" represents a central way in which independence is particularized within Mead's theory of self-construction. By reacting to the attitudes of the social group, which people have taken over into their own behavior and being, humans are neither homogeneous, nor are they reduced to acting as the passive marionettes of social forces. Instead, they are conceptualized as distinct and self-directing individuals who are capable of uniquely interpreting social attitudes by constructing their own goals, preferences, and ideas.

In addition, these independence dimensions of the "I" are inseparable from interdependence because an individual's attitudes are not only derived from social experiences but are also expressed within social contexts, thus enabling a person to establish and maintain his or her own differentiated position in relation to others. "I" and "Me" activities also represent interrelated or inseparable dimensions of independence and interdependence because they complement one another in the process of self-construction. As inseparable dimensions of self-construction, they enable individuals to contribute to and change the very structuring of the social attitudes and customary patterns of engagement that simultaneously shape their selfing activities. More specifically:

> The response of the "I" [to the "Me"] involves adaptation, but an adaptation which affects not only the self but also the social environment which helps

to constitute the self; that is, it implies a view of evolution in which the individual affects its own environment as well as being affected by it. . . . There is always a mutual relationship of the individual and the community in which the individual lives. (Mead, 1934/1962, pp. 214–215)

In this way, an individual's process of self-construction represents an individually active reflection of the social group's values and attitudes that is established through social interactions. The social group, in turn, is shaped by the unique reactions and ideas of its constituent individuals. Although the "I" and "Me" activities that together constitute the process of self-construction as a whole may be distinguished analytically, they are experientially inseparable aspects of human functioning. Thus, they occur in an ongoing interrelation (Marková, 2000), indicating how neither independence nor interdependence takes precedence within Mead's unifying framework.

Independence and Interdependence in Cooley's Conceptualization of Self-Construction

As another American pragmatist, Cooley (1864–1929) and his overall approach to human functioning shared Mead's emphasis on understanding and describing human functioning in relation to the exigencies of daily living and as socially constituted through symbolic mediation. Within the pragmatist framework, Cooley also eschewed dualisms, and his conceptualization of self-construction involved inseparable meanings and dimensions of independence and interdependence (Schubert, 1998). This inseparability between independence and interdependence was evident in Cooley's claim that, "A separate individual is an abstraction unknown to experience, and so likewise is society when regarded as something apart from individuals" (1902, p. 1). He went on to say:

> I do not see that life presents two distinct and opposing tendencies that can properly be called individualism and socialism, any more than that there are two distinct and opposing entities, society and the individual, to embody these tendencies. The phenomena usually called individualistic are always socialistic in the sense that they are expressive of tendencies growing out of the general life, and, contrariwise, the so-called socialistic phenomena have always an obvious individual aspect. (1902, p. 5)

Thus, within this framework, both independence and interdependence are implicated in self-construction, and any separation between these dimensions of self occurs only in analytic emphasis.

More specifically, according to Cooley (1902), a social self is "that which is designated in common speech by the pronouns of the first person singular, 'I,' 'me,' 'my,' 'mine,' and 'myself' " (p. 136), and this " 'I' of common language always has more or less distinct reference to other people as well as the speaker" (pp. 136–137). Insofar as any kind of "common speech" involves social interaction, self-construction, in turn, always involves a person's communicative expression of his or her own distinct and differentiated position as an individual in relation to others within cultural practices. In particular, when referring to his or her own position in relation to others through the use of varied personal pronouns, an individual is typically referring to his or her individual "opinions, purposes, desires, claims, and the like" (Cooley, 1902, p. 144).

Cooley further pointed out:

> What we call "me," "mine," or "myself" is, then, not something separate from the general life, but the most interesting part of it, a part whose interest arises from the very fact that it is both general and individual. That is, we care for it just because it is that phase of the mind that is living and striving in the common life, trying to impress itself upon the minds of others. "I" is a militant social tendency, working to hold and enlarge its place in the general current of tendencies. So far as it can it waxes, as all life does. To think of it as apart from society is a palpable absurdity of which no one could be guilty who really *saw* it as a fact of life. (1902, pp. 149–150)

Within this conceptualization of self-construction, dimensions of independence and interdependence are inseparably interrelated as an individual establishes, maintains, and expresses his or her differentiated position in a social network, thereby also ideally finding individual personal fulfillment through social relationships. In addition to providing a forum for self-expression, social interaction allows for individual self-enhancement because interacting with others, who occupy their own distinct positions within the social world, provides opportunities for exposure to new perspectives that an individual may appropriate. In this way, independence and interdependence are inseparable dimensions of self-construction as individuality is expressed socially and as social interactions provide fodder for transforming one's individuality.

More specifically, according to Cooley (1902), social self-construction is most often cast in the form of a "reflected or looking-glass self" (p. 152). A looking-glass self is constituted by imagining and reacting to others' judgments of one's own being and behavior in varied social situations. Cooley explained further that a looking-glass self consists of the following three component processes: "the imagination of our appearance to the other person; the imagination of his judgment of that appearance, and some sort of self-feeling, such as pride or mortification" (p. 152). Such a looking-glass self clearly involves interdependence insofar as it is constituted through imagining and reacting to other people. At the same time, the integration of these three component processes involves a mentally and physically independent or separate individual who constructs ideas about others' opinions and then also constructs his or her own positive or negative emotional reactions to those imagined opinions.

Another meaning of independence is further evident in this conceptualization of the looking-glass self in that there is an element of individual choice, or self-direction, regarding the others who serve as mirrors to an individual's own conduct. That is, it is the opinions of others whom an individual values, in some way, that contribute most to the phenomenon of the looking-glass self. As Cooley pointed out, a person "can hold on to some influences and reject others, choose his leaders, individualize his conformity; and so work out a characteristic and fairly consistent career" (1902, p. 207), thus enabling him or her to be a unique reflection of social processes.

Without identifying specific stages of self-construction, Cooley outlined a general sequence for the development of a looking-glass self that begins during infancy. Initially, children construct connections between their own actions and the effects of those actions on others. As he or she makes these connections, "The child appropriates the visible actions of his parent or nurse, over which he finds he has some control, in quite the same way as he appropriates one of his own members [i.e., body parts] or a plaything" (Cooley, 1902, pp. 164–165). Then, as children purposefully try to engage others in particular ways, "Strong joy and grief depend upon the treatment this rudimentary social self receives" (Cooley, 1902, p. 166).

Soon, children begin to differentiate among people, and then they move on to imagining the reactions of varied others who treat them in different ways. As children continue to make such discriminations among people, the looking-glass self ultimately involves a progressive appropriation of the opinions and judgments of valued others, which guide an individual's attitudes toward his or her own behavior and being, including his or her ongoing social action. In turn, being able to imagine the reactions of others in a coherent way also ultimately enables a person to engage in self-direction on the basis of an appropriated social self-structure. Cooley explained this process as follows: "When we speak of a person as independent of opinion, or self-sufficient, we can only mean that, being of a constructive and stable character, he does not have to recur every day to the visible presence of his approvers, but can supply their places by imagination" (1902, p. 207). Although self-sufficiency and having one's own opinions may be conceptualized as dimensions of independence, it is evident that within Cooley's framework it is impossible to define this (or any) aspect of self-construction as either wholly independent or interdependent.

With regard to imagining and reacting to the opinions of others, Cooley took pains to discuss the importance of maintaining a balance between interrelated individual or independent, and social or interdependent, self-dimensions. That is, a person should not be unduly influenced by the opinions of others, and a person should simultaneously not dismiss others' judgments as irrelevant to him or herself. As Cooley (1902) noted, "So long as a character is open and capable of growth it retains a corresponding impressibility, which is not weakness unless it swamps the assimilating and organizing faculty" (p. 176). In this way, openness to others makes continued individual self-progress possible. Using other words, Cooley also claimed that "A healthy self must be both vigorous and plastic, a nucleus of solid, well-knit private purpose and feeling, guided and nourished by sympathy [with others]" (p. 157). In addition to taking social sympathy as a guide for personal goals and feelings, people who avoid focusing excessively on either independent or interdependent dimensions of self-construction should be able to ward off any "peculiarity of self-feeling" that results from being "out of joint with their social environment" (Cooley, 1902, p. 227).

Independence and Interdependence in Erikson's Theory of Identity Construction

In his psychosocial theory of identity, Erikson (1902–1990) explicitly sought to explain individual identity construction in relation to the social experiences that are afforded by direct relationships, as well as wider sociocultural expectations and traditions (1950/1963, 1959/1980, 1968, 1982). According to Erikson, identity construction is a life-span process that consists of eight stages, each of which is characterized by a specific "psychosocial" conflict that enables a person to reorganize his or her identity, or sense of self, as a distinct mental and physical individual who engages with and is recognized by others. To further understand this view of self- or identity construction, we now turn to a consideration of the first five stages of Erikson's theory, which take place during infancy, childhood, and adolescence. Within Erikson's framework, each stage's psychosocial conflict may be resolved either positively or negatively, and my analysis focuses on the positive resolution to each conflict.

The first psychosocial stage or conflict experienced in infancy is known as *trust versus mistrust*. As the positive resolution to this conflict, developing trust involves a sense of trust in others, a basic sense of trust in oneself, and a sense of one's own trustworthiness to others. At least two of these three modes of trust (i.e., trusting others and viewing oneself as someone whom others can trust) point to how forming an identity begins with conceptions of interdependence, which further provide the basis for an individual's general approach to interpersonal interactions. In addition, being able to trust oneself as a separate person demonstrates how

Erikson's analysis includes conceptions of independence. According to Erikson, these varied aspects of trust are constructed through an infant's earliest caregiving interactions and relationships, which are characterized by mutual regulation.

The second psychosocial conflict or stage in Erikson's theory involves *autonomy versus shame and doubt*. Constructing autonomy at this time consists of a sense of oneself as a separate agent who makes individual choices, thus revealing another conception of independence. However, Erikson related this conception of autonomy to conceptions of interdependence by asserting that autonomy develops in the context of supportive social relationships, and that autonomous action requires social structuring within a wider institutional framework. Also indicating how conceptions of independence and interdependence are interrelated in Erikson's theory, a person's conception of his or her own autonomy ideally eventually extends to others who are increasingly recognized as autonomous agents with whom one can enter into social engagement. This idea that conceptualizing oneself and others as autonomous individuals who can enter into relationships with one another may be interpreted as representing a view of people as essentially separate. That is, rather than being fundamentally connected, people are separate and must explicitly arrange to have social contact with other isolated individuals. However, within Erikson's overall framework, constructing oneself as autonomous takes place in relation to others, suggesting that there is no autonomy without social connectedness. In addition, the idea that autonomous individuals enter into relationships with other autonomous individuals suggests that individuals may be temporally prior to some specific relationships, but not to relationships per se.

Once autonomy is established, the third psychosocial stage involves a conflict between *initiative and guilt*. With initiative comes a "truly free sense of enterprise" (Erikson, 1959/1980, p. 86) or a person's ability to establish and pursue his or her own goals. For a young child going through this stage, such self-directed initiative is inseparable from interdependence expectations because it involves imagining future social goals and social roles. Erikson explained further that a child with a sense of initiative is "eager and able to make things cooperatively, to combine with other children for the purpose of constructing and planning, and he is willing to profit from teachers and to emulate ideal prototypes" (Erikson, 1950/1963, p. 258). Independence and interdependence are again inherently intertwined within this conceptualization of initiative insofar as the goals that are initiated and pursued by a distinct individual are social goals that are shaped by and carried out with others. Moreover, as a child imagines him or herself pursuing future social goals within a wider societal context, he or she also begins to "gain some insight into the institutions, functions, and roles which will permit his responsible participation" as an adult (Erikson, 1950/1963, p. 256). This latter aspect of initiative reveals the importance of eventually viewing oneself as an individual whose initiative has wider societal significance.

The final psychosocial conflict to be resolved during childhood involves *industry versus inferiority*, when a child establishes a sense of being useful as he or she starts learning to "be a worker and potential provider" (Erikson, 1950/1963, pp. 258–259), and "to win recognition by producing things" (Erikson, 1950/1963, p. 259). In many cultures, such industry develops for children as they go to school. According to Erikson, industry in school settings is coupled with a developing sense of social duty or obligation as children engage in activities that are prescribed and structured by others. Somewhat idealistically, Erikson (1959/1980) described this stage as "socially a most decisive stage: since industry involves doing things beside and with others, a first sense of *division of labor* and of *equality of opportunity* develops at this time" (p. 93). Within this view, an industrious person is one whose individual productivity is connected to others. Moreover, conceptions of independence and interdependence are further interrelated as Erikson placed an individual's sense of industry within a wider socioeconomic context that expands the individual's identity beyond his or her immediate or direct social interactions and prepares the individual for functioning within wider societal networks.

Movement through these four stages during infancy and childhood provides the foundations for the critical stage of *identity versus identity diffusion or role confusion* during adolescence. Erikson posited that, during this stage, adolescents evaluate previous identifications and construct an integrated, continuous, and coherent sense of themselves in relation to others. Erikson (1959/1980) explained, "The conscious feeling of having a *personal identity* is based on two simultaneous observations: the immediate perception of one's selfsameness and continuity in time; and the simultaneous perception of the fact that others recognize one's sameness and continuity" (p. 22). In addition, for adolescents, "identity gains real strength only from wholehearted and consistent recognition of real accomplishment, that is, achievement that has meaning in their culture" (Erikson, 1959/1980, p. 95).

In this way, identity construction involves defining oneself as a separate individual, as well as in terms of specific relationships and a broader sociocultural context, all of which were taken by Erikson to be historically situated and shaped by cultural traditions (Sorrell & Montgomery, 2001). Constructing such an identity takes place through experimenting with some of the different possible social roles that are available to adolescents in their sociocultural contexts. Through such culturally situated experimentation, adolescents act as individuals who explore identity options and make identity choices to construct a coherent, integrated identity that permits a "temporal-spatial continuity" over time (Côté & Levine, 2002, p. 16).

In addition to exploring social roles, according to Erikson, this kind of experimentation requires the support and guidance of older generations, and thus does not necessarily imply breaking ties with parents or other older relatives (Roeser et al., 2000). Ultimately, an individual identifies "a niche in some section of his society, a niche which is firmly defined and yet seems to be uniquely made for him" (Erikson, 1959/1980, p. 120). Identifying such a niche represents an interrelation between independence and interdependence because it is not only identified through social engagement but it also enables a person to participate in society (Waterman, 1992) by expressing his or her separate individuality. Erikson further addressed how independence and interdependence dimensions are inseparable in adolescent identity construction:

> It is this identity of something in the individual's core with an essential aspect of a group's inner coherence which is under consideration here: for the young individual must learn to be most himself where he means most to others—those others, to be sure, who have come to mean most to him. The term "identity" expresses such a mutual relation in that it connotes both a persistent sameness within oneself (selfsameness) and a persistent sharing of some kind of essential character with others. (1959/1980, p. 109)

This description of adolescent identity construction, along with the ones quoted in the preceding paragraphs, does not portray adolescent identity formation as a time for separating oneself from others. On the contrary, according to Erikson, the identity transformations that individual adolescents undergo are inseparable from their connections to others and from their functioning within a wider societal network. Moreover, connections to others may be strengthened as an adolescent's sense of subjective continuity and sense of individuality are shared with others.

Elaborating on Erikson: The Inseparability of Independence and Interdependence Within Varied Domains of Identity. Empirical elaborations of Erikson's theory, beginning with Marcia's (1966) efforts to operationalize and investigate "degree of ego identity" (p. 551), revolve around the view that Erikson's "simple dichotomy of identity versus identity confusion" (Marcia, 1980, p. 161) does not adequately account for the complexities of adolescent identity construction. As Marcia (1980) pointed out, identity construction "does not happen neatly" (p. 160), but "gets done by bits and pieces" (p. 161). Accordingly, Marcia suggested that identity formation be analyzed in terms of the extent to which an adolescent has gone through a period of crisis or experimentation with different identity options, and also the extent to which an adolescent is committed to a particular identity option. Using interview and/or questionnaire methods, adolescents may be rated as high or low on these two dimensions, thus yielding four possible identity statuses.

The status of *identity achievement* refers to someone who has gone through a period of active questioning and identity exploration and is now committed to a particular identity. The *identity moratorium* status refers to someone who is currently in the midst of a period of active questioning or identity experimentation but is not committed to any particular identity. The *identity foreclosure* status refers to someone who is committed to a particular identity without having gone through a period of questioning or experimentation. Finally, the *identity diffusion* status characterizes someone who is not committed to any particular identity option and is also not actively exploring any identity options. During the course of the adolescent life phase, adolescents may change identity statuses in varied ways (Marcia, 1980; Waterman, 1982). For example, a person who is in identity diffusion may move into the moratorium status by starting to actively explore identity possibilities, or that person may move from diffusion into the foreclosure status by choosing a particular identity without exploring other possibilities.

Conceptualizing the identity statuses also turns on the idea that active exploration of identity options takes place in relation to multiple domains of behavior. When forming their identities, adolescents do not form just one overall identity but instead construct different identities or aspects of themselves in relation to their concrete activities and interactions in varied cultural practices. Thus, analyses of identity construction not only involve discerning overall shifts among the various identity statuses, but also require a consideration of identity status change within different domains of functioning. Marcia's and others' early attempts to investigate adolescent identity formation in relation to different domains of functioning included occupational aspirations, religious beliefs, and political ideology. However, it was argued that identity formation in relation to these domains is "intrapersonal," involving "an internalized process that impacts on the individual's purpose and direction in a rather singularized fashion" (Archer, 1992, p. 35). Accordingly, these domains were quickly pronounced to be male biased. To address female identity concerns, subsequent studies included other domains, such as family roles, gender roles, dating, and friendship. These domains are considered to be more relevant to women because they are "interpersonal" and "are primarily perceived as belief about self concerning connection with others" (Archer, 1992, p. 35).

With these definitions, we find ourselves confronting issues of independence and interdependence in relation to gender, and it is not surprising that identity researchers are engaged in vigorous debates about this issue (e.g., Archer, 1985, 1989, 1992; Archer & Waterman, 1988; Cramer,

2000; Patterson, Sochting, & Marcia, 1992; Thorbecke & Grotevant, 1982). Given the current approach to independence and interdependence, it is not my purpose here to consider whether males or females are more or less independent or interdependent, or whether some domains of functioning are more or less applicable to male or female experiences. Instead, the current approach leads to considering how issues of both independence and interdependence are theoretically implicated in the identity construction process no matter what the domain under consideration happens to be. It seems to me that all of the domains that have been studied—from political ideology to career choices to family life—involve issues of both independence and interdependence. Thus, labeling some domains as relatively intrapersonal and others as relatively interpersonal is problematic. As already noted, making choices about one's political ideology has been viewed as an intrapersonal or independence-oriented domain. Any political ideology, however, encompasses a host of interpersonal or interdependence issues, from the structuring of power relationships among people to pursuing the common goals of a collective. Career choices also entail orienting oneself in relation to wider social institutional and economic structures and, during the course of daily work, most careers involve concrete interactions with other people.

This point that it is problematic to demarcate strict boundaries between intrapersonal and interpersonal, or independent and interdependent, identity domains is not lost on contemporary Eriksonians. For example, Archer (1992) raised the following questions about labeling the varied identity domains as intrapersonal or interpersonal: "Are the terms *intrapersonal* and *interpersonal* useful and meaningful? How does one determine this? What determines which domains belong in each category?" (p. 36). Archer asserted that discerning whether and how independence and interdependence issues are particularized in identity constructions requires researchers "first to listen to the narratives of the many respondents to hear them tell us how they perceive their experiences within each of [the identity] domains" (pp. 36–37). The current conceptual approach also provides a way to address Archer's questions by leading us away from the idea that an identity domain can only be either intra- or interpersonal. Instead, the current approach leads to discerning how varied intra- and interpersonal issues are interrelated as adolescents construct identities during the course of participating with others in varied cultural practices.

SELF-CONSTRUCTING ACTIVITIES

Embedded within different conceptions of self, our central themes that independence and interdependence are essential to and inseparable within human experience are common to these three classic theorists. The theories of Mead, Cooley, and Erikson also point to some of the varied ways in which the word *self* has been conceptualized. Although increasing theoretical and empirical attention is being paid to self-issues, *self* remains a troublesome construct to define and investigate. In the context of the upcoming discussion, which is geared toward discerning how children and adolescents perceive and think about their own experiences, perspectives, and behavior, it is useful to borrow from these classic theorists and conceptualize self as an individual's ongoing and dynamic construction of his or her behavior, perspective, and experience. As such, self is not a static or tangible substance located deep within the individual, in some physical space, such as the pineal gland.

Claiming that a person "has" a self implies a single static substance or essence that a person carries around or possesses, as a person possesses an arm or a liver. Instead, rather than saying that people have selves, we may say that as self-aware individuals who are capable of self-reflection, people engage in varied self-organizing, self-constructing, or self-constituting activities that enable them to make sense of their lives and orient themselves in relation to others as they participate in cultural practices (Davies & Harré, 1990; Penuel & Wertsch, 1995; Youniss & Yates, 2000). Rather than claiming that people have a single static or essential self, I am taking the position that as people engage in self-constructing activities, they construct multiple selves in different situations and over time. At the same time that self-constructing activities are dynamic and support constructing oneself in different ways in different situations, there may simultaneously be continuity and consistency in a person's subjective experience across situations and over time (e.g., Chandler et al., 2003). A person may also construct some aspects of his or her perspective, behavior, and experience in relatively consistent ways across situations and over time.

More specifically, self-constructing activities may include thinking about and representing aspects of one's own behavior and experience to oneself. For example, an adolescent may lie awake at night, wondering, "Why did I do that stupid thing in math class today? I'm sure that the new kid in class hates me." Self-construction may also include thinking about and constructing aspects of one's own behavior, perspective, and experience while participating in cultural practices with others. For example, on the playground a child might ask another child, "Why is your jacket red?" or in school a child might be called on to tell the class what he or she did during a recent summer vacation. My observations of Euro-American parents' play practices with their 1- to 3-year-olds (presented in chap. 4) demonstrate how parents pose questions, providing the children with opportunities to think about and construct themselves socially. Based on the belief that a person cannot know another's perspective, Kaluli children may be asked to clarify their perspectives to others (Ochs & Schieffelin,

1984/1988). Or, in an interview with a psychologist, a child or adolescent may be asked to describe him or herself.

Without being asked specifically to describe or explain themselves, children and adolescents may also construct themselves by orienting or "positioning" (Bamberg, 2004; Davies & Harré, 1990) themselves in relation to others as they participate in cultural practices with their parents, peers, and teachers. For example, as adolescents spend increasing amounts of time with friends, they may discuss, and thereby construct, their perspectives, experiences, or future goals in relation to each other. Some studies of young children's speech during the course of social interaction also provide insight into how they go about constructing or positioning themselves as self-directed individuals in relation to others (Budwig, 1989; Budwig & Wiley, 1995; Imbens-Bailey & Pan, 1998). Although English-learning 2-year-olds often do not follow the grammatical rules of standard English when using self-reference pronouns (i.e., *I, my, me*), a functional analysis reveals that they do use these pronouns in systematic ways to mark varied aspects of their own self-direction or agency. Based on observations of play interactions between 2-year-olds and their caregivers, as well as peers, Budwig (1989) explained:

> *I* tends to be used in utterances expressing the children's internal states and intentions, utterances ranking Low in agentivity. In contrast *my* appears in clauses that often rank High in agentivity. In particular *my* appears in conjunction with highly kinetic verbs referring to telic actions. The uses of *my* link up with utterances in which the child acts as a prototypical agent bringing about a change of state. . . . In contrast to the use of *my*, in which the child acts to bring about a change in some object or activity, with *me* the child acts as instigator of actions that are directed back onto the Self. In such instances the child takes the view of Self as affected agent. (pp. 273–279)

Insofar as children are referring to and positioning themselves in a social context, such constructions of individual agency are inseparable from social concerns. As Cooley (1902) asserted, the use of self-referential pronouns during social communication always functions to position the speaker in relation to others. Thus, when a child uses personal pronouns, grammatically or extragrammatically, he or she is not expressing a kind of separate agency that reflects a wholly separate individual acting on or experiencing the world on his or her own. For example, a child might say "my pour the tea" while pouring pretend tea into his or her grandfather's pretend cup during a pretend tea party. In this situation, the child's declaration of agency through the use of "my" is inseparable from his or her interactions with the grandfather.

Given this conceptualization of self-construction, we may now consider how self-construction involves independence and interdependence. I focus on one of the self-constructing activities mentioned previously; namely, reflecting on and constructing oneself in relation to inquiring others, because so much developmental research to date has used interview methods that call on children and adolescents to represent themselves to others. The language data generated by interview methods are not taken to be direct manifestations of static or preexisting selves. Instead, they may be understood as ways of constructing aspects of one's behavior, perspective, and experience in relation to another person. As such, data from interview studies can be analyzed to discern how multifaceted and interrelated independence and interdependence meanings and activity dimensions are reflected in children's and adolescents' self-constructions.

More specifically, insofar as self-construction during the cultural practice of an interview involves a social situation in which someone is asking a child or adolescent to construct him or herself, that child or adolescent is constructing him or herself interdependently. In other words, the child's or adolescent's self-construction depends, in part, on interacting with the interviewer. At the same time, a child or adolescent is aware of him or herself and is actively thinking about his or her own experiences. Thus, self-construction clearly involves what I have been referring to as the independence activity dimension of self-awareness/reflection. In addition, as a self-directing individual, a person may actively choose to talk about certain aspects of his or her experience and not others, thus pointing to how independent self-direction is also involved in the process of self-construction.

In these ways, independence and interdependence represent inseparable dimensions of self-construction, just as any activities within a cultural practice involve inseparable independence and interdependence activity dimensions. Moreover, when specifically asked to reflect on themselves, people, including children and adolescents, cannot help but draw on their experiences as individuals in relation to others that have been particularized in varied cultural practices, such as parent–child interactions or during school. For example, a child might construct him or herself by claiming, "I'm friends with Gerti," or an adolescent might state, "I think I'm someone others can trust." In these cases, individual self-construction is inseparable from social experience, and thus connections to others partly constitute the process of self-construction.

In addition, as children and adolescents construct themselves, they may be expected to represent their socially situated behavior, perspectives, and experiences in ways that reflect multifaceted and interrelated cultural independence and interdependence meanings. This expectation is based on the position that any experiences as individuals in relation to others take place in specific cultures, where specific independence and interdependence meanings are enacted in cultural practices. Thus, it follows that anyone's self-constructions will reflect particular cultural meanings of independence and interdependence. In other words, self-constructing activities involve using or appropriating cultural independence and interdependence meanings to construct aspects of one's experience, perspective, and behavior.

SELF-CONSTRUCTION DURING CHILDHOOD AND ADOLESCENCE

Going Beyond First Glances to Discern the Inseparability of Independence and Interdependence

One comprehensive and in-depth self-interview study was conducted by Damon and Hart (1988) with racially mixed American middle-class 4- to 17-year-olds. This study was based on James' (1890/1983) theory of self-construction, thus requiring us to first briefly summarize James' position. According to James, the "Me" part of self-construction represents a person's constructions of his or her basic self-characteristics. Using Damon and Hart's (1988) contemporary terminology, the "Me" consists of physical, social, psychological, and active characteristics. Physical "Me" characteristics include constructions of one's physical features, as well as material possessions; social "Me" characteristics include a person's self-constructions in terms of social roles, relationships, and group memberships; psychological "Me" characteristics include constructions of personality characteristics, cognitive processes, beliefs, and values; and active "Me" characteristics include constructions of one's typical activities and skills.

Damon and Hart's interviews indicated that even children as young as 4 years old describe themselves in multifaceted ways, and in Damon and Hart's study, the participants' self-characteristics "were well distributed" (p. 97) among the four "Me" characteristic categories across all age groups. These findings have been corroborated by other studies showing that, toward the end of early childhood, Euro-American children's self-constructions include statements about their physical features, specific relationships, group memberships, and abilities or competencies within specific activities (Harter, 1999).

Although these studies point to how children and adolescents construct themselves in terms of multifaceted physical, social, psychological, and active "Me" characteristics, these findings cannot be translated into independence and interdependence issues in a straightforward way. At first glance, Damon and Hart's (1988) findings could lead to the conclusion that interdependence, in the form of social "Me" characteristics, comprises just one quarter of American children's self-constructions, whereas independence is more prevalent because physical, psychological, and active "Me" characteristics comprise the remaining bulk of the "Me" self.

However, a closer look at Damon and Hart's coding examples of the various "Me" characteristics shows how physical, psychological, and active "Me" characteristics are inseparable from interdependence. Consider, for instance, the following examples of psychological self-statements (Damon & Hart, 1988, p. 66): "I'm the kind of person who loves being with my friends" and "I'm really good with people." Although these statements represent personality characteristics, and thus classifying them as psychological "Me" characteristics makes sense, they cannot be separated from social concerns. Similarly, some active characteristics might include statements about social activities, such as playing varied team sports. We may recall that Mead used the game of baseball to explicate his ideas about social self-construction. As a team sport, baseball is an inherently social game that simply cannot be played alone, and it also involves clear roles for individuals in relation to others. Another striking example from Damon and Hart's interviews of a fundamentally social activity is, "Yesterday I went to visit my cousins at their new house" (p. 60). In this case, one might even envision a family getting together, with the new home owners welcoming their guests into their new house.

In addition to asking study participants to describe themselves, Damon and Hart's interviews further involved investigating how children and adolescents understand their varied stated "Me" characteristics. Toward that end, Damon and Hart asked participants to explain why their self-characteristics are important to them. Based on these explanations, Damon and Hart identified four levels of self-understanding during childhood and adolescence, which provide us with yet more ways to discern how independence and interdependence meanings are inseparable within self-constructing activities. According to Damon and Hart, the first level of self-understanding occurs during early childhood, when young children comprehend their self-characteristics in terms of simple ideas without further elaboration. During middle childhood, children become increasingly likely to discuss their self-characteristics in comparison to others (Level 2) and then later in terms of how their characteristics affect relationships with others (Level 3). An example of Level 3 could be of a girl who constructs herself in terms of some physical "Me" characteristics, such as being big and tall. When asked why these physical "Me" characteristics are important, this child might go on to explain that sometimes other people seem to be afraid of big and tall people, and so it is difficult for her to make friends. With regard to independence and interdependence, we may say that this child's construction of herself as a separate physical being is inseparable from constructing herself in relation to others.

Movement into the fourth level of self-understanding occurs during adolescence and involves understanding one's "Me" characteristics in terms of future goals and/or a personal value system. Again at first glance, this level of self-understanding might seem highly independence oriented because a person constructs him or herself in terms of individually chosen personal values or works toward achieving individually defined goals. However, as some of Damon and Hart's category examples indicate, an adolescent's future goals may include varied social aspirations ranging from establishing and maintaining direct personal relationships to being engaged with others in professional situations. In one interview excerpt, a study participant constructed him or herself in terms of a psychological "Me" characteristic as "I am someone who believes that everybody is created equal" (p. 69). This participant then went on to explain that this self-characteristic is important "Because I want to work for equal rights for everybody. I'm going to be a lawyer and take cases and see that everyone gets rights" (p. 69). This participant's claim of believing that everybody is created equal represents a psychological "Me" characteristic that is inseparable from interdependence issues because it is a belief about people. In addition, the participant's discussion of this self-characteristic in relation to his or her future goals even more clearly shows how he or she is conceptualizing him or herself in relation to a wider societal network in which he or she will eventually participate.

Although one can certainly argue over how to define "personal values," one function of personal values is that they provide people with standards for relating to others. Thus, although they may be individually chosen, they are also fundamentally social. In addition, as with any aspect of human behavior, personal values are constructed through social interactions, and they are also typically held in common with at least some others. Again, a closer look at Damon and Hart's interview examples points to how self-understanding in terms of personal values involves interrelated or inseparable independence and interdependence meanings. In one case, when asked, "What are you like?", a participant answered, "I don't have many things." The participant then said that this physical "Me" characteristic is important because "It's not fair to have a lot of things when some people don't have anything" (p. 67). In this case, understanding stated "Me" characteristics in terms of a personal value system involves orienting oneself within a wider societal network.

During the course of conducting numerous studies of self-development, Harter has also pointed out that as stated self-characteristics become increasingly differentiated during childhood and adolescence, the potential for contradictory or inconsistent self-characteristics increases (e.g., Harter, 1999; Harter, Bresnick, Bouchey, & Whitesell, 1997; Harter & Monsour, 1992). For example, a person might construct him or herself as both outgoing and shy. At first young children are unlikely to notice any inconsistencies in these self-characteristics, and then older children and young adolescents tend to find themselves rather confused by varied contradictory self-characteristics. Ultimately, older adolescents explain and integrate perceived contradictory characteristics by distinguishing among domains of self-construction or by appealing to social contextual issues. Thus, if asked how she can be both outgoing and shy, an adolescent might explain that she is reserved with her family and outgoing with her friends. In this way, using social relationships and social contexts to explain varied modes of self-construction points to how Euro-Americans do indeed define themselves contextually, and not solely in terms of immutable and decontextualized self-characteristics. Moreover, Harter's research shows that older adolescents even *seek* such social variability because they tend to "normalize potential contradictions, asserting that it is desirable to be different across relational contexts and that it would be weird or strange to be the same with different people" (Harter, 1999, p. 86).

The Inseparability of Independence and Interdependence in Adolescent Self-Construction

As adolescents undergo the biological changes associated with puberty, being physically separate may become an increasingly salient aspect of self-construction. At the same time, however, the physical changes of puberty place adolescents in relation to others in new ways, suggesting that adolescents' constructions of themselves as separate physical individuals are inseparable from their constructions of themselves in relation to others. In addition, as adolescents advance cognitively into the formal operational stage, they are able to reflect on themselves in increasingly complex ways. They are also likely to spend a lot of time engaging in self-reflection (Demo & Savin-Williams, 1992), but such self-reflection does not necessarily occur in isolation from others. Instead, based on research with primarily Euro-American samples, numerous studies of adolescence have suggested that self-construction becomes particularly or intensively social as children move from late childhood into the adolescent life phase (e.g., Brooks-Gunn & Paikoff, 1992; Csikszentmihalyi & Larson, 1984; Demo & Savin-Williams, 1992; Fasick, 1984; Greenberg, Siegel, & Leitch, 1983; Harter, 1999; Harter et al., 1997; Josselson, 1994; Newman & Newman, 1976; Offer et al., 1988; Ryan & Lynch, 1989; Steinberg & Silverberg, 1986).

The relatively intensive social nature of adolescent self-construction is often partly attributed to the increased time that adolescents spend with their peers, particularly their friends. Years of research demonstrate that friends and friendships are "transcendentally important" (Hartup, 1992, p. 186) to Euro-American children and adolescents, indicating the value of interdependence for developing Euro-Americans. Similarly, Csikszentmihalyi and Larson (1984) reminded readers that "Everybody knows that teenagers love being with each other—that they crave conversation with friends, in person or on the phone, almost more than they crave food" (p. 155).

The results of varied investigations show that friendships during childhood and adolescence are generally characterized by cooperation, reciprocal help, reciprocal consideration, and reciprocity in supporting and validating each other's perspectives (e.g., Aboud & Mendelson, 1996; Berndt, 1982; Buhrmester, 1996; Hartup, 1989, 1996; Newcomb & Bagwell, 1995; Rizzo, 1989; Youniss & Smollar, 1985). Increasingly, adolescent friendships and adolescents' conceptions of friendships also revolve around issues of equality, commitment, loyalty, and intimacy (Savin-Williams & Berndt, 1990). Adolescents from varied socioeconomic and ethnic backgrounds report that their friendships are characterized by mutual help and advice, and that they are prepared to sacrifice some of their own goals and preferences to help their friends. Friendships are also seen by adolescents as being enduring relationships of commitment that can transcend momentary conflicts and that oblige friends to settle conflicts to maintain their relationships.

In a rather detailed study conducted by Csikszentmihalyi and Larson (1984), middle-class American high school students reported on their activities when they were paged at random intervals during the course of a week. These high school students reported that when they talk to their friends, they typically "discuss themselves and what kind of people they are. By so doing, they forge social identities—of themselves as individuals, but also of themselves as a group" (Csikszentmihalyi & Larson, 1984, pp. 173–174). As adolescents spend more time with friends, they may congregate in small groups (sometimes known as cliques) that provide them with opportunities to construct themselves, not only in terms of dyadic friendships but also in terms of dynamic relationship networks (Brown, 1990/1995). Within mutually supportive and accepting group and dyadic relationships, adolescents understand friendships as contexts for expressing and validating both their individuality as well as their similarity and connectedness to others (Lightfoot, 1997; Youniss & Smollar, 1985).

Because close friends during adolescence provide mutual empathy and positive feedback, they act as safe sounding boards for each other to construct their own opinions and values, and also for mutually validating each other's self-constructions (Harter, 1999; Youniss & Smollar, 1985). In these ways, independence and interdependence are inseparable as adolescents construct their individual points of view in relation to each other. Ultimately, according to Youniss and Smollar (1985), adolescents come to "the realization that the self does not stand alone" (p. 168) because self-understanding involves both "being understood by others and understanding them" (p. 169). In addition, adolescents spend time discussing themselves with their friends, thereby situating and constructing themselves in relation to others. In doing so, the adolescents in Csikszentmihalyi and Larson's (1984) pager study reported that they "feel more clear, open, and free" (p. 165) with their friends. Along similar lines, many adolescents claim to feel most themselves and able to express their "true" feelings and opinions with friends (Harter, 1999; Youniss & Smollar, 1985). These analyses indicate how "feeling free" and "being oneself" are socially situated experiences, and thus are not tantamount to self-containment or to viewing oneself in isolation from others.

At the same time that adolescents are spending more time with friends, parent–child relationships also figure importantly as contexts for adolescent self-construction (Greenberg et al., 1983; O'Koon, 1997; Youniss & Smollar, 1985). Although adolescents may spend less time with their families, they do not typically seek to sever ties with their families in pursuit of some kind of wholly self-contained or unattached self. Instead, as we saw in chapter 4, family ties remain important to adolescents, and as adolescents participate in relationships of individuation with their parents they may encounter new opportunities for constructing themselves as individuals in relation to others. For example, parents may grant children more latitude in making their own decisions, and, as we have discussed before, such self-direction may occur in social situations. Specifically with regard to adolescents, they may be making all kinds of social choices—from how to deal with friends and teachers to decisions about future social roles. Also, as adolescents contribute more input into family decisions, their individual preferences and opinions are integrated into family functioning in new ways, enabling the adolescents to transform their constructions of themselves as family members. Even as there may be more conflict between adolescents and their parents, such conflict enables adolescents to consider and accommodate varied points of view, and also, through conflict negotiation, to construct their individual perspectives in relation to other family members.

William James and Multiple Social Selves

Children's and adolescents' constructions of multiple social selves in the context of varied social situations, as well as contemporary analyses thereof, reflect and build on a long-standing tradition in American psychology, going back at least to James (1842–1910), another American pragmatist of the late 19th and early 20th centuries. As already mentioned, according to James, the social self is a constituent of the "Me" self. More specifically, James (1890/1983) began his discussion of a "man's" social self by defining it as "the recognition which he gets from his mates" (p. 281). He then went on to explain that:

> Properly speaking *a man has as many social selves as there are individuals who recognize him* and carry an image of him in their mind. To wound any one of these his images is to wound him. But as the individuals who carry the images fall naturally into classes, we may practically say that he has as many different social selves as there are distinct *groups* of persons about whose opinion he cares. He generally shows a different side of himself to each of these different groups. Many a youth who is demure enough before his parents and teachers, swears and swaggers like a pirate among his "tough" young friends. We do not show ourselves to our children as to our club-companions, to our customers as to the laborers we employ, to our own masters and employers as to our intimate friends. From this there results what practically is a division of the man into several selves; and this may be a discordant splitting, as where one is afraid to let one set of his acquaintances know him as he is elsewhere; or it may be a perfectly harmonious division of labor, as where one tender to his children is stern to the soldiers or prisoners under his command. (pp. 281–282)

This description suggests that a person's social selves are constructed during direct interactions with others and also in terms of a person's individualized role within different social groups. Harmony among these varied social selves does not seem to involve being the same in all social situations, and there even seems to be an implication that rigid stasis across social situations would be problematic.

According to James (1890/1983), harmony among a person's multiple social selves involves a "subjective synthesis" (p. 315) that provides "an unceasing sense of personal existence" (p. 316). Thus, as people construct themselves in multiple or socially shifting ways, there is, in all human beings, a subjective experience of continuity and coordination among the different social selves. In this way, "Continuity makes us unite what dissimilarity might otherwise separate" (James, 1890/1983, p. 317). Using a cattle-herding metaphor, James further addressed how a person may subjectively experience continuity in the midst of different social selves:

> The various members of the collection thus set apart are felt to belong with each other whenever they are thought at all. The animal warmth . . . is their herd-mark, the brand from which they can never more escape. It runs through them all like a thread through a chaplet and makes them into a whole, which we treat as a unit, no matter how much in other ways the parts may differ. . . . The individual beasts do not stick together, for all that they wear the same brand. Each wanders with whatever accidental mate it finds. The herd's unity is only potential, its centre ideal, like the "centre of gravity" in physics, until the herdsman or owner comes. He furnishes a real centre of

accretion to which the beasts are driven and by which they are held. The beasts stick together by sticking severally to him. Just so, common-sense insists, there must be a real proprietor in the case of the selves, or else their actual accretion into a "personal consciousness" would never have taken place. (pp. 317–320)

In this explanation of continuity among multiple social selves, James acknowledged that a person's social self-constructions may be quite different across relationships and may seem unconnected at times. James even cautioned against making too much of any subjective experience of continuity or sameness among the varied social selves. Such caution suggests that James' conception of subjective continuity is not equivalent to an immutable and context-independent self, which (as mentioned in chap. 1) is so often taken to be the essence of Western self-construction, in contrast to what are often considered to be socially shifting non-Western self-constructions. Specifically, James wrote that such continuity:

must not be taken to mean more than these grounds warrant, or treated as a sort of metaphysical or absolute Unity in which all differences are overwhelmed. The past and present selves compared are the same just so far as they *are* the same, and no farther. A uniform feeling of "warmth," of bodily existence (or an equally uniform feeling of pure psychic energy?) pervades them all; and this is what gives them a *generic* unity, and makes them the same in *kind*. But this generic unity coexists with generic differences just as real as the unity. And if from the one point of view they are one self, from others they are as truly not one but many selves. And similarly of the attribute of continuity; it gives its own kind of unity to the self—that of mere connectedness, or unbrokenness, a perfectly definite phenomenal thing—but it gives not a jot or tittle more. (1890/1983, p. 318)

Based on this statement, I suspect that James might have considered contemporary accounts of a context-independent core Western self to be a tittle exaggerated. Instead, a core self was considered by James to be a subjective experience of oneself as a separate mental individual who is aware of his or her own continuity across social situations, as well as over time (Chandler, 2000; Chandler et al., 2003). Also comprising subjective experience as a separate mental being, James (1890/1983) suggested that all individuals feel or are aware of their own "palpitating inward life" (p. 287). This subjective experience involves being aware of oneself as a thinker and as an individual with distinct feelings, opinions, and goals. As a person constructs multiple social selves, he or she may still experience him or herself as separate and distinct from others in varied cultural practices. Thus, independence and interdependence represent inseparable dimensions of self-construction within James' theory insofar as a subjectively aware separate individual constructs him or herself in relation to others.

Although Western self-constructions may not be as static or context independent as sometimes described, they no doubt differ from self-constructions in other cultures in important ways. Accordingly, we now turn to a consideration of how independence and interdependence are particularized in Japanese self-constructions.

SELF-CONSTRUCTION IN JAPAN

In this section, I focus on some general considerations of Japanese self-construction because I have not come across enough studies in English to enable me to present an analysis of independence and interdependence that encompasses the childhood and adolescent years. Although my forays into the literature on Japanese self-construction are admittedly limited, I did not have to search far and wide before I came across varied analyses suggesting that it is inadequate to characterize Japanese self-construction as wholly interdependent (e.g., Kondo, 1987; Kuwayama, 1992/1995; Moeran, 1974/1986). Although interactive or social self-construction, involving "the awareness of self as defined, sustained, enhanced, or blemished through social interaction" (Lebra, 1992/1995, p. 106), is prevalent in Japan, much cultural room seems to exist for independent self-dimensions, just as we saw in chapters 4 and 5 that there is ample room for independence in Japanese parent–child interactions and school practices.

Different specific analytic approaches indicate that independence and interdependence are interrelated in varied ways, as Japanese self-constructing activities occur as people engage in relatively private or public cultural practices (e.g., Bachnik, 1992a/1995, 1992b, 1994; Doi, 1985/1988; Kondo, 1990, 1994; Lebra, 1992/1995; Odin, 1996; Rosenberger, 1992/1995; Tobin, 1992/1995). Alternating between public or outer and private or inner self-constructing activities may be understood in terms of varied Japanese independence and interdependence meanings. As noted in chapter 4, an individual is expected to engage in *enryo*, or restraint in public cultural practices, which then has implications for self-construction (Doi, 1973/2001). That is, *enryo* involves refraining from expressing one's personal opinions for the sake of maintaining social harmony. Thus, according to Lebra (1992/1995), people's behavior in public settings involves "self-effacement and modesty" (p. 108). Although practicing self-restraint in public is related to maintaining social harmony, independence is nevertheless implicated in public self-construction insofar as restraining oneself requires active self-direction on the part of an individual (Lanham

& Garrick, 1996; Lebra, 1994). Similarly, sensitivity to others is ideally "willing and self-generated" (Kondo, 1987, p. 261).

Although people may act with self-restraint in many cultural practices, it does not necessarily follow that the Japanese do not value individuality or that they do not express individual feelings, opinions, and ideas (Bachnik, 1994). Instead, the expression of those individual opinions may be reserved for private or informal social settings, in which conflicting opinions do not threaten a close relationship and in which *enryo* may be relaxed. Indeed, it is especially in the realm of one's private world, or ingroup, that unrestrained self-expression may be possible (Lebra, 1992/1995). As Kondo (1990) explained, "In one's inner circle there is no need to . . . worry about consequences of one's actions towards others. There is no need to hold back one's desires" (pp. 149–150). It is also in relationships characterized by *amae* that unrestrained self-expression may occur, thus providing a way for a person to construct and express his or her individuality as a separate mental being (Doi, 1973/2001, 1985; Kumagi & Kumagi, 1986).

According to Lebra (1992/1995), a social self or "interactional self is what occupies Japanese most of the time, and yet they are aware of its basically precarious, vulnerable, relative, unfixed nature" (p. 111). Invoking Mead, Lebra continued, "A more stable self, something like 'I,' more immune from social relativity, is sought inwardly. The socially, outwardly oriented interactional self is thus compensated for by the inner self" (p. 112). In addition, "It is the inner self that provides a fixed core for self-identity and subjectivity, and forms a potential basis of autonomy from the ever-insatiable demands from the social world. The inner self is also identified as the residence (shrine) of a god that each person is endowed with" (p. 112). Lebra (1992/1995) noted further that:

> At the center of the inner self is the *kokoro* which stands for heart, sentiment, spirit, will, or mind. While the outer self is socially circumscribed, the *kokoro* can be free, spontaneous, and even asocial. Further, the *kokoro* claims moral superiority over the outer self in that it is a reservoir of truthfulness and purity, uncontaminated by circumspections and contrivances to which the outer self is subject. (p. 112)

Along similar lines, Mathews' (1996) qualitative interview study of what makes life meaningful to adults in Japan and the United States pointed to independence as well as interdependence concerns in Japan. Using the Japanese word *ikigai* to connote that which makes life meaningful, Mathews claimed that, "while *ikigai as ittaikan* carries with it the premise that selves are most essentially their social roles, *ikigai as jiko jitsugen* carries with it the premise that there is an underlying self more essential than social role" (p. 18). Ultimately, when a person finds him or herself "under cross-pressures from inside and outside," Lebra (1992/1995) asserted that, "The imperative of conforming to interactional norms thus may give way to fidelity to one's inner self. 'Be faithful to yourself' (*jibun ni chujitsu ni*) becomes a final verdict" (p. 114).

If I may digress slightly for a moment, I would like to say that when I read that verdict, I was immediately reminded of Shakespeare's Western dictum, "To thine own self be true." This phrase from *Hamlet* implies a concern with constructing oneself as a separate or independent individual and as someone whose action is self-directed. However, understanding the full implications of the Shakespearean imperative requires reading at least two more lines. That is, Polonius instructed Laertes:

> This above all: to thine own self be true,
> And it must follow, as the night the day,
> Thou canst not then be fake to any man. (Shakespeare, 1963/1987, p. 52)

When viewed in context, being true to a separate self ultimately has implications for relationships, thus pointing to how self-direction and individuality are conceptualized in relation to social connections. These Shakespearean lines also suggest that being true to oneself as a separate individual is temporally prior to establishing and maintaining relationships with others, but it is not necessarily valued more than the relationships it facilitates.

Getting back to Japan, Doi (1973/2001) explained further that a person is considered "to have a self" (p. 132) if he or she "can maintain an independent self that is never negated by membership of the group" (p. 134). Within this framework, self-pathology may manifest itself in the form of an "individual's submersion in or submission to the group" (p. 138). If an individual submits to a group decision without "really" concurring, then he or she may lose a sense of individual control or self-direction. In contrast, when concurring with the group is experienced as an act of individual volition, individuality and self-direction are not suppressed and, hence, pathology is not manifest. These analyses take us back to issues raised in chapters 4 and 5 regarding the importance of willing conformity and how it may be fostered through Japanese parent–child interactions and some Japanese educational practices.

Some of these self-constructing issues are illustrated in a situation that arose in connection with Japan's role in Iraq during the spring of 2004. Specifically, on April 23, 2004, there was an article in *The New York Times* about the homecoming of three Japanese civilian aid workers who had been kidnapped in Iraq. *The New York Times* reported:

> The young Japanese civilians taken hostage in Iraq returned home this
> week, not to the warmth of a yellow-ribbon embrace but to a disapproving

nation's cold stare. Three of them, including a woman who helped street children on the streets of Baghdad, appeared on television two weeks ago as their knife-brandishing kidnappers threatened to slit their throats. A few days after their release, they landed here on Sunday, in the eye of a peculiarly Japanese storm. "You got what you deserve!" read one hand-written sign at the airport where they landed. "You are Japan's shame," another wrote on the Web site of one of the former hostages. They had "caused trouble" for everybody. The government, not to be outdone, announced it would bill the former hostages $6,000 for air fare. (Onishi, 2004)

Although no specific numbers were given, this report implied a rather widespread public condemnation of the hostages that seems to support a dichotomous interdependence view of Japanese culture. That is, instead of acting as good group members, and instead of heeding "a government advisory against traveling to Iraq" (Onishi, 2004), the three had acted to pursue their individual goals (in this case, risking their lives to help others), and thus had caused shame and trouble for the group, in this case all of Japan. By referring to the homecoming situation as "a peculiarly Japanese storm," *The New York Times* report also implied a contrast with cultures in which concerns for others and the wider social group are not emphasized over individual goals. Clearly, this report could be taken as a blow to the current theoretical approach to independence and interdependence. However, in keeping with the current theoretical approach and based on the research that I had been reading on Japanese culture, I suspected that there must be more to this story. Accordingly, I went to the Internet and Googled "Japan and Iraq." Google led me to *The Japan Times*, an English-language Japanese newspaper, and as I read through varied articles on the hostage situation, a complex situation began to unfold.

I found out that on April 9, 2004, *The Japan Times* reported that "Three Japanese civilians have been taken hostage in Iraq by a terrorist-related group that has threatened to kill them if Japan does not withdraw its troops from the country in three days." The hostages were released and eventually returned to Tokyo in mid-April. This hostage situation raised public questions about and criticisms of the Japanese Prime Minister's earlier controversial decision to deploy Japanese Self-Defense Forces in Iraq to contribute nonmilitary humanitarian and reconstruction assistance. Such questioning and criticism placed Prime Minister Junichiro Koizumi in a problematic political position, and on April 11 it was reported that an opposition leader of the Social Democratic Party "demanded Saturday that Prime Minister Junichiro Koizumi resign over the kidnapping of three Japanese citizens in Iraq."

On April 15, *The Japan Times* reported that, "Criticism of the three Japanese taken hostage in Iraq has been heard among ruling coalition lawmakers since the crisis surfaced last Thursday" (Shimoyachi, 2004). Subsequent reports in *The Japan Times* mentioned the *government's* criticism of the hostages, but I did not find an article that specified the extent of *public* criticism, suggesting that the criticism may have been an attempt on the government's part to deflect public questioning of its Iraq policy. Indeed, on April 18, *The Japan Times* reported:

> Foreign Ministry officials in Tokyo were pleasantly surprised Saturday by the news that two Japanese hostages were abruptly freed by their captors in Baghdad. Their freedom effectively enabled Prime Minister Junichiro Koizumi to avert the biggest political crisis he has had to face since taking office, because any Japanese casualties in Iraq could deal a heavy blow to the prime minister, who has supported the U.S.-led war against Iraq even though the public is divided over the issue. (Yoshida, 2004)

Regardless of whether the public condemnation of the hostages was extensive, *The Japan Times* reported on April 19 that one of the former hostages said, "I feel sorry for causing everybody to be concerned. But I do not think my actions were wrong. I don't want to apologize for what I did." In other words, this former hostage was remaining faithful to himself and, to paraphrase Doi, was maintaining an independent self that was not negated by group membership. This former hostage's claim, coupled with the prime minister's political pickle, suggests that characterizing the hostages' homecoming only in terms of Japanese conceptions of interdependence obscures some of the complexities of this situation, including how it implicates independence issues. In this case, the former hostage's claim points to the importance of individuality and self-direction in self-construction.

By considering how Japanese self-construction reflects or enacts independence meanings, I do not mean to ignore or deny the existence of the huge body of research that addresses the relational nature of Japanese self-construction. Indeed, it is impossible to ignore this research given its size and the ubiquity of claims that Japanese self-construction is more interdependent than is Western, especially Euro-American, self-construction. Instead, I am suggesting that we look at independence and interdependence from a theoretical vantage point that moves cultural analyses beyond questions of more or less independence or interdependence, to also asking questions that enable us to discern how both independence and interdependence, as fundamental to the human condition, are understood, enacted, and interrelated in different cultures. Such analyses can further our understanding of the integrated complexities of human culture, behavior, and development.

SOME GENERAL REMARKS

With regard to self-construction, the current conceptual approach has enabled us to consider how interrelated independence and interdependence activity dimensions and meanings are implicated in the process of self-construction. In conjunction with the current conceptual approach to independence and interdependence, Mead's, Cooley's, and Erikson's classic theories of self provided a conceptual backdrop for considering self-construction as a form of activity that takes place within cultural practices, and thus implicates independence and interdependence.

In addition, Mead's and Cooley's theories highlight the role of social processes in self-construction, and thus it is not surprising that they are often invoked as exceptions to the general rule that American psychology has been rather unidimensionally focused on the individual. In this chapter, I too have invoked Mead and Cooley, in part, because of their focus on interdependence. At the same time, however, characterizing Mead and Cooley as essentially interdependence oriented would be just as problematic as would be a claim that a particular culture is essentially independence or essentially interdependence oriented. Instead, Mead's and Cooley's perspectives reveal not only the importance of interdependence in American intellectual traditions, but they also indicate how interdependence is taken to be inseparable from independence in the process of self-construction.

Following a different path, Erikson's theory, as well as recent research on adolescent self-construction, takes us to the same conclusion. That is, Erikson's theory is sometimes criticized for an undue focus on individual processes, suggesting that the main goal of identity construction is to define oneself in separation from others. However, in this chapter I have tried to show that within Erikson's framework, individuals construct personal identities in relation to specific others and also in relation to wider societal functioning. Going beyond Erikson, this chapter has also more generally included considerations of how Euro-American adolescents construct themselves as individuals in relation to others in varied ways. These analyses indicate that adolescent self-construction cannot be fully understood as involving more or less independence or interdependence, but requires analyzing how independence and interdependence are interrelated during the course of identity construction.

Similarly, as mentioned in this chapter, Erikson's theory and Marcia's early elaborations on Erikson have been criticized for focusing on so-called intrapersonal domains of identity. The subsequent introduction of so-called interpersonal identity domains was used to more adequately understand differences in self-construction during adolescence. However, the distinction between intrapersonal and interpersonal modes of self-construction is based on the conceptual premise that identity domains differ in amounts of independence and interdependence. In contrast, the current conceptual approach shifts analytic attention toward discerning how identities are constructed in specific cultural practices that are made up of interrelated independence and interdependence activity dimensions, which reflect interrelated conceptions of human separateness and connectedness. Thus, any attempts to suggest that either independence or interdependence prevails during the course of self-construction in any culture is considered to be incomplete.

The discussion of Japanese self-constructions illustrates how independence is fully implicated in what have traditionally been characterized as interdependent modes of self-construction. Some research even suggests that Japanese self-constructions include a core sense of self that is considered to be stable across social contexts. Although it is commonplace to attribute a core sense of self to Westerners, the current approach enables us to discern how the notion of a core sense of self is particularized in a non-Western culture. In addition, the notion of a core sense of self helps to understand the complexities of the situation of the Japanese volunteers in Iraq.

The analysis of the Japan–Iraq situation also points to how analyzing independence and interdependence is not just an idle academic exercise. Instead, the current conceptual approach helps to shed light on some of the complexities of how independence and interdependence are interrelated as people construct themselves in varied "real-life" situations. Moreover, rather than jumping to the conclusion that the Japanese aid worker's reluctance to apologize for going to Iraq represents an anomaly within the overall interdependence of Japanese culture, the current approach enables us to see how independence and interdependence were inseparable in the aid worker's self-construction. In particular, his statement suggests that he was expressing his individuality in relation to Japanese conceptions of maintaining social cohesion. That is, he expressed his individuality by refusing to apologize for going to Iraq while simultaneously maintaining social cohesion by saying he felt sorry for causing people to be concerned.

Although the issues discussed in this chapter demonstrate some of the complexities of independence and interdependence in relation to self-construction, many issues remain open for further study. For example, it is important to further discern how specific independence and interdependence meanings are invoked as children and adolescents construct themselves in the context of varied cultural practices. Further understanding of children's and adolescents' subjective constructions of what it means to be independent and interdependent is also required. To begin addressing some of these issues, we now turn to chapter 7 and to a study of how independence and interdependence are particularized in late adolescent self-constructions.

Independence and Interdependence in Late Adolescent Self-Constructions

Although varied research directions have pointed to the utility of the current conceptual position, there is much room for conducting research that is explicitly based on this conceptualization. Thus, in this chapter, I present a study I conducted to discern how independence and interdependence are particularized in late adolescent self-constructions. More specifically, the current conceptual framework leads to investigating how late adolescent self-constructions reflect multifaceted and interrelated cultural independence and interdependence meanings.

As in many previous studies, this study consisted of semi-structured interviews in which the participants were asked to describe themselves. As explained in chapter 6, interview studies make possible a particular form of self-construction; namely, reflecting on and constructing one's behavior, perspective, and experience in relation to an inquiring other. In keeping with the current conceptual approach, as people engage in this kind of self-constructing activity, their claims about themselves may be analyzed in terms of how they reflect multifaceted and interrelated independence and interdependence meanings. In addition to asking participants to describe themselves, in this study, they were also explicitly asked to discuss whether and how they think of themselves as independent and interdependent.

Given my interest in trying to understand the complexities of Euro-American independence and interdependence meanings, the study sample consisted of 36 Euro-American college undergraduates between the ages of 18 and 21 (19 males, 17 females) from middle and lower socioeconomic status (SES) families. This research also included a group of 11 Vietnamese adolescents between the ages of 17 and 22 (7 females, 4 males), living in and attending high school or college in Albuquerque, New Mexico. One Vietnamese participant was born in the United States, and the other 10 Vietnamese participants had lived in the United States for 5 to 10 years. All of these Vietnamese adolescents lived with their parents, except for one female who lived with her aunt and uncle and one male who lived on his own in a spare room in the building where the Buddhist temple to which he belongs is housed. The interviews were conducted in English, and except for the one participant who was born in the United States, the Vietnamese participants were not native speakers of English. It certainly would have been ideal to conduct their interviews in Vietnamese, as their discussions were not as elaborate as were those of the Euro-American participants. Nevertheless, the Vietnamese participants understood the questions and were able to convey complex ideas about themselves in English. Thus, despite some language constraints, the interviews still provided an informative source of data about these Vietnamese adolescents' self-constructions as independent and interdependent.

The following discussion highlights qualitative analyses of how the two groups of late adolescents construct themselves in terms of varied and inseparable independence and interdependence issues. As I analyze the interviews, I present many interview excerpts to provide illustrations of the richness and complexity of some of these adolescents' self-constructions. No doubt for different reasons, the Euro-American and Vietnamese adolescents' statements were riddled with grammatical errors. The interviews were transcribed, and, to preserve the participants' voices, I have not made any grammatical adjustments, nor have I deleted the innumerable "you knows" and "likes."

OVERALL SELF-CONSTRUCTIONS

Multifaceted Independence and Interdependence Self-Characteristics

To investigate how independence and interdependence are particularized in these adolescents' overall self-constructions (at least within the context of an interview study), the interviews opened with the following general questions, taken from Damon and Hart's (1988) self-understanding interview protocol: "How would you describe yourself; tell me about yourself; who are you?" For each characteristic mentioned in response to those questions, participants were asked the follow-up question, "Why is that important to you?" This follow-up question enabled the participants to further reflect on and construct their understandings of their stated self-characteristics.

The participants' audiotaped interviews were transcribed, and responses to the open-ended self-questions were coded according to a theoretically and empirically derived category system of multifaceted independence and interdependence characteristics, as presented in Tables 7.1 and 7.2. The results for inseparable independence and interdependence characteristics are given separately. Interrater reliability for these coding categories between two judges on 28% of the Euro-American interviews, using Cohen's Kappa coefficient, was 82%. Interrater reliability for these coding categories between two judges on 27% of the Vietnamese interviews, using Cohen's Kappa coefficient, was 90%.

In keeping with the current conceptual position, the interviews yielded multifaceted independence and interdependence characteristics for both cultural groups. The findings for the Euro-American participants' overall self-constructions have already been reported (Raeff, 2004), but I briefly reiterate them here so that the self-constructions of both cultural groups may be considered. Thirty-three Euro-American participants (92%) discussed at least one interdependence characteristic, and a mean of 41% of their self-statements consisted of interdependence characteristics. Twenty-three Euro-American participants (64%) discussed at least one independence characteristic, and a mean of 21% of their self-

TABLE 7.1
Multifaceted Interdependence Self-Characteristics

1. *General sociability*—constructing oneself in terms of being able to interact with varied people.
   Interview examples:
   • Euro-American: "I'm very outgoing," "I'm a people person."
   • Vietnamese: "I'm friendly," "I'm nice."
2. *Wider social concerns*—constructing oneself in terms of wider social issues, social standards, social roles, or group membership.
   Interview examples:
   • Euro-American: "I follow the rules," "I was on student council."
   • Vietnamese: "I'm a Vietnamese girl," "I'm a schoolgirl."
3. *Social activities*—constructing oneself in terms of activities carried out with others.
   Interview examples:
   • Euro-American: "I play baseball."
   • Vietnamese: "I play soccer."
4. *Specific relationships*—constructing oneself in terms of direct relationships.
   Interview examples:
   • Euro-American: "I have friends and acquaintances," "I'm pretty much my father's son."
   • Vietnamese: "I like my family most."

TABLE 7.2
Multifaceted Independence Self-Characteristics

1. *Physically separate*—constructing oneself as a physically separate person.
   Interview examples:
   • Euro-American: "I'm athletic," "I'm in good health."
   • Vietnamese: "Well, physically, I'm short," "Really athletic."
2. *Self-direction*—constructing oneself as the source of one's own actions, or as a person who makes his/her own choices, judgments, and decisions.
   Interview examples:
   • Euro-American: "I'm determined," "I make my own decisions."
   • Vietnamese: "If I want to do something, I will do it."
3. *Separate activities*—constructing oneself in terms of activities conducted alone or in terms of finding fulfillment through activities conducted alone.
   Interview examples:
   • Euro-American: "I'd rather stay home and study," "I like to read."
   • Vietnamese: "Just want to [be] at home by myself," "I enjoy reading a book."
4. *Mentally separate*—constructing oneself as a mentally or cognitively separate person.
   Interview examples:
   • Euro-American: "I'm intelligent," "I'm opinionated."
   • Vietnamese: "I got a sense of humor."
5. *Self-reliant*—constructing oneself as a person who can handle varied life tasks on one's own.
   Interview examples:
   • Euro-American: "I can handle a lot of stuff," "I don't have to depend on anyone else to get along."
   • Vietnamese: "I live on my own."
6. *Self-insulation*—constructing oneself as a person who protects him or herself from stress or problems.
   Interview examples:
   • Euro-American: "I'm easygoing," "I don't let many things get to me."
7. *Self-confidence*—constructing oneself as a person who is confident in his or her own abilities.
   Interview example:
   • Euro-American: "I've just got uh, high self-confidence I guess. I'm sure of myself. I don't second guess myself a lot."
8. *Self-fulfillment*—constructing oneself in terms of being fulfilled as a separate person.
   Interview example:
   • Euro-American: "What I do is what makes me happy."

statements consisted of independence characteristics. When asked to describe themselves in general, all of the 11 Vietnamese adolescents discussed at least one interdependence characteristic, and a mean of 39% of their self-statements consisted of interdependence characteristics. Eight (73%) Vietnamese participants discussed at least one independence characteristic, and a mean of 30% of their self-statements consisted of independence characteristics.

More specifically, varied independence and interdependence character-istics comprised the Euro-American and Vietnamese self-constructions. For both groups, most participants constructed themselves in terms of general sociability. General sociability has been discussed in the preceding chapters in relation to Euro-American interaction patterns that involve being able to establish relationships within a diverse, and often shifting, network of peo-ple. For the Vietnamese, it is not clear if or how considerations of general sociability may reflect acculturation to American patterns and meanings of interdependence. In addition to general sociability, Euro-American and Vietnamese participants constructed themselves in terms of wider societal concerns, social activities, and specific relationships.

With regard to the independence characteristics, the Euro-Americans tended to construct themselves in terms of being mentally separate, physi-cally separate, self-directed, and in terms of engaging in separate activities. These characteristics, coupled with the relatively low proportion of Euro-Americans who constructed themselves as self-reliant, reflect the experi-ences of college students who are making some of their own decisions but are not yet financially self-reliant adults. In their overall self-constructions, most Vietnamese adolescents discussed being mentally separate, and many also discussed being physically separate. The finding that many of the Viet-namese adolescents constructed themselves in terms of mental separate-ness indicates how they were constructing themselves as separate individu-als with their own preferences and perspectives. Some of the Vietnamese adolescents also constructed themselves in terms of being self-directed and engaging in separate activities. Self-reliance was perhaps not such a preva-lent independence characteristic for the Vietnamese participants because most were living at home and contributing to their families' incomes.

Inseparable Independence and Interdependence Self-Characteristics

With regard to their general self-constructions, 35 (97%) of the 36 Euro-American participants constructed themselves in terms of interrelated or inseparable independence and interdependence characteristics, and a mean of 36% of their self-statements consisted of interrelated independ-ence and interdependence characteristics. Of these 35 Euro-American participants, 27 (77%) constructed themselves as being fulfilled and/or supported through being generally sociable, through their specific rela-tionships with others, and/or through their social activities. For example, when describing herself in terms of having close relationships, one partici-pant went on to explain that close relationships are important "just to, you know, help you through rough times. You know, just enjoy the good

ones." These findings point to how individual self-fulfillment is inseparable from social connections for Euro-Americans, and they suggest further
that the Euro-Americans' self-constructions do not revolve around self-
containment, in the form of "needing or wanting no one" (Sampson,
1977, p. 770). At least these Euro-Americans seemed to very much need
and want others.

For the Vietnamese sample, 10 out of the 11 (91%) participants discussed inseparable independence and interdependence characteristics.
Similar to the Euro-Americans, 9 (90%) of these 10 participants discussed
how they found fulfillment and/or support through being generally sociable, through their social relationships, and/or through participating in social activities. For example, one Vietnamese participant explained, "I like
my family the most. And I stay with them . . . umm, because they help me a
lot." Another Vietnamese participant explained that relationships with
others are a source of personal support " 'Cause when you're on you own,
you know, if you need somebody there, when you're down, or something,
you know. And somebody is there for you."

With regard to some other inseparable independence and interdependence characteristics, 11 (31%) of the 35 Euro-American participants discussed how their separate cognitive abilities were inseparable from their
wider social concerns and their general sociability. For example, one participant described himself as "intellectually focused," and this individual
cognitive ability was important to him because it was enabling him to pursue his goal of being a Supreme Court justice, which, in turn, would enable him to have a wide impact on society.

Another person described herself as "insightful," which by itself seems
to represent a separate cognitive ability. However, when asked why being
insightful is important, this participant answered:

> Well, for me it's very important because communication's obviously an im-
> portant thing for everything and every facet of life. But I just, it makes me
> feel good to have that insight because. I don't know. I feel like I'm helping
> them in a way by trying to understand them. . . . It makes me feel like I've
> put forth an effort and. I don't know.

When asked to further clarify her ideas, this participant went on to say:

> An effort to understand where someone's coming from. And some people.
> You know like most people I would say, kind of with their busy lives, kind of
> just, you know [say], uh, this is what I need, this is what I want. You know,
> and sometimes it's nice to have insight into what somebody else is thinking
> and feeling.

For this young woman, constructing herself as insightful was inseparable
from issues of general sociability and also enabled her to establish rela-

tionships with others in ways that went beyond superficial social pleasant-ries. Her discussion also reflects the value of understanding and communicating with others as separate individuals for the sake of enhancing social connections.

CONSTRUCTING ONESELF AS INDEPENDENT

To investigate the participants' subjective constructions of themselves as independent, they were first asked, "Would you say that you are independent?" If they answered this question affirmatively, they were next asked, "How or in what ways are you independent, or what does it mean to you to be independent?" Finally, they were asked, "Why is it good or important to be independent?" The coding categories for these issues are presented along with the results. Using Cohen's Kappa coefficient, the reliability for coding the participants' self-constructions was .78 for the Vietnamese sample and .97 for the Euro-American sample.

When asked whether they would say that they were independent, three (27%) Vietnamese adolescents said yes unequivocally, and the other eight (73%) participants claimed that they were partially but not completely independent. These partially independent Vietnamese participants explained that they were not completely independent because they lived at home and/or were dependent on their parents. When asked to discuss what it means to be independent or how they were independent, nine (82%) Vietnamese adolescents said that being independent involves being self-directed or being able to make their own decisions and choices. For example, different Vietnamese participants claimed:

- If everybody wants to do something, and I want to do something else, then I'll do it. . . . Just to decide by myself what to do.
- I can do whatever I want.
- In life, I make my own decisions.
- I have my own choice. I can make my own decisions.

In addition to constructing independence in terms of self-direction, two (18%) Vietnamese participants defined independence in terms of liking or wanting to be alone. One said, "Sometimes I just don't want to talk with anybody. Just like to be myself. And when, even though I stay home, I still don't talk to anybody." The other participant said, "Sometimes I like to be alone, just to read a book or something. Like just to read on my own. Or just go on a mountain, and just sit there to think. Just some times to myself, just to think or something." Also, only two (18%) of the Vietnamese participants defined independence in terms of practical self-reliance.

When asked whether they would say that they were independent, 22 (61%) of the Euro-American participants said yes without hesitation, and 1 (3%) said no. The remaining 13 (36%) Euro-American participants gave qualified affirmative answers, claiming that they were partially but not completely independent, or that they were becoming increasingly independent. Except when noted otherwise, the percentages given for the Euro-American discussions of independence are based on the 35 participants who claimed to be independent, partially independent, or becoming increasingly independent.

With regard to becoming increasingly independent, one Euro-American participant said:

> I think I'm becoming more independent because I've noticed that I'm not going home as often this year as I did last year. Last year I'd probably say I went home like once a month. This year I've been home twice so far, and that's because like my dad made me come home last weekend. . . . So I went home, you know what I mean? But like, you know, I've found more that I want to stay here now.

With regard to being partially but not completely independent, one Euro-American adolescent noted:

> I would say I'm both dependent and independent. I mean, I'm independent in a way that, like I said before, I'm not gonna follow other people around. I'm gonna do what I want to do, what keeps me happy. But I'm dependent on other people also I guess to be happy. 'Cause, I mean, without my friends and family, I guess I wouldn't be as happy as I am.

In addition to indicating how this person was constructing herself as partially independent, this last quotation suggests that independence means being self-directed or making one's own choices, and that personal happiness requires relationships with others. Similarly, another participant stated, "I'm not totally independent. I mean there are some people that I depend on for things. I don't think anyone is totally independent. Everyone needs somebody to lean on." Based on this statement, we also begin to see how needing others and living in relation to others are assumed to be part of human nature.

The interview excerpts just presented to illustrate constructing oneself as partially independent also point to the now rather well-worn theme of contrasting independence with dependence, and this theme is discernible throughout many of the interviews. Indeed, 28 (80%) of the Euro-American participants explicitly contrasted independence with dependence, implying that independence does not preclude the importance and even necessity of social connectedness. In fact, many participants maintained that they liked being around other people and that friends and family were central to their lives. In addition, when asked specifically to consider whether they preferred to be alone or with other people, 28 (78%) of the total sample of 36 Euro-American participants said they preferred to be with other people, and the remaining 8 (22%) discussed the importance of balancing being alone and being with others. None of these Euro-American adolescents claimed to prefer being alone, thus echoing James (1890/1983), who long ago pointed out that humans are "gregarious animal[s]" and "To be alone is one of the greatest of evils" for them (p. 1047).

For the Euro-Americans, when asked to discuss what it means to be independent, several or multifaceted meanings of independence emerged, including and also going beyond opposing independence to dependence. For 27 (77%) of the Euro-American participants, being independent involved constructing oneself as self-reliant or being able to deal with the practicalities of life on one's own. It is interesting to note that being instrumentally self-reliant did not figure prominently in the participants' overall self-constructions, but it did emerge as the most commonly discussed meaning of independence, thus pointing to the dynamic nature of self-constructing activities. As examples of this independence meaning, consider the following interview excerpts, which show some of the varied ways in which a person may be self-reliant in practical matters:

- I'm independent, like I never ask my parents for money. Like I have, I brought all my own money up here.
- I have my own living. Nobody gives me anything. I earn everything I get. Nothing is given to me.
- Like I pay for all my bills, I pay for everything. So umm, and I think that I'm independent that way, 'cause I don't really depend on my parents. I don't depend on really anybody else. Like I do my work. I don't usually ask people.
- I guess I could function every day by myself. I don't have to have somebody tell me what to do, and where to go, and how to do things or whatever. I can handle a schedule. . . . I guess just, if you just handle everyday things by yourself. I guess that's being independent.
- I can survive on my own, and not have to depend on other people to do things for me.

It is important to point out that, for the Euro-Americans, being self-reliant in these ways did not preclude either being connected to others or valuing one's connections to others. Indeed, only two (6%) Euro-American participants specifically said that being independent means being alone or doing things alone. Moreover, many Euro-American participants made sure to point out that just as they valued being self-reliant, they also valued being with others. For example, consider the following interview passages:

- I like to be on my own as much as possible. But at the same time I like to be with other people. You know what I mean? Like, I like having a boyfriend. . . . But like, we had our apartment, I paid half of everything. And umm, I don't know, I guess in just ways like that. I just don't like people doing things for me. Like, it's hard for me to accept people doing things for me.
- I can take care of myself, cook, clean, do my laundry. I don't need mommy to tuck me in at night or anything like that. So, I guess that goes with being adaptive I guess. If you throw me somewhere, like I'll survive. I'll learn to deal with it.

This person also quickly pointed out that "Sometimes I prefer to have someone with me." And when asked why, he said, "Uh, it's more comfortable. It's always fun to have a friend with you."

These Euro-American statements suggest that the participants seemed to be insisting on dealing with life's practical exigencies on their own, but when it comes to their subjective well-being, they did not shy away from claiming the necessity of relationships. Thus, once again their constructions of themselves as independent, in the form of self-reliance, did not entail self-containment, in the form of "needing or wanting no one" (Sampson, 1977, p. 770).

For 13 (37%) of the Euro-American participants, being independent meant being self-directed, which involves constructing oneself as someone who makes one's own decisions and choices. This meaning of independence is illustrated in the following interview excerpts:

- Well. When I'm 750 miles away from, you know, home, and it's all me, I decide, you know, what to do, when to do it. You know, I go to class when I want to go to class.
- I always have my own way of making decisions.
- I'm gonna do what I want to do.
- I motivate myself.
- If I don't want to do something, if I don't feel comfortable in the surroundings, I'm gonna leave. . . . I'm not a follower at all. I make my own decisions.

Another participant discussed independent self-direction in conjunction with being mentally separate, and also immediately went on to discuss her emotional dependence on her friends:

And if you don't believe in doing something and somebody says to do it, you're not gonna do it, you know. But, I'm pretty dependent though on like my friends where I feel like I'm kind of. 'Cause I need them for like, you know, for security and for friendship. And like the ones up here, like I don't think I could like live without like them. And also like my boyfriend and everything like that. Everyone. Like I really need to depend on them to just, for security to like make you happy and to share your experiences with. . . . Um, but I'm pretty independent.

When asked, "How else are you independent, when you say you're pretty independent?", she replied:

Well. I do things like that, without you know, asking my friends for their permission. Like once I went to a pet store and saw a dog that I liked and I bought it. And like we didn't know where she was gonna live 'cause she can't live in the dorm room or anything. So, I do stuff like that, I guess which makes me independent. And, 'cause I have a car, so I'm independent. Like if I want to stay here or go somewhere else.

This somewhat meandering discussion again illustrates the view that people may find emotional fulfillment through relationships, but remain self-reliant when handling daily life issues.

A few other categories of independence also emerged in the Euro-Americans' discussions of independence, but they occurred less frequently than did constructing independence in terms of practical self-reliance and self-direction. For example, four (11%) participants discussed being independent in terms of being mentally separate, as illustrated in the following quotations:

- I'm an independent thinker. I think, like if the whole, if there are gonna be 50 people there that are saying one thing. If I don't agree with I'll tell all 50 of them that I don't agree. I have my own ideas, and it doesn't matter what other people think.
- Yeah, 'cause I have like my own views.
- I have my own feelings about things.

These statements are in keeping with long-standing Euro-American traditions of conceptualizing independence in terms of thinking for oneself without coercion from others. Given these long-standing traditions, one may wonder why so few Euro-American adolescents discussed independence in terms of thinking for oneself. This finding may reflect the homogenization of some aspects of contemporary life in the United States. However, simply because many participants did not construct themselves in terms of being mentally separate at that point in the interview, it does not mean that thinking for oneself was not important to them, nor does it mean that they did not think for themselves. As we see later in this chapter, ideas about thinking for oneself did crop up in other ways during the interviews. In addition, thinking for oneself is similar to being self-directed, and thus further research is needed to disentangle how these constructs may be differentiated as people reflect on and construct themselves.

Also for the Euro-American participants, one set of independence meanings revealed how constructing oneself as independent is explicitly inseparable from interdependence issues, supporting the current theoretical position that people's self-constructions reflect inseparable independence and interdependence meanings. That is, for three (9%) participants, being independent meant being able to help others. For example, one of the participants explained that she was independent because "I like to help other people. Like if I know they have to do something, and I can help them do it, I am going to do it for them, whether they ask me or not." When asked why this made her independent, the participant responded that being independent "makes me feel like I can do things for them. I don't have to depend on other people. I can do things for myself and also for other people without having to depend on somebody to help me."

Another participant said, "Um, I help other people fix their cars, their computers. Anything they're having trouble with. You know, I help them." When asked why helping others in this way made him independent, he replied, "Because it shows that you're able to do stuff for yourself. Enough that you're able to give your knowledge to somebody else. Give your experiences, or do something for somebody else." These findings, along with the issues discussed previously, indicate that when a Euro-American claims to be self-reliant or generally independent, one cannot immediately assume that he or she conceptualizes him or herself as unidimensionally independent or in isolation from interpersonal relationships.

WHY INDEPENDENCE IS GOOD OR IMPORTANT

In addition to constructing themselves as independent in varied ways, the participants also discussed varied reasons for why it is good or important to be independent. Again pointing to the importance of self-direction, for five (45%) of the Vietnamese participants, being independent was good because it allowed them to make their own decisions and choices. As some of the participants put it:

- Then you can, make like, choose what you can do, and decide what you want to do.

- 'Cause, umm. I think that's what helps me make me have my own decisions. So, that's better than like just listening to people.

Eight (23%) Euro-American participants also claimed that being independent was important because it enabled them to make their own decisions and choices. For example, reflecting the importance of not being coerced into decisions by others, one Euro-American participant said, "Uh, you can go do what you want. You don't have to sit and wait for somebody to tell you what to do, or follow somebody else." In the context of not waiting for others to tell one what to do, the statement "Uh, you can go do what you want" does not necessarily imply self-containment or disregard for others, but instead seems to reflect the value of not having to depend on others for self-direction.

Among the Euro-Americans, 12 (34%) participants explained that, in one way or another, other people may not always be around, and therefore it is important to be able to do for oneself in life. This advantage of being independent is illustrated in the following interview excerpts:

- I guess 'cause someone is not always gonna be there for you. There's gonna be times that you gotta make your own decisions, do things your own way, and kind of get on with your life.
- What's good about being independent? You don't have to rely on anybody else, 'cause somebody might not be there for you when you actually need them and depend on them.
- Well, nobody's gonna do things for you all your life, and you're gonna have to do things for yourself some time. So, you might as well start it early.

Some Euro-American participants also made sure to discuss the advantages of being independent in case others are not around, in conjunction with highlighting the importance of relationships. For example, two participants claimed:

- Well it's good that if you, umm if you're independent and you can do things on your own and you don't have to rely on others. I mean it's good to have other people there for you to help you, but you don't always have to have someone. If you need to do something by yourself, then you can do it, and then you don't have to be reliant on people.
- Uh, well I think that you do need the relationships obviously. You do need people around you, but being independent. I mean, if you're stuck in the middle of nowhere and you can survive, then I think you're independent, you know. I mean if you can survive without other people, then I guess I think that's good. I mean I think you should have other people obviously, but if you can [survive], then I think that's good.

In this last quotation, the participant's two-time use of the word *obviously* to explain the necessity of relationships suggests that, although independence is important in emergencies, being connected to others is basic to human experience.

For the Vietnamese participants, concern that others might not be around was mentioned by only two (18%) participants. They stated:

- When my family like. My family, they have to die too. Can't live forever with me. And my sister, when they married, they have to move out too. And my brother too.
- I think it's good being independent 'cause you need help, and nobody is really [there to] help you.

In addition to living with their families, many of the Vietnamese participants talked about how they would provide for their parents later in life. Thus, the possibility of others not being around was probably rather remote for them.

For the Euro-Americans, another advantage of independence revolved around the notion that being independent enables one to evaluate oneself positively or to feel good about oneself. This advantage of independence was discussed by nine (26%) participants and is illustrated in the following interview excerpts from three participants:

- Uh, gives you a good feeling when you know you did it yourself, and you didn't need anybody to help. That gives you more confidence, I think.

When asked why he thought that independence gave him confidence, this participant responded:

Um, 'cause you feel, hey, I can conquer this job by myself. What else can I do by myself? Like, I'm sure I can do harder things than this, or whatever.
- You don't feel helpless. If you have to depend on everybody, you just feel, like, helpless.
- I think you should be able to have your own opinions about things. And if you don't have your own opinion, then that means you don't respect yourself. And if you don't respect yourself then, like I said before, then you have nothing.

This last quotation also demonstrates how positive self-evaluation, in the form of self-respect, may be enhanced by formulating one's own opinions, reflecting long-standing traditions of not being coerced by others.

For one Euro-American participant, the self-esteem advantages of being independent were inseparable from social concerns:

> It makes me feel good. You know what I mean? Like I know I'm. Me and my two friends are looking for apartments and houses for next year which is like the biggest pain in the world. And um, like, I think, you know, telling my dad that, you know, I'm getting an apartment. And he didn't want me to at first. And I told him that I was going to do it, like with him or without him. You know what I mean? I, you know, I said, if you don't want to pay for it, that's fine. Like, I will pay for it, you know. He didn't think I was ready to get one for next year. But umm, you know, we had a big argument over it of course, and then he gave in. He was like, okay, you know. You will be 21 next year, you know. You will, you know, you're old enough, you know what I mean, you know, to have your own place and pay utility bills, and stuff like that, you know. So, I think in that aspect. Just doing for yourself, you know. It makes me feel good that, you know, I'm out looking for places. And, you know, that I'm going to be paying my own bills and stuff like that. That makes me feel good.

In this case, the participant's construction of herself as independent involved living separately from her family. However, her construction of independence also implicated constructions of interdependence insofar as being independent, to her, involved living with other people as well as coping with a wider economic institutional framework.

Seven (20%) Euro-American participants explained that being independent is good because it is a sign of stable functioning and makes life easier or enables people to survive. For example, some of them commented:

- I think it's very good to be independent, that way you can get on with your life. You don't need somebody to tell you to go ahead and get on with your life. I just think it makes your life easier. Umm, a whole lot easier. I mean you might be able to get something done if you're extremely dependent, but it will take you longer and you won't be as efficient, and you'll just be feeling worse.
- Like you know, you have to learn how to do, you have to. It's like healthy to be able to take care of yourself.

Five (14%) Euro-American and four (36%) Vietnamese participants asserted that independence is good because it can promote development or facilitate learning and self-improvement. As two Vietnamese participants put it:

- Independence can like, make you, like experiment. . . . When you have something difficult, and you try to decide. And then you, you make stronger on that. You know.

- 'Cause it allows you to. Independence. It teach you lessons. You learn something. In life you got to learn stuff by yourself.

As one Euro-American participant explained, being independent is good because one can, "You know, kind of, develop yourself to make you the kind of person you want to be." Another Euro-American participant noted:

> You learn a lot. You learn a lot being independent. I think you learn a lot more than being dependent. I think, umm, people that are dependent on other people don't learn as much, learn the value of life and stuff like that. Because I know, like I said before, like people that are dependent on their parents they don't. They take things for granted.

In this case, I again cannot refrain from pointing out that conceptualizing the self as independent was being contrasted with being dependent. When asked to further explain what can be learned by being independent, a discussion ensued that also illustrated that independence stands in contrast to dependence, but not interdependence per se:

Participant: Um, just learn um. Like the, I know, being independent you learn the value of money a lot better than being, if somebody was dependent. Um. And what else? Being independent you learn. I think you learn, umm, people. I think you learn people too. You learn about people more 'cause you uh. I think interact more with people I would say if you're independent.

Interviewer: How does that work?

Participant: Well, now that I was thinking about it. Umm. Because I think, uh, if you're a dependent person, I think you kind of depend on other people. I mean, but you don't really get to know them. Like you kind of just depend on like one or two people. Or you just, you don't. You don't really care to know people. But I think when you're independent, I think you do.

Interviewer: And how do you care about them in a way that's different?

Participant: Uh, I think people that are dependent don't care. I don't. I really don't. I don't think they. They don't care. They're just like, "oh whatever." And, but I think when you're independent you care, and you want to know people, I think. You want to get to know people.

In this discussion, we see how independence enhances interdependence and enabled this participant to know and establish relationships with others as individuals and on their terms. Moreover, in highlighting responsivity to others, this participant seemed to be speaking against an instrumental or egocentric approach to relationships, which, in her view, results from being dependent on others for self-serving purposes.

The interviews also revealed other advantages of independence that point to ways in which constructions of being independent are inseparable from connections to other people. That is, for three (9%) Euro-American participants, being independent is important because it prevents a person from being a burden to others, thereby also indicating how the participants construed themselves in terms of consideration for others. For example, one participant said that one advantage of being independent is that "people don't have to worry about you." Along similar lines, another participant explained that independence, in the form of being self-reliant, is important because it is a sign of maturity, which is good "Because you don't have someone like worrying if you get in trouble for doing certain things." Another participant who viewed independence in terms of being self-reliant maintained that such self-reliance is important because if one starts to rely on others, "sometimes you can get lax and rely on them too much, and you don't do your part. And I've seen a lot of people do that, and it's just irritating because everybody else has to pick up what you are laxing in, and it makes for a lot of problems then later on." This explanation of self-reliance seems inseparable from a view of people as embedded in relationships and social groups with responsibilities and obligations to each other.

Another way in which conceptions of independence are inseparable from conceptions of interdependence was discussed by two (6%) Euro-American participants and it involves the idea that independence enables a person to be respected or trusted by others. For example, one person said, "I think people have more respect for you if you're independent. Like, oh she can do this by herself, she doesn't need help doing it. People have more respect." Another participant noted that by being self-reliant:

> people can rely on you. . . . So that they know, you know, they don't have to do everything themselves. I can, you know, I can pick up the slack wherever is necessary. . . . If like somebody's having problems because they're just getting mobbed with other things, you know that they can rely on me to go out and do it. So, like I can be the person, the outside person that people can rely on. I can be trusted in any sort of fashion if necessary.

Overall, for the Euro-American participants who discussed the advantages of independence in relation to interdependence, independence and interdependence seemed to be interrelated in rather positive ways. For only three (9%) participants did some negative conceptions of interdependence emerge in their discussions of the advantages of independence.

That is, these three participants mentioned that independence is important because it freed them from having to be burdened or distracted by others. For example, one of these participants said, "You don't have to wait for everyone else . . . you don't have to worry about making everyone else happy." Another participant said that independence, in the form of being self-reliant, is "good because you're gonna get done what you want to get done. I mean rather than if you're gonna depend on somebody else, then sometimes you're gonna end up falling on them. You might be doing some of what you want to do, but you're gonna. I mean, sooner or later you're gonna get off track of what you want to do."

FEELING "REALLY" INDEPENDENT

The Euro-American participants were also asked to describe a time when they felt "really" independent. Half of the entire Euro-American sample talked about living away from home or being on their own. Once again, these descriptions focused on issues of instrumental or practical self-reliance, as is evident in the following interview excerpts:

- I guess probably the most is, probably it's not that much, but it's when I went to school. And, I was like far away from my parents. I just talked to them on the phone and whatever. I didn't see them much or whatever. I didn't depend on them too much, so that was probably about the most.
- When I had my own apartment. I was doing everything for myself. Paying the bills, doing all the cooking, the cleaning, the laundry.
- Well, I'm living totally like, I'm like physically on my own. I'm still like getting income from my parents, but it's my responsibility to budget, to have, for different things that I need, to pay for bills, groceries, weekends, whatnot. So. And I have to schedule myself, which I don't do yet. But, you know, so right now is probably like the most independent I've ever been.
- Coming to school. Like, my first day of school because you're on your own. I mean, my parents left, and it was just like, here you are. I mean, it's all up to you. I mean I had to go. You know, I mean they brought me food up, but I still had to go shopping and buy my own food sometimes. And like you have to go to, you have to eat on your own. I mean, there's not someone standing over your shoulder telling you that you have to do your homework, or you have to get this done, or you have to do that. You have to do it on your own.
- Umm, probably just right now. Um, in college, just. You know, away from family and away from all my old friends. Just doing everything for myself.

Somewhat related to practical self-reliance, some Euro-American participants discussed how living on their own enabled them to make their own

choices and decisions and to be generally self-directed. As different participants explained:

- I had to start like thinking for myself. Like learning a job, like I didn't have
  somebody there telling me every little step to do or like what to do. I kinda
  had to like guide myself.
- It's kind of exciting 'cause you're on your own. You make your own decisions.
- You know, I controlled whatever I did. Nobody breathing down my neck
  saying do this, do that.

In this last statement, we can also discern the idea that being independent
involved not being coerced by others.

Twelve (33%) of the participants' descriptions of feeling really independent indicate how independence is related to interdependence issues.
For example, one participant commented:

That was this summer. This summer which I really felt really independent.
It's just because I was on my own. Like I was on my own. I had to do everything on my own. Like I was getting money. I had to take care of my money
and things because I had to pay, I had to pay for like everything. Umm, I had
to pay for my place down there. And I was also doing my internship there, so
I was paying for my internship credits. And then when I came back to school,
I had to pay for my apartment. So like I had to manage all my money down
there, and you know, I had to be living down there. And like pay for my
food, and still have time to like, want to go out and have fun, you know. And
so, I had to like manage everything. Working, like I was working seventy
hours a week. So I had to manage doing that, getting enough sleep, doing
my stuff for my internship.

In this case, the participant was indeed describing varied aspects of being
self-reliant, but part of her time management included going out, which
probably involved going out with others, at least some of the time. In addition, her self-reliance included managing the social role of being an in-
tern. Moreover, when asked where she lived during this time, it became
even clearer that her independent life took place in relation to others as
she said, "I lived with umm. It was like. I lived with three, it was four of us
in like this little apartment."

Similarly, for another participant, a time of independence involved:

Probably, probably when I came down here. Like the first few days, uhh, after my parents dropped me off. And like, I was here, and I was basically by
myself, and I didn't know anybody. I was pretty much independent then. I
had to go out and find my own friends, and learn how to get around. And

that's probably like the biggest independency. It was fun. Uh, it was fun finding new friends, and making new friends.

In this case, besides some practical self-reliance, being independent involved establishing social connections in a new social context.

The following interview excerpts elucidate some other ways in which independence events are considered to be inseparable from connections to other people, including being trusted by others and wider social concerns:

- Probably, my junior year to here. I never had to, you know, check in with my mom or anything. It was just as long as I, as long as I knew what was best for me, and not. I'm not like a bad kid. So they trusted me, and I made the right choices.
- Umm. I guess maybe like the first time like my dad went out of town for a while, and left me home by myself. I guess maybe. Just like, you know, like taking care of my little brother. You know what I mean? Having to go like grocery shopping and stuff. I mean and that was, that wasn't bad. And that just happened like I guess two years ago. I guess my senior year of high school, he let me actually like, like watch my brother, you know what I mean, for like a week. . . . I mean it felt good that my dad trusted me enough to let me go by myself like, and taking care of my brother who was only 14 at the time. So, I mean, a 14-year-old boy can be a handful.

When asked how this event made her feel, this participant went on to say:

It made me, it made me feel trusted. It made me feel like my dad could actually trust me. You know what I mean? Trust me enough, you know, to, you know, make sure nothing happened to the house. To not throw like a huge party. You know what I mean? To actually take care of my brother . . . taking care of my brother, I mean, that, it was a big responsibility. And it made me feel trusted, like he could trust me.

Taking these two cases together, independence is tied to interdependence in two ways. That is, both participants described feeling independent when they were trusted by other people. Also, in the second interview excerpt, the participant was being trusted not just to take care of herself, but to take care of another person.

Another participant described feeling really independent in relation to wider social concerns:

Right now I'm involved in a lot of political battles, I guess. Actually with the state. Um, and there's a few other individuals that are in agreement with me. . . . Right now I'm the only recruiter for the national guard. And every other school [in the state] gets one hundred percent college tuition, and we get two thirds. I've written letters to a lot of people. And a lot of people don't agree with what I'm doing. And I'm really sticking my head out on the chopping block. You know what I mean? Either they're gonna grab my head and kiss me, or they're gonna cut it off. And I don't, I don't know. But I'm trying to do what I think is best, not only for me, but for the other sixty thousand guard members that are in college right now. And if I'm the only one, and so far I don't think anyone else has written this kind of letter. There's sixty thousand people. And if I'm the only one that writes a letter, if that makes a difference, then that's what I'm gonna do.

For this participant, independence involved political action, with the hope of benefiting not only himself but others as well. When asked why this experience makes him feel independent, he replied, "It's like. I don't know. It's like, I'm the only one that. I know I'm not the only one that cares. It's just I'm the only one that's actually getting involved and trying to do something about it."

CONSTRUCTING ONESELF AS INTERDEPENDENT

To investigate the participants' constructions of themselves as interdependent, they were first asked, "Would you say that you are interdependent or connected to others?" If they answered this question affirmatively, they were next asked, "How or in what ways are you interdependent or connected to others, or what does it mean to you to be connected to others?" Finally, they were asked, "Why is it good or important to be connected to others?" The coding categories for these issues are presented along with the results. Using Cohen's Kappa coefficient, the reliability for coding these self-constructions was .83 for the Vietnamese sample and .81 for the Euro-American sample.

When asked if they considered themselves to be interdependent or connected to others, 35 (97%) of the 36 Euro-American participants said yes and 1 (3%) said no. Thus, the same people who constructed themselves as independent also constructed themselves as interdependent. Moreover, although many Euro-American adolescents claimed to be partially independent, none claimed to be only partially interdependent. Except when otherwise noted, the percentages given for the Euro-American discussions of interdependence are based on the 35 participants who claimed to be interdependent.

When asked what it meant to be interdependent or connected, or how they were connected to others, 32 (91%) Euro-Americans said they were connected to specific people, including family members and friends with whom they enjoyed spending time, or who provided emotional or financial support. Interestingly, although the Euro-Americans' overall self-descriptions mostly included conceptions of general sociability, their more explicit considerations of themselves as being interdependent highlighted specific relationships. The participants' constructions of how they were connected to specific others are evident in the following varied interview excerpts:

- Yeah. I mean, I'm connected with my family and friends.
- Uh, yeah, I'm connected, uh. Like I'm real close to mom and dad. My grandmother especially. I only have one of my grandparents still living. And when I'm home during summer, I'm always in there doing something little for her so she doesn't have to do it. So, I'm close to her that way. Mom and dad I'm close to. We're always doing stuff. Brothers and sisters and nine nieces and nephews. It just brings the whole family closer together.
- I still have friends that, you know, that I made years before that I still talk to. I keep in touch with them. They're probably my best friends, and you know, I bounce my ideas off them, and they talk to me about anything you can talk about. You know, that kind of thing, everything.
- Yeah, through all my friends. I have some friends who go here, so like I can rely on them. If I need talk to somebody about anything, or something. Or if I want to go eat with someone else, then I can go call some of my friends.
- One thing because I have such a large family, that's most of my connections, and all my friends. And then my boyfriend. So I have a bunch of different connections to other people.
- Well, I'm living with my best friend. So, and then I talk to my parents every day. So, yeah, I'm still connected to them.

When asked to elaborate on how she was connected to these people, this participant said:

Well, I'm connected to my best friend 'cause I live with her, and we do like a lot of things together. Like, whenever I hang out or do anything, like study, or go to class, usually with her. . . . But my mom and dad like like they support me, and like financially and like mentally and all that stuff. So, I'm still like connected to them.

One participant discussed how he was connected to varied specific people by engaging in different activities with them, thus also pointing to how he constructed himself differently in relation to different people:

Certain things I do with other people. Like I work out with certain people just I guess they're similar and they want to go do something. And I'm friends with certain people. There are certain people that I can talk to about my feelings. There's other people who I can't, there's other people where I work with them or like I help them do something. Um. Certain people that, uh, you know, I can just make laugh. I guess I can be funny with other people. Some people find me funny, other people don't. Um, I can just be goofy. Like if I just want to be goofy, my one friend, like he's all for it. I mean we'll just be silly all day, and it's fun. It's like a good release. I can be loving with my girlfriend and my family. With my mom I can do anything. I can be goofy and chase her around the house, or you know, talk to her about something serious. My dad I can probably do the same thing, but he's not as sensitive.

When asked whether they would say that they were interdependent or connected to others, all 11 of the Vietnamese participants said yes. As with the Euro-Americans, when asked to discuss what it means to be interdependent or how they are connected to others, nine (82%) Vietnamese said that being connected involved direct or specific relationships with family or friends with whom they enjoyed spending time, or who provided emotional and/or financial support. For example, some of the Vietnamese participants commented:

- My girlfriend. Yeah. 'Cause she's always there for me. And, my uncle. Yeah, but he, he's from another state though. So, he's always calling me and asking me how are things going.
- I mean. Since I grow up with a lot of people, so, they're like my own brothers and sisters. So we're connected all through the way.

One Vietnamese participant said she was connected to, "Umm, my best friend. And my parents. And my aunt."

Two (18%) Vietnamese participants noted that being interdependent or connected meant being connected to all people in general, as human beings, perhaps reflecting a Buddhist view of life's ongoing interrelations. These two participants explained:

- In my thinking and my way of doing things. Umm, sometimes, like people have the same thinking and the same, like, things that I do. So that's how the connection is.
- Well. Just like. If you. For example, you drink this cup of soy bean milk, right? Uhh. It must be some people that produced it. So, you are connected. They produced, you buy, you drink, they make money. So, it's connected. Everybody are connected together.

WHY INTERDEPENDENCE IS GOOD OR IMPORTANT

When asked why it is good or important to be connected to others, 28 (80%) of the Euro-American participants discussed variations on the theme of having a support network. This theme included discussions of how being connected to others provided support, help, or company. This theme also included the participants' discussions of how being connected to others made them feel a sense of belongingness, as well as being cared for, secure, and understood. As some participants maintained:

- I think everybody needs to have like a home feeling. Like a place where they can, people and place where they can kind of let their guard down, and say, oh this is where I'm really comfortable. And I think people aid in that. And I think a connectedness with people really aids in feeling at home. And I think that's very important.
- I think it's just human nature. You want to feel that you fit in, that you belong. And so having a group of friends, having a connection, or a church connection, or whatever it is, it gives you that sense of belonging.
- What's good about being connected? Um. Well I don't know. I guess I'm getting kind of broad. But I guess it's good to be connected to people to have some kind of unifying feeling, you know. I would hate to think that we all walk around and have no idea what anybody else is thinking. Or, you know, like that much like, like in a box you know.
- I guess I don't want to be lonely. . . . Just being around people or whatever. Not being like isolated from the world or whatever.
- That you don't have to, that you're not alone, I guess. You don't have to be alone on a lot of things. Like I, I thought I was. I was always afraid of going out and getting a job, and um going to school, and when I was in high school and all that. And umm, I've realized that, you know, I'm not alone in a lot of my fears either. Like talking to people you realize how scared people are too.

Similarly, when asked why it is good or important to be connected to others, all of the Vietnamese participants discussed variations on the theme of having a support network as defined earlier. As some of them pointed out:

- It's very good because, you know. Friend beside you, just make you. Like sometimes you're sad, and then they can make you happy. Uhh. And then sometimes when you want to talk about something. You're very upset, and you want a person to listen to you, they can listen. That's why.
- 'Cause umm. Because you can't. Well, if you don't have anybody to talk to, you feel trapped because you can't say anything. Like you can say it, but you're just gonna have to say it to yourself. And, it's not healthy 'cause

you're gonna have to explode sometimes. And like, you need somebody there to support you, to give you support. And then you need somebody there to listen to you.

For many of the participants, being part of a supportive social network entailed not only feeling supported by others, but also being there to provide support to others. For example, different Euro-American participants explained how they supported the people who supported them:

- Just the fact that they, they care for you and enjoy your company. And you can do the same in return.
- It's good 'cause they're always there to help you. If you run into a problem, then you have someone that can, like maybe help you out. Or if they run into a problem, and then you can help them out.

Similarly, some Vietnamese participants explained the reciprocity of being part of a social network:

- Well. I guess they are important because. To me, family and friends are, you know, what you have. If you don't have them, then you're gonna be like all by yourself. You know. . . . My family, you know. To me, they're gonna be there for me any time, every time, whatever happens. . . . It's fun to have them. You know. Because we do family things and go out and stuff. And you have people like looking after you, and you're looking after other people. It's just the way it is.
- So you could have like, you could help each other out.
- Lets you know that they're gonna be there for you. And you're gonna be there for them. And. I mean. You need everyone. You need all the help you can get when you, going through life and everything. . . . It's like, when I need help they would be there for me, and when they need help, I'm gonna be there. And I know I would because they have helped me through what I've been through, and they deserve help from me.

For one (9%) Vietnamese and seven (20%) Euro-American adolescents, being interdependent or connected to others was understood as a source of individual development or improvement. The one Vietnamese participant said:

- Umm. I think. Like. No matter, you can't learn anything by yourself. So, it's good to connect with other people, where you can learn from them. And all that. They have more experience than you or, like, there are some things they know, but you don't know.

Some of the Euro-American participants claimed:

- Um, I guess it helps you develop who you are, what you want to be.
- 'Cause I think it makes you umm, overall a better person because other people have different opinions than you do. So, I mean, if you interact with other people, you have a more diverse way of thinking.

When asked why that was important, this participant said:

Um. 'Cause the world. There are a lot of different people out there in the world. And if you think that you're the only, the only right way, then that's bad, I think. Like the more people that you know, the more experiences, different personalities, and stuff like that.

- You just need somebody else . . . to learn from.
- Um, just people to talk to, and like, know different things about people or. Probably like a one-track mind, knowing the same thing and things becoming redundant. I don't think that's really good for a person. I think it's good for a person to, things to like change a little bit. Learn a little bit about somebody else, hear about what's going on in their life. Talk to different people every day.

When asked why it was important to talk to different people, this participant responded, "Like broader. Like you have broader views and umm. I think that's good because you're more compatible with people and just like. That's why like, just getting to know lots of people is healthy for you." This last quotation indicates ongoing interrelations between conceptions of independence and interdependence because connections to others facilitated self-improvement, which in turn involved enhancing social connections.

For five (14%) of the Euro-American participants, the advantages of being connected to others revolved around being able to get input and advice from varied sources so that one could ultimately make the best possible individual decision based on considering different perspectives. The advantages of talking to other people when trying to make individual decisions are evident in the following interview quotation: "And you get different point of views from it 'cause sometimes your family has one point of view and other people have a different point of view." When asked to elaborate on why it was important to get different points of view, this participant replied, "In case you have like a hard decision to make, if you have different choices, they have different opinions about it."

Another participant maintained:

Having someone there for you if you need them 'cause. Like if you have a problem, your family is going to give you one perspective from it. Your friends are going to give you another. You know your boyfriend's going to give you another. I think that's important, to have, you know, more than one perspective on something. You know, if you're having a problem, you know of course, your mom's going to tell you something completely different from what your friends are going to tell you. You know what I mean? I think it's important to take all those things into consideration. You know, from what they tell you and you know. And I think putting them all together will give you like a final answer.

Putting various aspects of being interdependent together, one Euro-American participant indicated how social connections ultimately keep people healthy because, as has been pointed out already, social connections are simply basic to human nature:

'Cause um, like if nobody had friends, then they would lack like such incredible social ties. And like, you need social ties to be happy. Like you can't live in a cardboard box away from like the world and be happy. Like a lot of people think they could, but you just, you need somebody else, like to share your experiences with or talk to, to learn from. They did like research on it and everything. Like that they found that babies who weren't talked to or really touched or anything like that were like very lacking in like intelligence and everything like that. Stuff like that. It's like, it's genetic. It's like human nature, like, you need people. Like we're social animals. Like we really need like each other for security and things like that.

Echoing this idea, another person claimed, "I guess interacting with other people is, is good for everything, I guess. Keeps you sane."

FEELING "REALLY" INTERDEPENDENT

The Euro-American participants were also asked to describe a time when they felt "really" connected to others or interdependent. Eleven (31%) participants discussed a specific event when they felt close to or supported by someone. For example, the following interview excerpts demonstrate how some of the participants' connectedness events involved feeling close to others:

- Uh. I think that um. There were other people in the car with me when I wrecked. And I think that like brought us all closer together . . . 'cause we went through like a very traumatic thing, and we all came out okay. That helped to bring us all together. . . . I think that it, it felt good 'cause we were really. You know, we were good friends, but I think it's just made it even better. I just think we just like love each other a lot more as a result.

- Um. Let's see. When I was really connected to people? Probably like, when I was in my fraternity. When I was pledging with my pledge brothers. I was really connected to all that. I don't know, we just like, we knew everything about each other. We were going through the same things, and we were really good friends. We really bonded.

The following interview excerpts indicate how some participants' interdependence or connectedness events enabled them to feel supported by others:

- Probably, um, when one of my friends died in high school in a car accident, and everyone was there for me. . . . Just knowing that they were there for me.
- Uh. Maybe when, my senior year during the individual golf playoffs there. Uh, I was going through my bag to get ready to go out, and I found a card in my bag. And here it was from my mother saying, hey good luck, you can do it, just try hard, and you can be able to do it. And I feel that way it brought me that, it was like we were connected there. I knew she was there with me. Maybe not physically, but through the mentally. While she was working, she was thinking, well I wonder how he's doing today. So I think that way, I felt a connection there.
- I know there is a time. I always go back to this one. I have asthma really bad. And I was in the hospital, and my mom was there for me. And I just, I felt really really connected to my mom there. 'Cause like, when I'm, if I'm in the hospital, she's always been there for me. Like then, she'd always just, you know, calm me.

Rather than focusing on one particular event, 23 (64%) Euro-American participants described how they felt ongoing connections to specific people, such as relatives, friends, or teammates, because they were there for each other, could talk to each other about anything, had common interests, had common attitudes or opinions, had shared various experiences, or enjoyed being together. This experience of ongoing mutuality in connectedness is evident in the following quotations:

- Uh. Yeah, pretty much my whole life, you know like growing up with sports, like people on my teams or whatever. You know my dad was always like coaching. You know he was pretty much my coach in basketball, football, baseball, you know. And there was always that connection there. Like you just develop, uh, relationships with these people that you're with. You know, you're all striving to achieve the same goal. You know, to win, to the championship or whatever. To be the best team that you could be. So, it like gives you all kind of a focus and it helps you, umm, just kind of strengthen relationships with people. I've always felt like a part of something, you know, a group.

- Uh. I feel really connected to my girlfriend because we've been going out for three years. And we can tell each other anything, and do anything together. We would like drop anything to like help them out, without it being a problem or anything.
- Hmm. I don't know. That's a pretty big question. Uh. I'm gonna have to get back again to the training for the military. And uh. Another guy, the guy that lives, his bunk was across from mine. He goes to [to school here] too. And that was one of the reasons I came to this school was because he was here. And I've known him for about four years. . . . We joined, we joined on the same day. We did training together. I mean, we've been through, we've been through a lot. . . . And uhh, I think I'm more connected to him than anybody right now. . . . Yeah, we share a lot of the same, the same views and opinions. Our career goals are totally different, but uh we're a lot alike when it really comes down to it. And when push comes to shove, I know that he'd do anything for me, and uh, I'd do anything for him too.

Another participant explained how her connections to particular friends enhanced her self-awareness, thus linking interdependence to conceptions of independence. She said that she felt close to a specific person because:

Like I can tell him anything and he can tell me anything and like. Just some of the conversations we have, it's like, wow, I never knew that about myself. Or, I don't know, like some of like the friends I have up here. Like, how like very nice a lot of people are here. And like, I'll just sit down and have like conversations with them for like hours and that really makes you feel close to them. Like you just talk about everything and you, they feel comfortable around you, and you feel comfortable around them.

The end of this explanation also shows the importance of reciprocal self-expression for enhancing relationships.

SOME GENERAL REMARKS

This chapter furthered our understanding of how older adolescents construct themselves in terms of multifaceted and inseparable independence and interdependence meanings in the context of going to college, which provides varied opportunities for dealing with a host of independence and interdependence issues, from making self-directed choices to negotiating the rather socially saturated context of student life. Moreover, the interviews show that when specifically asked about independence and inter-dependence, the participants did not necessarily construe independence and interdependence in mutually exclusive terms. Sometimes their conceptions of independence explicitly entailed conceptions of interdependence, and similarly their conceptions of interdependence sometimes explicitly entailed conceptions of independence.

In addition to revealing multifaceted and inseparable independence and interdependence issues, the study presented in this chapter points to the advantages of semistructured interviews as a method for discerning some of the complexities of independence and interdependence (Raeff, 2004). In particular, this study suggests that simply asking study participants to generate a list of self-characteristics, or to rate themselves with respect to varied preconceived independence and interdependence issues, is not sufficient for analyzing how they construct themselves as independent and interdependent. It is not sufficient because an apparently independent self-characteristic may be understood in relation to interdependence issues and vice versa. For example, in this chapter, we have seen how independence may be construed as being able to make friends on one's own or using one's individual abilities to contribute to society. Thus, once an individual lists some self-characteristics, it is important to go further in an effort to discern the importance or meaning of those characteristics to the individual. Moreover, this point is not exclusive to studies of self-construction. Indeed, this notion came up in chapter 4 with regard to parents' claims about wanting their children to be self-directed in relation to varied social situations, such as making friends and choosing careers.

The issue of finding individual fulfillment through interdependence came up several times in this chapter and has also been addressed in previous chapters. Actually, this topic takes us back to some basic conceptual issues regarding cultural differences in the meanings of independence and interdependence. Going back to dichotomous conceptions of independence and interdependence, the idea that others can serve as a source of personal fulfillment or support is related to the idea that relationships may serve instrumental and self-serving purposes within so-called *individualistic* cultures. As mentioned in chapter 1, the tone of such characterizations is rather pejorative, implying that individualists use others for personal benefit and would be less concerned about another person for that person's own sake or for the sake of their relationship. However, I wonder if some instrumentality does not also play a role in the structuring of independence and interdependence in some other cultures, perhaps even in all cultures in some situations. For example, we have seen how the realization of group goals requires the contributions of individuals, suggesting that it is possible for individuals to be the instruments of group goals.

Instrumentality is also evident in claims that, in allegedly interdependence-oriented cultures, people are not valued as individuals, but rather valued insofar as they fulfill certain roles within the group. The idea that a parent expects to live with his or her children during old age could also be linked to an instrumental view of others. Some analyses suggest that an instrumental form of financial *amae* "can be observed in older children. They may exhibit *amae* behaviors toward parents with less purely affective motives but more in relation to financial needs. Children as old as high-school or even college age do approach their parents in helpless and desperate manners when they want new clothes, shoes, or cars" (Behrens, 2004, p. 15).

These different modes of instrumentality suggest that, as social beings, people everywhere fulfill and support others in some way. However, rather than being instrumentally self-serving, the idea that one can find fulfillment through social relationships may be interpreted alternatively as reflecting a view of people as fundamentally connected. If people were not taken to be fundamentally connected, one would find fulfillment elsewhere, and it could then be argued that such asocial self-fulfillment epitomizes an independence orientation. In addition, as we have seen in this chapter, varied modes of instrumentality may be construed as mutual or reciprocal aspects of relationships. Thus, just as others may be sources of someone's personal fulfillment, that someone can and probably expects or wants to play a role in the fulfillment of others. Using the term *instrument* as a metaphor connotes the idea of an unfeeling, almost inhuman, approach to others and relationships, and there are certainly cases of human conduct that can aptly be characterized by this metaphor. However, the instrument metaphor may not be applicable for characterizing people's constructions of themselves as fundamentally connected to others.

These Euro-American and Vietnamese adolescents' self-constructions encompassed many of the issues discussed throughout this book. Thus, the time appears to have come to step back and synthesize varied issues that have been addressed in this text, as well as to consider how steps forward may be taken to further our understanding of independence and interdependence.

CHAPTER EIGHT

Recurring Themes

STEPPING BACK

The current conceptual approach has guided analyses of cultural contexts of development in ways that can advance our understanding of how independence and interdependence enter into human behavior and development. Thinking back to chapter 2, we may recall the basic claims of this conceptual approach. The current conceptual approach holds that independence and interdependence are constructs that refer to multifaceted and interrelated dimensions of activity that make up the cultural practices in which children participate. In addition, the current approach provides conceptual tools for analyzing activity dimensions of cultural practices by defining independence activity dimensions in terms of individuality, subjectivity, self-direction, and self-awareness/reflection, and by defining interdependence activity dimensions in terms of cultural interaction patterns, social relationships, social roles, and links to wider societal functioning. The current conceptual approach also holds that independence and interdependence are constructs that refer to multifaceted and interrelated cultural meanings regarding human separateness and human connectedness that are enacted as children participate in varied cultural practices.

To offer some general conclusions regarding the issues discussed in this book, it is useful to also reiterate the three organizing goals that are derived from the current conceptual approach and that guided my analyses of independence and interdependence in previous chapters:

1. To show that independence meanings are prevalent in cultures that
   have traditionally been characterized as interdependent, as well as to
   show that interdependence meanings are prevalent in cultures that
   have traditionally been characterized as independent.
2. To explore how independence and interdependence may be understood and valued in multifaceted ways.
3. To explore some of the interrelations between independence and
   interdependence meanings, and some of the interrelations between
   independence and interdependence activity dimensions, as they are
   particularized in the cultural practices in which children participate.

Let us now consider issues pertaining to each of these goals in turn.

Independence and Interdependence in Varied Cultures

In the preceding chapters, considerations of research in varied non-
Western cultures have pointed to the importance of independence in cultures that have traditionally been characterized as interdependent. For example, analyses of the Kaluli reveal the importance of clearly articulating
one's individual perspective to others during social interaction. Also, a
conception of people as separate mental individuals is evident in the
Kaluli belief that people cannot know what others are thinking or feeling.
For Marquesas Islanders, as well as for Guatemalan and Mexican Mayans,
self-direction is valued. Studies of African-American storytelling practices
reveal the importance of expressing one's individuality and asserting oneself as a separate individual. Studies of Japanese parent–child interactions,
school practices, and self-constructions point to varied independence
meanings, including conceptions of self-direction, self-awareness, individual self-expression, and satisfying individual desires. Additionally, varied
analyses suggest that, in some situations, the Japanese think it is important not to conform to others and instead to steadfastly adhere to one's
own opinions.

In the preceding chapters, our considerations of research with Euro-
American samples have noted the importance of interdependence for this
cultural group that is so often characterized in terms of independence.
For example, interdependence has been emphasized for generations of
Euro-Americans, beginning with the Puritans who valued communal living, conformity to social norms, and service to others. Euro-American
childrearing practices have long emphasized the value of fostering family
ties, consideration for others, and being able to establish and maintain relationships with varied others in a diverse social network. With regard to
education, collaborative learning is increasingly being incorporated into

American school practices. Additionally, studies of self-construction show how Euro-American children and adolescents define themselves in relation to others and in terms of their behavior in social situations.

Multifaceted Independence and Interdependence Meanings

Moving beyond simply claiming that both independence and interdependence are evident in some way in all cultures, the current conceptual approach provides a framework for considering some of the cultural complexities of infants', children's, and adolescents' developmental experiences by directing our attention to multifaceted cultural meanings of independence and interdependence. Focusing on multifaceted cultural meanings and how they are enacted in cultural practices also takes us beyond asking only if one culture values independence or interdependence more than another culture, to discerning how independence and interdependence may be construed in different cultures.

In addition, analyzing multifaceted meanings of independence and interdependence as they are embedded in cultural practices moves us toward discerning how independence and interdependence are construed by a group of people. For example, we have seen that independence meanings include values and expectations for taking care of one's physical needs, reflecting on one's own behavior, directing one's own behavior, and understanding oneself and others in terms of individual preferences and abilities. Interdependence can mean being generally sociable, defining oneself in relation to other individuals (e.g., a particular friend), defining oneself in relation to a group, conforming to authority, empathizing with others, engaging in group interactions, engaging in dyadic interactions, and following social norms.

The findings discussed throughout this book also suggest that important cultural similarities and differences lie in independence and interdependence meanings and how they are enacted in the structuring of independence and interdependence activity dimensions within different cultural practices. For example, although self-construction may involve identifying oneself with a group in some cultures and with individuals in other cultures, self-construction in both cases involves interdependence. Another example of cultural similarities and differences in independence and interdependence meanings concerns the pursuit of common goals, which has emerged as an interdependence issue in varied cultural contexts. Although pursuing common goals may be important around the world, such goals may be structured and construed differently in different cultures. Indeed, as we have seen, the pursuit of common goals in varied cultures has included community subsistence goals, chores in nuclear families, membership in voluntary associations, cooperative learning activities, and contributing to democratic societal goals. These findings suggest that it is not necessarily the case that the pursuit of common goals is more or less important in some cultures than in others. Rather, the pursuit of common goals around the world occurs in the context of different cultural practices in which independence and interdependence meanings may be construed and enacted differently.

The Inseparability of Independence and Interdependence

Based on the position that independence and interdependence are interrelated or inseparable, identifying independence and interdependence meanings in isolation from each other provides only a partial view of independence and interdependence issues within and across cultures. Similarly, analyzing the structuring of independence and interdependence activity dimensions in isolation from each other obscures some of the complexities of independence and interdependence. According to the current approach, the key to understanding how both independence and interdependence are particularized in children's developmental experiences is to discern how they are interrelated or inseparable within cultural practices. Analyzing some of the ways in which independence and interdependence are interrelated reveals similarities and differences in how they are particularized in varied cultural contexts of development, and it also takes us beyond first-glance analyses that may deceptively suggest a dominance of either independence or interdependence.

Cultural Similarities and Differences. By drawing on diverse studies, we have been made aware of some of the ways in which independence and interdependence are interrelated or inseparable in varied cultures, making it possible to tentatively identify some systematic similarities in how they are interrelated across cultures. For example, we have seen how pursuing common goals in varied cultures is inseparable from individual self-direction. In addition, individual self-expression is considered to play a role in facilitating interpersonal interaction among both Euro-Americans and the Kaluli. Similarly, in the Japanese context of inner cultural practices, expressing one's individuality is implicated in the structuring of social interactions.

At the same time that there seem to be some cultural similarities in how independence and interdependence are interrelated, there are also cultural differences. For example, although Euro-American and Japanese interpersonal interactions involve expressing individuality, this similarity seems to specifically involve Japanese inner cultural practices and is not necessarily evident when Euro-American and Japanese outer cultural practices are compared. Interpersonal interactions in Japanese outer cultural practices seem more likely to involve the suppression of individuality for the sake of maintaining social cohesion.

Also, although some of the research discussed in previous chapters suggests that the same independence and interdependence activity dimensions are inseparable across cultures, the more specific structuring of those activity dimensions may be different across cultures in relation to different cultural practices. For example, Rogoff's observations in a Guatemalan Mayan village indicate how self-direction is related to social nurture, which includes community members beyond a child's immediate family. Although self-direction is seen in relation to social nurture by some Euro-American parents, responsibility for the care of Euro-American children is taken to lie primarily within the nuclear family. In addition, although both Guatemalan Mayan and Euro-American children become increasingly capable of directing their own behavior as they pursue common goals, those common goals will be constituted differently in the two cultures. Also, in varied cultures, children may be aware of themselves in relation to others, but the structuring of such relational self-awareness may be different in different cultures. For example, Japanese schoolchildren may construct themselves as members of a particular kindergarten class, whereas Euro-American kindergartners may be more likely to construct themselves in relation to particular classmates.

Beyond First Glances.   The evidence in support of the current view that independence and interdependence are inseparable also takes us beyond discerning whether a culture emphasizes either independence or interdependence more or less than the other or more or less than another culture. The research discussed throughout this book indicates that even if a culture appears at first glance to value interdependence over independence, or independence over interdependence, an emphasis on one does not in any way preclude the other. More important, values regarding one also most likely implicate the other, making for interrelated or inseparable independence and interdependence meanings, and interrelated or inseparable independence and interdependence activity dimensions.

For example, in chapter 4 we encountered some cultural groups, such as Mexican Mayans, Guatemalan Mayans, and Marquesas Islanders, for whom much of life revolves around group-subsistence economic activities. At first glance, the pursuit of group-subsistence goals makes it rather tempting to characterize these cultures as interdependence oriented. However, children's socialization experiences indicate how the realization of group goals implicates and requires independence expectations, such as engaging in self-directed work and being physically self-reliant. Another example of how a seemingly interdependence-oriented practice is related to conceptions of independence comes from our discussion of Japanese educational practices in chapter 5. If we start with the importance of belonging to a group in Japan, we soon find that the group is taken to be constituted through willing individual conformity, by the enthusiastic contributions of individually distinct participants, as well as by people who understand each other as mentally separate individuals.

With regard to the American case, it has long been evident that independence meanings are central to Euro-American cultural traditions and practices. Nevertheless, the research discussed in previous chapters shows that issues of independence, although key, are only part of Euro-American developmental experiences. Even if one starts from the premise that Euro-Americans emphasize certain independence issues over interdependence, one soon finds that those independence issues are inseparable from interdependence issues.

For example, in chapter 7 we saw how some Euro-American adolescents' constructions of themselves as independent implicate conceptions of interdependence in different ways. That is, some of them explained that independence involves being able to help others, being trusted by others, being able to make friends, responding to others, and living with other people. In chapters 4 and 5 we saw how Euro-American parents and teachers view children as mentally separate beings with their own individual preferences, talents, and perspectives. At the same time, Euro-Americans are likely to see these kinds of individual characteristics in relation to interdependence in varied ways. That is, these individual characteristics are taken to require nurture, indicating that individual characteristics cannot develop without being embedded in social connections. Moreover, establishing and maintaining interpersonal relationships involve expressing one's individual characteristics to others, pointing to the relational value of individual self-expression. In addition to direct relationships, we have seen that the expression of one's individuality is taken to be central for enhancing the collective functioning of a democratic society, thus linking self-expression to wider societal interdependence.

I realize that many findings from research with Euro-Americans can be interpreted as illustrations of the idea that people are isolated individuals who enter into relationships with other isolated individuals when they take a notion to, only to exit them and return to their self-contained lives. For example, going back to the Puritans, we may recall that in his arrival sermon Winthrop (1630/1988) offered "two rules whereby wee are to walke one towards another" (p. 23). This remark suggests that individuals are initially separate, and thus require specifically contrived rules for approaching one another. There is also an implication that if separate individuals can walk toward one another, they can choose to walk away from one another. However, this one clause from Winthrop's sermon is embedded within the wider context of Puritan life, in which the inherent interdependence of human experience was also emphasized. Moreover, before Winthrop and his fellow Puritans banded together to settle in the New World, they may have conceptualized themselves as separate from one another, but not necessarily from relationships per se.

We may consider again a study finding mentioned in chapter 4 that Euro-American parents typically want their children to eventually "make their own decisions and establish separate existences" (Richman et al., 1988, p. 68). By itself, this childrearing aspiration may be interpreted as a classic example of how Euro-American goals of development revolve around separation. These Euro-American parents may recognize that children are initially connected to others (i.e., the parents), but the goal could be interpreted as implying that such connections are merely a precondition to an independence ideal of separation and self-direction.

Ultimately, however, this one childrearing goal is a single finding in the midst of many studies. Within the wider context of Euro-American life, we have also seen that children are viewed as initially separate individuals who must be taught how to relate to others. Taken together, we find that children are understood as both separate and connected. In addition, we have seen varied interrelations between self-direction and interdependence insofar as making one's own decisions involves making decisions in social situations and making decisions that are in keeping with social norms. We have also seen that eventually establishing a separate existence does not mean severing parent–child connections, but instead typically involves individuation in family relationships, establishing oneself in relation to others besides one's parents, and finding a place within a wider social network. These examples indicate the utility of casting a wide empirical and interpretive net that places a finding from any single study in relation to the systemic complexities of a broader cultural context.

With regard to the issue of considering findings from varied studies, the current conceptual approach provides a framework for integrating disparate studies from several, rather artificially divided academic disciplines. These studies, distributed throughout numerous disciplinary outlets, demonstrate the importance of considering varied cultural practices as sites for enacting different independence and interdependence meanings within as well as across cultures. For example, the Japanese distinction between inner and outer social practices quite starkly points to how conceptions of independence and interdependence may be interrelated differently in different cultural practices. Even in cultures where distinctions among practices are not as stark, we have seen how independence and interdependence meanings may be interrelated differently in different cultural practices. For example, Euro-American parent–child interactions are generally characterized by communicative symmetry and mutual self-expression, but teacher–student interactions in whole-class practices are asymmetrical and tend to inhibit individuality.

Although it offers a basis for identifying some systematic cultural patterns or networks of inseparable independence and interdependence meanings and activity dimensions, the extant research does not currently allow us to construct a comprehensive taxonomy of such cultural patterns. Although more research in different cultures is needed, the disproportionately massive number of studies with Euro-American samples enables us to identify a Euro-American network of some inseparable independence and interdependence meanings and some inseparable independence and interdependence activity dimensions across several cultural practices. Figure 8.1 offers a graphic representation of such a network of Euro-American independence and interdependence meanings and activity dimensions as they are enacted in children's developmental experiences.

Insofar as independence and interdependence are inseparable, we can enter Fig. 8.1 at any point and we will end up making our way through the entire network, enabling us to consider varied independence and interdependence issues along the way. To begin, let us start at the bottom right corner of the figure, with the values of maintaining social cohesion and facilitating social interaction, and the lines that immediately connect us to individuality and self-direction. Varied studies with Euro-American samples indicate how social interactions are facilitated, and social cohesion is maintained when people—who are viewed as separate individuals with

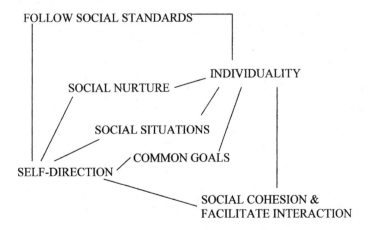

FIG. 8.1.   A network of independence and interdependence meanings and activity dimensions in Euro-American developmental experiences.

their own preferences, goals, and talents—express their individuality to others.

We have also discussed how social interactions and social cohesion in a diverse society are established and maintained through individual self-direction. In addition to being tied to maintaining social cohesion and facilitating social interaction, both individuality and self-direction, as independence activity dimensions, are structured in relation to varied other conceptions of interdependence. That is, there are lines from both individuality and self-direction to following social standards insofar as expressing one's individuality and self-direction ideally involve following social standards, such as being considerate of others. Individuality and self-direction are also connected to common goals insofar as studies suggest that achieving some common goals (e.g., household chores, cooperative learning goals) requires the contributions of distinct individuals who can direct their own behavior without being constantly told what to do. Varied studies suggest further that individuality and self-direction are understood by Euro-American parents and teachers to require social nurture. In addition, the line between self-direction and social situations is based on studies that indicate how self-direction is particularized in situations with peers or in career contexts, and we have also seen how individual self-expression takes place in such varied social situations.

FUTURE DIRECTIONS

Despite varied conceptual advantages and some compelling evidence for the current approach, much remains unknown about developmental and cultural aspects of independence and interdependence. Explicating the current conceptual approach is just the beginning, and I now end by suggesting a few ways in which this approach provides a systematic framework for future research.

First, there is a need to better integrate contemporary findings about any culture's independence and interdependence meanings and activity dimensions with a consideration of that culture's historical traditions. For example, contemporary Japanese independence and interdependence meanings are rooted in centuries of Japanese culture. They are also related to the varied political, educational, and economic changes that have occurred quite rapidly in Japan since World War II and that were influenced by the post-World War II American occupation of Japan. Not only can historical analyses enhance our understanding of changing independence and interdependence meanings, and the structuring of independence and interdependence activity dimensions in any single culture, but they can also enhance our understanding of how and why independence and interdependence have come to be construed, enacted, and interrelated similarly and differently around the world.

Around the world, historical analyses might include discerning how industrial capitalism, globalization, immigration, and access to formal education have and continue to affect the patterning of both independence and interdependence in children's developmental experiences. For example, higher levels of formal education may be related to an increasing emphasis on independence insofar as Western-style formal education is oriented around individual achievement and competition. However, some analyses of education in the United States suggest that educational achievement:

> has little effect on . . . informal social connectedness, like visiting friends or family dining . . . On the other hand, education is an especially powerful predictor of participation in public, formally organized activities. Having four additional years of education (say, going to college) is associated with 30 percent more interest in politics, 40 percent more club attendance, and 45 percent more volunteering. College graduates are more than twice as likely to serve as an officer or committee member of a local organization, to attend a public meeting, to write Congress, or to attend a political rally. The same basic pattern applies to both men and women and to all races and generations. Education, in short, is an extremely powerful predictor of civic engagement. (Putnam, 2000, p. 186)

These findings show how education may widen the scope of interdependence beyond direct relationships and suggest that increasing access to formal education may be related to changes in how both independence and interdependence are particularized in relation to each other. In addition, these specific findings of expanding interdependence to include civic participation are likely related to American democratic practices. Indeed, throughout the previous chapters, our discussions of Euro-American independence and interdependence meanings have been linked to issues regarding the organization of democratic societies. These considerations also demonstrate the importance of exploring how changing political institutions around the world may frame children's participation in varied cultural practices.

In exploring cultural independence and interdependence meanings as they are enacted in the structuring of independence and interdependence activity dimensions, I have been rather general in my approach, and there is much room for research into the nitty-gritty of independence and interdependence in different cultures. For example, exploring gender similarities and differences in independence and interdependence meanings, both within and across cultures, constitutes an interesting line of "nitty-gritty research." In addition, it would likely prove fruitful to investigate some of the nuanced ways in which parents around the world understand varied independence and interdependence issues, including conformity, obedience, self-direction, and happiness. Other possibilities for investigating more specific aspects of cultural independence and interdependence meanings and activity dimensions might involve studies of children's participation in cultural practices with varied others, including and moving beyond the interaction partners mentioned in this book. For example, the vast area of research on peer interactions (briefly alluded to in chaps. 4 and 6) indicates that they provide children with complex opportunities to engage as individuals in relation to others.

Some of the research discussed in this book further indicates that there are important within-culture differences in the meaning and structuring of independence and interdependence, thus pointing to another issue that requires more detailed empirical analysis. For example, we have considered how different independence and interdependence issues are particularized in different cultural practices for both Euro-American and Japanese children. In the Japanese case, within-culture differences are apparent in relation to how independence and interdependence are particularized in inner and outer cultural practices. For Euro-Americans, some of the research discussed in previous chapters indicates that independence and interdependence may be played out differently in home and school practices. The studies reviewed suggest that independence and interdependence may also be particularized differently within cultures during the course of children's development. However, there is no doubt much more to understand about the complexities of independence and interdependence within cultures as children participate in varied cultural practices during the course of development.

Moving beyond middle-class Euro-Americans, research also suggests that, in the United States, some aspects of independence and interdependence may be understood and structured differently for children of differing socioeconomic and ethnic backgrounds. However, there is no doubt more to understand about how independence and interdependence are understood and interrelated in the developmental experiences of children from different socioeconomic circumstances and ethnic backgrounds.

Exploring more detailed aspects of different cultural practices could also shed further light on how and when independence and interdependence meanings and activity dimensions come into conflict in children's developmental experiences. I recognize that in this book I have barely considered situations of conflict, although in chapter 2 I specifically pointed out that, theoretically, cultural independence and interdependence meanings and activity dimensions may be both harmonious and conflicting, and that empirical analyses are required to discern the patterning of such harmony and conflict in varied cultures. I have focused mostly on how independence and interdependence may be interrelated in harmonious ways in part to argue against conceptualizing independence and interdependence as opposing dimensions of human functioning. An important research direction will involve discerning how independence and interdependence may conflict in different cultural practices within and across cultures. In addition, it is important to discern whether and how such conflicts are resolved.

In addition to pointing to topics for future research, the current conceptual approach offers some methodological and analytical guidance for pursuing these lines of research. To begin, this approach reveals the importance of investigating independence and interdependence as they are particularized in the cultural practices in which children participate. Then, armed with the conceptual tools of the current approach, analyzing those cultural practices would involve discerning how multifaceted independence and interdependence activity dimensions are structured and interrelated, and how they reflect multifaceted and inseparable cultural independence and interdependence meanings. Studies of parents' childrearing ideas, teachers' ideas about children, and children's and adolescents' self-constructions may also be guided by the current approach. For example, with regard to parents' ideas, the research reviewed in this book shows that parents construe independence and interdependence in multifaceted ways. The current approach points to the utility of interview methods that give participants a chance to expand on their initial statements about varied independence and interdependence issues.

Finally, with regard to future research, the current conceptual approach leads us toward the major work of discerning developmental changes in children's abilities to engage in cultural practices that reflect cultural independence and interdependence meanings. Based on the current conceptual approach, developmental analyses would be directed toward discerning transformations in children's abilities to act as separate individuals in relation to others. More specifically, developmental analyses would involve identifying changes in children's abilities to engage in self-directed action, be self-aware, express individuality, and interact with varied others. Based on the orthogenetic principle, developmental analyses of these kinds of changes would involve exploring how these dimensions of behavior are differentiated and integrated in relation to cultural goals of development.

Within the current theoretical context, analyzing the development of children's abilities to act as both separate individuals and in relation to others would not only be focused on discerning whether development involves becoming more or less likely to act as a separate individual or in relation to others. Instead, I am suggesting that when development is understood in terms of increasing differentiation and integration, developmental analyses involve assessing how a person's abilities to act as a separate individual and in relation to others are differentiated and integrated over time in relation to varied cultural practices. For example, one might investigate how children's abilities to engage in self-directed action are differentiated from and integrated with their abilities to interact with others (e.g., peers) in culturally appropriate ways. With regard to self-construction, developmental analyses might involve analyzing how independence and interdependence meanings are differentiated and integrated in children's and adolescents' representations of themselves.

Pursuing these varied lines of research requires more nuanced conceptualizations of independence and interdependence in relation to such thorny issues as motivation, consciousness, intentionality, and goal directedness. In addition, as more is learned about cultural independence and interdependence meanings and activity dimensions, the current conceptual approach will undoubtedly benefit from theoretical refinement. For example, it is important to conceptualize independence activity dimensions in terms of more nuanced conceptions of self-direction, subjectivity, self-awareness/reflection, and individuality. These dimensions of independence have certainly long been topics of theoretical and empirical consternation in the social sciences. However, rather than focusing on social scientists' conceptions of these issues, my focus in this book has been on how these dimensions of human functioning are construed in everyday life and enacted in some of the cultural practices in which children participate. Ultimately, analyses will require integrating more elaborate theoretical conceptions of independence and interdependence with how they are particularized in everyday life during development in different cultures.

It will also likely prove fruitful to conceptualize independence and interdependence in relation to more nuanced conceptions of "cultural practices" and "activities." In referring to cultural practices and activities, I have been plagued by some nagging conceptual questions that are related to ongoing efforts to identify and explicate a unit of analysis in psychology that encompasses the interrelations among individual, social, and cultural processes (e.g., Cole, 1995; Wertsch, 1998). In particular, I wonder if it would be useful for understanding issues of independence and interdependence to demarcate activities within cultural practices more precisely, and to identify some parameters that distinguish one cultural practice from another within the relatively seamless conduct of human life.

Pursuing these and other empirical and theoretical directions will undoubtedly encompass yet more independence and interdependence issues beyond the ones included in this book. In doing so, future research will also hopefully enable us to identify patterns or networks of multifaceted and inseparable independence and interdependence meanings and activity dimensions in varied cultures, and to graphically represent them as I did in Fig. 8.1 for the Euro-American case.

Going back to Fig. 8.1, it is important to note that this figure is just one way of graphically representing Euro-American independence and interdependence meanings and activity dimensions. It is also a representation of Euro-American independence and interdependence meanings and activity dimensions at a particular point in time. Insofar as cultures are dynamic and under ongoing change, future analyses may render Fig. 8.1 a historical relic. Indeed, I would suggest that we cannot count on future research to identify definitive or final networks of independence and interdependence meanings and activity dimensions for any culture because in all cultures they have changed historically and will continue to change. Instead, by recognizing the dynamic and systemic nature of human experience, future analyses may be directed toward investigating the ongoing human construction of independence and interdependence meanings and activity dimensions. Ultimately, the current conceptual approach will hopefully provide a productive framework for organizing our continued understanding of the ongoing and inseparable dynamics of independence and interdependence as people go about their lives in all corners of the world.

References

Abbott, S. (1992). Holding on and pushing away: Comparative perspectives on an Eastern Kentucky child-rearing practice. *Ethos, 20*, 33–65.

Aboud, F. E., & Mendelson, M. J. (1996). Determinants of friendship selection and quality: Developmental perspectives. In W. M. Bukowski, A. F. Newcomb, & W. W. Hartup (Eds.), *The company they keep: Friendship in childhood and adolescence* (pp. 87–112). Cambridge, UK: Cambridge University Press.

Adams, G. R., & Marshall, S. K. (1996). A developmental social psychology of identity: Understanding the person-in-context. *Journal of Adolescence, 19*, 429–442.

Ames, C. (1984). Competitive, cooperative, and individualistic goal structures: A cognitive-motivational analysis. In R. Ames & C. Ames (Eds.), *Research on motivation in education: Vol. 1. Student motivation* (pp. 177–207). Orlando: Academic Press.

Antil, L. R., Jenkins, J. R., Wayne, S. K., & Vadasy, P. F. (1998). Cooperative learning: Prevalence, conceptualizations, and the relation between research and practice. *American Educational Research Journal, 35*, 419–454.

Archer, M. S. (1988/1994). *Culture and agency: The place of culture in social theory*. Cambridge, UK: Cambridge University Press.

Archer, S. L. (1985). Career and/or family: The identity process for adolescent girls. *Youth and Society, 16*, 289–314.

Archer, S. L. (1989). Gender differences in identity development: Issues of process, domain and timing. *Journal of Adolescence, 12*, 117–138.

Archer, S. L. (1992). A feminist's approach to identity research. In G. R. Adams, T. P. Gullotta, & R. Montemayor (Eds.), *Adolescent identity formation* (pp. 25–49). Newbury Park, CA: Sage.

Archer, S. L., & Waterman, A. S. (1988). Psychological individualism: Gender differences or gender neutrality? *Human Development, 31*, 65–81.

Aronson, E., & Patnoe, S. (1997). *The jigsaw classroom: Building cooperation in the classroom*. New York: Longman.

Bachnik, J. (1992a/1995). *Kejime*: Defining a shifting self in multiple organizational modes. In N. R. Rosenberger (Ed.), *Japanese sense of self* (pp. 152–172). Cambridge, UK: Cambridge University Press.

Bachnik, J. M. (1992b). The two "faces" of self and society in Japan. *Ethos, 20*, 3–32.

Bachnik, J. M. (1994). Indexing self and society in Japanese family organization. In J. M. Bachnik & C. J. Quinn, Jr. (Eds.), *Situated meaning: Inside and outside in Japanese self, society, and language* (pp. 143–166). Princeton, NJ: Princeton University Press.

Baker, J. A., Terry, T., Bridger, R., & Winsor, A. (1997). Schools as caring communities: A relational approach to school reform. *School Psychology Review, 26*, 586–602.

Ball, H. L., Hooker, E., & Kelly, P. J. (1999). Where will the baby sleep? Attitudes and practices of new and experienced parents regarding cosleeping with their newborn infants. *American Anthropologist, 101*, 143–151.

Bamberg, M. (2004). Form and function of "slut bashing" in male identity constructions in 15-year-olds. *Human Development, 47*, 331–353.

Barry III, H., Child, I. L., & Bacon, M. K. (1959). Relation of child training to subsistence economy. *American Anthropologist, 61*, 51–63.

Bartz, K. W., & Levine, E. S. (1978). Childrearing by Black parents: A description and comparison to Anglo and Chicano parents. *Journal of Marriage and the Family, 40*, 709–719.

Baumrind, D. (1967). Child care practices anteceding three patterns of preschool behavior. *Genetic Psychology Monographs, 75*, 43–88.

Baumrind, D. (1989). Rearing competent children. In W. Damon (Ed.), *Child development today and tomorrow* (pp. 349–378). San Francisco: Jossey-Bass.

Baumrind, D. (1996). The discipline controversy revisited. *Family Relations: Journal of Applied Family and Child Studies, 45*, 405–414.

Beales, R. W., Jr. (1985). In search of the historical child: Miniature adulthood and youth in colonial New England. In N. R. Hiner & J. M. Hawes (Eds.), *Growing up in America: Children in historical perspective* (pp. 7–24). Urbana: University of Illinois Press.

Behrens, K. Y. (2004). A multifaceted view of the concept of *amae*: Reconsidering the indigenous Japanese concept of relatedness. *Human Development, 47*, 1–27.

Bell, R. Q. (1968). A reinterpretation of the direction of effects in studies of socialization. *Psychological Review, 75*, 81–95.

Bell, R. Q., & Harper, L. V. (1977). *Child effects on adults*. New York: Wiley.

Bellah, R. N., Madsen, R., Sullivan, W. M., Swidler, A., & Tipton, S. M. (1985/1986). *Habits of the heart: Individualism and commitment in American life*. New York: Harper & Row.

Ben-Ari, E. (1996). From mothering to othering: Organization, culture, and nap time in a Japanese day-care center. *Ethos, 24*, 136–164.

Benedict, A. E. (1939, September). Threshold years. *Parents' Magazine*, pp. 24–25, 73–75.

Berlin, I. (1958/1969). Two concepts of liberty. In I. Berlin (Ed.), *Four essays on liberty* (pp. 118–172). London: Oxford University Press.

Berndt, T. J. (1982). The features and effects of friendship in early adolescence. *Child Development, 53*, 1447–1460.

Berry, J. W. (1969). On cross-cultural comparability. *International Journal of Psychology, 4*, 119–128.

Betts, E. M., & Bear, J. A., Jr. (Eds.). (1966/1986). *The family letters of Thomas Jefferson*. Charlottesville: University Press of Virginia.

Bhavnagri, N. P., & Parke, R. D. (1991). Parents as direct facilitators of children's peer relationships: Effects of age of child and sex of parent. *Journal of Social and Personal Relationships, 8*, 423–440.

Boatright, M. C. (1968). The myth of frontier individualism. In R. Hofstadter & S. M. Lipset (Eds.), *Turner and the sociology of the frontier* (pp. 43–64). New York: Basic Books.

Boocock, S. S. (1992). The social construction of childhood in contemporary Japan. In G. Levine (Ed.), *Constructions of the self* (pp. 165–188). New Brunswick, NJ: Rutgers University Press.

Bornstein, M. H., Tal, J., & Tamis-LeMonda, C. (1991). Parenting in cross-cultural perspective: The United States, France, and Japan. In M. H. Bornstein (Ed.), *Cultural approaches to parenting* (pp. 69–90). Hillsdale, NJ: Lawrence Erlbaum Associates.

Bowlby, J. (1969/1982). *Attachment*. New York: Basic Books.

Bowlby, J. (1973). *Separation: Anxiety and anger*. New York: Basic Books.

Brazelton, T. B. (1982). Joint regulation of neonate–parent behavior. In E. Z. Tronick (Ed.), *Social interchange in infancy: Affect, cognition, and communication* (pp. 7–22). Baltimore: University Park Press.

Briggs, J. L. (1991). Expecting the unexpected: Canadian Inuit training for an experimental lifestyle. *Ethos, 19*, 259–287.

Briggs, J. L. (1992). Mazes of meaning: How a child and a culture create each other. *New Directions for Child Development, 58*, 25–49.

Brody, G. H., & Stoneman, Z. (1992). Child competence and developmental goals among rural Black families: Investigating the links. In I. E. Sigel, A. V. McGillicuddy-DeLisi, & J. J. Goodnow (Eds.), *Parental belief systems: The psychological consequences for children* (pp. 415–431). Hillsdale, NJ: Lawrence Erlbaum Associates.

Bronfenbrenner, U. (1958). Socialization and social class through time and space. In E. E. Maccoby, T. M. Newcomb, & E. L. Hartley (Eds.), *Readings in social psychology* (pp. 400–425). New York: Holt, Rinehart & Winston.

Brooks-Gunn, J., & Paikoff, R. L. (1992). Changes in self-feelings during the transition towards adolescence. In H. McGurk (Ed.), *Childhood social development: Contemporary perspectives* (pp. 63–97). Hillsdale, NJ: Lawrence Erlbaum Associates.

Brown, A. L. (1997). Transforming schools into communities of thinking and learning about serious matters. *American Psychologist, 52*, 399–413.

Brown, B. B. (1990/1995). Peer groups and peer cultures. In S. S. Feldman & G. R. Elliott (Eds.), *At the threshold: The developing adolescent* (pp. 171–196). Cambridge, MA: Harvard University Press.

Bruner, J. (1983). *Child's talk: Learning to use language*. New York: Norton.

Bruner, J. (1990). *Acts of meaning*. Cambridge, MA: Harvard University Press.

Budwig, N. (1989). The linguistic marking of agentivity and control in child language. *Journal of Child Language, 16*, 263–284.

Budwig, N., & Wiley, A. (1995). What language reveals about children's categories of personhood. In L. L. Sperry & P. A. Smiley (Eds.), Exploring young children's concepts of self and other through conversation. *New Directions for Child Development, 69*, 21–32.

Buhrmester, D. (1996). Need fulfillment, interpersonal competence, and the developmental contexts of early adolescent friendship. In W. M. Bukowski, A. F. Newcomb, & W. W. Hartup (Eds.), *The company they keep: Friendship in childhood and adolescence* (pp. 158–185). Cambridge, UK: Cambridge University Press.

Bumpus, M. F., Crouter, A. C., & McHale, S. M. (2001). Parental autonomy granting during adolescence: Exploring gender differences in context. *Developmental Psychology, 37*, 163–173.

Burton, L. M., Allison, K. W., & Obeidallah, D. (1995). Social context and adolescence: Perspectives on development among inner-city African-American teens. In L. J. Crockett & A. C. Crouter (Eds.), *Pathways through adolescence: Individual development in relation to social contexts* (pp. 119–138). Mahwah, NJ: Lawrence Erlbaum Associates.

Cauce, A. M., Hiraga, Y., Graves, D., Gonzales, N., Ryan-Finn, K., & Grove, K. (1996). African American mothers and their adolescent daughters: Closeness, conflict, and control. In B. J. R. Leadbeater & N. Way (Eds.), *Urban girls: Resisting stereotypes, creating identities* (pp. 100–116). New York: New York University Press.

Caudill, W., & Plath, D. W. (1966). Who sleeps by whom? Parent–child involvement in urban Japanese families. *Psychiatry, 29*, 344–366.

Caudill, W., & Weinstein, H. (1969). Maternal care and infant behavior in Japan and America. *Psychiatry, 32*, 12–43.

Cazden, C. B. (2001). *Classroom discourse: The language of teaching and learning*. Portsmouth, NH: Heinemann.

Chandler, M. (2000). Surviving time: The persistence of identity in this culture and that. *Culture and Psychology, 6,* 209–231.

Chandler, M. J., Lalonde, C. E., Sokol, B. W., & Hallett, D. (2003). Personal persistence, identity development, and suicide. *Monographs of the Society for Research in Child Development, 68*(2, Serial No. 273).

Chen, S. (1996). Are Japanese young children among the gods? In D. W. Shwalb & B. J. Shwalb (Eds.), *Japanese childrearing: Two generations of scholarship* (pp. 31–43). New York: Guilford.

Child, L. (1831/1972). *The mother's book.* New York: Arno Press/New York Times.

Chirkov, V., Ryan, R. M., Kim, Y., & Kaplan, U. (2003). Differentiating autonomy from individualism and independence: A self-determination theory perspective on internalization of cultural orientations and well-being. *Journal of Personality and Social Psychology, 84,* 97–110.

Clancy, P. M. (1986). The acquisition of communicative style in Japanese. In B. B. Schieffelin & E. Ochs (Eds.), *Language socialization across cultures* (pp. 213–250). Cambridge, UK: Cambridge University Press.

Cohen, E. G. (1994). Restructuring the classroom: Conditions for productive small groups. *Review of Educational Research, 64,* 1–35.

Cole, M. (1995). The supra-individual envelope of development: Activity and practice, situation and context. In J. J. Goodnow, P. J. Miller, & F. Kessel (Eds.), *Cultural practices as contexts for development. New Directions for Child Development, 67,* 105–118.

Cole, M. (1996). *Cultural psychology: A once and future discipline.* Cambridge, MA: Belknap Press/Harvard University Press.

Collins, W. A., & Laursen, B. (1992). Conflict and relationships during adolescence. In C. U. Shantz & W. W. Hartup (Eds.), *Conflict in child and adolescent development* (pp. 216–241). Cambridge, UK: Cambridge University Press.

Collins, W. A., & Luebker, C. (1994). Parent and adolescent expectancies: Individual and relational significance. In J. G. Smetana (Ed.), Beliefs about parenting: Origins and developmental implications. *New Directions for Child Development, 66,* 65–80.

Colt, M. D. (1862/1966). *Went to Kansas.* New York: Readex Microprint.

Conroy, M., Hess, R. D., Azuma, H., & Kashiwagi, K. (1980). Maternal strategies for regulating children's behavior: Japanese and American families. *Journal of Cross-Cultural Psychology, 11,* 153–172.

Cooley, C. H. (1902). *Human nature and the social order.* New York: Scribner's.

Coontz, S. (1988/1991). *The social origins of private life: A history of American families 1600–1900.* London: Verso.

Coontz, S. (1992). *The way we never were: American families and the nostalgia trap.* New York: Basic Books.

Cooper, C. R. (1999). Multiple selves, multiple worlds: Cultural perspectives on individuality and connectedness in adolescent development. In A. S. Masten (Ed.), *Cultural processes in child development. The Minnesota Symposia on Child Psychology* (Vol. 29, pp. 25–57). Mahwah, NJ: Lawrence Erlbaum Associates.

Côté, J. E., & Levine, C. G. (2002). *Identity formation, agency, and culture: A social psychological synthesis.* Mahwah, NJ: Lawrence Erlbaum Associates.

Cramer, P. (2000). Development of identity: Gender makes a difference. *Journal of Research in Personality, 34,* 42–72.

Csikszentmihalyi, M., & Larson, R. (1984). *Being adolescent.* New York: Basic Books.

Cushman, P. (1995). *Constructing the self, constructing America: A cultural history of psychotherapy.* Reading, MA: Addison-Wesley.

Damon, W. (1983). *Social and personality development.* New York: Norton.

Damon, W., & Hart, D. (1988). *Self-understanding in childhood and adolescence.* Cambridge, UK: Cambridge University Press.

Danziger, K. (1990/1998). *Constructing the subject: Historical origins of psychological research.* Cambridge, UK: Cambridge University Press.

Davies, B., & Harré, R. (1990). Positioning: The discursive production of selves. *Journal for the Theory of Social Behaviour, 20,* 43–63.

Demo, D. H., & Savin-Williams, R. C. (1992). Self-concept stability and change during adolescence. In R. P. Lipka & T. M. Brinthaupt (Eds.), *Self-perspectives across the life span* (pp. 116–148). Albany: State University of New York Press.

Demos, J. (1970). *A little commonwealth: Family life in Plymouth Colony.* London: Oxford University Press.

Demos, J. (1986). *Past, present, and personal.* New York: Oxford University Press.

Dennis, T. A., Cole, P. M., Zahn-Waxler, C., & Mizuta, I. (2002). Self in context: Autonomy and relatedness in Japanese and U.S. mother–preschooler dyads. *Child Development, 73,* 1803–1817.

de Tocqueville, A. (1835/1945). *Democracy in America.* New York: Vintage Books.

Dewey, J. (1897/1974a). Ethical principles underlying education. In R. D. Archambault (Ed.), *John Dewey on education: Selected writings* (pp. 108–138). Chicago: University of Chicago Press.

Dewey, J. (1897/1974b). My pedagogic creed. In R. D. Archambault (Ed.), *John Dewey on education: Selected writings* (pp. 427–439). Chicago: University of Chicago Press.

Dewey, J. (1900/1990). *The school and society.* Chicago: University of Chicago Press.

Dewey, J. (1902/1990). *The child and the curriculum.* Chicago: University of Chicago Press.

Dewey, J. (1916/1997). *Democracy and education: An introduction to the philosophy of education.* New York: The Free Press.

Dewey, J. (1933/1974). The process and product of reflective activity: Psychological process and logical form. In R. D. Archambault (Ed.), *John Dewey on education: Selected writings* (pp. 242–259). Chicago: University of Chicago Press.

Dewey, J. (1934/1974). The need for a philosophy of education. In R. D. Archambault (Ed.), *John Dewey on education: Selected writings* (pp. 3–14). Chicago: University of Chicago Press.

Dewey, J. (1937/1939). The democratic form. In J. Ratner (Ed.), *Intelligence in the modern world: John Dewey's philosophy* (pp. 400–404). New York: Modern Library.

Dewey, J. (1938/1997). *Experience and education.* New York: Touchstone.

Doi, L. T. (1962/1974/1986). *Amae:* A key concept for understanding Japanese personality structure. In T. S. Lebra & W. P. Lebra (Eds.), *Japanese culture and behavior: Selected readings* (pp. 121–129). Honolulu: University of Hawaii Press.

Doi, T. (1973/2001). *The anatomy of dependence* (J. Bester, Trans.). Tokyo: Kodansha International.

Doi, T. (1985/1988). *The anatomy of self: The individual versus society* (M. A. Harbison, Trans.). Tokyo: Kodansha International.

Downs, J. F. (1972/1984). *The Navajo.* Prospect Heights, IL: Waveland.

Doyle, D. H. (1978). *The social order of a frontier community: Jacksonville, Illinois, 1825–1870.* Urbana: University of Illinois Press.

Dunn, J. (1996). The Emanuel Miller memorial lecture 1995: Children's relationships: Bridging the divide between cognitive and social development. *Journal of Child Psychology and Psychiatry, 37,* 507–518.

Dunn, J., Cutting, A. L., & Fisher, N. (2002). Old friends, new friends: Predictors of children's perspective on their friends at school. *Child Development, 73,* 621–635.

Egan, K. (1992). The roles of schools: The place of education. *Teachers College Record, 93,* 641–655.

Eisenberg, M., & Mussen, P. H. (1989). *The roots of prosocial behavior in children.* Cambridge, UK: Cambridge University Press.

Emde, R. N., & Buchsbaum, H. K. (1990). "Didn't you hear my Mommy?" Autonomy *with* connectedness in moral self emergence. In D. Cicchetti & M. Beeghly (Eds.), *The self in transition: Infancy to childhood* (pp. 35–60). Chicago: University of Chicago Press.

Erikson, E. H. (1950/1963). *Childhood and society.* New York: Norton.

Erikson, E. H. (1959/1980). *Identity and the life cycle.* New York: Norton.

Erikson, E. H. (1968). *Identity: Youth and crisis.* New York: Norton.

Erikson, E. H. (1982). *The life cycle completed.* New York: Norton.

Escalona, S. (1949). A commentary upon some recent changes in child rearing practices. *Child Development, 20,* 157–162.

Fasick, F. A. (1984). Parents, peers, youth culture and autonomy in adolescence. *Adolescence, 19,* 143–157.

Fernald, A., & Morikawa, H. (1993). Common themes and cultural variations in Japanese and American mothers' speech to infants. *Child Development, 64,* 637–656.

Feshbach, N. D. (1969). Student teacher preferences for elementary school pupils varying in personality characteristics. *Journal of Educational Psychology, 60,* 126–132.

Fijneman, Y. A., Willemsen, M. E., Poortinga, Y. H., Erelcin, F. G., Georgas, J., Hui, C. H., Leung, K., & Malpass, R. S. (1996). Individualism-collectivism: An empirical study of a conceptual issue. *Journal of Cross-Cultural Psychology, 27,* 381–402.

Flowerday, T., & Schraw, G. (2000). Teacher beliefs about instructional choice: A phenomenological study. *Journal of Educational Psychology, 92,* 634–645.

Fogel, A., Stevenson, M. B., & Messinger, D. (1992). A comparison of the parent–child relationship in Japan and the United States. In J. L. Roopnarine & D. B. Carter (Eds.), *Parent–child socialization in diverse cultures: Advances in applied developmental psychology* (Vol. 5, pp. 35–51). Norwood, NJ: Ablex.

Fogel, A., Toda, S., & Kawai, M. (1988). Mother–infant face-to-face interaction in Japan and the United States: A laboratory comparison using 3-month-old infants. *Developmental Psychology, 24,* 398–406.

Ford, D. H., & Lerner, R. M. (1992). *Developmental systems theory: An integrative approach.* Newbury Park, CA: Sage.

Fowler, B. P. (1934, May). Encourage your children to think for themselves. *Parents' Magazine,* pp. 22–23, 65–67.

Furman, W., & Buhrmester, D. (1992). Age and sex differences in perceptions of networks of personal relationships. *Child Development, 63,* 103–115.

Gadlin, H. (1978). Child discipline and the pursuit of self: An historical interpretation. In H. W. Reese & L. P. Lipsitt (Eds.), *Advances in child development and behavior* (Vol. 12, pp. 231–265). New York: Academic Press.

Gans, H. J. (1988/1991). *Middle American individualism: Political participation and liberal democracy.* New York: Oxford University Press.

Gaskins, S. (1996). How Mayan parental theories come into play. In S. Harkness & C. M. Super (Eds.), *Parents' cultural belief systems: Their origins, expressions, and consequences* (pp. 345–363). New York: Guilford.

Gaskins, S. (1999). Children's daily lives in a Mayan village: A case study of culturally constructed roles and activities. In A. Göncü (Ed.), *Children's engagement in the world: Sociocultural perspectives* (pp. 25–61). Cambridge, UK: Cambridge University Press.

Geertz, C. (1973). *The interpretation of cultures.* New York: Basic Books.

Geertz, C. (1974/1988). "From the native's point of view." On the nature of anthropological understanding. In R. A. Shweder & R. A. LeVine (Eds.), *Culture theory: Essays on mind, self, and emotion* (pp. 123–136). Cambridge, UK: Cambridge University Press.

Getis, V. L., & Vinovskis, M. A. (1992). History of child care in the United States before 1950. In M. E. Lamb, K. J. Sternberg, C. Hwang, & A. G. Broberg (Eds.), *Child care in context* (pp. 185–206). Hillsdale, NJ: Lawrence Erlbaum Associates.

Gilligan, C. (1982). *In a different voice.* Cambridge, MA: Harvard University Press.

Gjerde, P. F. (2004). Culture, power, and experience: Toward a person-centered cultural psychology. *Human Development, 47,* 138–157.

Gjerde, P. F., & Onishi, M. (2000). Selves, cultures, and nations: The psychological imagination of "the Japanese" in the era of globalization. *Human Development, 43,* 216–226.

Glendon, M. A. (1991). *Rights talk: The impoverishment of political discourse.* New York: The Free Press.

Goodnow, J. J. (1996). From household practices to parents' ideas about work and interpersonal relationships. In S. Harkness & C. M. Super (Eds.), *Parents' cultural belief systems: Their origins, expressions, and consequences* (pp. 313–344). New York: Guilford.

Goodnow, J. J., & Delaney, S. (1989). Children's household work: Task differences, styles of assignment, and links to family relationships. *Journal of Applied Developmental Psychology, 10,* 209–226.

Goodnow, J. J., & Warton, P. M. (1991). The social bases of social cognition: Interactions about work and their implications. *Merrill-Palmer Quarterly, 37,* 27–58.

Gottlieb, G. (1991). Experiential canalization of behavioral development: Theory. *Developmental Psychology, 27,* 4–13.

Gottlieb, G., Wahlsten, D., & Lickliter, R. (1998). The significance of biology for human development: A developmental psychobiological systems view. In W. Damon (Ed.), *Handbook of child psychology: Vol. 1. Theoretical models of human development* (pp. 233–273). New York: Wiley.

Gralinski, J. H., & Kopp, C. B. (1993). Everyday rules for behavior: Mothers' requests to young children. *Developmental Psychology, 29,* 573–584.

Greenberg, M. T., Siegel, J. M., & Leitch, C. J. (1983). The nature and importance of attachment relationships to parents and peers during adolescence. *Journal of Youth and Adolescence, 12,* 373–386.

Greenfield, P. J. (1996). Self, family, and community in White Mountain Apache society. *Ethos, 24,* 491–509.

Greenfield, P. M. (2000). Three approaches to the psychology of culture. Where do they come from? Where can they go? *Asian Journal of Social Psychology, 3,* 223–240.

Greenfield, P. M. (1994). Independence and interdependence as developmental scripts: Implications for theory, research, and practice. In P. M. Greenfield & R. R. Cocking (Eds.), *Cross-cultural roots of minority child development* (pp. 1–40). Hillsdale, NJ: Lawrence Erlbaum Associates.

Greenfield, P. M., & Suzuki, L. K. (1998). Culture and human development: Implications for parenting, education, pediatrics, and mental health. In I. E. Sigel & K. A. Renninger (Eds.), *Handbook of child psychology* (Vol. 4, pp. 1059–1109). New York: Wiley.

Grotevant, H. D., & Cooper, C. R. (1985). Patterns of interaction in family relationships and the development of identity exploration in adolescence. *Child Development, 56,* 415–428.

Grotevant, H. D., & Cooper, C. R. (1986). Individuation in family relationships: A perspective on individual differences in the development of identity and role-taking skill in adolescence. *Human Development, 29,* 82–100.

Grotevant, H. D., & Cooper, C. R. (1998). Individuality and connectedness in adolescent development. Review and prospects for research on identity, relationships, and context. In E. Skoe & A. von der Lippe (Eds.), *Personality development in adolescence: A cross national and life span perspective* (pp. 3–37). London: Routledge.

Gruenberg, B. C., & Gruenberg, S. M. (1932, May). Are ideals out of date? *Parents' Magazine,* pp. 24–25, 58–60.

Gruenberg, S. M. (1930, May). Guiding the adolescent in a changing world. *Parents' Magazine,* pp. 17, 63–64.

Guisinger, S., & Blatt, S. J. (1994). Individuality and relatedness: Evolution of a fundamental dialectic. *American Psychologist, 49,* 104–111.

Hamilton, V. L., Blumenfeld, P. C., Akoh, H., & Miura, K. (1989). Citizenship and scholarship in Japanese and American fifth grades. *American Educational Research Journal, 26*, 44–72.

Harari, S. E., & Vinovskis, M. A. (1989). Rediscovering the family in the past. In K. Kreppner & R. M. Lerner (Eds.), *Family systems and life-span development* (pp. 381–394). Hillsdale, NJ: Lawrence Erlbaum Associates.

Hareven, T. K. (1992). Continuity and change in American family life. In L. S. Luedtke (Ed.), *Making America: The society and culture of the United States* (pp. 308–326). Chapel Hill: University of North Carolina Press.

Harkness, S., Super, C. M., & van Tijen, N. (2000). Individualism and the "Western mind" reconsidered: American and Dutch parents' ethnotheories of the child. In S. Harkness, C. Raeff, & C. M. Super (Eds.), Variability in the social construction of the child. *New Directions for Child and Adolescent Development, 87*, 23–39.

Harter, S. (1999). *The construction of the self: A developmental perspective*. New York: Guilford.

Harter, S., Bresnick, S., Bouchey, H. A., & Whitesell, N. R. (1997). The development of multiple role-related selves during adolescence. *Development and Psychopathology, 9*, 835–853.

Harter, S., & Monsour, A. (1992). Developmental analysis of conflict caused by opposing attributes in the adolescent self-portrait. *Developmental Psychology, 28*, 251–260.

Hartup, W. W. (1989). Behavioral manifestations of children's friendships. In T. J. Berndt & G. W. Ladd (Eds.), *Peer relations in child development* (pp. 46–70). New York: Wiley.

Hartup, W. W. (1992). Conflict and friendship relations. In C. U. Shantz & W. W. Hartup (Eds.), *Conflict in child and adolescent development* (pp. 186–215). Cambridge, UK: Cambridge University Press.

Hartup, W. W. (1996). The company they keep: Friendships and their developmental significance. *Child Development, 67*, 1–13.

Harwood, R. L., Handwerker, W. P., Schoelmerich, A., & Leyendecker, B. (2001). Ethnic category labels, parental beliefs, and the contextualized individual: An exploration of the individualism-sociocentrism debate. *Parenting: Science and Practice, 1*, 217–236.

Hattwick, L. A. (1941, May). Cultivating self-reliance. *Parents' Magazine*, pp. 24–25, 44, 79–80.

Hawthorne, N. (1850/1994). *The scarlet letter*. New York: Dover.

Heath, S. B. (1983/1992). *Ways with words: Language, life, and work in communities and classrooms*. Cambridge, UK: Cambridge University Press.

Hendry, J. (1986). *Becoming Japanese: The world of the pre-school child*. Honolulu: University of Hawaii Press.

Hertz-Lazarowitz, R., & Shachar, H. (1990). Teachers' verbal behavior in cooperative and whole-class instruction. In S. Sharan (Ed.), *Cooperative learning: Theory and research* (pp. 77–94). New York: Praeger.

Hess, R. D., & Azuma, H. (1991). Cultural support for schooling: Contrasts between Japan and the United States. *Educational Researcher, 20*, 2–8, 12.

Hess, R. D., Kashiwagi, K., Azuma, H., Price, G. G., & Dickson, P. (1980). Maternal expectations for mastery of developmental tasks in Japan and the United States. *International Journal of Psychology, 15*, 259–271.

Hewlett, B. S. (1992/1994). The parent–infant relationship and social-emotional development among Aka pygmies. In J. L. Roopnarine & D. B. Carter (Eds.), *Parent–child socialization in diverse cultures* (pp. 223–243). Norwood, NJ: Ablex.

Hill, B. (1996). Breaking the rules in Japanese schools: *Kōsoku ihan*, academic competition, and moral education. *Anthropology and Education Quarterly, 27*, 90–110.

Hill, J. P., & Holmbeck, G. N. (1987). Disagreements about rules in families with seventh-grade girls and boys. *Journal of Youth and Adolescence, 16*, 221–246.

264

Hoff-Ginsberg, E., & Tardif, T. (1995). Socioeconomic status and parenting. In M. H. Bornstein (Ed.), *Handbook of parenting* (Vol. 2, pp. 161–188). Mahwah, NJ: Lawrence Erlbaum Associates.

Hoffman, D. M. (2000). Pedagogies of self in American and Japanese early childhood education: A critical conceptual analysis. *The Elementary School Journal, 101,* 193–208.

Hofstede, G. (1980/2001). *Culture's consequences: Comparing values, behaviors, institutions, and organizations across nations.* Thousand Oaks, CA: Sage.

Hofstede, G. (1994). Forward. In U. Kim, H. C. Triandis, Ç. Kağitçibaşi, S. Choi, & G. Yoon (Eds.), *Individualism and collectivism: Theory, method, and applications* (pp. ix–xiii). Thousand Oaks, CA: Sage.

Hollan, D. (1992). Cross-cultural differences in the self. *Journal of Anthropological Research, 48,* 283–300.

Holland, D. (1997). Selves as cultured: As told by an anthropologist who lacks a soul. In R. D. Ashmore & L. Jussim (Eds.), *Self and identity: Fundamental issues* (pp. 160–190). New York: Oxford University Press.

Holland, D., & Kipnis, A. (1994). Metaphors for embarrassment and stories of exposure: The not-so-egocentric self in American culture. *Ethos, 22,* 316–342.

Holloway, S. D. (1999). Divergent cultural models of child rearing and pedagogy in Japanese preschools. *New Directions for Child and Adolescent Development, 83,* 61–75.

Holmbeck, G. N., Paikoff, R. L., & Brooks-Gunn, J. (1995). Parenting adolescents. In M. H. Bornstein (Ed.), *Handbook of parenting* (Vol. 1, pp. 91–118). Mahwah, NJ: Lawrence Erlbaum Associates.

Howard, A. (1985). Ethnopsychology and the prospects of a cultural psychology. In G. M. White & J. Kirkpatrick (Eds.), *Person, self, and experience: Exploring Pacific ethnopsychologies* (pp. 401–420). Berkeley: University of California Press.

Imbens-Bailey, A., & Pan, B. A. (1998). The pragmatics of self- and other-reference in young children. *Social Development, 7,* 219–233.

James, W. (1890/1983). *The principles of psychology.* Cambridge, MA: Harvard University Press.

The Japan Times. (2004, April 9). Japanese trio held hostage in Iraq. (online version with no page numbers)

The Japan Times. (2004, April 11). SDP chief says Koizumi should resign over crisis. (online version with no page numbers)

The Japan Times. (2004, April 19). Freed captive not sorry he went to Iraq. (online version with no page numbers)

Johnson, D. W., & Johnson, R. T. (1987). *Learning together and alone: Cooperative, competitive, and individualistic learning.* Englewood Cliffs, NJ: Prentice-Hall.

Josselson, R. (1994). Identity and relatedness in the life cycle. In H. A. Bosma, T. L. G. Graafsma, H. D. Grotevant, & D. J. de Levita (Eds.), *Identity and development: An interdisciplinary approach* (pp. 81–102). Thousand Oaks, CA: Sage.

Kagan, S. (1985). Learning to cooperate. In R. E. Slavin, S. Sharan, R. H. Lazarowitz, C. Webb, & R. Schmuck (Eds.), *Learning to cooperate, cooperating to learn* (pp. 365–370). New York: Plenum.

Kağitçibaşi, Ç. (1994). A critical appraisal of individualism and collectivism: Toward a new formulation. In U. Kim, H. C. Triandis, Ç. Kâğitçibaşi, S. Choi, & G. Yoon (Eds.), *Individualism and collectivism: Theory, method, and applications* (pp. 52–65). Thousand Oaks, CA: Sage.

Kağitçibaşi, Ç. (1996). *Family and human development across cultures: A view from the other side.* Mahwah, NJ: Lawrence Erlbaum Associates.

Kaplan, B. (1967). Meditations on genesis. *Human Development, 10,* 65–87.

Kaye, K. (1982). *The mental and social life of babies: How parents create persons.* Chicago: University of Chicago Press.

Kedar-Voivodas, G. (1983). The impact of elementary children's school roles and sex roles on teacher attitudes: An interactional analysis. *Review of Educational Research, 53,* 415–437.

Keliher, A. V. (1941, September). Understanding themselves and others. *Parents' Magazine,* pp. 23, 70–73.

Keller, H. (2003). Socialization for competence: Cultural models of infancy. *Human Development, 46,* 288–311.

Kelley, M. L., Power, T. G., & Wimbush, D. D. (1992). Determinants of disciplinary practices in low-income Black mothers. *Child Development, 63,* 573–582.

Killen, M., & Sueyoshi, L. (1995). Conflict resolution in Japanese social interactions. *Early Education and Development, 6,* 317–334.

Killen, M., & Wainryb, C. (2000). Independence and interdependence in diverse cultural contexts. In S. Harkness, C. Raeff, & C. M. Super (Eds.), Variability in the social construction of the child. *New Directions for Child and Adolescent Development, 87,* 5–21.

Kitayama, S., Markus, H. R., & Matsumoto, H. (1995). Culture, self, and emotion: A cultural perspective on "self-conscious" emotions. In J. P. Tangney & K. W. Fischer (Eds.), *Self-conscious emotions: The psychology of shame, guilt, embarrassment, and pride* (pp. 439–464). New York: Guilford.

Kohn, M. L. (1963). Social class and parent–child relationships: An interpretation. *The American Journal of Sociology, 68,* 471–480.

Kohn, M. L. (1969/1977). *Class and conformity: A study in values.* Chicago: University of Chicago Press.

Kojima, H. (1986). Japanese concepts of child development from the mid-17th to the mid-19th century. *International Journal of Behavioral Development, 9,* 315–329.

Kondo, D. K. (1987). Creating an ideal self: Theories of selfhood and pedagogy at a Japanese ethics retreat. *Ethos, 15,* 241–272.

Kondo, D. K. (1990). *Crafting selves: Power, gender, and discourses of identity in a Japanese workplace.* Chicago: University of Chicago Press.

Kondo, D. K. (1994). *Uchi no kaisha:* Company as family? In J. M. Bachnik & C. J. Quinn, Jr. (Eds.), *Situated meaning: Inside and outside in Japanese self, society, and language* (pp. 169–191). Princeton, NJ: Princeton University Press.

Kruper, J. C., & Užgiris, I. Č. (1987). Fathers' and mothers' speech to young infants. *Journal of Psycholinguistic Research, 16,* 597–614.

Kumagi, H. A., & Kumagi, A. K. (1986). The hidden "I" in *amae:* "Passive love" and Japanese social perception. *Ethos, 14,* 305–320.

Kusserow, A. S. (1999). De-homogenizing American individualism: Socializing hard and soft individualism in Manhattan and Queens. *Ethos, 27,* 210–234.

Kuwayama, T. (1992/1995). The reference other orientation. In N. R. Rosenberger (Ed.), *Japanese sense of self* (pp. 121–151). Cambridge, UK: Cambridge University Press.

Labaree, D. F. (1997). Public goods, private goods: The American struggle over educational goals. *American Educational Research Journal, 34,* 39–81.

Ladd, G. W., LeSieur, K. D., & Profilet, S. M. (1993). Direct parental influences on young children's peer relations. In S. Duck (Ed.), *Learning about relationships* (pp. 152–183). Newbury Park, CA: Sage.

Ladd, G. W., Profilet, S. M., & Hart, C. H. (1992). Parents' management of children's peer relations: Facilitating and supervising children's activities in the peer culture. In R. D. Parke & G. W. Ladd (Eds.), *Family–peer relationships: Modes of linkage* (pp. 215–253). Hillsdale, NJ: Lawrence Erlbaum Associates.

Lanham, B. B., & Garrick, R. J. (1996). Adult to child in Japan: Interaction and relations. In D. W. Shwalb & B. J. Shwalb (Eds.), *Japanese childrearing: Two generations of scholarship* (pp. 97–124). New York: Guilford.

Laursen, B., Coy, K. C., & Collins, W. A. (1998). Reconsidering changes in parent–child conflict across adolescence: A meta-analysis. *Child Development, 69*, 817–832.

Lebra, T. S. (1992/1995). Self in Japanese culture. In N. R. Rosenberger (Ed.), *Japanese sense of self* (pp. 105–120). Cambridge, UK: Cambridge University Press.

Lebra, T. S. (1994). Mother and child in Japanese socialization: A Japan–U.S. comparison. In P. M. Greenfield & R. R. Cocking (Eds.), *Cross-cultural roots of minority child development* (pp. 259–274). Hillsdale, NJ: Lawrence Erlbaum Associates.

Levine, L. W. (1977). *Black culture and Black consciousness: Afro-American folk thought from slavery to freedom.* Oxford, UK: Oxford University Press.

LeVine, R. A. (1990). Infant environments in psychoanalysis: A cross-cultural view. In J. W. Stigler, R. A. Shweder, & G. Herdt (Eds.), *Cultural psychology: Essays on comparative human development* (pp. 454–474). Cambridge, UK: Cambridge University Press.

Lewis, C. C. (1984). Cooperation and control in Japanese nursery schools. *Comparative Education Review, 28*, 69–84.

Lewis, C. C. (1995/1999). *Educating hearts and minds: Reflections on Japanese preschool and elementary education.* Cambridge, UK: Cambridge University Press.

Lienhardt, G. (1985/1991). Self: Public, private. Some African representations. In M. Carrithers, S. Collins, & S. Lukes (Eds.), *The category of the person: Anthropology, philosophy, history* (pp. 141–155). Cambridge, UK: Cambridge University Press.

Lightfoot, C. (1997). *The culture of adolescent risk-taking.* New York: Guilford.

Lingeman, R. (1992). A consonance of towns. In L. S. Luedtke (Ed.), *Making America: The society and culture of the United States* (pp. 95–109). Chapel Hill: University of North Carolina Press.

Luther, M. (1517/1957). *Ninety-five theses* (C. M. Jacobs, Trans.). Philadelphia: Fortress.

Luther, M. (1520/1943). A treatise on Christian liberty (W. A. Lambert, Trans.). In *Three treatises* (pp. 251–290). Philadelphia: Muhlenberg.

Lutz, C. (1985). Ethnopsychology compared to what? Explaining behavior and consciousness among the Ifaluk. In G. M. White & J. Kirkpatrick (Eds.), *Person, self, and experience: Exploring Pacific ethnopsychologies* (pp. 35–79). Berkeley: University of California Press.

Maccoby, E. E., & Martin, J. A. (1983). Socialization in the context of the family: Parent–child interaction. In P. H. Mussen (Ed.), *Handbook of child psychology* (Vol. IV, pp. 1–101). New York: Wiley.

Mann, L., Mitsui, H., Beswick, G., & Harmoni, R. V. (1994). A study of Japanese and Australian children's respect for others. *Journal of Cross-Cultural Psychology, 25*, 133–145.

Marcia, J. E. (1966). Development and validation of ego-identity status. *Journal of Personality and Social Psychology, 3*, 551–558.

Marcia, J. E. (1980). Identity in adolescence. In J. Adelson (Ed.), *Handbook of adolescent psychology* (pp. 159–187). New York: Wiley.

Marková, I. (2000). The individual and society in psychological theory. *Theory and Psychology, 10*, 107–116.

Markus, H. R., & Kitayama, S. (1991). Culture and the self: Implications for cognition, emotion, and motivation. *Psychological Review, 98*, 224–253.

Martini, M. (1994). Peer interactions in Polynesia: A view from the Marquesas. In J. L. Roopnarine, J. E. Johnson, & F. H. Hooper (Eds.), *Children's play in diverse cultures* (pp. 73–103). Albany: State University of New York Press.

Martini, M., & Kirkpatrick, J. (1981). Early interactions in the Marquesas Islands. In T. M. Field, A. M. Sostek, P. Vietze, & P. H. Leiderman (Eds.), *Culture and early interactions* (pp. 189–213). Hillsdale, NJ: Lawrence Erlbaum Associates.

Martini, M., & Kirkpatrick, J. (1992/1994). Parenting in Polynesia: A view from the Marquesas. In J. L. Roopnarine & D. B. Carter (Eds.), *Parent–child socialization in diverse cultures* (pp. 199–222). Norwood, NJ: Ablex.

Mascolo, M. F., Misra, G., & Rapisardi, C. (2004). Individual and relational conceptions of self in India and the United States. In M. F. Mascolo & J. Li (Eds.), Culture and developing selves: Beyond dichotomization. *New Directions for Child and Adolescent Development, 104*, 9–26.

Mather, C. (1699/2001). *A family well-ordered*. Morgan, PA: Soli Deo Gloria.

Mather, C. (1706/1973). Some special points, relating to the education of my children. In P. J. Greven, Jr. (Ed.), *Child-rearing concepts, 1628–1861* (pp. 42–45). Iasca, IL: F. E. Peacock.

Mathews, G. (1996). *What makes life worth living? How Japanese and Americans make sense of their worlds*. Berkeley: University of California Press.

Matthews, S. R. (1936/1992). *Interwoven: A pioneer chronicle*. College Station: Texas A & M University Press.

Mead, G. H. (1934/1962). *Mind, self, & society*. Chicago: University of Chicago Press.

Meek, L. H. (1928, January). Obedience and character. *Parents' Magazine*, pp. 9, 43.

Mehan, H. (1979). *Learning lessons: Social organization in the classroom*. Cambridge, MA: Harvard University Press.

Meyer, J. W. (1986). Myths of socialization and of personality. In T. C. Heller, M. Sosna, & D. E. Wellberry (Eds.), *Reconstructing individualism: Autonomy, individuality, and the self in Western thought* (pp. 208–221). Stanford, CA: Stanford University Press.

Miller, D. L. (1973). *George Herbert Mead: Self, language, and the world*. Austin: University of Texas Press.

Miller, P. (1986). Teasing as language socialization and verbal play in a white working-class community. In B. B. Schieffelin & E. Ochs (Eds.), *Language socialization across cultures* (pp. 199–212). Cambridge, UK: Cambridge University Press.

Miller, P. J., & Goodnow, J. J. (1995). Cultural practices: Toward an integration of culture and development. In J. J. Goodnow, P. J. Miller, & F. Kessel (Eds.), Cultural practices as contexts for development. *New Directions for Child Development, 67*, 5–16.

Miller, P., & Sperry, L. L. (1987). The socialization of anger and aggression. *Merrill-Palmer Quarterly, 33*, 1–31.

Mintz, S., & Kellogg, S. (1988). *Domestic revolutions. A social history of American family life*. New York: The Free Press.

Minuchin, P. P., & Shapiro, E. K. (1983). The school as a context for social development. In P. H. Mussen (Ed.), *Handbook of child psychology* (Vol. IV, pp. 197–274). New York: Wiley.

Moeran, B. (1984/1986). Individual, group and *seishin*: Japan's internal cultural debate. Reprinted in T. S. Lebra & W. P. Lebra (Eds.), *Japanese culture and behavior: Selected readings* (pp. 62–79). Honolulu: University of Hawaii Press.

Montemayor, R. (1983). Parents and adolescents in conflict: All families some of the time and some families most of the time. *Journal of Early Adolescence, 3*, 83–103.

Morelli, G. A., Rogoff, B., Oppenheim, D., & Goldsmith, D. (1992). Cultural variation in infants' sleeping arrangements: Questions of independence. *Developmental Psychology, 28*, 604–613.

Morris, C. (1972). *The discovery of the individual: 1050–1200*. New York: Harper Torchbooks.

Murdoch, D. H. (2001). *The American West: The invention of a myth*. Reno: University of Nevada Press.

Murray, D. W. (1993). What is the Western concept of the self? On forgetting David Hume. *Ethos, 21*, 3–23.

Nakane, C. (1970/1986). Criteria of group formation. In T. S. Lebra & W. P. Lebra (Eds.), *Japanese culture and behavior: Selected readings* (pp. 171–187). Honolulu: University of Hawaii Press.

Nasaw, D. (1979/1981). *Schooled to order: A social history of public schooling in the United States*. Oxford, UK: Oxford University Press.

Neff, K. (2003). Understanding how universal goals of independence and interdependence are manifested within particular cultural contexts. *Human Development, 46,* 312–318.

New, R. S., & Richman, A. L. (1996). Maternal beliefs and infant care practices in Italy and the United States. In S. Harkness & C. M. Super (Eds.), *Parents' cultural belief systems: Their origins, expressions, and consequences* (pp. 385–404). New York: Guilford.

Newcomb, A. F., & Bagwell, C. L. (1995). Children's friendship relations: A meta-analytic review. *Psychological Bulletin, 117,* 306–347.

Newman, P. R., & Newman, B. M. (1976). Early adolescence and its conflict: Group identity versus alienation. *Adolescence, 11,* 261–274.

Nucci, L., & Smetana, J. G. (1996). Mothers' concepts of young children's areas of personal freedom. *Child Development, 67,* 1870–1886.

Ochs, E., & Schieffelin, B. B. (1984/1988). Language acquisition and socialization: Three developmental stories and their implications. In R. A. Shweder & R. A. LeVine (Eds.), *Culture theory: Essays on mind, self, and emotion* (pp. 276–320). Cambridge, UK: Cambridge University Press.

Odin, S. (1996). *The social self in Zen and American pragmatism.* Albany: State University of New York Press.

O'Donnell, A. M., & O'Kelly, J. (1994). Learning from peers: Beyond the rhetoric of positive results. *Educational Psychology Review, 6,* 321–349.

Offer, D., Ostrov, E., Howard, K. I., & Atkinson, R. (1988). *The teenage world: Adolescents' self-image in ten countries.* New York: Plenum Medical.

Ogbu, J. U. (1985). A cultural ecology of competence among inner city Blacks. In M. B. Spencer, G. K. Brookins, & W. R. Allen (Eds.), *Beginnings: The social and affective development of Black children* (pp. 45–66). Hillsdale, NJ: Lawrence Erlbaum Associates.

O'Koon, J. (1997). Attachment to parents and peers in late adolescence and their relationship with self-image. *Adolescence, 32,* 471–482.

Onishi, N. (2004, April 23). Freed from captivity in Iraq, Japanese return to more pain. *The New York Times.* (Online version with no page numbers)

Osterweil, Z., & Nagano, K. N. (1991). Maternal views on autonomy: Japan and Israel. *Journal of Cross-Cultural Psychology, 22,* 362–375.

Oyserman, D., Coon, H. M., & Kemmelmeier, M. (2002). Rethinking individualism and collectivism: Evaluation of theoretical assumptions and meta-analyses. *Psychological Bulletin, 128,* 3–72.

Patterson, S. J., Sochting, I., & Marcia, J. E. (1992). The inner space and beyond: Women and identity. In G. R. Adams, T. P. Gullotta, & R. Montemayor (Eds.), *Adolescent identity formation* (pp. 9–24). Newbury Park, CA: Sage.

Peak, L. (1991). *Learning to go to school in Japan: The transition from home to preschool life.* Berkeley: University of California Press.

Pearson, G. H. J. (1931, January). What the preschool child needs. *Parents' Magazine,* pp. 12–13, 32.

Penuel, W. R., & Wertsch, J. V. (1995). Vygotsky and identity formation: A sociocultural approach. *Educational Psychologist, 30,* 83–92.

Pettit, G. S., & Mize, J. (1993). Substance and style: Understanding the ways in which parents teach children about social relationships. In S. Duck (Ed.), *Learning about relationships* (pp. 118–151). Newbury Park, CA: Sage.

Piaget, J. (1953). *The origin of intelligence in the child* (M. Cook, Trans.). London: Routledge & Kegan Paul.

Pipp, S. (1990). Sensorimotor and representational internal working models of self, other and relationship: Mechanisms of connection and separation. In D. Cicchetti & M. Beeghly (Eds.), *The self in transition* (pp. 243–264). Chicago: University of Chicago Press.

Power, T. G., Kobayashi-Winata, H., & Kelley, M. L. (1992). Childrearing patterns in Japan and the United States: A cluster analytic study. *International Journal of Behavioral Development, 15,* 185–205.

Prawat, R. S. (1985). Affective versus cognitive goal orientations in elementary teachers. *American Educational Research Journal, 22*, 587–604.

Preston, G. H. (1929, September). Fit your child for living. *Parents' Magazine*, pp. 18, 62–63.

Putnam, R. D. (2000). *Bowling alone: The collapse and revival of American community*. New York: Simon & Schuster.

Raeff, C. (1997a). Individuals in relationships: Cultural values, children's social interactions, and the development of an American individualistic self. *Developmental Review, 17*, 205–238.

Raeff, C. (1997b). Maintaining cultural coherence in the midst of cultural diversity. *Developmental Review, 17*, 250–261.

Raeff, C. (2000). European-American parents' ideas about their toddlers' independence and interdependence. *Journal of Applied Developmental Psychology, 21*, 183–205.

Raeff, C. (2003). Patterns of culturally meaningful activity: Linking parents' ideas and parent–child interactions. In C. Raeff & J. B. Benson (Eds.), *Social and cognitive development in the context of individual, social, and cultural processes* (pp. 35–53). London: Routledge.

Raeff, C. (2004). Within-culture complexities: Multifaceted and interrelated autonomy and connectedness characteristics in late adolescent selves. In M. F. Mascolo & J. Li (Eds.), Culture and developing selves: Beyond dichotomization. *New Directions for Child and Adolescent Development, 104*, 61–78.

Ramirez, M. C. (2003). Play as a context for the socialization of interpersonal relationships. In C. Raeff & J. B. Benson (Eds.), *Social and cognitive development in the context of individual, social, and cultural processes* (pp. 84–102). London: Routledge.

Reeve, J., Bolt, E., & Cai, Y. (1999). Autonomy supportive teachers: How they teach and motivate students. *Journal of Educational Psychology, 91*, 537–548.

Rice, E. F., Jr. (1970). *The foundations of early modern Europe, 1460–1559*. New York: Norton.

Richman, A. L., Miller, P. M., & LeVine, R. A. (1992). Cultural and educational variations in maternal responsiveness. *Developmental Psychology, 28*, 614–621.

Richman, A. L., Miller, P. M., & Solomon, M. J. (1988). The socialization of infants in suburban Boston. In R. A. LeVine, P. M. Miller, & M. M. West (Eds.), Parental behavior in diverse societies. *New Directions for Child Development, 40*, 65–74.

Rizzo, T. A. (1989). *Friendship development among children in school*. Norwood, NJ: Ablex.

Roeser, R. W., Eccles, J. S., & Sameroff, A. J. (2000). School as a context of early adolescents' academic and social-emotional development: A summary of research findings. *The Elementary School Journal, 100*, 443–471.

Rogoff, B. (1990). *Apprenticeship in thinking: Cognitive development in social context*. New York: Oxford University Press.

Rogoff, B. (2003). *The cultural nature of human development*. Oxford, UK: Oxford University Press.

Rogoff, B., Mistry, J., Göncü, A., & Mosier, C. (1993). Guided participation in cultural activity by toddlers and caregivers. *Monographs of the Society for Research in Child Development, 58*(7, Serial No. 236).

Rosenberger, N. R. (1992/1995). Tree in summer, tree in winter: Movement of self in Japan. In N. R. Rosenberger (Ed.), *Japanese sense of self* (pp. 67–92). Cambridge, UK: Cambridge University Press.

Rothbaum, F., Pott, M., Azuma, H., Miyake, K., & Weisz, J. (2000). The development of close relationships in Japan and the United States: Paths of symbiotic harmony and generative tension. *Child Development, 71*, 1121–1142.

Rubin, Z., & Sloman, J. (1984). How parents influence their children's friendships. In M. Lewis (Ed.), *Beyond the dyad* (pp. 223–250). New York: Plenum.

Ryan, M. P. (1981/1998). *Cradle of the middle class: The family in Oneida County, New York, 1790–1865.* Cambridge, UK: Cambridge University Press.

Ryan, R. M., & Lynch, J. H. (1989). Emotional autonomy versus detachment: Revisiting the vicissitudes of adolescence and young adulthood. *Child Development, 60,* 340–356.

Sampson, E. E. (1977). Psychology and the American ideal. *Journal of Personality and Social Psychology, 35,* 767–782.

Sampson, E. E. (2000). Reinterpreting individualism and collectivism: Their religious roots and monologic versus dialogic person-other relationships. *American Psychologist, 55,* 1425–1432.

Savin-Williams, R. C., & Berndt, T. J. (1990). Friendship and peer relations. In S. S. Feldman & G. R. Elliot (Eds.), *At the threshold: The developing adolescent* (pp. 277–307). Cambridge, MA: Harvard University Press.

Schaffer, H. R. (1979). Acquiring the concept of the dialogue. In M. H. Bornstein & W. Kessen (Eds.), *Psychological development from infancy* (pp. 279–305). Hillsdale, NJ: Lawrence Erlbaum Associates.

Schaffer, H. R. (1984). *The child's entry into a social world.* London: Academic Press.

Schieffelin, B. B. (1990/1993). *The give and take of everyday life: Language socialization of Kaluli children.* Cambridge, UK: Cambridge University Press.

Schlissel, L. (1982). *Women's diaries of the Westward journey.* New York: Schocken.

Schlissel, L. (1992). The frontier family: Dislocation and the American experience. In L. S. Luedtke (Ed.), *Making America: The society and culture of the United States* (pp. 83–94). Chapel Hill: University of North Carolina Press.

Schmuck, R. (1985). Learning to cooperate, cooperating to learn: Basic concepts. In R. E. Slavin, S. Sharan, R. H. Lazarowitz, C. Webb, & R. Schmuck (Eds.), *Learning to cooperate, cooperating to learn* (pp. 1–4). New York: Plenum.

Schubert, H. (Ed.). (1998). *Charles Horton Cooley: On self and social organization.* Chicago: University of Chicago Press.

Schulze, P. A., Harwood, R. L., Schoelmerich, A., & Leyendecker, B. (2002). The cultural structuring of parenting and universal developmental tasks. *Parenting: Science and Practice, 2,* 151–178.

Schwartz, S. H. (1990). Individualism-collectivism: Critique and proposed refinements. *Journal of Cross-Cultural Psychology, 21,* 139–157.

Sears, R. R., Maccoby, E. E., & Levin, H. (1957). *Patterns of child rearing.* Evanston, IL: Row, Peterson.

Shain, B. A. (1994). *The myth of American individualism.* Princeton, NJ: Princeton University Press.

Shakespeare, W. (1963/1987). *The tragedy of Hamlet Prince of Denmark* (E. Hubler, Ed.). New York: Penguin.

Shantz, C. U., & Hobart, C. J. (1989). Social conflict and development: Peers and siblings. In T. J. Berndt & G. W. Ladd (Eds.), *Peer relationships in child development* (pp. 71–94). New York: Wiley.

Sharan, S., & Sharan, Y. (1976). *Small-group teaching.* Englewood Cliffs, NJ: Educational Technology Publications.

Sharan, S., & Shaulov, A. (1990). Cooperative learning, motivation to learn, and academic achievement. In S. Sharan (Ed.), *Cooperative learning: Theory and research* (pp. 173–202). New York: Praeger.

Shimizu, H. (2000). Beyond individualism and sociocentrism: An ontological analysis of the opposing elements in personal experiences of Japanese adolescents. *Human Development, 43,* 195–211.

Shimoyachi, N. (2004, April 15). Families caught in cross fire over Iraq hostage ordeal. *The Japan Times.* (online version with no page numbers)

Shwalb, D. W. (2000). The "overwhelming importance of personal relationships" in Japanese adolescents' thinking on achievement and morality. *Human Development, 43,* 230–234.

Shwalb, D. W., Shwalb, B. J., & Shoji, J. (1996). Japanese mothers' ideas about infants and temperament. In S. Harkness & C. M. Super (Eds.), *Parents' cultural belief systems: Their origins, expressions, and consequences* (pp. 169–191). New York: Guilford.

Shweder, R. A., & Bourne, E. J. (1984/1988). Does the concept of the person vary cross-culturally? In R. A. Shweder & R. A. LeVine (Eds.), *Culture theory: Essays on mind, self, and emotion* (pp. 158–199). Cambridge, UK: Cambridge University Press.

Shweder, R. A., Jensen, L. A., & Goldstein, W. M. (1995). Who sleeps by whom revisited: A method for extracting the moral goods implicit in practice. In J. J. Goodnow, P. J. Miller, & F. Kessel (Eds.), Cultural practices as contexts for development. *New Directions for Child Development, 67,* 21–39.

Silverman, K. (1984/2002). *The life and times of Cotton Mather.* New York: Welcome Rain.

Singelis, T. M. (1994). The measurement of independent and interdependent self-construals. *Personality and Social Psychology Bulletin, 20,* 580–591.

Sinha, D., & Tripathi, R. C. (1994). Individualism in a collectivist culture: A case of coexistence of opposites. In U. Kim, H. C. Triandis, Ç. Kağitçibaşi, S. Choi, & G. Yoon (Eds.), *Individualism and collectivism: Theory, method, and applications* (pp. 123–136). Thousand Oaks, CA: Sage.

Slavin, R. E. (1983). *Cooperative learning.* New York: Longman.

Slavin, R. E. (1985). An introduction to cooperative learning research. In R. E. Slavin, S. Sharan, R. H. Lazarowitz, C. Webb, & R. Schmuck (Eds.), *Learning to cooperate, cooperating to learn* (pp. 5–15). New York: Plenum.

Slavin, R. E. (1991). *Student team learning: A practical guide to cooperative learning.* Washington, DC: National Education Association.

Smetana, J. G. (1988). Adolescents' and parents' conceptions of parental authority. *Child Development, 59,* 321–335.

Smetana, J. G. (1989). Adolescents' and parents' reasoning about actual family conflict. *Child Development, 60,* 1052–1067.

Smetana, J. G. (1994). Parenting styles and beliefs about parental authority. In J. G. Smetana (Ed.), Beliefs about parenting: Origins and developmental implications. *New Directions for Child Development, 66,* 21–36.

Smetana, J. G. (2000). Middle-class African American adolescents' and parents' conceptions of parental authority and parenting practices: A longitudinal investigation. *Child Development, 71,* 1672–1686.

Smetana, J. G., Abernethy, A., & Harris, A. (2000). Adolescent–parent interactions in middle-class African American families: Longitudinal change and contextual variations. *Journal of Family Psychology, 14,* 458–474.

Smetana, J. G., & Asquith, P. (1994). Adolescents' and parents' conceptions of parental authority and personal autonomy. *Child Development, 65,* 1147–1162.

Smetana, J., & Gaines, C. (1999). Adolescent–parent conflict in middle-class African-American families. *Child Development, 70,* 1447–1463.

Smith, R. J. (1983/1993). *Japanese society: Tradition, self, and the social order.* Cambridge, UK: Cambridge University Press.

Sorell, G. T., & Montgomery, M. J. (2001). Feminist perspectives on Erikson's theory: Their relevance for contemporary identity development research. *Identity: An International Journal of Theory and Research, 1,* 97–128.

Spelke, E. S., & Cortelyou, A. (1981). Perceptual aspects of social knowing: Looking and listening in infancy. In M. E. Lamb & L. R. Sherrod (Eds.), *Infant social cognition: Empirical and theoretical considerations* (pp. 61–84). Hillsdale, NJ: Lawrence Erlbaum Associates.

Spiro, M. E. (1993). Is the Western conception of the self "peculiar" within the context of the world cultures? *Ethos, 21,* 107–153.

Sroufe, L. A. (1990). An organizational perspective on the self. In D. Cicchetti & M. Beeghly (Eds.), *The self in transition: Infancy to childhood* (pp. 281–307). Chicago: University of Chicago Press.

Steinberg, L. (1990). Autonomy, conflict, and harmony in the family relationship. In S. S. Feldman & G. R. Elliot (Eds.), *At the threshold: The developing adolescent* (pp. 255–276). Cambridge, MA: Harvard University Press.

Steinberg, L., & Silverberg, S. B. (1986). The vicissitudes of autonomy in early adolescence. *Child Development, 57*, 841–851.

Stephan, C. W., Stephan, W. G., Saito, I., & Barnett, S. M. (1998). Emotional expression in Japan and the United States: The nonmonolithic nature of individualism and collectivism. *Journal of Cross-Cultural Psychology, 29*, 728–748.

Stern, D. (1977). *The first relationship: Mother and infant.* Cambridge, MA: Harvard University Press.

Stern, D. N. (1985). *The interpersonal world of the infant.* New York: Basic Books.

Stevenson, H. W. (1991). Japanese elementary school education. *The Elementary School Journal, 92*, 109–120.

Stevenson, H. W., Lee, S., Chen, C., Stigler, J. W., Hsu, C., & Kitamura, S. (1990). Contexts of achievement: A study of American, Chinese, and Japanese children. *Monographs of the Society for Research in Child Development, 55*(1–2, Serial No. 221).

Strauss, C. (2000). The culture concept and the individualism-collectivism debate: Dominant and alternative attributions for class in the United States. In L. P. Nucci, G. B. Saxe, & E. Turiel (Eds.), *Culture, thought, and development* (pp. 85–114). Mahwah, NJ: Lawrence Erlbaum Associates.

Stuhr, J. J. (2000). Dewey's life: Cultural context and philosophical background. In J. J. Stuhr (Ed.), *Pragmatism and classical American philosophy: Essential readings and interpretive essays* (pp. 431–444). New York: Oxford University Press.

Suina, J. H., & Smolkin, L. B. (1994). From natal culture to school culture to dominant society culture: Supporting transitions for Pueblo Indian students. In P. M. Greenfield & R. R. Cocking (Eds.), *Cross-cultural roots of minority child development* (pp. 115–130). Hillsdale, NJ: Lawrence Erlbaum Associates.

Sunley, R. (1955). Early nineteenth-century American literature on child-rearing. In M. Mead & M. Wolfenstein (Eds.), *Childhood in contemporary cultures* (pp. 150–167). Chicago: University of Chicago Press.

Takahashi, K., Ohara, N., Antonucci, T. C., & Akiyama, H. (2002). Commonalities and differences in close relationships among the Americans and Japanese: A comparison by the individualism/collectivism concept. *International Journal of Behavioral Development, 26*, 453–465.

Taylor, C. (1985/1991). The person. In M. Carrithers, S. Collins, & S. Lukes (Eds.), *The category of the person: Anthropology, philosophy, history* (pp. 257–281). Cambridge, UK: Cambridge University Press.

Tharp, R. G., & Gallimore, R. (1988). *Rousing minds to life: Teaching, learning, and schooling in social context.* Cambridge, UK: Cambridge University Press.

Thorbecke, W., & Grotevant, H. D. (1982). Gender differences in adolescent interpersonal identity formation. *Journal of Youth and Adolescence, 11*, 479–492.

Tobin, J. J. (1992/1995). Japanese preschools and the pedagogy of selfhood. In N. R. Rosenberger (Ed.), *Japanese sense of self* (pp. 21–39). Cambridge, UK: Cambridge University Press.

Tobin, J. J., Wu, D. Y. H., & Davidson, D. H. (1987). Class size and student/teacher ratios in the Japanese preschool. *Comparative Education Review, 31*, 533–549.

Tobin, J. J., Wu, D. Y. H., & Davidson, D. H. (1989). *Preschool in three cultures: Japan, China, and the United States.* New Haven, CT: Yale University Press.

Toma, C., & Wertsch, J. V. (2003). The multiple agendas of intersubjectivity in children's group writing activity. In C. Raeff & J. B. Benson (Eds.), *Social and cognitive development in the context of individual, social, and cultural processes* (pp. 131–146). London: Routledge.

Trevarthen, C. (1979). Communication and cooperation in early infancy: A description of primary intersubjectivity. In M. Bullowa (Ed.), *Before speech* (pp. 321–347). Hillsdale, NJ: Lawrence Erlbaum Associates.

Trevarthen, C. (1980). The foundations of intersubjectivity: Development of interpersonal and cooperative understanding in infants. In D. R. Olson (Ed.), *The social foundations of language and thought: Essays in honor of Jerome S. Bruner* (pp. 316–342). New York: Norton.

Triandis, H. C. (1989). The self and social behavior in differing cultural contexts. *Psychological Review, 96*, 506–520.

Triandis, H. C. (1994). Theoretical and methodological approaches to the study of collectivism and individualism. In U. Kim, H. C. Triandis, Ç. Kağitçibaşi, S. Choi, & G. Yoon (Eds.), *Individualism and collectivism: Theory, method, and applications* (pp. 41–51). Thousand Oaks, CA: Sage.

Triandis, H. C. (1995). *Individualism and collectivism*. Boulder, CO: Westview.

Tsuneyoshi, R. (1994). Small groups in Japanese elementary school classrooms: Comparisons with the United States. *Comparative Education, 30*, 115–129.

Tudge, J., Hogan, D., Lee, S., Tammeveski, P., Meltsas, M., Kulakova, N., Snezhkova, I., & Putnam, S. (1999). Cultural heterogeneity: Parental values and beliefs and their preschoolers' activities in the United States, South Korea, Russia, and Estonia. In A. Göncü (Ed.), *Children's engagement in the world: Sociocultural perspectives* (pp. 62–96). Cambridge, UK: Cambridge University Press.

Turiel, E. (1983/1985). *The development of social knowledge: Morality and convention*. Cambridge, UK: Cambridge University Press.

Turiel, E. (1996). Equality and hierarchy: Conflict in values. In E. S. Reed, E. Turiel, & T. Brown (Eds.), *Values and knowledge* (pp. 75–101). Mahwah, NJ: Lawrence Erlbaum Associates.

Turiel, E., & Perkins, S. A. (2004). Flexibilities of mind. Conflict and culture. *Human Development, 44*, 158–178.

Turiel, E., Smetana, J. G., & Killen, M. (1991). Social contexts in social cognitive development. In W. M. Kurtines & J. L. Gewirtz (Eds.), *Handbook of moral behavior and development* (Vol. 2, pp. 307–332). Hillsdale, NJ: Lawrence Erlbaum Associates.

Turiel, E., & Wainryb, C. (2000). Social life in cultures: Judgments, conflict, and subversion. *Child Development, 71*, 250–256.

Užgiris, I. Č. (1981). Two functions of imitation during infancy. *International Journal of Behavioral Development, 4*, 1–12.

Užgiris, I. Č. (1984). Imitation in infancy: Its interpersonal aspects. In M. Perlmutter (Ed.), *The Minnesota symposia on child psychology* (Vol. 17, pp. 1–32). Hillsdale, NJ: Lawrence Erlbaum Associates.

Užgiris, I. Č. (1989). Infants in relation: Performers, pupils, and partners. In W. Damon (Ed.), *Child development today and tomorrow* (pp. 288–311). San Francisco: Jossey-Bass.

Užgiris, I. Č. (1991). The social context of infant imitation. In M. Lewis & S. Feinman (Eds.), *Social influences and socialization in infancy* (pp. 215–251). New York: Plenum.

Užgiris, I. Č. (1996). Together and apart: The enactment of values in infancy. In E. S. Reed, E. Turiel, & T. Brown (Eds.), *Values and knowledge* (pp. 17–39). Mahwah, NJ: Lawrence Erlbaum Associates.

Užgiris, I. Č., Benson, J. B., Kruper, J. C., & Vasek, M. E. (1989). Contextual influences on imitative interactions between mothers and infants. In J. J. Lockman & N. L. Hazen (Eds.), *Action in social context: Perspectives on early development* (pp. 103–127). New York: Plenum.

Valsiner, J. (1997). *Culture and the development of children's action: A theory of human development*. New York: Wiley.

Vincent, C. E. (1951). Trends in infant care ideas. *Child Development, 22*, 199–209.

von Bertalanffy, L. (1968). *Organismic psychology and systems theory*. Barre, MA: Clark University Press (with Barre Publishers).

von Bertalanffy, L. (1969). *General system theory*. New York: George Braziller.

Wainryb, C. (1995). Reasoning about social conflicts in different cultures: Druze and Jewish children in Israel. *Child Development, 66*, 390–401.

Wainryb, C., & Turiel, E. (1994). Dominance, subordination, and concepts of personal entitlements in cultural contexts. *Child Development, 65*, 1701–1722.

Waterman, A. S. (1981). Individualism and interdependence. *American Psychologist, 36*, 762–773.

Waterman, A. S. (1982). Identity development from adolescence to adulthood: An extension of theory and a review of research. *Developmental Psychology, 18*, 341–358.

Waterman, A. S. (1992). Identity as an aspect of optimal psychological functioning. In G. R. Adams, T. P. Gullotta, & R. Montemayor (Eds.), *Adolescent identity formation* (pp. 50–72). Newbury Park, CA: Sage.

Webb, N. M. (1982). Group composition, group interaction, and achievement in cooperative small groups. *Journal of Educational Psychology, 74*, 475–484.

Weisner, T. S., & Gallimore, R. (1977). My brother's keeper: Child and sibling caretaking. *Current Anthropology, 18*, 169–190.

Wentzel, K. R. (1991). Social competence at school: Relation between social responsibility and academic achievement. *Review of Educational Research, 61*, 1–24.

Wentzel, K. R. (1993). Does being good make the grade? Social behavior and academic competence in middle school. *Journal of Educational Psychology, 85*, 357–364.

Werner, H., & Kaplan, B. (1963/1984). *Symbol formation: An organismic developmental approach to the psychology of language*. Hillsdale, NJ: Lawrence Erlbaum Associates.

Wertsch, J. V. (1998). *Mind as action*. New York: Oxford University Press.

West, E. (1989). *Growing up with the country: Childhood on the far Western frontier*. Albuquerque: University of New Mexico Press.

White, L. K., & Brinkerhoff, D. B. (1981). Children's work in the family: Its significance and meaning. *Journal of Marriage and the Family, 43*, 789–798.

White, M. (1987). *The Japanese educational challenge: A commitment to children*. New York: The Free Press.

White, M. I., & LeVine, R. A. (1986). What is an "*ii ko*" (good child)? In H. W. Stevenson, H. Azuma, & K. Hakuta (Eds.), *Child development and education in Japan* (pp. 55–62). New York: W. H. Freeman.

Whiting, B. B., & Edwards, C. P. (1988). *Children of different worlds: The formation of social behavior*. Cambridge, MA: Harvard University Press.

Wiley, A. R., Rose, A. J., Burger, L. K., & Miller, P. J. (1998). Constructing autonomous selves through narrative practices: A comparative study of working-class and middle-class families. *Child Development, 69*, 833–847.

Winthrop, J. (1630/1988). A model of Christian charity. In R. N. Bellah, R. Madsen, W. M. Sullivan, A. Swidler, & S. M. Tipton (Eds.), *Individualism and commitment in American life: Readings on the themes of* Habits of the Heart (pp. 22–27). New York: Harper & Row.

Wishy, B. (1968). *The child and the republic*. Philadelphia: University of Pennsylvania Press.

Wolf, A. W., Lozoff, B., Latz, S., & Paludetto, R. (1996). Parental theories in the management of young children's sleep in Japan, Italy, and the United States. In S. Harkness & C. M. Super (Eds.), *Parents' cultural belief systems: Their origins, expressions, and consequences* (pp. 364–384). New York: Guilford.

Wolfenstein, M. (1953). Trends in infant care. *American Journal of Orthopsychiatry, 23*, 120–130.

Woolley, H. T. (1926, October). Before your child goes to school. *Parents' Magazine*, pp. 8–11.

Yamada, H. (2004). Japanese mothers' views of young children's areas of personal discretion. *Child Development, 75*, 164–179.

Yoshida, R. (2004, April 18). Pair's release takes the heat off Koizumi. *The Japan Times.* (online version with no page numbers)

Young, V. H. (1970). Family and childhood in a Southern Negro community. *American Anthropologist, 72*, 269–288.

Youniss, J., & Smollar, J. (1985). *Adolescent relations with mothers, fathers, and friends.* Chicago: University of Chicago Press.

Youniss, J., & Yates, M. (2000). Adolescents' public discussion and collective identity. In N. Budwig, I. Č. Užgiris, & J. V. Wertsch (Eds.), *Communication: An arena of development* (pp. 215–233). Stamford, CT: Ablex.

Zachry, C. B. (1933, September). Your child's need of security. *Parents' Magazine*, pp. 15, 62–63.

Zukow-Goldring, P. (1995). Sibling caregiving. In M. H. Bornstein (Ed.), *Handbook of parenting* (Vol. 3, pp. 177–208). Mahwah, NJ: Lawrence Erlbaum Associates.

Author Index

A

Abbott, S., 107, *256*
Abernethy, A., 137, *271*
Aboud, F. E., 200, *256*
Adams, G. R., 35, *256*
Akiyama, H., 26, *272*
Akoh, H., 170, 171, *263*
Allison, K. W., 120, *258*
Ames, C., 156, *256*
Ames, R., *256*
Antil, L. R., 159, 160, 162, *256*
Antonucci, T. C., 26, *272*
Archer, M. S., 45, *256*
Archer, S. L., 191, 192, *256*
Aronson, E., 160, 161, 162, *256*
Asquith, P., 137, *271*
Atkinson, R., 135, 199, *268*
Azuma, H., 116, 140, 143, 145, 170, 171, *259, 263, 269*

B

Bachnik, J., 139, 204, *256*
Bachnik, J. M., 139, 204, *257*
Bacon, M. K., 8, *257*
Bagwell, C. L., 200, *268*
Baker, J. A., 151, *257*
Ball, H. L., 107, *257*

Bamberg, M., 194, *257*
Barnett, S. M., 26, *272*
Barry, H., III, 8, *257*
Bartz, K. W., 105, 110, *257*
Baumrind, D., 111, *257*
Beales, R. W., Jr., 65, *257*
Bear, J. A., Jr., 70, 71, 72, 73, 74, 75, 76, *257*
Behrens, K. Y., 142, 146, 241, *257*
Bell, R. Q., 4, *257*
Bellah, R. N., 29, 99, *257*
Ben-Ari, E., 169, *257*
Benedict, A. E., 92, *257*
Benson, J. B., 124, *273*
Berlin, I., 77, 78, *257*
Berndt, T. J., 200, *257, 270*
Berry, J. W., 23, *257*
Beswick, G., 142, *266*
Betts, E. M., 70, 71, 72, 73, 74, 75, 76, *257*
Bhavnagri, N. P., 116, *257*
Blatt, S. J., 35, *262*
Blumenfeld, P. C., 170, 171, *263*
Boatright, M. C., 85, 86, 87, *257*
Bolt, E., 158, *269*
Boocock, S. S., 163, 172, *257*
Bornstein, M. H., 13, *257*
Bouchey, H. A., 198, 199, *263*
Bourne, E. J., 12, 17, 20, *271*
Bowlby, J., 34, *257, 258*

Brazelton, T. B., 123, *258*
Bresnick, S., 198, 199, *263*
Bridger, R., 151, *257*
Briggs, J. L., 40, 121, *258*
Brinkerhoff, D. B., 111, 112, *274*
Brody, G. H., 121, *258*
Bronfenbrenner, U., 91, 105, *258*
Brooks-Gunn, J., 135, 136, 199, *258*, *264*
Brown, A. L., 178, *258*
Brown, B. B., 200, *258*
Bruner, J., 32, 43, 124, *258*
Buchsbaum, H. K., 34, *261*
Budwig, N., 194, *258*
Buhrmester, D., 33, 136, 200, *258*, *261*
Bumpus, M. F., 136, *258*
Burger, L. K., 118, *274*
Burton, L. M., 120, *258*

C

Cai, Y., 158, *269*
Cauce, A. M., 137, *258*
Caudill, W., 9, 107, 139, *258*
Cazden, C. B., 156, *258*
Chandler, M., 20, 203, *259*
Chandler, M. J., 14, 20, 193, 203, *259*
Chen, C., 146, 170, 171, *272*
Chen, S., 139, 145, *259*
Child, I. L., 8, *257*
Child, L., 81, 82, 83, 84, *259*
Chirkov, V., 26, *259*
Clancy, P. M., 139, 142, *259*
Cohen, E. G., 159, 162, *259*
Cole, M., 23, 38, 40, 43, 254, *259*
Cole, P. M., 30, *260*
Collins, W. A., 135, 136, 138, *259*, *266*
Colt, M. D., 86, 87, *259*
Conroy, M., 144, *259*
Cooley, C. H., 184, 185, 186, 187, 194, *259*
Coon, H. M., 26, *268*
Coontz, S., 64, 69, 81, 82, 83, 87, 89, 91, *259*
Cooper, C. R., 35, 136, *259*, *262*
Cortelyou, A., 123, *271*
Côté, J. E., 190, *259*
Coy, K. C., 135, 136, *266*
Cramer, P., 191, *259*
Crouter, A. C., 136, *258*
Csikszentmihalyi, M., 136, 199, 200, 201, *259*

Cushman, P., 99, *259*
Cutting, A. L., 97, *260*

D

Damon, W., 33, 196, 197, 198, 212, *259*, *260*
Danziger, K., 21, *260*
Davidson, D. H., 15, 104, 116, 158, 163, 164, 165, 166, 167, 168, 169, 170, 171, 172, 173, 174, 175, *272*
Davies, B., 193, 194, *260*
de Tocqueville, A., 6, 7, 78, 79, 80, 90, *260*
Delaney, S., 111, *262*
Demo, D. H., 199, *260*
Demos, J., 62, 64, 65, 82, *260*
Dennis, T. A., 30, *260*
Dewey, J., 151, 152, 153, 154, 155, *260*
Dickson, P., 116, 140, 143, 145, *263*
Doi, L. T., 142, *260*
Doi, T., 139, 141, 143, 204, 205, 206, *260*
Downs, J. F., 18, *260*
Doyle, D. H., 87, 89, 90, *260*
Dunn, J., 97, *260*

E

Eccles, J. S., 35, 190, *269*
Edwards, C. P., 107, 111, 112, 113, 114, 115, *274*
Egan, K., 151, *260*
Eisenberg, M., 159, *261*
Emde, R. N., 34, *261*
Erelcin, F. G., 26, *261*
Erikson, E. H., 187, 188, 189, 190, *261*
Escalona, S., 105, *261*

F

Fasick, F. A., 120, 199, *261*
Fernald, A., 139, *261*
Feshbach, N. D., 157, 159, *261*
Fijneman, Y. A., 26, *261*
Fisher, N., 97, *260*
Flowerday, T., 158, *261*
Fogel, A., 139, 143, *261*
Ford, D. H., 38, *261*
Fowler, B. P., 95, *261*
Furman, W., 136, *261*

G

Gadlin, H., 81, 82, 84, *261*
Gaines, C., 137, *271*
Gallimore, R., 115, 157, *272, 274*
Gans, H. J., 6, *261*
Garrick, R. J., 140, 204, *265*
Gaskins, S., 106, 109, 112, 113, *261*
Geertz, C., 9, 43, *261*
Georgas, J., 26, *261*
Getis, V. L., 64, *262*
Gilligan, C., 28, *262*
Gjerde, P. F., 26, 45, *262*
Glendon, M. A., 99, *262*
Goldsmith, D., 107, *267*
Goldstein, W. M., 107, *271*
Göncü, A., 18, 19, 124, *269*
Gonzales, N., 137, *258*
Goodnow, J. J., 32, 38, 40, 43, 111, 112, *262, 267*
Gottlieb, G., 38, *262*
Gralinski, J. H., 104, 105, 106, 109, 111, 112, *262*
Graves, D., 137, *258*
Greenberg, M. T., 199, 201, *262*
Greenfield, P. J., 18, *262*
Greenfield, P. M., 10, 29, 107, 175, *262*
Grotevant, H. D., 35, 136, 192, *262, 272*
Grove, K., 137, *258*
Gruenberg, B. C., 92, 94, *262*
Gruenberg, S. M., 92, 94, *262*
Guisinger, S., 35, *262*

H

Hallett, D., 14, 20, 193, 203, *259*
Hamilton, V. L., 170, 171, *263*
Handwerker, W. P., 26, *263*
Harari, S. E., 65, 81, *263*
Hareven, T. K., 64, 81, 82, *263*
Harkness, S., 26, *263*
Harmoni, R. V., 142, *266*
Harper, L. V., 4, *257*
Harré, R., 193, 194, *260*
Harris, A., 137, *271*
Hart, C. H., 116, *265*
Hart, D., 196, 197, 198, 212, *260*
Harter, S., 14, 20, 196, 198, 199, 200, 201, *263*
Hartup, W. W., 199, 200, *263*
Harwood, R. L., 26, 105, *263, 270*

Hattwick, L. A., 94, *263*
Hawthorne, N., 64, *263*
Heath, S. B., 118, 124, 125, *263*
Hendry, J., 139, 140, 142, 143, 145, 163, 164, 165, 166, 167, 169, 170, 171, 173, *263*
Hertz-Lazarowitz, R., 156, *263*
Hess, R. D., 116, 140, 143, 144, 145, 170, 171, *259, 263*
Hewlett, B. S., 18, *263*
Hill, B., 163, *263*
Hill, J. P., 112, 137, *263*
Hiraga, Y., 137, *258*
Hobart, C. J., 33, *270*
Hoff-Ginsberg, E., 119, *264*
Hoffman, D. M., 165, 166, 170, 171, *264*
Hofstede, G., 9, 10, 11, 13, 15, 16, 27, 30, *264*
Hollan, D., 18, *264, 273*
Holland, D., 21, 26, *264*
Holloway, S. D., 139, 165, *264*
Holmbeck, G. N., 112, 135, 136, 137, *263, 264*
Hooker, E., 107, *257*
Howard, A., 18, *264*
Howard, K. I., 135, 199, *268*
Hsu, C., 146, 170, 171, *272*
Hui, C. H., 26, *261*

I, J

Imbens-Bailey, A., 194, *264*
James, W., 201, 202, 203, 219, *264*
Jenkins, J. R., 159, 160, 162, *256*
Jensen, L. A., 107, *271*
Johnson, D. W., 162, *264*
Johnson, R. T., 162, *264*
Josselson, R., 35, 199, *264*

K

Kagan, S., 159, *264*
Kağitçibaşi, Ç., 8, 14, 31, *264*
Kaplan, B., 38, 39, *264, 274*
Kaplan, U., 26, *259*
Kashiwagi, K., 116, 140, 143, 144, 145, *259, 263*
Kawai, M., 139, *261*
Kaye, K., 123, 124, *264*
Kedar-Voivodas, G., 157, *265*

Keliher, A. V., 96, 97, 99, *265*
Keller, H., 13, 16, *265*
Kelley, M. L., 119, 143, *265*, *268*
Kellogg, S., 64, 65, 69, 81, 82, 87, 91, *267*
Kelly, P. J., 107, *257*
Kemmelmeier, M., 26, *268*
Killen, M., 26, 31, 168, *265*, *273*
Kim, Y., 26, *259*
Kipnis, A., 21, *264*
Kirkpatrick, J., 106, 107, 113, 115, 116, 121, 128, *266*
Kitamura, S., 146, 170, 171, *272*
Kitayama, S., 5, 12, 13, 17, 20, 30, 112, *265*, *266*
Kobayashi-Winata, H., 143, *268*
Kohn, M. L., 24, 119, 120, 146, *265*
Kojima, H., 170, *265*
Kondo, D. K., 139, 141, 142, 171, 204, 205, *265*
Kopp, C. B., 104, 105, 106, 109, 111, 112, *262*
Kruper, J. C., 124, *265*, *273*
Kulakova, N., 24, *273*
Kumagi, A. K., 205, *265*
Kumagi, H. A., 205, *265*
Kusserow, A. S., 22, 118, *265*
Kuwayama, T., 204, *265*

L

Labaree, D. F., 151, *265*
Ladd, G. W., 116, *265*
Lalonde, C. E., 14, 20, 193, 203, *259*
Lanham, B. B., 140, 204, *265*
Larson, R., 136, 199, 200, 201, *259*
Latz, S., 107, *274*
Laursen, B., 135, 136, *259*, *266*
Lebra, T. S., 139, 140, 143, 204, 205, 206, *266*
Lee, S., 24, 146, 170, 171, *272*, *273*
Leitch, C. J., 199, 201, *262*
Lerner, R. M., 38, *261*
LeSieur, K. D., 116, *265*
Leung, K., 26, *261*
Levin, H., 105, 108, 110, 112, 114, 117, 118, 119, *270*
Levine, C. G., 190, *259*
Levine, E. S., 105, *257*
Levine, L. W., 126, *266*
LeVine, R. A., 23, 123, 166, 171, *266*, *269*, *274*

Lewis, C. C., 164, 165, 166, 167, 168, 169, 170, 171, 172, *266*
Leyendecker, B., 26, 105, *263*, *270*
Lickliter, R., 38, *262*
Lienhardt, G., 18, *266*
Lightfoot, C., 200, *266*
Lingeman, R., 87, *266*
Lozoff, B., 107, *274*
Luebker, C., 135, 138, *259*
Luther, M., 60, *266*
Lutz, C., 107, *266*
Lynch, J. H., 199, *270*

M

Maccoby, E. E., 105, 108, 109, 110, 112, 114, 117, 118, 119, *266*, *270*
Madsen, R., 29, 99, *257*
Malpass, R. S., 26, *261*
Mann, L., 142, *266*
Marcia, J. E., 190, 191, 192, *266*, *268*
Marková, I., 184, *266*
Markus, H. R., 5, 12, 13, 17, 20, 30, 112, *265*, *266*
Marshall, S. K., 35, *256*
Martin, J. A., 109, *266*
Martini, M., 106, 107, 113, 115, 116, 121, 128, *266*
Mascolo, M. F., 26, *267*
Mather, C., 65, 66, 67, 68, *267*
Mathews, G., 205, *267*
Matsumoto, H., 13, *265*
Matthews, S. R., 88, *267*
McHale, S. M., 136, *258*
Mead, G. H., 180, 181, 182, 183, 184, *267*
Meek, L. H., 93, 94, *267*
Mehan, H., 156, 157, *267*
Meltsas, M., 24, *273*
Mendelson, M. J., 200, *256*
Messinger, D., 139, 143, *261*
Meyer, J. W., 80, *267*
Miller, D. L., 182, *267*
Miller, P., 119, *267*
Miller, P. J., 32, 38, 40, 43, 118, *267*, *274*
Miller, P. M., 103, 104, 107, 108, 110, 116, 123, 248, *269*
Mintz, S., 64, 65, 69, 81, 82, 87, 91, *267*
Minuchin, P. P., 157, *267*
Misra, G., 26, *267*
Mistry, J., 18, 19, 124, *269*

Mitsui, H., 142, *266*
Miura, K., 170, 171, *263*
Miyake, K., 140, *269*
Mize, J., 104, *268*
Mizuta, I., 30, *260*
Moeran, B., 204, *267*
Monsour, A., 20, 198, *263*
Montemayor, R., 137, *267*
Montgomery, M. J., 189, *271*
Morelli, G. A., 107, *267*
Morikawa, H., 139, *261*
Morris, C., 59, *267*
Mosier, C., 18, 19, 124, *269*
Murdoch, D. H., 85, *267*
Murray, D. W., 14, *267*
Mussen, P. H., 159, *261*

N

Nagano, K. N., 143, 145, *268*
Nakane, C., 15, 141, *267*
Nasaw, D., 151, *267*
Neff, K., 26, *268*
New, R. S., 105, 108, *268*
Newcomb, A. F., 200, *268*
Newman, B. M., 199, *268*
Newman, P. R., 199, *268*
Nucci, L., 104, 105, *268*

O

O'Donnell, A. M., 159, 160, *268*
O'Kelly, J., 159, 160, *268*
O'Koon, J., 201, *268*
Obeidallah, D., 120, *258*
Ochs, E., 123, 124, 126, 193, *268*
Odin, S., 151, 204, *268*
Offer, D., 135, 199, *268*
Ogbu, J. U., 125, *268*
Ohara, N., 26, *272*
Onishi, M., 26, *262*
Onishi, N., 207, *268*
Oppenheim, D., 107, *267*
Osterweil, Z., 143, 145, *268*
Ostrov, E., 135, 199, *268*
Oyserman, D., 26, *268*

P

Paikoff, R. L., 135, 136, 199, *258*, *264*
Paludetto, R., 107, *274*
Pan, B. A., 194, *264*
Parke, R. D., 116, *257*
Patnoe, S., 160, 161, 162, *256*
Patterson, S. J., 192, *268*
Peak, L., 143, 163, 164, 166, 168, 169, 170, 173, *268*
Pearson, G. H. J., 93, 94, *268*
Penuel, W. R., 193, *268*
Perkins, S. A., 26, 45, *273*
Pettit, G. S., 104, *268*
Piaget, J., 42, *268*
Pipp, S., 34, 41, *268*
Plath, D. W., 107, *258*
Poortinga, Y. H., 26, *261*
Pott, M., 140, *269*
Power, T. G., 119, 143, *265*, *268*
Prawat, R. S., 159, *269*
Preston, G. H., 92, *269*
Price, G. G., 116, 140, 143, 145, *263*
Profilet, S. M., 116, *265*
Putnam, R. D., 99, *269*
Putnam, S., 24, *273*

R

Raeff, C., 8, 103, 104, 116, 213, *269*
Ramirez, M. C., 128, *269*
Rapisardi, C., 26, *267*
Reeve, J., 158, *269*
Rice, E. F., Jr., 60, *269*
Richman, A. L., 103, 104, 105, 107, 108, 110, 116, 123, 248, *268*, *269*
Rizzo, T. A., 200, *269*
Roeser, R. W., 35, 190, *269*
Rogoff, B., 18, 19, 32, 38, 43, 107, 113, 114, 115, 124, *267*, *269*
Rose, A. J., 118, *274*
Rosenberger, N. R., 204, *269*
Rothbaum, F., 140, *269*
Rubin, Z., 116, *269*
Ryan, M. P., 64, 69, 81, 82, 83, 87, 89, *270*
Ryan, R. M., 26, 199, *259*, *270*
Ryan-Finn, K., 137, *258*

S

Saito, I., 26, *272*
Sameroff, A. J., 35, 190, *269*
Sampson, E. E., 9, 60, 216, 220, *270*
Savin-Williams, R. C., 199, 200, *260, 270*
Schaffer, H. R., 123, 124, *270*
Schieffelin, B. B., 121, 123, 124, 126, 193, *268, 270*
Schlissel, L., 85, 86, 88, *270*
Schmuck, R., 159, *270*
Schoelmerich, A., 26, 105, *263, 270*
Schraw, G., 158, *261*
Schubert, H., 151, 184, *270*
Schulze, P. A., 105, *270*
Schwartz, S. H., 11, 21, *270*
Sears, R. R., 105, 108, 110, 112, 114, 117, 118, 119, *270*
Shachar, H., 156, *263*
Shain, B. A., 62, 64, 69, 77, 80, *270*
Shakespeare, W., 206, *270*
Shantz, C. U., 33, *270*
Shapiro, E. K., 157, *267*
Sharan, S., 156, 162, *270*
Sharan, Y., 162, *270*
Shaulov, A., 156, *270*
Shimizu, H., 34, 139, *270*
Shimoyachi, N., 208, *270*
Shoji, J., 143, *271*
Shwalb, B. J., 143, *271*
Shwalb, D. W., 26, 143, *270, 271*
Shweder, R. A., 107, *271*
Siegel, J. M., 199, 201, *262*
Silverberg, S. B., 199, *272*
Silverman, K., 62, 65, *271*
Singelis, T. M., 30, *271*
Sinha, D., 26, *271*
Slavin, R. E., 160, 162, *270, 271*
Sloman, J., 116, *269*
Smetana, J., 137, *271*
Smetana, J. G., 31, 104, 105, 137, 138, *268, 271, 273*
Smith, R. J., 140, 171, *271*
Smolkin, L. B., 18
Smollar, J., 34, 135, 136, 200, 201, *275*
Snezhkova, I., 24, *273*
Sochting, I., 192, *268*
Sokol, B. W., 14, 20, 193, 203, *259*
Solomon, M. J., 103, 104, 107, 108, 110, 116, 248, *269*
Sorell, G. T., 189, *271*
Spelke, E. S., 123, *271*

Sperry, L. L., 119, *267*
Spiro, M. E., 18, 20, *271*
Sroufe, L. A., 34, *271*
Steinberg, L., 135, 199, *272*
Stephan, C. W., 26, *272*
Stephan, W. G., 26, *272*
Stern, D., 42, 123, *272*
Stern, D. N., 34, 41, 97, 124, *272*
Stevenson, H. W., 146, 167, 170, 171, *272, 274*
Stevenson, M. B., 139, 143, *261*
Stigler, J. W., 146, 170, 171, *272*
Stoneman, Z., 121, *258*
Strauss, C., 33, *272*
Stuhr, J. J., 180, *272*
Sueyoshi, L., 168, *265*
Suina, J. H., 18, *272*
Suizzo, M., 26
Sullivan, W. M., 29, 99, *257*
Sunley, R., 81, *272*
Super, C. M., 26, *263*
Suzuki, L. K., 7, 29, 107, *262*
Swidler, A., 29, 99, *257*

T

Takahashi, K., 26, *272*
Tal, J., 13, *257*
Tamis-LeMonda, C., 13, *257*
Tammeveski, P., 24, *273*
Tardif, T., 119, *264*
Taylor, C., 21, 22, *272*
Terry, T., 151, *257*
Tharp, R. G., 157, *272*
The Japan Times, 207, 208, *264*
Thorbecke, W., 192, *272*
Tipton, S. M., 29, 99, *257*
Tobin, J. J., 15, 104, 116, 139, 158, 163, 164, 165, 166, 167, 168, 169, 170, 171, 172, 173, 174, 175, 204, *272*
Toda, S., 139, *261*
Toma, C., 139, *272*
Trevarthen, C., 123, 124, *273*
Triandis, H. C., 17, 30, 31, 141, *273*
Tripathi, R. C., 26, *271*
Tsuneyoshi, R., 173, *273*
Tudge, J., 24, *273*
Turiel, E., 17, 26, 27, 31, 45, *273, 274*

U

Užgiris, I. Č., 4, 38, 42, 123, 124, *265, 273*

V

Vadasy, P. F., 159, 160, 162, *256*
Valsiner, J., 21, 38, *273*
van Tijen, N., 26, *263*
Vasek, M. E., 124, *273*
Vincent, C. E., 91, 105, *274*
Vinovskis, M. A., 64, 65, 81, *262, 263*
von Bertalanffy, L., 38, *274*

W

Wahlsten, D., 38, *262*
Wainryb, C., 17, 26, 31, 45, *265, 273, 274*
Warton, P. M., 112, *262*
Waterman, A. S., 5, 190, 191, *256, 274*
Wayne, S. K., 159, 160, 162, *256*
Webb, N. M., 162, *274*
Weinstein, H., 9, 139, *258*
Weisner, T. S., 115, *274*
Weisz, J., 140, *269*
Wentzel, K. R., 151, 157, 159, *274*
Werner, H., 38, *274*
Wertsch, J. V., 32, 38, 139, 157, 254, 193, *268, 272, 274*
West, E., 85, 87, 89, *274*
White, L. K., 111, 112, *274*

White, M., 165, 166, 171, 173, *274*
White, M. I., 166, 171, *274*
Whitesell, N. R., 198, 199, *263*
Whiting, B. B., 107, 111, 112, 113, 114, 115, *274*
Wiley, A., 194, *258*
Wiley, A. R., 118, *274*
Willemsen, M. E., 26, *261*
Wimbush, D. D., 119, *265*
Winsor, A., 151, *257*
Winthrop, J., 62, 63, 247, *274*
Wishy, B., 81, 82, 83, 84, *274*
Wolf, A. W., 107, *274*
Wolfenstein, M., 91, 105, *274*
Woolley, H. T., 93, *275*
Wu, D. Y. H., 15, 104, 116, 158, 163, 164, 165, 166, 167, 168, 169, 170, 171, 172, 173, 174, 175, *272*

Y

Yamada, H., 139, 144, *275*
Yates, M., 193, *275*
Yoshida, R., 208, *275*
Young, V. H., 125, *275*
Youniss, J., 34, 135, 136, 193, 200, 201, *275*

Z

Zachry, C. B., 95, 96, *275*
Zahn-Waxler, C., 30, *260*
Zukow-Goldring, P., 115, *275*

Subject Index

A

A Family Well-Ordered, 65–66
A Treatise on Christian Liberty, 60
Acceptance speeches, 2
Acculturation, 215
Activity, dimensions, 40–43, 49
Adolescence
  early self-construction, 196–204
  independence/interdependence
    dimensions of activity, 41
    inseparability, 190
    self-concepts and moving beyond, 34
  late and self-construction
    constructing oneself as independent,
      217–222
    constructing oneself as interdepend-
      ent, 231–233
    feeling really independent, 228–231
    feeling really interdependent, 237–239
    overall, 212–217
    why independence is good or impor-
      tant, 222–228
    why interdependence is good or im-
      portant, 234–237
  parent–child relationships, 135–138
  role confusion and Erikson's theory of
    identity construction, 189
Adult children, 65
Advice, 236
Affect attunement, 124

African Americans
  cultural practices and obedience, con-
    formity, and dependence, 121
  importance of independence, 243
  parent–child relationships
    adolescence, 136–137
    infancy/childhood, 125–126
  social class concepts of independence/
    dependence, 118
Age, 132, 133, 134, 135
Aging mother, 15
Agricultural societies, 8–9
Allocentric, 30
Aloneness, 217, 219, 220
Amae, 142–144, 146, 205
American culture, 6, 29
American individualism, 5–6, 22–23, *see
  also* Individualism
American school practices, *see* School
  practices, American
Americans, *see also* Euro-Americans
  community/peer relationships and inde-
    pendence/interdependence, 114
  family values, 15
  Japanese culture comparison of child-
    rearing, 9, 144–145
  parents
    individual inviolability, 18–19
    Estonian and Russian comparison of
      self-direction, 24–25
  self-conceptions, 5

Animal companions, 15
Animals, interactions, 84
Appropriation of sociocultural norms and values, 182
Assertiveness, 125
Attitudes, negative, 135–136
Authoritative parenting, 111
Autonomous selves, 118
Autonomy versus shame/doubt, 188

B

Beginning of day activities, 174, *see also* Japanese
Behavior, 123, 193
  cooperative, 109

C

Calvinism, 62
Caregiving, 115, 188
Childhood
  parent–child interactions, 122–129
  self-construction, 196–204
Childrearing, independence/interdependence
  culture and inseparability, 248
  Euro-Americans and value of interdependence, 243
  goals/ideas, 103–104
  historical study
    19th century in middle class, 81–82
    Parents' Magazine and early 20th century, 91, 92–93
    Puritan cultural traditions, 65–68
Children
  autonomy and individual inviolability across cultures, 18–19
  cultural contexts of development, 51
  cultural similarities/differences and inseparability of independence/interdependence, 246
  hand shaking and culture, 43–44
  household chores and parent–child relationships, 111–113
  self-constructing activities, 195
Choices, 175–176, 189–190
Christians, 59–63
Civic duties, 74
Clarification requests, 126

Class size, 164
Classrooms
  contemporary American, 155–159
  regulation in Japan, 166–170
Cleanup notice, 1
Cleanup song, 1–2
Collective goals, 7, *see also* Goals
Collectivism, 5, 6–7
Colonial period, 65
Colombian parents, 128
Commands, 131–132, 133, 134
Communication, 123–124, 135, 139
Community, 79, 114
  standards, 64
Community subsistence, 113, *see also* Subsistence
Competency, 44–45
Competitive system, 155–159
Compliance, 143–144
Conduct standards, 68
Confidence, 224
Conflict
  independence/interdependence changes over time, 109–111
  dimensions of activity, 42–43
  investigating, 253
  peer and inseparability, 168
  parent–child relationships during adolescence, 135–136, 137–138
Conformity
  childrearing goals/ideas of parents, 108
  fostering independence or undermining interdependence, 159
  within-culture differences, 117–121
Congregationalism, 62
Connectedness, 238
Constitution, 77
Continuity, 202–203
Conventional behavior, 125–126
Co-occurrence of independence/interdependence model, 33–35
Cooley theory, 184–187
Cooperation, 163–166
Cooperative behavior, *see* Behavior
Cooperative learning, 159–162
Cosleeping practices, 106, 107
Creativity, 157
Cross-cultural studies, 26
Cultural conceptions, dynamic, 24–26
Cultural development, 46–55
Cultural differences, 115
Cultural emphasis, 29–31, 32

Cultural heterogeneity, 31, 32
Cultural meanings, 21–24, 44–45
Cultural practices, independence/interdependence
  conceptualizing the dynamics in contexts of development, 49, 52–53
  constructs, 242, 244
  context of inner/outer in Japan, 139–142, 163
  dimensions of activity, 40–41, 42
  historical case study, 63–65
  inseparability, 104–105, 191, 248–249
  meanings of, 252–254
  obedience, conformity, and dependence, 120–121
  parent–child interactions in infancy/childhood, 122–123
  self-constructing activities, 193, 195–196, 204
  systems framework and new conceptual approach, 40
  Western versus non-Western and rise of dichotomous conceptions, 27
Cultural traditions, 189, 250
Culture
  independence/interdependence
    conceptualizing, 43–46
    different and interrelatedness, 2–3, 4
    individual across cultures and complexities, 17–19
    meanings, 251, 252
    similarities/differences and inseparability, 245–246
    variability and moving beyond dichotomous conceptions, 29–31, 32
    varied, 243–244
  independence- versus interdependence-oriented, 9–12
Culture's Consequences, 9–10

D

de Tocqueville, A., 6–7, 78, 79, 82, 89, 153
Decade of I/C (individualism/collectivism), 8
Decision making
  independence/interdependence
    contemporary classrooms, 158–159
    cultural similarities/differences and inseparability, 248

individual inviolability and complexities, 18
Parents' Magazine and historical study in early 20th century, 94
parent–child relationships during adolescence, 136
why independence is good or important, 223
Declaration of agency, 194
Declaration of Independence, 76, 77
Degree of ego identity, 190, see also Identity
Democracy, 152
Democracy in America, 6
Dependence, independence distinction, 226
Development, children's, 3, 25, 70–71, 254
Dewey, John, 151–155
Dichotomous conceptions
  independence and interdependence, 8–14
    moving beyond, 28–35
    understanding rise of, 26–28
    theoretical problems, 14–17
Discipline, 92–93, 144–145
Diversity, 84
Division of labor, 189
Doubt, see Autonomy versus shame/doubt
Dualisms, 11, 16, 184
Dyadic interactions, 127–129, 130

E

Eating practices, 104–109
Economic production, 89
Education, 67, 243–244, 251
Educational reform, 152, 178
Educational settings
  American school practices
    contemporary American classrooms, 155–159
    inseparability and cooperative learning, 159–162
    John Dewey and education of individuals in relation to others, 151–155
  pre- and elementary school in Japan
    enacting conceptions in a typical preschool, 172–176
    individualized learning, 170–172

Educational settings *(cont.)*
  pre- and elementary school in Japan
    (cont.)
    inseparability in classroom regulation,
      166–170
    structuring cooperation and group
      life, 163–166
Egalitarianism, 81, 170
Eighteenth century
  historical case study of Euro-American
    cultural traditions, 69–80
  norms and freedom in America, 77
Elementary school, 162–166, *see also* Edu-
    cation
Emic methods, 23–24
Empathy, 139, 167–168, 200
Enryo, 139, 141, 204, 205
Equality, 78, 198
Equality of opportunity, 189
Erikson's theory, 187–192
Estonia, 24–25
Ethnicity, 252
Ethnographic analyses, 18
Etic methods, 23–24
Euro-American
  concepts of independence, 117
  constructing oneself as independent,
    217–222
  constructing oneself as interdependent,
    231–233
  feeling really independent, 228–231
  feeling really interdependent, 237–239
  historical case study
    nineteenth-century families, 81–90
    Parents' Magazine in the early 20th
      century, 91–97
    Puritan beginnings, 59–68
    revolutionary and early national peri-
      ods, 69–80
  importance of independence and inter-
    dependence, 243
  inseparability of independence/interde-
    pendence
    cultural similarities/differences,
      245–246, 247, 248, 249
    dyadic and group interactions, 128
    eating practices, 105
    self-construction in adolescents,
      199–200
    sleeping practices, 107–108
  Japanese comparison of childrearing
    practices, 138

parent–child relationships
  household chores, 112
  infancy/childhood, 123
  parental talk, 129–130, 132, 133
  structuring of independence/interde-
    pendence, 110
parents, 104, 116
self-constructing activities, 193
self-construction studies, 244
  late adolescence, 212–217
social class concepts of independence/
  dependence, 118
why independence is good or important, 222–228
why interdependence is good or important, 234–237
Expectations, independence/interdepend-
  ence
  changes over time and potential con-
    flict, 109–111
  changing with children's development
    and cultural conceptions, 25
  eating practices and childrearing goals/
    ideas of parents, 106
  household chores in structuring,
    111–112

F

Face-to-face interactions, 123, 128
Faith, 60–61, 62
Family, 15, 64, 232
Family ties, 71–73
Father–son relationships, 82
Feedback, 200
Feminist movement, 28
Financial independence, 119–120, 215
Flexibility, 92
Formal operations stage, 199
Founding Fathers, 77
Fraternal organizations, 90
Free play, 173, 174, *see also* Preschool
Freedom, 7, 76–80
Friendships, 200, *see also* Peers
Frontier lives, 85–89

G

Games, organized, 182, *see also* Self-
  construction

Gender, 28, 191–192, 251
Generalized other, 182, 183
Goals, independence/interdependence
    community and structuring, 113
    dimensions of activity and conceptual-
        izations, 42
    historical case study, 94–95
    inseparability in context of cooperative
        learning, 160
    parent–child relationships and structur-
        ing, 109, 110
    pursuit and multifaceted meanings,
        244–245
    self-chosen in relation to culture, 45
    structuring cooperation in educational
        settings in Japan, 164
    theory of self-construction, 198
Grandsons, 74
Great Depression, 95–96
Group, submersion, 206
Group identification, 164, see also Japan
Group interactions, 127–129
Group members, 165, see also Japan
Group practices, 95
Group subsistence, 246–247, see also
        Goals; Subsistence
Guidance, 92
Guilt, see Initiative versus guilt
Gusii people of Kenya, 23

H

Hamlet, 206, see also Self-construction
Hand waving, 43–44
Happiness, 116
Hard defensive individualism, 22–23
Hard offensive individualism, 22
Harmony, see Conflict/harmony
Heterogeneous groupings, 160
Historical background, individualism ver-
        sus collectivism, 9–11
Historical derivations, independence/inter-
        dependence, 45
History analysis, 250–251
Hoikuen, 172
Hostages, 206–208
Household chores, 111–114
Household freedom, 80
Human companions, 15
Human connectedness, 71, see also Social
        connectedness

Human functioning
    American school practices and Dewey's
        philosophy, 152
    independence/interdependence
        investigating cultural meanings, 21–22
        new conceptual approach, 38, 39
    individualistic versus collectivistic cul-
        tures, 9–13, 16
Hunting/fishing societies, 8

I

"I" activities, 183–184
Identity, independence/interdependence
    adolescent and moving beyond the di-
        chotomy, 34–35
    Erikson's theory of construction,
        187–192
    inseparability, 191
Idiocentric, 30
Ikigai, 205, see also Japan
Imaginary friends, 182
Imitation, 124
Immigrants, 90
Independence, see also Interdependence
    characteristics and self-construction in
        late adolescence, 214, 215
    constructing oneself as, 217–222
    use of terminology, 56–57
    why is it good or important, 222–228
Independence activity dimensions, 57
Independence/interdependence
    multifaceted meanings, 244–245
    theoretical foundations
        context-dependent/context-
            independent selves, 20–21
        dichotomous conceptions, 8–14
        dynamic cultural conceptions, 24–26
        dynamics in cultural contexts of de-
            velopment, 46–55
        individual inviolability across cultures,
            17–19
        investigating cultural meanings, 21–24
        moving beyond dichotomous concep-
            tions, 28–35
        new conceptual approach, 38–46
        preliminaries, 3–8
        problems and empirical discrepancies,
            14–17
        trying to understand the rise of di-
            chotomous conceptions, 26–28

Independent, feeling, 228–231
Independent judgment, 95
Independent meanings
  conceptualizing the dynamics in cultural
    contexts, 47, 49, 54
  future directions of research, 250–251
Individual accountability, 162
Individual feelings, 140, see also Japan
Individual goals, 110, see also Goals
Individual inclinations, 154
Individual persistence, 171
Individual space, 112
Individual variability, 29–31, 32
Individualism
  collectivism comparison in studies, 9–11
  independence/interdependence
    human separateness and preliminar-
      ies, 5, 6, 7–8
    score, 16
Individuality, independence/interdepend-
    ence
  cultural similarities/differences and in-
    separability, 246
  fostering or undermining in classrooms,
    157
  historical case study
    early 20th century, 96–97
    19th century in middle class, 82–84
  Japan
    amae practice and childrearing prac-
      tices, 143
    inner/outer cultural practices, 140
    self-construction, 208
    typical preschool, 173
  Kaluli parent–child interactions, 127
Individualized learning, 170–172, see also
    Japan
Individuation, 136
Industry versus inferiority, 189
  school, 189
Infancy, independence/interdependence
  childrearing goals/ideas of parents, 105,
    107
  dimensions of activity and conceptual-
    izations, 41–42
  parent–child interactions, 122–129
Inferiority, see Industry versus inferiority
Ingroup–outgroup, 141
Initiative taking, 116–117
Initiative versus guilt, 188–189
Inseparability, independence/interdepend-
    ence

adolescent self-construction, 199–201
American school practices in Dewey's
    philosophy, 152–153
concept, 245–250
constructing oneself as independent,
    222
Cooley's theory of self-construction,
    184, 185
domains of identity, 190–192
dyadic and group interactions, 127–129
dynamics in cultural contexts of devel-
    opment, 47–48, 51, 54
feeling really independent, 230
frontier life, 87–89
individuality and political freedom,
    77–80
Japan
  childrearing practices, 142–146
  classroom regulation, 166–170
Revolution-era cultural traditions, 75–76
self-constructing activities, 195
self-construction in late adolescence,
    215–217
use of terminology, 57
why independence is good or impor-
    tant, 227
why interdependence is good or impor-
    tant, 236
Insightfulness, 216
Interaction patterns, 40–41
Interactional self, 205, see also Japan; Self
Interdependence
  activity dimensions, 57
  constructing oneself as, 231–233
  independence enhancement and why it
    is good or important, 226
  meanings
    dynamics in cultural contexts of de-
      velopment, 47, 49, 54
    future directions of research, 250–251
    historical case study in early 20th cen-
      tury, 95
    use of terminology, 57
  self-construction in late adolescence,
    213, 215
  use of terminology, 56–57
  with autonomy, 19
Interdependent, feeling, 237–239
Interpersonal domains, 191
Interrater reliability, 130–131, 213
Interwoven: A Pioneer Chronicle, 88
Intrapersonal domains, 191

Inviolability, 17–19
Iraq, 206–208
IRE/F format, 156–157

J

James' theory, self-construction, 196
James, William, 201–204
Japan, independence/interdependence
adolescent self-concepts, 34
childrearing practices, 138–146
American culture comparison, 9
educational setting in pre- and elementary school, 162–166
family values, 15
importance of independence, 243
inseparability, 245–246, 247
peer relationships, 116–117
self-construction, 204–208
Jefferson, Thomas, 69–76
Jigsaw, 160–161, 162
Joint attention, 131–132, 133, 134
Justice, 63

K

Kaluli society, 121, 126–127, 193–194, 243
Kappa coefficient, 131, 231
Kindness, 71
Kokoro, 205, *see also* Japan
Komatsudani, 172, *see also* Japan; Preschool

L

Learning, 156–157
Leave-taking, 44–45
Liberal social activism, 28
Likert scale, 10–11
Linguistic markers, 12
Living separately, 15
Looking-glass self, 185–186, *see also* Self
Lutheranism, 59–62

M

Male-biased domains, 191
Marquesas Islands, 106–107, 115, 116, 121, 128, 243
Massachusetts Bay Colony, 62–63

Mather, Cotton, 65–68
Mayan society, independence/interdependence
childrearing goals/ideas of parents, 106, 109
cultural similarities/differences and inseparability, 246
household chores and parent–child relationships, 112–113
individual inviolability, 18–19
neighborhood connections and peer relationships, 115
self-direction and importance of independence, 243
"Me" activities, 183–184
"Me" characteristics, 196–197, 198, 201
Mead's theory, self-construction, 180–184
Meanings, independence/interdependence, 244–245
Men, 28, 85
Mental separateness, 215, 220
Mercy, 63
Middle class, independence/interdependence
concepts, 117–120
19th century, 81–84
parental childrearing goals/ideas and expectations, 103
parent–child relationships and household chores, 111
relational individuation during adolescence, 136–137
self-construction in adolescents, 200
study of parental utterances, 130
Ministers, 65
Misbehavior, 174–175, *see also* Behavior
Mistrust, *see* Trust versus mistrust
Monitors, 167
Mother–child relationships, 172, *see also* Japan
Mother's Book, The, 81–82, 83–84
Motives, 83
Multiple selves, 21, *see also* Self
Mutual gazing, 123
Mutuality, 136, 238–239
My Pedagogic Creed, 154

N

Navajo Indians, 17
Negotiations, 110–111, *see also* Parent–child relationships

Neighborhood, 114–117
Neonatal functioning, 41–42
New England parents, 117
Niche, identification, 190
Nineteenth century, historical study, 81–90
Ninety-Five Theses, 59
Non-Western cultures, 23, 243
Novel objects, working with, 18–19

O

Obedience, independence/interdependence
  African American parent–child interactions, 125
  historical case study, 69, 73, 83
  Japanese childrearing practices, 144–145
  within-culture differences and what they reveal, 117–121
Oneness, 173
Opinions, 132, 186–187, 201, 221
Organismic developmental theory, 38, 39
Others, relationships, independence/interdependence
  Cooley theory of self-construction, 186
  dimensions of activity in conceptualizations, 42
  historical case study, 73–74
  parent–child interactions in infancy/childhood, 123–124, 125–126
  self-concepts and moving beyond the dichotomy, 34
  self-construction in late adolescence, 215–216
Outer/inner activities, 204, *see also* Japan
Outgroup, *see* Ingroup–outgroup

P

Parent–child relationships, independence/interdependence
  adolescence, 135–138
  childrearing ideas and goals
    eating and sleeping practices, 104–109
    expectations, 103–104
    life at home and structuring, 109–113
    neighborhood and peer relationships, 114–117
    within-culture differences, 117–121

dynamics in cultural contexts of development, 52
frontier life, 89
how parents talk about, 129–135
infancy and childhood, 122–129
Japanese childrearing practices, 138–146
meanings, 252
19th century in middle class, 81
self-construction in adolescents, 201
why independence is good or important, 224
Parents' Magazine, 91–97
Participation, educational settings, 165, *see also* Japan
Passivity, 157
Patriotism, 45
Peer conflict, 168, *see also* Peers
Peers, independence/interdependence
  connectedness and constructing oneself, 232
  dimensions of activity and conceptualizations, 41
  fostering, 114–117
  self-construction in adolescents, 194, 199–200
Performance goals, 156, *see also* Goals
Personal attributes, 20–21
Personal values, 198
Persuasion, 144–145
Physical exercise, 173
Physical "Me" characteristics, 196, 197
Physical objects, concern for, 86
Pioneers, 85–87
Piousness, 66, 67–68
Play, 182, 194
Play dates, 116
Playmate choices, 104
Political freedom, 7, 77–80
Political institutions, 7
Population growth, 69
Positioning, 194, *see also* Self-construction
Predestination, 61–62
Preferences, child, 129–139
Preschool, independence/interdependence
  structuring cooperation in educational settings in Japan, 162–166
  typical Japanese, 172–176
Preschool in Three Cultures, 15, 172
Preschoolers, 91, *see also* Preschool
Primary/secondary orientations, 29, 32
Privacy, 64
Privatization, 82

Pronouns, 184–185, 194
Protestants, 59–63
Psychological "Me" characteristics, 196, 197, 198, *see also* Self-construction
Psychological paradigm, traditional, 21–22
Psychosocial conflict, 187
Public condemnation, 207–208, *see also* Japan
Pueblo Indians, 18
Puritans, independence/interdependence
   cultural similarities/differences and inseparability, 247–248
   historical case study of Euro-Americans, 59–68
   value of, 243

Q

Q sort, 24
Questions, use of, 131, 132, 134
Quizzes, 162

R

Reciprocity, 200, 235
Regulation, classroom, 166–170
Regulatory role, government, 78, 79
Relationships, necessity, 223, 224
Religious instruction, 67
Representation, others, 195, *see also* Self-construction
Responsivity, to others, 227
Revolutionary period, 69–80
Role confusion, 189
Rule-based games, 182
Rules, 93, 109, 166, 169–170
Rules of conduct, 90
Russian parents, 24–25

S

Salvation, 60–61, 62, 65, 67
Scarlet Letter, The, 64
Schedules, 105, 173–175
School practices, American
   contemporary classrooms, 155–159
   inseparability of independence/interdependence and cooperative learning, 159–162

John Dewey and education of individuals in relation to others, 151–155
School property, 164
Secondary orientations, *see* Primary/secondary orientations
Security, 95–96
Self, *see also* Individual entries
   characteristics, 197, 198–199, 212–215
   conceptualizations, 20–21, 34, 193
Self-awareness, 166, 203, 239, 246
Self-chosen goals, 171, *see also* Goals
Self-consciousness, 181, 183
Self-constructing activities, 192–196
Self-construction, independence/interdependence
   childhood and adolescence, 196–204
   classic Western theories
      Cooley's theory, 184–187
      Erikson's theory of identity construction, 187–192
      Mead's theory, 180–184
   Japan, 204–208
   multifaceted meanings, 244
   self-constructing activities, 192–196
Self-containment, 9
Self-definition, 33–34, 64–65
Self-demand, 105
Self-development, 182, 226
Self-direction, independence/interdependence
   American school practices
      Dewey's philosophy, 153–154
      fostering independence or undermining interdependence, 158
   constructing oneself as independent, 217, 218, 220, 221
   feeling really independent, 229
   historical case study
      early 20th century, 93, 94, 95
      Euro-American cultural traditions, 62
      19th century in middle class, 82–84
   household chores and parent–child relationships, 113
   inseparability
      childrearing goals/ideas of parents, 104, 106, 107, 108
      frontier life, 88–89
      self-construction in adolescents, 201
   Japanese childrearing practices, 145–146
   neighborhood and peer relationships, 114, 115, 116–117

Self-direction, independence/interdepend-
    ence *(cont.)*
  parent–child play and dynamics in cul-
    tural contexts, 52
  parent–child relationships and structur-
    ing, 110
  self-construction in late adolescence,
    215
  typical Japanese preschool, 175–176
  urban parents comparison, 24–25
  why independence is good or impor-
    tant, 223
Self-esteem, 225
Self-evaluation, 224
Self-expression, 158, 185, 245
Self-feeding, 105
Self-fulfillment, 45
Self-identity, 205, *see also* Identity
Self-improvement, 225, 235–236
Self-pathology, 206
Self-progress, 187
Self-reflection, 67–68, 83, 166, 178, 199
Self-reliance, independence/interdepend-
    ence
  constructing oneself as independent,
    217, 219, 221, 222
  feeling really independent, 228–230
  financial of working-class children, 119
  fostering using household chores, 112
  historical case study, 75–76, 93–96
  inseparability, 106, 168
  Japanese childrearing practices, 145–146
  parent–child play and conceptualizing
    the dynamics in cultural contexts,
    52
  self-construction in late adolescence,
    215
  why independence is good or impor-
    tant, 227
Self-restraint, 204, 205
Self-sufficiency, 186
Self-understanding, 197–198, 200–201
Selfishness, 6
Separate individualism, 19, *see also* Indi-
    viduality
SES, *see* Socioeconomic status
Shame, *see* Autonomy versus shame/doubt
Shared meanings, 43, 45
Siblings, 81, 115
Sin, freedom from, 61
Singing, 82, 173–174
Sleeping practices, 106–109

Small-group practices, 165, *see also* Japan
Sociability, 216
Social burden, 14–15
Social class, 118–119
Social cohesion, 140, 158
Social connectedness
  constructing oneself as independent,
    218–219, 220, *see also* Others, rela-
    tionships
  different cultures, 4
  Erikson's theory of identity construc-
    tion, 188
  feeling really independent, 230
  frontier life, 87–88
  historical case study, 96
  independent individuals, 2
  why independence is good or impor-
    tant, 223
  why interdependence is good or impor-
    tant, 236
Social development, 33
Social engagement, 78, 83, 188
Social goals, 152, 153, *see also* Goals
Social harmony, 139, 204
Social identities, 200, *see also* Identity
Social interactions, 123, 180–181, 185,
    194
Social knowledge, 193
Social "Me" characteristics, 196
Social nurture, 71
Social partners, 40–41
Social progress, 155
Social regulation, 79–80
Social role playing, 182
Social roles, 82, 113, 188, 197
Social self, 184–185, *see also* Self
  multiple, 201–204
Social space, 112
Socialization, 117
Socially approved behavior, 109, *see also*
    Behavior
Societal cohesion, 96–97
Societal concerns, 215, 216, 230–231
Sociocultural theory, 38, 39
Socioeconomic institutions, 41
Socioeconomic status (SES), 211, 252
Soft offensive individualism, 23
Sometimes independence–sometimes in-
    terdependence models, 28–33
Sorority, 2
Souls, separate, 59
Spiritual freedom, 60

STAD, *see* Student Teams–Achievement Divisions
Standards, 198
Statements, 131, 132, 134
Storytelling, 125–126
Stranger friends, 86
Strangers, 84, 141–142
Student Teams–Achievement Divisions (STAD), 161
Student–student interaction, 159
Subsistence, 8–9
Support networks, 215–216, 234
Survival, 83
Systems framework, 39–40
Systems theory, 38, 39–40

T

Talk, 129–135
Talking, 123–124
Teachers, independence/interdependence
  child interactions and conceptualizations, 40
  fostering or undermining, 156, 157, 158, 159
  individualized learning, 170–171
  inseparability, 159, 166
Teasing practices, 125
Terminology, 3–8
Thinking, for oneself, 222
Toddlers, 115
Tolerance, 92
Trust, 25, 230
  versus mistrust, 187
Twentieth century, 91–97

U

Utterances, 130–132
  forms, 132

V

Verbal assertiveness, 140–141
Verbal self-expression, 158
Vietnamese
  constructing oneself as independent, 217–222
  constructing oneself as interdependent, 231–233
  feeling really independent, 228–231
  feeling really interdependent, 237–239
  study of self-construction in late adolescence, 212–217
  why independence is good or important, 222–228
  why interdependence is good or important, 234–237
Viewpoints, 235, 236–237
Voluntary associations, 89–90, 91

W

Waving bye-bye, 44
Western cultures, 4, 27, 112
White Mountain Apache, 18
Whole-class instruction, 15
Whole-class practices, 156–158, 165
Winthrop, John, 62–63, 247
Within-culture differences, 117–121, 252
Women, 28
Work, 113
Working class, 118–120, 125, 171–172
  study of parental utterances, 130

Y

Yōchien, 172